CRISIS OF THE TWO CONSTITUTIONS

CHARLES R. KESLER

CRISIS OF THE TWO CONSTITUTIONS

The Rise, Decline, and Recovery of American Greatness

NEW YORK · LONDON

First American edition published in 2021 by Encounter Books,
an activity of Encounter for Culture and Education, Inc.,
a nonprofit, tax-exempt corporation.
Encounter Books website address: www.encounterbooks.com

Frontispiece by Elliott Banfield

Manufactured in the United States and printed on
acid-free paper. The paper used in this publication meets
the minimum requirements of ANSI/NISO Z39.48–1992
(R 1997) (*Permanence of Paper*).

FIRST AMERICAN EDITION

LIBRARY OF CONGRESS CATALOGING-IN-PUBLICATION DATA

Names: Kesler, Charles R., author.
Title: Crisis of the two constitutions : the rise, decline, and recovery of
American greatness / Charles R. Kesler.
Description: First American edition. | New York : Encounter Books, 2021. |
Includes bibliographical references and index.
Identifiers: LCCN 2020003421 (print) | LCCN 2020003422 (ebook) |
ISBN 9781641771023 (cloth) | ISBN 9781641771030 (epub)
Subjects: LCSH: Constitutional history—United States. | United States—Politics
and government. | Conservatism—United States.
Classification: LCC KF4541.K47 20201 (print) | LCC KF4541 (ebook) |
DDC 342.7302/9—dc23
LC record available at https://lccn.loc.gov/2020003421
LC ebook record available at https://lccn.loc.gov/2020003422

CONTENTS

To the memory of

Harry V. Jaffa
Peter W. Schramm
Thomas B. Silver

INTRODUCTION

In New York City on July 9, 1776, after hearing a public reading of the Declaration of Independence, George Washington returned on horseback to his headquarters, leaving a crowd of soldiers and civilians to surge down Broadway to Bowling Green, where a gilt George III sat atop his horse. Some excited young men broke through the iron fence, climbed the marble pedestal, and "lassoed the equestrian figure," as Rick Atkinson puts it in *The British Are Coming*, the first of his three-volume military history of the American Revolution. Down came the massive statue. It was decapitated, stripped of its gold leaf, and shot through several times by musket fire. But the indignities it would suffer had only begun. The head was impaled on a spike outside a nearby tavern. The rest of the king and his horse were soon melted down and molded into 42,088 lead bullets for use by the Continental Army. History does not record if the bullets were marked, Return to Sender.

Toppling a tyrant's statue is nothing new. It is a fairly routine part of the heady early days of revolutions across the globe, though it is rarely done with such panache. From the Baltic to the Balkans, for example, as the Soviet empire collapsed around them, statues of Stalin and Lenin disappeared from the public squares of the former "captive nations."

But what are we to make of the mobs in America who started pulling down, or otherwise vandalizing, statues? They began with Confederate generals but quickly graduated to George Washington, Thomas Jefferson, Abigail Adams, Ulysses S. Grant, Abraham Lincoln, various abolitionists and Catholic saints, and Saint-Gaudens's great bronze bas-relief monument to the 54th Massachusetts Volunteer

Regiment, the storied all-black regiment that fought so nobly in the Civil War. What message are our twenty-first century rebels trying to send? What revolution are they inaugurating?

They protested the horrific death of George Floyd in police custody in Minneapolis, but their broader target was what they called the "systemic racism" of American police departments, and of America. *The New York Times,* in its "1619 Project," helpfully provided them a manifesto. At the root of systemic racism, according to the *Times,* is the original American system of slavery, which began long before but was protected, promoted, and made official in the Declaration of Independence and the Constitution. America was born racist and remains so today. It doesn't get more systemic than racism being in "the very DNA of this country," as the Project's originator, Nikole Hannah-Jones, charged.

When I suggested in the *New York Post* that our civil unrest should be called "the 1619 riots," she accepted my criticism as a compliment, replying in a tweet, which soon disappeared from the Web, "It would be an honor. Thank you." One has to admire her belated, even if temporary, candor. *The New York Times* doesn't apparently regard the violence as a mere matter of collateral damage, regrettable but unavoidable. It's more like America's "chickens coming home to roost," as the Rev. Jeremiah Wright, Barack Obama's pastor for twenty years, said of the 9/11 terrorist attacks.

How far we have come from the America whose *anti-slavery* principles were invoked by the Rev. Martin Luther King, Jr., at the Lincoln Memorial in 1963. He repeated the majestic words of the Declaration of Independence without irony or bitterness, hailing them as a "promissory note" of American freedom and equality.

If anti-black racism is in our national DNA, however, those promises were hypocritical at best. Still more depressing is the implication of today's woke wisdom that there is very little Americans can do about racism (the new original sin) even if we wanted to. You can't change your DNA. At least you can't make the wholesale change that would be needed to produce a new, non-racist American. Hence the only cure is "anti-racism," the never-ending repression of never-ending racism, the proscription of offensive words, sentiments, opinions, and people, which exchanges the old for a new hypocrisy. This is the continuing moral revolution that the progressive Left, in its latest version, is bringing to America.

But it is only the latest version. Two years ago it was the #MeToo movement that seized Brett Kavanaugh, then a Supreme Court nominee, in its coils, insisting on a new, postmodern test of truth: "Believe the woman." "Her truth," the protestors proclaimed, is stronger than any objective or disinterested truth that might emerge from an adversarial process weighing evidence and testimony. Two years before that, the new revolutionary creed was socialism – "democratic socialism," as updated by Bernie Sanders, who had no doubt learned a lot about it in his travels to Cuba, Nicaragua, and the Soviet Union. He took that show on the road again this year, and though it got mixed reviews and closed out of town, it managed to write itself into the Democratic Party platform.

One thing we all should have learned, therefore, is that the fall of the Soviet Union did not end the revolutionary challenge to America. Whether the country is guilty of systemic racism, sexism, or capitalism, it is sure as hell guilty of *something* systemic and evil. The very idea of "the System" was one of those 1960s slogans (coined by a president of Students for a Democratic Society) that proclaimed its own immoderation, its simplifying antinomianism: whatever the specific vices of the deplorable (American) System – it must be overthrown, or at least fundamentally transformed. As Joe Biden declared, "I will be an ally of the light, not the darkness."

We have come a long way from Barack Obama's debut on the national stage at the 2004 Democratic convention, when he assured the delegates, "There's not a liberal America and a conservative America. There's the United States of America." At this year's virtual Democratic convention, Michelle Obama corrected the record. "We live in a deeply divided nation," she warned. "If you think things cannot possibly get worse, trust me, they can." That was one point at least, on which both sides could agree. In Donald Trump's words, "We are in a fight for the survival of our nation and civilization itself."

Angelo Codevilla was not the first analyst to describe our political disorders as a cold civil war, but after him the term resonated. A cold civil war is better than a hot (i.e., a shooting) one, but it's not a healthy situation for a country to be in. Underlying our cold civil war is the fact, described in this book, that America increasingly is torn between two rival cultures, two constitutions, two ways of life. This mutual estrangement has been going on for a long time, but the pace accelerated beginning in the Sixties and accelerated again after the end of the Cold War.

Political scientists sometimes distinguish between normal politics and regime politics. Normal politics takes place within an accepted political and constitutional order, and concerns means, not ends. That is, the purposes and limits of politics are agreed; the debate is over how to achieve those purposes while observing those limits. By contrast, regime politics is about who rules and for the sake of what ends or principles. It unsettles any existing political order, as well as its limits. It raises anew the basic questions of who counts as a citizen, what are the goals of the political community, and what do we honor or revere together as a people.

This book explains why America may be leaving the world of normal politics and entering the dangerous world of regime politics – in which our political loyalties diverge more and more, as they did in the 1850s, between two contrary visions of what constitutes the country.

One vision is based on the founders' Constitution – written in 1787 and ratified in 1788, grounded in the natural rights and practical wisdom of the Declaration, interpreted in *The Federalist*, and expounded in their best moments by subsequent American jurists and statesmen. In keeping with its own provisions, this Constitution has been amended – some vital improvements, some not – but is broadly recognizable still as the founders' handiwork.

The other vision is based on what progressives and liberals for more than a century now have called "the living constitution." The term implies that the original Constitution is *dead* – or at least on life support, in which case, in order to remain relevant to our national life, the old frame of government must continually receive life-giving infusions of new meaning, and along with them new duties, rights, and powers. The doctors who are qualified to diagnose our constitutional maladies and to prescribe and administer these transfusions form a nascent elite or ruling class who attended the best colleges and universities, and who trust themselves and people like themselves with virtually unchecked power. For example, under the living constitution they favor new kinds of administrative agencies, which concentrate legislative, executive, and even judicial power in the same expert hands, even though the founders warned that such concentrations would satisfy "the very definition of tyranny." But why worry about the misuse of power if your motives are pure, your degrees Ivy League, and history is on your side?

The resulting constitution – the progressives' constitution – is not a regime of unchanging natural rights or equal individual rights, but of rights that travel in groups and that vary with the historical moment. The *right* to health care, for example, is emphatically part of the constitution of what's happening now: it is impossible to imagine such a moral claim outside of our stage of economic and social development in a very rich country in a largely peaceful world with doctors, drugs, and hospitals in what is fancied, at least, to be surplusage. To borrow Walter Berns's quip, the founders tried to keep the times in tune with the Constitution; the progressives want to keep the constitution in tune with the times. Or should I say, with the *Times*?

Until the 1960s most American liberals believed it was inevitable that their constitution would overtake and absorb the founders' Constitution in a kind of evolutionary convergence. Their progressivism was more post- than anti-Constitutional for that reason. But the Civil Rights movement had been waiting a long time for "inevitable" progress down South, and even in northern cities. Its decision to take history into its own hands helped to inspire the New Left, which dreaded apathy above all, and eventually led large numbers of mainstream liberals, under pressure from the Vietnam War, to lose faith in the progressive gradualism of their fathers' generation. Other tributaries of revolutionary zeal poured in as well, like the Frankfurt School's with-it combination of Marxism and Freudianism. As the Civil Rights movement gave way to Black Power, and the New Left switched from nonviolence to Revolution, the progressives' constitution became more aggressive, more eager for Supreme Court justices to overrule popular majorities and precedents, more anti-Constitutional, more openly contemptuous of the unenlightened masses, more anti-American.

American conservatives had seen the disguised or latent radicalism in American liberalism early on. They set out at first to limit the damage, then to reverse it. The latter was the planted assumption of Ed Meese's epic call, as Ronald Reagan's attorney general, for a return to a jurisprudence of "original intent." Long before that, however, conservatives had contemplated a return to the founders' Constitution, via both jurisprudence and elective politics. Their mixed reaction to the 1964 Civil Rights Act included many qualms about its conformity to the original Constitution, but their subsequent half-hearted fight over the Act's interpretation (particularly over the rise of affirmative action) exposed qualms about their earlier qualms. The multiplying varieties of originalism showed as well that, for all of the conservatives' supposed determination to return to the founders' Constitution, they couldn't agree about the content or principles of that Constitution, nor about how to recover them.

As for elective politics, the greatest of conservative statesmen, Ronald Reagan, repeatedly urged a return to the old Constitutional consensus, but the means to that end eluded him. Amid the great and enduring successes of the Reagan Revolution, its failure to rise to the level of "a second American Revolution," as he called it, stands out. It haunts his otherwise sunny Farewell Address. If you want to know why he failed, and if conservatives can do better than that – read on.

When it became clear to liberals *and* conservatives that neither was going away anytime soon, the cold civil war was on. As a result, the gap between the two constitutions became a gulf, to the extent that today we are two countries – or we are fast on the road to becoming two countries with divergent ways of life. We increasingly read different books and newspapers, watch different shows, get our news from different networks, worship in different churches and synagogues, live in different parts of the country, attend different colleges and study different disciplines, admire different sports and sportsmen, and may even have to eat at different restaurants in order to avoid ugly, partisan mobs. The tradition of the loyal opposition – meaning, opposed to the party in power but loyal to the same Constitution – is yielding to a new norm of fierce and implacable Resistance to the other party's very legitimacy. Our polarization is pervasive and deepening, though it isn't yet, I hope, at the point of no return.

That's why this volume, though it speaks frequently of two constitutions, is not (you may be relieved to hear) about constitutional law. Few court decisions are so much as mentioned here. There are plenty of books rehearsing the struggle between judicial activism and judicial restraint. This one concerns the much larger political, intellectual, and moral divide in America – its origins, nature, and prospects.

There is an old distinction – between constitutional law and the law of the Constitution – that might be repurposed here. In this inquiry we focus on the latter – that is, how each of these competing constitutions claims to be lawful *for us*, what is the ground of its authority, and how do its intellectual, moral, and legal assumptions translate into a whole political-cultural order, and ultimately two such orders? Insofar as federal court decisions are not caught up in this larger conflict, they belong to normal jurisprudence and are not of interest to us. Con law cases that do involve regime questions are relevant but are less interesting to us than the regime questions themselves.

What about that point of no return – is it possible that America's cold civil war could be dialed back or even resolved? There seem to me basically five possibilities along those lines. The most obvious would be victory by one side or the other. Perhaps liberals or conservatives could persuade a majority of their fellow citizens to embrace their party's agenda and constitution, to win in the polling booth (quaint idea) a decisive verdict. In the past, that's how Americans settled their swelling differences, in so-called realigning elections that handed control to a majority party for a generation or two, as in Thomas Jefferson's breakthrough in 1800 or Andrew Jackson's in 1828. In the twentieth century, however, only two presidents were able to make enduring changes in public opinion and voting patterns – Franklin Roosevelt and Ronald Reagan. FDR reaped an electoral realignment that lasted for about two generations, lifting the Democratic Party to majority status. Reagan effected a realignment of public policy and voting blocs but wasn't able to make the GOP the majority party. Since 1968, you see, the norm has been divided government: the people have preferred to split control of the national government between Democrats and Republicans rather than entrust it for the most part to a single, majority party.

Trump has so far not been able to break out of this new pattern of stalemate. Both parties continue to lust after old-fashioned overwhelming victories, but the American people seem disinclined to make those dreams come true. If the new pattern holds, the parties will continue to alternate control of the presidency and routinely share control of the government, which means that embittering conflict between the two constitutions will continue. But how long can believers in the country's systemic injustice and believers in its systemic justice continue to keep house together?

If Americans can't change one another's minds, then there is the second possibility of changing the subject. Reagan used to say that when the little green men arrive from outer space, all of our political differences will be transcended and humanity will unite. Similarly, if some jarring event occurs like a major war or a natural calamity it might change the focus of, and thus reset, our politics. But the COVID-19 pandemic was a pretty severe shock to the system, and it didn't succeed in redrawing our political lines. On the contrary, it quickly became captured by the ongoing political war. Now the two sides may disagree about face masks, quarantines, vaccines, lockdowns, and reopenings in addition to the usual issues.

So if we can't change our minds and won't change the subject, we are left with but three ways out of the conflict between the two constitutions. The happiest of these would be a vastly reinvigorated federalism. If we had a re-flowering of federalism, some of the differences between blue states and red states could be handled at the state level. The most disruptive issues could be denationalized. Let New York have a permissive abortion policy and let Utah have a very restrictive one. But having built a national regulatory state and spent the last century doing everything it could to create a national political community, with interest and identity groups sharing in a national agenda of consciousness-raising and programmatic rights, it's hard to see how, at this late juncture, liberalism could imagine, much less accede to, a revival of federalism.

That leaves two possibilities. One, alas, is secession – a danger to any federal system, as Alexander Hamilton and James Madison explained long ago. The Czech Republic and Slovakia went their separate ways peacefully, just within the last generation. Great Britain seceded, in effect, from the European Union after much toing and froing. In America, despite the Great Sorting, liberals and conservatives remain intermingled in many regions of the country; secession would be messy, and therefore would probably not be entirely voluntary. In other words, secession might be more an intensification than a termination or alleviation of the cold civil war. Years ago I saw a bumper-sticker that read: "If at first you don't secede, try, try, again." The United States did try it once, which led to the fifth and worst possibility, namely, bloody Civil War. I doubt we want to try it again.

Which is why, under present circumstances, America seems to be approaching some kind of crisis – a crisis of the two constitutions, from which none of the possible exit ramps offers a sure escape.

The crisis could be triggered by a disputed election, a Supreme Court decision (on abortion, gun rights, immigration policy, etc.) that many state governments refused to accept and sought to nullify, an ultimatum over trade or foreign policy, an impeachment gone very wrong – any number of causes. Nor is simply protracting the cold civil war until the people got sick of it necessarily a better outcome. As the conflict has gone on the disagreements, generally speaking, have gotten worse, not better. The tectonic plates of the two constitutions, already grinding away at each other for more than a century, may eventually produce a "Big One" but certainly will produce in the meantime many lesser but severe shocks to the country.

I am loath to write "the two countries." The original basis of American greatness and unity is still available to us. To appeal to the better angels of our nature we must first reacquaint ourselves with that nature. *Crisis of the Two Constitutions* thus proceeds by exploring the case for the founders' Constitution as they made it; then explaining the development of the arguments for the progressives' ("living") constitution, roughly from Woodrow Wilson to our own age's Woke Social Justice Warriors; and finally examining American conservatives' attempts, from William F. Buckley, Jr., and Ronald Reagan to Donald Trump, and so far mostly unavailing, to revive the founders' wise principles and fortify them again with prudent statesmanship.

The book began as a collection of essays written over many

years, but I have revised, expanded, and updated them, as well as added several new chapters, so as to bring a fresh perspective to the whole. I confess to having preserved some repetitions of ideas for heuristic purposes. This is above all a book of arguments with thinkers, some of them friends, on the contemporary Left and Right – with progressives, socialists, multiculturalists, postmodernists, "Eastern" Straussians, Southern conservatives, neoconservatives, "rad trads" (radical traditionalists), and many others, all of whom doubt that America was ever that great, or could be made so again.

PART I

THE FOUNDERS' CONSTITUTION

CHAPTER ONE

THE FOUNDERS AND THE CLASSICS

Constitutionalism in the United States today is often thought to be a matter for the courts, which in the course of deciding cases must often pronounce on the meaning of the Constitution. Indeed, judges are not the least of those who think this way, often being willing to assume the burden of interpreting, enforcing, and updating the Constitution almost alone. Their solicitude might be accepted as *noblesse oblige* were there more *noblesse* to it; as it is, the obligations seem to be wholly on the part of the people of the United States, by and for whom the Constitution was made the fundamental law, and not on the part of judges who are sworn to uphold that law.

To this complaint, the liberal members of the judiciary who are not ashamed to be called "judicial activists" might respond that the Constitution's meaning is not necessarily the same thing as its framers' intentions, that in any case the framers' intentions will probably not square with the political agenda of the judges' contemporary critics, and that the best guide to the meaning of the Constitution today is a moral and political theory that is in touch with today's conditions, which theory can be found in law schools and in woke philosophy departments. According to this view, it is necessary to add a political theory to the Constitution either because the document itself lacks one (the wording of the Preamble is vague, the meaning of "due process" and "equal protection" is mysterious, and so forth), or because the Constitution's own theory is antiquated

and undemocratic (embodying the eighteenth century's commitment to the defense of property and to the Lockean or even Hobbesian view of man as irredeemably self-interested).

Strangely, the conservatives' response to this critique has been
not so much to dispute as to celebrate it. They have either agreed
that the Constitution contains no theory and in fact stands oppressed
to all abstract theories, or have rejoiced in the Constitution's no-nonsense commitment to the Lockean or Hobbesian view of man – and
of Americans – as base but reliable. True, the partisans of judicial
restraint do draw opposite conclusions from the same analysis of the
Constitution, but there is less to this opposition than meets the eye:
the conservatives want laws made by legislative majorities, the activists want judge-made law, but neither side seems to doubt the law is
whatever the law-making authority says it is. In short, the premises
of both activism and restraint are grounded in a theory of legal positivism, which under the pressure of adapting to changing circumstances becomes either fast-forward or slow-motion historicism

To escape the confines of the contemporary debate therefore
requires that we reopen questions so basic that we have long
assumed we knew their answers: questions like, "Is there a political
theory of the Constitution of the United States?" Before we can take
up that inquiry, however, an even more basic one presents itself: Is
there such as a thing as political theory? At least according to one
great student of constitutions, the answer would seem to be no. For
Aristotle, theory, *theoria*, means observation or contemplation, and
particularly the contemplation of the highest things in nature; it is
the leisured activity of studying those things which cannot be other
than they are, which are not directed to any end that is attainable by
action. Theoretical wisdom, he writes, "will contemplate none of
the things that will make a man happy (for it is not concerned with
any coming-into-being)." Politics, by contrast, is concerned with the
human good, with happiness understood as living well in accordance
with virtue; justice, the political virtue par excellence, is partly by
nature, partly not, yet "all of it is changeable." "Political theory"
would therefore appear to be a contradiction in terms, a combination of the human and changeable with the divine (or suprahuman)
and unchangeable. Yet Aristotle does speak of political science and

political philosophy, which receive justification and guidance from the fact that, despite the variety of actual regimes, there is "one which is everywhere by nature the best." Political science is a practical science, whose goal is not to *study* the things that ought to be done, for the sake of study, but to *do* them, to teach men to possess and use virtue, to help men to become good. But the good for man is an object of study, even as how best to make men good is an object of study. The union of the two is the culmination of political science as well as the standard of the political art: the idea of the best regime.[1]

In the modern understanding of politics, however, political theory is not only possible but inevitable. A product of the revolutionary turn begun by Niccolò Machiavelli and Thomas Hobbes, political theory now means a political science that does not try or does not need to try to make men better and that does not orient itself by the notion of the best regime. It takes men as they are, which is not identical with the way we find them around us, that is, living in families, neighborhoods, and cities in many countries with a variety of forms of government, but rather as they are when they are abstracted from the social and political – what was once seen as the natural – context. When stripped of the accretions of time and the veils of propriety, man is an abstract "self" in (what beginning with Hobbes was called) the state of nature: a self oriented primarily, ineluctably, to its own preservation and interest. Political theory reckons on and only on this fundamental natural impulse or passion, which, precisely because its promptings are universal and efficacious, guarantees that whatever chains of reasoning issue from it will be universally valid and applicable. Therefore, the problem of mediating between the best regime and all, or nearly all, actual regimes – of deciding the relation between the best everywhere and always, and what is best here and now – ceases to be a problem. Prudence or practical wisdom, which was once thought to provide the solution to that problem, is either dismissed as illusory or admitted only as the clever voice of experienced self-interestedness.[2] In short, it becomes possible to have a theory of politics because there is a universally valid and applicable solution to the problem of politics: the "best regime," understood now as whatever form of administration best secures men's life and property, can be made practicable anywhere, hence everywhere.

To determine whether there is a political theory of the American Constitution requires, then, that we bear in mind this ambiguity in the notion of "political theory." On the one hand, speaking loosely, the term may mean the more theoretical part of the practical science of politics: that combination of the principles of human excellence with the knowledge of how to make men better that distinguishes the idea of the best regime. On the other hand, the term may mean the theoretical science of politics, the universal doctrine based on the knowledge that men ought not and do not have to be made better, which can safely dispense with prudence because it replaces the best regime with itself – with techniques for the manipulation and channeling of human passions. It is important to remind ourselves of the ambiguity within the question, so that we do not presuppose our answer to it. We must be open to the possibility of prudence in the American Constitution and in the American founding more generally. At the least, we ought not to assume that the possibility of practical wisdom has been abolished in the modern world, either by positivist science or by history – not even by the history of modern political philosophy. It is quite possible, as I shall argue, for prudence to use the insights of modern political philosophy for its own ends. The reverse may happen too, but we shall be blind to both possibilities if we assume that the conquest of prudence by theory is inevitable.

For the same reason, we must beware of the perils of what is today called intellectual history, which so often ends by subordinating the intellect to history. For example: according to the Preamble, "We the People of the United States" ordained and established the Constitution, though it was actually written by a few men met in convention on behalf of the people (about which more presently). Neither consideration suggests that there was a preexisting theory to which the people's or their representatives' wishes were conformed, or by which they were necessarily guided. Yet it is common to hear that the theory of the Constitution emerged from or was influenced by many preexisting theories – those of Machiavelli, Bacon, Hobbes, Locke, and Montesquieu, among others. This attempt to trace the efficient causes of the Constitution's theory or principles leads to the following difficulty. On the one hand, if these authorities disagree among themselves on important issues, then the attempt to clarify the Constitution on the basis of their theories would result in obscurity. The Constitution would represent at best an eclectic combination of principles – that is, a combination that could not itself be justified by any principle – and at worst a "bundle of compromises" assembled in explicit opposition to the irreconcilable demands of conflicting theories and interests. On the other hand, if these thinkers agree, *per impossibile*, on all of the important issues, then the Constitution as a product of this general, not to say monolithic, theoretical agreement would be of only secondary interest. Study of the Constitution would be reduced to that peculiar academic pastime, the "case study." The conclusion from either direction would be the same: the American Constitution would become an epiphenomenon of theory, that is, of the new political science, which virtually reduces practice to the application of theory. The Constitution would cease to be interesting, inasmuch as it could be studied only as the result of, or as a link in, a chain of efficient causation – of intellectual causation, of "ideology," to be sure, but an unfreedom in principle no different from the economic determinism peddled by Charles Beard and the Progressive historians.[3]

The shadows cast by this approach would eventually overwhelm the light of the Constitution. We would be seduced by the play of shadows into forgetting that the Constitution is the product of the Federal Convention's deliberations, and was ratified by special conventions in the states called to deliberate yet again on the merits of the new plan. But deliberating well is, according to Aristotle, the mark of a prudent man. The Constitution could therefore be said to be a work of prudent men or of prudence, of practical wisdom, not theoretical wisdom. Even as, properly speaking, there can be no theory of prudence, so there can be no theory of the Constitution. This answer would be definitive, except that we cannot assume *a priori* that the Convention did in fact deliberate well, nor that prudence is in fact self-sufficient and independent of theoretical wisdom. But these considerations do remind us that our attention should be directed toward the men who deliberated over and framed the Constitution, if we are to understand their handiwork. It will not do to construct imaginary chains of influence based on the books these men had or might have read, any more than it will suffice to attribute

their thoughts to the spirit of their age. Counting the founders' citations of particular thinkers is also bound to be misleading, unless
the citations are interpreted in the context of the arguments that the
founders are advancing. Only then may we say that we begin our
efforts to understand the American founding with the way in which
the founders understood themselves – rather than with a way in
which they could not have understood themselves, the consciousness of their limited historical horizon not having been vouchsafed
to them.

Contemporary scholarship appears to be of two minds concerning the founders' relation to the Classics. It is well established
that education in the colonies and in the new nation was anchored,
from the primary school to college, in the study of classical languages and literature. By comparison with much instruction in the
classics today, this study was serious: it did not regard Greece and
Rome as two unusually interesting cultures, an acquaintance with
which is mildly diverting and sometimes useful in decoding high-
brow literature and middlebrow crossword puzzles. For the founders, instruction in the classics was, to a great extent, the study of
living wisdom that happened to have been written centuries ago in
different languages. To be sure, some parts of ancient learning had to
be rejected or questioned in light of Christian revelation and later
discoveries in the sciences, but as guides to logic, rhetoric, ethics,
history, politics, poetry, mathematics, and even some parts of theology, the classical writers remained, if not always authoritative, nonetheless principal authorities in the curriculum of schools and of life.[4]

Yet if there is a scholarly consensus on anything regarding the
founding, it is that the founding was essentially a modern enterprise.
Pamphlets, newspaper articles, sermons, and political debates of the
day may have been strewn with classical quotations and allusions,
but these must be understood to have been cultural reflexes or
examples of forensic showmanship. "The classics … are everywhere
in the literature of the Revolution," Bernard Bailyn writes, "but they
are everywhere illustrative, not determinative, of thought. They
contributed a vivid vocabulary but not the logic or grammar of
thought, a universally respected personification but not the source
of political and social beliefs."[5] That the source of the founders'

thought is modern, specifically the modern political philosophy of Hobbes, Locke, and Montesquieu, has by now become almost a commonplace, due chiefly to the influential scholarship of Martin Diamond. Although *The Federalist* "rejects the 'chains of despotism,' i.e., the Hobbesian solution to the problem of self-preservation," Diamond wrote, "it nonetheless seems to accept the Hobbesian statement of the problem." American liberalism and republicanism, based on the premise of the paramount natural right of self-preservation, are therefore "not the means by which men may ascend to a nobler life; rather they are simply instrumentalities which solve Hobbesian problems in a more moderate manner." The American regime marks a fundamental break with the premodern tradition. "Other political theories had ranked highly, as objects of government, the nurturing of a particular religion, education, military courage, civic-spiritedness, moderation, individual excellence in the virtues, etc. On all of these *The Federalist*," and by implication the American regime, "is silent, or has in mind only pallid versions of the originals, or even seems to speak with contempt."[6]

The notion that the origins of the American regime are basically Hobbesian or, as it is more often contended, Lockean, has of course been around longer than the essays of Martin Diamond. In one form or another it has been a staple of twentieth-century criticism of the regime: one thinks, for instance, of the widely differing interpretations of Richard Hofstadter, Louis Hartz, and Carl Becker.[7] Its alleged Lockeanism was in this century employed as an indictment of the regime more often by the Left than by the Right, leaving aside the memorable protest of Aleksandr Solzhenitsyn. In the nineteenth century it was an attack favored more by the Right than the Left, particularly by the bitterenders who defended the positive good of slavery, notably the audacious George Fitzhugh, but also by more elegant critics of modern civilization like Henry Adams. In the lates 1960s a protest against the supposed influence of Locke on the founders blossomed into a whole school of revisionist history. The principal figures of this school are Bernard Bailyn, Gordon Wood, and J.G.A. Pocock, though they are indebted to the previous researches of Zera Fink and Caroline Robbins, and all are beholden to the seminal inquiries of Douglass Adair. Here the argument is that

Locke's influence has been overstated, at the expense of the radical Whig pamphleteers of eighteenth-century England, who were the direct sources of America's revolutionary doctrines. What His Majesty George III should have taxed, in short, was not American imports of tea but of the ideas of classical republicanism or civic humanism. Still, in the end these dissenters agree with the prevailing interpretations that the Constitution is a work of modern or Lockean political theory, though they maintain that the new science of politics came to prominence only in the 1780s, and only by supplanting the older paradigm of American politics that traced its roots to classical republicanism. The Revolution of 1776 had been made in the name of a virtuous people against a corrupt British Empire. The Constitution, these scholars assert, was made in the name of a modern political theory suited for a modern commercial republic.[8]

The view of the Constitution, or of the founding more generally, as a work inspired by modern political theory is thus not new, but what is new is the extent to which the question of America's modernity has eclipsed the question of our form of government. As the controversy between ancients and moderns has come to dominate the foreground, the regime question as such, the controversy between republican government and monarchical government, or (to use Tocqueville's formulation) between democracy and aristocracy, has receded into the background. American liberalism, that is, the doctrine of freedom flowing from the modern definition of natural rights, has become central to understanding ourselves; American republicanism has been relegated to the role of handmaid to freedom, or, at best, to the role of freedom's bumptious understudy. But this represents a decisive change in America's self-understanding: before, with few exceptions, liberalism had been seen as subordinate, to one degree or another, to American republicanism, hence had not, to one degree or another, been seen as liberalism at all. In itself this development is startling. Its political implications deserve to be pursued at greater length elsewhere, but its effects on our view of the founders' relation to the classics may properly be considered now.[9] For insofar as the founders were concerned primarily with the regime question, they were, roughly speaking, acting like ancients.

Insofar as they regarded that question as secondary to or derivative from the distinction between ancients and moderns – from the modern discovery of the abstract "self" with natural rights arising from the passions – then they were acting like moderns.

The one is political, understanding American life to be organized, finally and no matter how indirectly, by the "regime," by a structure of authoritative principles, institutions, and types of character. The other is theoretical, asserting that the American regime was subordinated to or was absorbed by a theory of human nature (stemming from Machiavelli and Hobbes) so open-ended that ultimately it outgrew the idea of nature and evolved into a theory of history. Many Straussian scholars tend to take the latter viewpoint, assuming too readily that the history of political philosophy is itself the key to modern political history: that America is, to quote Joseph Cropsey, "an arena in which modernity is working itself out," because it is "the microcosm of modernity, repeating in its regime, on the level of popular consciousness, the major noetic events of the modern world."[10] This theoretical view of American politics thus transforms itself into the historical or historicist view. Leo Strauss, in his unforgettable critique of the new political science, condemned it on its own grounds – that it was unscientific or unempirical because, when confronted with Nazi and Communist tyranny, it could not recognize the phenomenon *as tyranny*. Today, some disciples of Strauss seem untrue to the phenomena in a similar way, for by viewing American politics primarily through the lenses of the theoretical distinction between ancients and moderns, they are no longer able to recognize *politics* when they see it.

Let us look, then, at the two greatest documents of the founding as they bear on the question of the founders' relation to the classics, keeping in mind that by that question we mean not simply the classics' influence on the founders but, more importantly, the founders' position vis-a-vis the classical understanding of politics as a practical science; or, to put the matter another way, the founders' understanding of the meaning of liberalism and republicanism. The place to begin is with the Declaration of Independence, and then we will turn to the Constitution as articulated and defended in *The Federalist*.

THE PRUDENT DECLARATION

The Declaration announces the independence of the United States from Great Britain, and justifies the dissolution of the "political bands" that had formerly connected the two peoples on the grounds that the king of Great Britain now has "in object the establishment of an absolute Tyranny over these States." Tyranny is destructive of the ends for which government is instituted, namely the securing of equal men's "unalienable rights," among which are "Life, Liberty, and the pursuit of Happiness." The ends of government include, however, the people's "Safety and Happiness," and since no man is by nature the ruler of another, it is the people's right to decide when their safety and happiness have been violated and what they wish to do about it. But the people's right "to alter or to abolish" their government is conjoined to their right "to institute new Government," and nowhere in the Declaration is government's dissolution spoken of without immediate reference to its reinstitution. The people do not seem to have a right to go without government: the existence of a people implies – obliges – the constitution of a government. When they are threatened by "absolute Despotism," says the Declaration carefully, "it is their right, it is their duty" to "throw off such Government" and to "provide new Guards for their future security." Right and duty are brought together in a statesmanlike decision under the pressure of circumstances. Their future security extends to the choice of a principled "foundation" that will "effect" their safety, and an organization of "Powers" will "effect" their happiness. This distinction between safety and happiness corresponds, by the way, to the two parts of *The Federalist*: the Union, discussed in Nos. 1 through 36, is especially for the sake of the people's safety; but "the merits of this Constitution," its "particular structure" as discussed in *Federalist* 37 to 85, is more for the sake of the people's happiness.

Now, the people may not exercise their right "to alter or to abolish" and "to institute new Government" on a whim. The Declaration restricts that right to "whenever any Form of Government becomes destructive of these ends," and lest the message be misunderstood, confirms that "Prudence, indeed, will dictate that Governments long established should not be changed for light and transient causes."

The Declaration even offers evidence that this right will not be abused: "[A]ll evidence hath shown, that mankind are more disposed to suffer, while evils are sufferable, than to right themselves by abolishing the forms to which they are accustomed." Of course, being "more disposed" to suffer is different from being always or entirely disposed. Perhaps "mankind" does not always listen to the dictates of prudence, or perhaps prudence speaks not about suffering but about "causes," connecting "a long train of abuses and usurpations" to an "Object" that "evinces a design." Prudence teaches both the advantages of government – how "Governments long established" conduce to the serious and enduring "Safety and Happiness" of the people – and the necessity to look into "causes," to scan the designs of men, to infer motives based on the repeated acts of men, to read the intentions of men's characters. Thus it is not simply "a long train of abuses and usurpations" that the Declaration charges, and recounts, against George III; it is a "long train" that culminates in a judgment of his character. "A Prince, whose character is thus marked by every act which may define a Tyrant, is unfit to be the ruler of a free People." This judgment implies in turn that, if a ruler may be "unfit" for a people, a people may be unfit for a certain kind of ruler. George III, the Declaration states, has commanded actions "totally unworthy the Head of a civilized nation," and "scarcely paralleled in the most barbarous ages," including, infamously, the endeavor "to bring on the inhabitants of our frontiers, the merciless Indian Savages, whose known rule of warfare, is an undistinguished destruction of all ages, sexes, and conditions." Distinctions of character are as important among peoples as among rulers. Unless the distinction is preserved between "civilized" peoples and barbarians – between those who make war honorably and "Savages" who do not – then the distinction cannot be sustained between heads of government who act worthily and those who act unworthily. Hence the contrast, developed towards the end of the Declaration, between "our British brethren" who, though apparently possessing a "native justice and magnanimity," yet are "deaf to the voice of justice and of consanguinity," and the "good People of these Colonies," in whose name and by whose authority the signers of the Declaration act.

A "good People" is deaf neither to the voice of justice and

consanguinity, nor to the dictates of prudence: it hears the claims of others, of kindred, and of wisdom. Americans are both a "free People" and a "good People," and a free people must apparently be a good people if it is to be worthy of its freedom. On this basis the prudent men who sign the Declaration take upon themselves the grave responsibility of submitting "Facts" to "a candid world," of imputing to the king the intention to reduce the colonies "under absolute Despotism," and, of course, of leading their fellow Americans in the Revolution against this despot. These signers pledge "to each other" – not to the people, as one might expect – "our lives, our fortunes, and our sacred honor." As individuals men are "created equal" and endowed with certain "unalienable rights"; but it is their collective right, "the Right of the People," to alter or abolish the existing government and to institute a new one. The Declaration acknowledges this right only in the context of a judgment establishing the tyrannical character of an already existing government, which judgment is both circumstantial and principled – prudential, in other words. "The Right of the People" depends upon the prudence of a few, therefore upon the character of a people who are disposed to heed the dictates of a prudent few.

For Aristotle, election is the aristocratic way of choosing office holders. Lot, or chance, is the democratic way. The American people become an elect, in effect, in the act of electing others. They are in a sense defined by their admirations. Their appeals to the "native justice and magnanimity" of "our British brethren" went unanswered, perhaps because George III *was* fit to rule the British people. But the appeals themselves reflected that the American people, as brethren of the British, have their own justice and magnanimity. This magnanimity is evinced in the people's support for the "manly firmness" with which their representatives in the colonial assemblies resisted George III's encroachments; in their support for laws "the most wholesome and necessary for the public good"; and, above all, in their refusal to "relinquish the right of Representation in the Legislature, a right inestimable to them and formidable to tyrants only." An "inestimable" right is one that cannot be estimated or calculated, that is of surpassing value or excellence. It is a right too precious to be exchanged for any other good. It is something honorable and noble, pointing toward the nobility of the best regime. The doctrine of the Declaration of Independence is unintelligible apart from the idea of the best regime – the idea of a people worthiest of freedom, of a government worthiest of man.[11]

If this interpretation is correct, then the Declaration is not an expression of "political theory" in the modern sense of the term, but is an eminently practical statement of the practical science of politics. The Declaration, after all, proclaims that a political action has been taken and gives the reasons why it has been taken. Neither the American people nor their representatives disdain to explain their actions, for they desire to show to "a candid world" that the course they have decided upon is just, prudent, honorable, and deserving of the world's support. To make their case, it is true, the Americans give reasons that go to the ends for which government is instituted, but these theoretical principles, the highest principles of political science, require prudence to supplement them or to translate them into terms of political art. Therefore the Americans must show (as previously noted) not only that "it is their right" to throw off despotism and institute new government, but that "it is their duty" to do so – that is, that a prudent reading of the situation authorizes, indeed necessitates, their action. The principles of just government proclaimed in the Declaration begin, practically enough, from the difference between man and beasts on the one hand, and between man and God on the other. But this very distinction requires that the secondary differences among men also be recognized by political science. "Our British brethren" are said to be "deaf" to the "voice of justice and of consanguinity." Insofar as they are deaf, nature's intention to make human beings with full use of their senses, with their faculties functioning perfectly, is thwarted. But something similar is true of "Savages" and barbarians, even "civilized" ones like George III. To some extent they are not, so to speak, fully functioning human beings, insofar as they do not understand or respect the principles of "a civilized nation." It is the task of prudence to judge the defects, infirmities, and special circumstances of peoples and regimes, as well as the distinctions among men within regimes, and to choose so far as possible what is suitable to each. Hence the Declaration implies there could be a variety of possible legitimate regimes corresponding to the character of various peoples, ranked according to their potential for self-government.

Is this making a mountain out of a molehill, reading into the Declaration a classicism that is simply not there or only barely there? John Adams, writing in 1774, identified these "revolution principles," as he called them, with "the principles of Aristotle and Plato, of Livy and Cicero, and [Algernon] Sidney, [James] Harrington, and Locke; the principles of nature and eternal reason."[12]

Examples of this sort, deriving the principles of the Declaration and the Revolution from ancient as well as modern authors, could be multiplied. But none is so authoritative, or so interesting, as Thomas Jefferson's letter to Henry Lee of May 8, 1825. Jefferson was responding to a remark of Timothy Pickering's which Adams had repeated, and Pickering had subsequently published, to the effect that the Declaration did not contain an idea "but what had been hackneyed in Congress two years before." Jefferson wrote:

> But with respect to our rights, and the acts of the British government contravening those rights, there was but one opinion on this side of the water. All American Whigs thought alike on these subjects. When forced, therefore, to resort to arms for redress, an appeal to the tribunal of the world was deemed proper for our justification. This was the object of the Declaration of Independence. Not to find out new principles, or new arguments, never before thought of, nor merely to say things which had never been said before; but to place before mankind the common sense of the subject, in terms so plain and firm as to command their assent, and to justify ourselves in the independent stand we are compelled to take.

Jefferson's appeal to common sense put the colonists' case on non-theoretical grounds, on grounds that could be made more intelligible by Aristotle than, say, by Hobbes. Jefferson continued:

> Neither aiming at originality of principle or sentiment, nor yet copied from any particular and previous writing, it was intended to be an expression of the American mind, and to give to that

expression the proper tone and spirit called for by the occasion. All its authority rests then on the harmonizing sentiments of the day, whether expressed in conversation, in letters, printed essays, or in the elementary books of public right, as Aristotle, Cicero, Locke, Sidney, etc.[13]

What are we to make of the fact that the principal author of the Declaration of Independence thought his work the expression of an American mind whose common sense was harmonious with the political principles of Aristotle, Cicero, Locke, and Sidney, to say nothing of "etc."? If the notion strikes us as naive or perverse, perhaps it is because we have studied the "elementary books of public right" from the theoretical rather than the practical viewpoint. If we could suspend our disbelief at this heretical combination of ancients and moderns, maybe we could see a reasonable, a common sense agreement among them on certain points. To begin with, all were republicans or were reputed to be republicans. (Recall Hobbes excoriating "the democratical principles of Aristotle and Cicero."[14]) For Jefferson, the "elementary books of public right" were elementary books of *republican* right. In this broad sense of the term, "republican" stands for government in which the people have a voice; in which there is some form of public debate or deliberation over public policy; the public good is the end of government; laws and not men may be said to rule; and priests do not rule. As commonly used, the term thus includes free, mixed governments as well as moderate democracies. *Republican* stands particularly in opposition to absolute, hereditary, patriarchal, arbitrary, divine right monarchy or, more simply, it stands in opposition to tyranny.

But a fuller account of the reasonable agreement between ancients and moderns may be found in Sidney's political thought. He is hardly studied today, but for the founders he was a figure of great moral and intellectual authority.[15] A martyr to the "old cause" – he was beheaded in 1683 after a show-trial on the charge of high treason, being accused of plotting to depose the king and set up a republic – he was also the author of the celebrated *Discourses Concerning Government*, published in 1698. Like Locke, Sidney wrote against Robert Filmer (the defender of absolute monarchy on patriarchal grounds), invoking Richard Hooker (the "Anglican Aquinas," as someone called him) as his ally; but unlike Locke, Sidney explicitly attacked Hobbes and reserved his greatest admiration for Plato and Aristotle. Jefferson frequently mentions Sidney in the same breath with Locke, so perhaps it is not unreasonable to suggest that he viewed Locke in the light of Sidney.[16] In outline, Sidney's argument does resemble Locke's: the "natural universal liberty" of mankind, arising from the equality of men – from the fact that God did not cause some men "to be born with crowns upon their heads, and all others with saddles upon their backs" – obliges that government be instituted by the consent or "contract" of the governed. The people have the right to choose the form of government that "according to their own prudence or convenience" they think best. If the government threatens to subvert the public good, the people have the right to revolt and to institute new government.[17]

Nevertheless, the differences are significant. Man's "natural love to liberty," as Sidney calls it, is not the whole or the most important part of his nature. "Liberty without restraint" is inconsistent with "the good which man naturally desires for himself, children, and friends." Therefore, when man enters civil society he is "hereunto led by reason, which is his nature." Though each man enters society with a view to his (and his children's and friends') own good, "this general consent of all to resign such a part of their liberty as seems to be for the good of all, is the voice of nature." The movement out of the state of nature into civil society is not a movement away from nature, according to Sidney, but is a hearkening to the voice of a higher nature. It is not so much fear of violent death impelling man out of the state of nature, but nature's voice calling him into civil society that is the efficient cause of the body politic. Despite his republican credentials, therefore, Sidney does not reject the idea of the absolute monarchy of the best man, which is discussed in the third book of Aristotle's *Politics*. Such a man of surpassing virtue "ought to govern," Sidney writes, "because it is better for a people to be governed by him, than to enjoy their liberty; or rather they do enjoy their liberty, which is never more safe, than when it is defended by one who is a living law to himself and others." But, Sidney explains, the point of Aristotle's discussion is not thereby to approve absolute monarchy for just anyone. "Wheresoever such a man appears, he ought to reign: he bears in his person the divine character of a sovereign: God has raised him above all: and such as will not submit to him, ought to be accounted sons of Belial, brought forth and slain. But … if no such man be found, there is no natural king." To insist upon absolute monarchy when the requisite virtues do not exist is the height of injustice. Absent such "excellency of virtue," "the right and power is by nature equally lodged in all."[18]

The absolute monarchy of the best man serves as a standard and a limit for politics in Aristotle's understanding; for Sidney it is much more of a limit than a standard, but it continues to perform both functions. For example, in the *Discourses* regimes do not simply protect "the lives, lands, liberties, and goods" of their citizens, but also act as "nurses of virtue." The best regime is a mixed government in which *detur digniori* is the rule: "Plato, Aristotle, Hooker, and (may I say in short) all wise men have held, that order required, that the wisest, best, and most valiant men," should be placed in the leading offices of the regime. "All will confess, that if there be any stability in man, it must be in wisdom and virtue," and hence stability in civil and military affairs demands that the wisest and best be rulers.[19]

It appears, then, that in Sidney's doctrine ancients and moderns have a common ground not only in the idea that "man's natural love to liberty is tempered by reason, which originally is his nature," but by the larger idea that "nature, which is reason" can speak to man.[20] To understand this better, it may help to refer to Rousseau's critique of the natural rights liberalism of Hobbes and Locke. In the *Second Discourse*, Rousseau accused the early liberals of not going back far enough in their quest to find natural man, man in the state of nature. As described by Hobbes and Locke, the individual in the state of nature is much too advanced, much too reasonable: he must be almost a philosopher to imagine and then create the way out of the state of nature that leads into civil society.[21] Unless man in his natural state is not only prepolitical but also *prerational*, the attempt to locate human nature prior to and abstracted from civil society must fail. For man's reason is the mark of civil society; or rather it is the mark of a long historical development in the state of nature, preparing and conditioning man to enter the social contract. In the end (or, properly speaking, from the very beginning) Hobbes and Locke had therefore vitiated their attempt to understand man nonteleologically – that is, in opposition to the way the ancients had understood him, as the political animal, as the being whose natural end (*telos*) is fulfilled in civic life – by in effect smuggling a hidden or implicit teleology into their account of natural man, who, in following out his interest, would wish to escape the state of nature as soon as possible, for his comfortable home in civil society. The individual in the state of nature was still a man naturally meant to live in, or constituted for, civil society.

In short, Sidney agreed with Rousseau's critique, but drew the opposite conclusion. There *was* an implicit teleology in the Lockean account of the state of nature: rational man did imply political man. So an unbridgeable gap between ancients and moderns did not exist, insofar as modern political philosophy could be interpreted teleologically. From the point of view of political practice – that is, of practical wisdom as opposed to theoretical wisdom, not to mention defective theoretical wisdom or philosophical hebetude – this assimilation of moderns to ancients was, well, natural. It was the only way to make sense of the republican liberalism of Locke. As statesmen, the founders never doubted for a moment that human beings were a species in nature distinct from and superior to other animals, or that the self-evident truth that "all men are created equal" could be the foundation of just government precisely because it recognized the differences between man and beast on the one hand, and between man and the Creator on the other.

Man's unalienable rights are not, after all, his creation. Men are "endowed by their Creator" with these rights, and an endowment is not an arbitrary grant but something meant to be used for certain essential and recurring purposes. Apparently, the Creator endows men with these rights in the full knowledge that it is up to men to "secure" them, inasmuch as it is to judge men's intentions and efforts that the divine nature has as one of its names, the "Supreme Judge of the World." Yet "nature's God" is also a legislator and an executive, and the uses to which men put their natural rights seem finally to have to be reconciled with "the law of nature and of nature's God." Otherwise, the "Protection of Divine Providence," on which the signers of the Declaration rely, could not be justly forthcoming. Men are therefore meant to secure their rights in such a way as to effect their safety and happiness in a separate and equal people: they have to choose a "form of government" for themselves. In making that choice, their individual rights become "ends" that encompass an opinion or judgment of their safety and happiness. Their consent encompasses, too, the means (the "principles" and "powers") they judge conducive to those ends. But from the standpoint of the divine nature, in thus securing their rights men are in fact using or exercising them, and are answerable to the divine nature in its legislative, executive, and judicial aspects. In any case, far from being the *summum malum* or (in Hobbes's words) the "dissolute condition of masterless men," nature is in the Declaration the cause of responsibility, in both senses: it is the ground of human freedom, and it points to the end or standard of human freedom. The Declaration culminates in "sacred Honor."

THE FEDERALIST ON FOUNDING

Let us look now at the effort to secure these rights in *The Federalist*'s account of the Constitution. For present purposes, we shall confine our interest in this account to its bearing on the founders and the classics. Now, *The Federalist* presents a famous defense of republicanism, as well as of certain modern improvements in the science of politics. What is the relation between the two? Surely the place to begin is with the surface. *The Federalist* was written by Alexander Hamilton, James Madison, and John Jay, but not under their own names; they used the pseudonym of "Publius." What is the significance of the fact that the most authoritative defense of the Constitution claims to have been written by a Roman – by one of the founding statesmen of the Roman republic?

Some biography would seem to be in order. Publius Valerius, whose life is recounted in Livy and Plutarch, fought alongside Lucius Junius Brutus in expelling the last Roman king. Although he served as consul four times, Publius accomplished his best and most important measures when he held the office alone, following the death of his fellow consul Brutus. Then he enacted a series of reforms: he increased the size of the Senate; granted a defendant's right to appeal a consul's judgment to the people; reduced tax rates to encourage manufactures and commerce; and ordered that the lictors' rods, when a consul came into the popular assembly, be lowered not toward him but toward the people, thus emphasizing, as Plutarch puts it, "the majesty of the democracy." By such measures Publius quickly succeeded in augmenting his authority over the people, "not by humbling himself, as they thought, but by checking and removing their envious feelings through moderation on his part." With each renunciation of his kingly or consular authority, his own influence grew, so that the people "submitted to him with pleasure and bore his yoke willingly," even honoring him with the name "Publicola," which means lover or cherisher of the people. Publius's regime endured in Rome until the time of the civil wars, whereas Solon (whose life is parallel to Publius's in Plutarch) saw with his own eyes the collapse of his regime into the tyranny of Peisistratus.[22]

It is not necessary to draw out the analogy at every point to catch its overall significance. Our Publius wishes to seize the fleeting moment that is favorable to constitution making, the moment of maximum influence of the wise and moderate men of the Federal Convention, to form a just and enduring republic in an extensive land. To accomplish this he must speak moderately, "emphasizing the majesty of the democracy" at the same time that he increases his own and the regime's authority. Unlike Solon, who after making his laws deserted Athens for ten years, the American Publius will follow the Roman Publius in remaining in his country, always ready to counsel it and thus to extirpate tyranny's hopes of return. As for the original Publius, his was a career of broadening the popular basis of the republic while stabilizing and guiding it aristocratically. Could the American Publius have attempted something similar in our regime?

Once past the ancient portals of *The Federalist*, however, we find little deference to the theory or practice of classical politics. In No. 9 we have Publius's lamentations on the instability of the ancient republics:

It is impossible to read the history of the petty republics of Greece and Italy without feeling sensations of horror and disgust at the distractions with which they were continually agitated, and at the rapid succession of revolutions by which they were kept in a state of perpetual vibration between the extremes of tyranny and anarchy. If they exhibit occasional calms, these only serve as short-lived contrasts to the furious storms that are to succeed. If now and then intervals of felicity open themselves to view, we behold them with a mixture of regret, arising from the reflection that the pleasing scenes before us are soon to be overwhelmed by the tempestuous waves of sedition and party rage. (No. 9, p. 66)[23]

To which Publius, however, conjoins the hope of better things to come:

If it had been found impracticable to have devised models of a more perfect structure, the enlightened friends to liberty would have been obliged to abandon the cause of that species of government as indefensible. The science of politics, however, like most other sciences, has received great improvement. The efficacy of various principles is now well understood, which were either not known at all, or imperfectly known to the ancients. The regular distribution of power into distinct departments; the introduction of legislative balances and checks; the institution of courts composed of judges holding their offices during good behavior; the representation of the people in the legislature by deputies of their own election: these are wholly new discoveries, or have made their principal progress towards perfection in modern times ... To this catalogue of circumstances that tend to the amelioration of popular systems of civil government, I shall venture, however novel it may appear to some, to add one more ... I mean the ENLARGEMENT of the ORBIT within which such systems are to revolve. (No. 9, p. 67)

These improvements might seem dangerous or inadvisable precisely because of their novelty. But in No. 14 Publius assures his readers that it is the glory of the people of America "that they have not suffered a blind veneration for antiquity, for custom, or for names." "Happily for America, happily we trust for the whole human race,"

Publius continues, "they pursued a new and more noble course. They accomplished a revolution which has no parallel in the annals of human society" (pp. 99–100). Shortly thereafter, Publius compares favorably the sciences of ethics and politics to the science of mathematics: "Though it cannot be pretended that the principles of moral and political knowledge have, in general, the same degree of certainty with those of the mathematics, yet they have much better claims in this respect than to judge from the conduct of men in particular situations we should be disposed to allow them" (No. 31, p. 190).

These statements, together with others that could be collected, especially from Nos. 10 and 51, seem to add up to *The Federalist*'s clear endorsement of the superiority of modern to ancient political science, and to constitute a sort of pledge of allegiance to modern principles. But, on closer examination, *The Federalist*'s allegiance to political theory in the modern sense becomes much more ambiguous. The "great improvement" in the science of politics is explicitly said to concern "means," albeit "powerful means, by which the excellencies of republican government may be retained and its imperfections lessened or avoided" (p. 67). No "great improvement" in understanding the ends of government is claimed; in fact, the goal is to retain the "excellencies" of republicanism while mitigating or curing its historic ills. The "novelty" of American government has perhaps also been misunderstood. Publius says: "But why is the experiment of an extended republic to be rejected merely because it may comprise what is new?" Now, to "comprise" what is new is to include what is new, suggesting that it also comprises what is old. Hence the next sentence: "Is it not the glory of the people of America that, whilst they have paid a decent regard to the opinions of former times and other nations, they have not suffered a blind veneration for antiquity, for custom, or for names, to overrule the suggestions of their own good sense, the knowledge of their own situation, and the lessons of their own experience?" A "blind" veneration for antiquity must be distinguished from a sighted or insightful veneration, which may well be compatible with the suggestions of good sense, self-knowledge, and the lessons of experience. Even a "decent regard" to the opinions of former times would be, however, incompatible with the new political theory. But it is not this political theory to which

Publius appeals: it is a kind of practical knowledge, a statesman's knowledge. It is the sort of wisdom able to learn new lessons from experience, but also to learn that America will not be exempt from "a common portion of the vicissitudes and calamities which have fallen to the lot of other nations," that in many cases we shall have to follow "the customary and ordinary modes practiced in other governments," that we shall never be able to desert "all the usual maxims of prudence and policy" (No. 14, p. 99; No. 30, p. 189; No. 23, p. 151; No. 24, p. 158).

Mathematics, too, may be less of a help in, or less of an analogy to, ethical and political matters than Publius might seem to indicate. While acknowledging that there are axioms in the human sciences even as there are in geometry, Publius distinguishes "other truths" that "cannot pretend to rank in the class of axioms," but nevertheless are "such direct inferences" from the axioms, "and so obvious in themselves, and so agreeable to the natural and unsophisticated dictates of common sense that they challenge the assent of a sound and unbiased mind with a degree of force and conviction almost equally irresistible" (No. 31, p. 189). Here "the natural and unsophisticated dictates of common sense" are a standard independent of mathematical science, or perhaps are a standard to which mathematics itself must in practice conform. Nor can everything in ethics and politics be understood quantitatively, or be reduced to certainties. "[T]he saying is as just as it is witty," Publius observes, "that 'in political arithmetic, two and two do not always make four'" (No. 21, p. 138). In the human sciences, it is the mean between two extremes that is the usual guide to action, or that at least is the common desideratum, and rightly judging what is the mean is the work of prudence, not of a deductive or mathematical science. "Nothing can be more fallacious," Publius concludes, "than to found our political calculations on arithmetical principles" (No. 55, p. 339).

These considerations deserve to be amplified by reference to the problem of founding itself. According to the classics, founding is the highest task of the political art, the work of prudence in its most universal sense. Has the new science of politics improved the understanding or the practice of founding? Publius addresses this question in Nos. 37 through 40 in the course of introducing the second part of *The Federalist*. The first part of the book (through No. 36) concerned the Union, or, one might say, the matter of the new country. The second half discusses the Constitution itself, the form of the nation, and Nos. 37 through 40 serve as a prelude to the consideration of the separation of powers – of the distinctive elements of America's republican form that make it worthy of choice. In contrast to the stirring introduction to the first part in *The Federalist* No. 1, the introduction to the second stresses the limits of human wisdom: reflecting men "will keep in mind that they themselves are but men, and ought not to assume an infallibility in rejudging the fallible opinion of others"; they should know "that a faultless plan was not to be expected" from the Convention or from any body of men (No. 37, p. 222).

Publius gives five reasons for the innate difficulties of the Convention's task. First, "the novelty of the undertaking." This was counted the "glory" of the American "experiment" in No. 14, but now we are reminded of the disadvantages of novelty – particularly that our experience can provide only "warning of the course to be shunned, without pointing out that which ought to be pursued." The reason of man, Publius later observes, is "timid and cautious" when left alone; the laws are frail and unlovely when deprived of "reverence" or "veneration," which only time and recollections of good can bestow. Novelty, in short, both piles difficulties before reason and cuts away prejudices useful for the support of even the most rational government (No. 37, p. 222; No. 49, pp. 311–12). Second, the difficulty of combining stability and energy with liberty. The republican genius seems to demand "not only that all power should be derived from the people," but that it be kept in close dependence upon them by means of short terms and frequent rotations of office. Yet energy, which enters "into the very definition of good government," and stability, which is "essential to national character," demand the opposite. Third, the difficulty of distinguishing the authority of the federal and the state governments. Here Publius's disquisition turns metaphysical, as he ponders the obstacles to distinguishing as such. The faculties of the mind have not yet been distinguished and defined by "the most acute and metaphysical philosophers," nor have the boundaries between the animal, vegetable, and material parts of nature been identified by "the most sagacious and laborious naturalists." There is an order in nature, but its articulation is not readily understandable by man. Human institutions, however, are even less intelligible. The "greatest adepts in political science" are puzzled by questions that "daily occur in the course of practice," and by the difficulties of discriminating and defining the three powers of government. Contrary to Hobbes, we have a more lucid understanding of the things of nature than of the things we ourselves make. It follows, therefore, that words are a "cloudy medium" through which to express ideas, because words are equivocal and are imperfectly matched to the articulations of nature. Even the "Almighty himself," when He speaks to men in their language, has His meaning, "luminous as it must be ... rendered dim and doubtful" by the obscurities of words (No. 37, pp. 222–25).

In short, neither philosophers, naturalists, political scientists, nor theologians have achieved wisdom; they should, in a certain sense, be more impressed by what they do not know, than by what they do know. Accordingly, none is entitled to rule simply on the basis of his wisdom. They are "but men," not the human divinity who deserves to rule in the absolute monarchy of the best man. To these theoretical obstacles to the Convention's task, Publius adds two practical ones: the "interfering pretensions of the larger and smaller states," and the "variety of interests" in the country as a whole. These fourth and fifth difficulties facing the Convention show that the necessity of gaining the consent of the governed, in addition to the complications of the pursuit of wisdom, should moderate our political expectations. But the point of Publius's entire discourse in No. 37 is not to apologize for the work of the Federal Convention, but to teach respect, reverence, even "wonder" and "astonishment" for its accomplishments. Given these awesome difficulties, given the remarkable fact that the Convention nevertheless "surmounted" them "with a unanimity almost as unprecedented as it must have been unexpected, ... [i]t is impossible for the man of pious reflection not to perceive" in the Constitution "a finger of the Almighty hand which has been so frequently and signally extended to our relief" (No. 37, pp. 222, 225–27). Reason and revelation seem to concur in regarding the founding as the work of more-than-human legislators, of the "demi-gods" of whom Jefferson once spoke.

If this is an example of mixing the "authority of superstition" into the founding, then it is but an instance of the nature of foundings in general, which is the theme of No. 38. There we discover that the new science of politics has not in any significant way improved upon the ancient, in respect of the difficulties of founding. Ancient foundings were not always "clothed with the legitimate authority of the people." Publius seems to believe that the American Founding was so clothed, and to regard it as an "improvement" on the ancient mode, but in No. 40 he will admit the possible "defect of regular authority" in the Convention (No. 38, pp. 228–29; No. 40, p. 248). Ancient foundings were also the work of one man, and Publius reviews thirteen ancient lawgivers. The American founding was the work of an assembly of men – but it seems to require the defense and explication and sense of wonder supplied by one man, Publius. Ancient foundings involved "expedients," which the lawgivers were "obliged to employ in order to carry their reforms into effect." Solon confessed to having indulged "a more temporizing policy," not giving his countrymen "the government best suited to their happiness, but most tolerable to their prejudices." Could Publius also have been obliged to tolerate the perhaps too democratic or confederal prejudices of the Americans? Lycurgus, "more true to his object, was under the necessity of mixing a portion of violence with the authority of superstition, and of securing his final success by a voluntary renunciation, first of his country and then of his life" (No. 38, p. 229). Publius's own use of superstition has been suggested (compare No. 2, p. 32, and No. 1, p. 29), and his portion of violence may be said to consist in the dire warnings he gives and the dark pictures he draws of a disunited, warring, unfree America, the inevitable result of the imprudent rejection of the proposed Constitution (see, e.g., Nos. 2–9, 15–22, and 24–28).

The conjunction of wisdom with consent (and of consent with violence and superstition) is nowhere better exemplified in The Federalist than in the innocuous analogy of the patient and his doctor in this same number. "A patient who finds his disorder daily growing

worse," Publius writes, "and that an efficacious remedy can no longer be delayed without extreme danger, after coolly revolving his
situation and the characters of different physicians, selects and calls
in such of them as he judges most capable of administering relief,
and best entitled to his confidence" (No. 38, pp. 220–31). We note
that a patient threatened with "extreme danger" may nonetheless
"coolly revolve" his situation and call in his preferred physician. In
this analogy, the members of the Convention are made doctors to
America's political health. But it is not on the basis of their knowledge alone that they are entitled to prescribe for their patient; they
must also possess a certain character that the patient judges worthy
of his confidence, because the art and science alone could as easily
be used to injure as to cure him. Any art or science, in its purely cognitive aspect, is indifferent to the morality or immorality governing
its use. This is why the character of the physician, his allegiance to
the Hippocratic oath, and his interest in his own prosperity and reputation combine to inspire the patient's confidence that the doctor's
skill will be used to heal rather than to enfeeble. In the same manner,
the presence of the moral virtues is the touchstone of the intellectual virtues. Prudence or practical wisdom is one of the theoretical
virtues: it is the virtue of deliberating well on the means to the ends
set by moral virtue. Thus prudence presupposes the presence of
moral virtue, and no one who supposes himself to give prudent
advice or even to teach philosophy (so far as the intellectual virtues
include prudence) has a right to be taken seriously if his character
does not inspire confidence. Otherwise, it would be impossible to
trust such a figure or to befriend him, because one would always fear
that his advice or his teachings were duplicitous and meant to serve
only his advantage. In this regard *The Federalist* is one with the classical, particularly the Aristotelian, tradition.

The subject of No. 39 is the Constitution's conformity to republican and federal principles, and Publius's reassuring answer is that
it conforms easily to both. His reassurance is based, however, on a
redefinition of republicanism and federalism. The implications of
the latter do not become clear until somewhat later, and will not be
pursued here. But the former is of direct concern. Whereas in No. 37
republicanism seemed to require "that all power be derived from the

people," with short terms and frequent rotations in office, in No. 39 republicanism has been redefined to include the requirements of good government, namely energy and stability. To wit, a republic is "a government which derives all its powers directly or indirectly from the great body of the people; and is administered by persons holding their offices during pleasure for a limited period, or during good behavior" (No. 37, p. 223; No. 39, p. 237). By this transformation, Publius is allowed both to reestablish his republican bona fides after his tantalizing discussion of ancient foundings and of the relation of wisdom to consent, and to prepare for the discussion of the separation of powers as an invention of wisdom meant to perfect republicanism. At the same time he is able discreetly to separate the two parts of his rather undemocratic account of the problem of founding, in Nos. 38 and 40, with the orthodox professions of No. 39.

It is only in No. 40 that Publius confesses to the possible "defect of regular authority" in the Federal Convention. It appears that the patient did not "coolly revolve" his situation and call in his physician, after all. But then there are emergencies when the physician must act without the patient's consent but in his interest, cases in which the patient himself will approve the action retroactively. To some extent, Publius suggests, these were the circumstances of the American case, and so he must justify the conduct of the Convention. In "all great changes of established governments forms ought to give way to substance," because "a rigid adherence in such cases to the former would render nominal and nugatory the transcendent and precious right of the people to 'abolish or alter their governments as to them shall seem most likely to effect their safety and happiness.'" Notice that Publius abridges his quotation from the Declaration of Independence, pretermitting the people's right "to institute new government, laying its foundations on such principles, and organizing its powers in such form, as to them shall seem most likely to effect their safety and happiness." He seems, therefore, to deny that the people can actually institute their own government, and remarks explicitly that "since it is impossible for the people spontaneously and universally, to move or concert towards their object, it is therefore essential that such changes be instituted by some *informal and unauthorized* propositions, made by some patriotic and respectable citizen or number of citizens" (No. 40, p. 249). Once again, the character of the leading citizens is essential to their trustworthiness: there are "considerations of duty arising out of the case itself" that may supply any "defect of regular authority," but it is only "patriotic and respectable" citizens who can be counted on to perform the duty. Exactly what makes them "patriotic and respectable" Publius does not say, perhaps leaving it to the reader to recall that, in a previous case of a lack of "regular authority" – that of the feudal sovereign prince as against his barons – the prince was said to acquire "personal weight and influence" by his "vigorous and warlike temper and ... superior abilities" (No. 40, pp. 248–49; No. 17, p. 116). Perhaps then the presence of men of superior abilities, especially of men who had fought the Revolution through to a successful conclusion, supplied the defect of authorized republican authority with a kingly virtue all their own.

But Publius goes further. Even if circumstances had not justified the Convention in proposing a new Constitution, it still would be the prudent thing to do. Absent delegated authority, absent compelling circumstances, the dictates of prudence remain a rule to be obeyed. If, Publius asks, it is a "noble precept" to accept good advice even from an enemy, "shall we set the ignoble example of refusing such advice even when it is offered by our friends?" American republicanism must be open to good advice even from its enemies – from monarchy and perhaps even from the modern political philosophers who defended absolute or mixed monarchy. "The prudent inquiry, in all cases, ought surely to be not so much from whom the advice comes, as whether the advice be good" (No. 40, p. 250). The inquiries of prudence follow the noble or aristocratic precept of looking to the end, to the goodness, of advice, rather than to its origins or authorization. When we learn that the "auxiliary precautions" of American republicanism are "inventions of prudence," we therefore behold a regime in whose republicanism is combined democratic consent and aristocratic prudence (No. 51, p. 319). In the contrast between the introduction of these auxiliary devices – separation of powers, an independent judiciary, the extended sphere, and so forth – in *Federalist* No. 9 as improved products of the science of politics, and their later explication in *Federalist* No. 51 as "inventions of prudence," Publius shows us by example how prudence may use the discoveries or insights of modern political science for its own good purposes.

In interpreting the Constitution, we must not forget that Publius himself regards the principal mechanisms of government established under it as "auxiliary devices" designed to help perfect republican government, and that as "inventions of prudence," these devices, like prudence itself, concern only means to be employed in the service of ends that are not themselves expressly discussed in the Constitution. To locate "the fundamental principles of the Revolution" we must instead turn to "the transcendent law of nature and of nature's God, which declares that the safety and happiness of society are the objects to which all political institutions aim and to which all such institutions must be sacrificed" (No. 39, p. 236; No. 43, p. 276). In the American regime, the ends to which prudence ministers are proclaimed in the fundamental justification of the Revolution, the Declaration of Independence. It is above all because of this connection between the Constitution and the Declaration that American constitutionalism cannot be mainly a matter for judges, however enlightened they may be. For the purpose of American constitutionalism is to produce a certain kind of human being and citizen – an American, whose character reflects the ends of our republicanism. In this respect, the political theory of the Constitution cannot be understood apart from the principles of the Declaration of Independence, and the political theory of the American regime cannot be understood apart from the political science of the classics.

CHAPTER TWO

RELATIVISM AND THE DECLARATION
OF INDEPENDENCE

For decades now, commencement speakers, editorial writers, and others who ought to know better have hailed each graduating class of American high school and college seniors as the vanguard of the brightest and best-educated generation in our history. If only it were so! The truth, alas, is humbler. Although in certain technical and scientific fields today's students may see farther than their predecessors, in the liberal arts generally – in moral and political subjects, particularly – this is simply not the case.

Reports by the U.S. Department of Education, the National Endowment for the Humanities, the National Association of Scholars, and other groups have drawn attention to many students' appalling ignorance of history, geography, literature, and other departments of learning, thus affording commencement speakers a delicious new topic for declamation. But in my experience as a college teacher, this deplorable ignorance is matched, in a few students' cases, by equally shallow pretensions to knowledge. Some young men and women arrive in class stuffed with facts. What the two kinds of students have in common is that neither can conceive of knowledge as anything other than an accumulation of facts. The one type cannot see the value of collecting what, bereft of any larger associations, is essentially trivia. The other students enjoy this trivial pursuit precisely because it is a game they can win; and the rewards of winning can be substantial.

Stricter high school and college standards, more Advanced Placement courses and tests, and "back to basics" instruction may result in more facts being learned in American schools, but they cannot by themselves redress the fundamental problem, which is that the *value* of learning, the ultimate purpose of education, is no longer apparent. In short, we are in danger of killing our young people's appetite to learn – so deadening and tranquilizing their sense of wonder that education becomes something either to be endured or exploited, but never to be loved.

I see this every year in my freshman course in American politics, which typically begins with a discussion of the Declaration of Independence. Invariably, there are loads of bright young students who know all about it and who can discourse plausibly on the Declaration's roots in the Enlightenment, John Locke's influence on its authors, the economic interests that actuated its signers, and so forth. What these students have trouble with is the most basic question: Is its central and most memorable claim *true*? Are men created equal and endowed with certain unalienable rights? The question never fails to floor them. After all, it seems impossibly naïve. Who would have thunk it, as Pogo might say, that a college professor could ask such a question? "In *their* [the founders'] opinion, it was true," a freshman will volunteer, finally. When students understand that this revelation is not the end but the beginning of the discussion, their education has begun.

It takes a while, I am saying, before students recognize that the really interesting question is precisely whether the proposition at the heart of the Declaration is true or not. It is only the concern with such ultimate questions that justifies paying serious attention to everything else there is to know about the document. Who can blame students for *not* remembering the dates of the American Revolution, for example, if they have been taught not that the Declaration is "that immortal emblem of humanity" (Lincoln's words), as previous generations learned, but that it is (ho-hum) an eruption of Enlightenment optimism, a footnote to Locke's *Second Treatise*, or a hostile takeover bid by some greedy and racist colonials?

Now I wish to make clear that this is not an indictment of contemporary students. The fault, I am tempted to say, is not in them, nor in their stars, but more likely in the star faculty of their universities, whose teaching has trickled down to their high school instructors. Students today labor under the weight of the accumulated dogmas of the modern academy, superstitions that are crushing the life out of modern education as well as politics – chief among them, a set of ideas whose family name is "relativism."

VALUE JUDGMENTS

Relativism is the notion that all judgments of right and wrong, of noble and base, are relative to the person or persons making them. That is to say, it assumes there are no reasonable, independent, objective standards of right and wrong available to man as such. Rather, every such judgment, whether the person making it acknowledges it or not, is in fact nothing more than an expression of personal preference. "Cultural relativism" modifies this definition by suggesting that persons do not, in fact, at least regarding the most serious "value" questions, judge relative to themselves alone – as if everyone could create his own values out of the depths of his self. Instead, men receive their most important values from a larger and more comprehensive authority, from a "culture," which is, as the name suggests, a kind of growth. One version of cultural relativism, once prevalent in anthropology departments but with roots going back at least to Romanticism, understands this growth to be spontaneous and unplanned, a matrix resulting from myriad particular actions or reactions to surrounding conditions. Another (less popular) version, indebted in different ways to Thomas Carlyle and Friedrich Nietzsche, explains cultures as the product of willful creativity on the part of a few heroic men of vision – creative artists who establish the horizons within which human life can alone have meaning.

Whatever the ground of culture, however, cultural relativism teaches that all opinions of good and evil are "values" – that is, they have significance only because they happen to be valued by somebody – and that values vary from culture to culture much more fundamentally than they do from person to person within a culture. In this way, cultural relativism tries to shy away from the final *reductio* of deconstructionism and existentialism, that every individual or "self" inhabits and creates its own world of meaning. Though existentialism seemed daring and new to countless mid-twentieth-century readers, its roots went back to the origins of modern philosophy.

In early modern philosophy, the problem was how to connect the consciousness or ego (*res cogitans*) with the external world (*res extrensa*), given the radical separation between them introduced by Descartes for the sake of liberating man from his tutelage to nature or God. Only if man were alone with his own thoughts – not bound by his place in nature or his communion with God – could he originate and so test his own concepts as to be *certain* of his knowledge, which for confirmation required exerting human power over an otherwise unintelligible nature in order to order, or re-create, it according to his own will. In latter-day deconstructionism, this enterprise is reduced to the problem of relating a reader to a text. According to deconstructionism, every reading of a text is transformed into an act of appropriation or re-creation, because there is no objective intent or meaning in the words – and no relation between the words and the entities to which they seem to refer – to which the mind can have access. Every text, therefore, eventually becomes a battleground over which readers attempt to exert power. Thus modern (political) philosophy may be said to begin with Hobbes's books discovering the state of nature, and to end with books *becoming* the state of nature – a literary *bellum omnium contra omnes*.

Try as it may, however, cultural relativism cannot escape the logic of radical existentialism; it can only transfer it to the level of cultures. Accordingly, every culture stands in relation to other cultures as one self does to other selves, each building and dwelling in its own world of meaning. From this fact cultural relativism usually concludes that all cultures are equal and also, quite illogically (about which more in a moment), that toleration of all cultures is the only appropriate moral policy. This sentiment, of course, forms the basis of students' reluctance to evaluate the Declaration of Independence, not to mention the contrary claims made by Communist, Islamist, and other forms of government. In the ethics of the contemporary academy, passing value judgments on other cultures or ways of life is a mistake typically inspired by "racism" or what an earlier generation called "ethnocentrism," which means here not the excessive or unjustified love of one's own group, but, in principle, *any preference* for one's own over others – the assumption being that any preference for one's own is by definition irrational and therefore immoral.

If reason cannot pronounce one set of values to be superior to another, it would indeed be irrational to prefer one's own values to those of others. But it would be *just as irrational* to prefer others' to one's own. If all values are relative, one cannot reasonably prefer any values to any others. The practical result of this, in America, is in the first place a reflexive but shallow toleration for all points of view – the "openness" of the American mind that Allan Bloom famously diagnosed – which turns into a kind of false and mindless cosmopolitanism. And so today, professors and students who do not take values seriously can hardly believe that anyone else does or ever did. This easy-going toleration or acceptance of different values might seem to run up against hard cases very quickly. For instance, connoisseurs and cannibals both enjoy their food, and though the difference between having people to dinner and having them for dinner may seem fundamental to any idea of human dignity, it is, in the eyes of the consistent cultural relativist, strictly a cultural phenomenon, like preferring baguettes to bagels. In their own defense, the relativists will assert that no serious value relativist has ever defended cannibalism. But even if that is so, it would prove not that relativism is civilized, but only that its advocates are inconsistent. They dispose of cases they do not want to think about – by not thinking about them.

Cultural relativism might seem to resemble a view so old that it antedates Socrates and the beginnings of the natural right tradition. I mean the view, often called conventionalism, that justice has no roots in nature but is entirely conventional, i.e., a product of custom and legislation, varying from city to city or from country to country. But conventionalism pointed to the distinctiveness of conventions (*nomoi*), to the laws and customs and opinions (including opinions about the gods) that distinguished one city from another, and thus to the importance of politics as the art of choosing such conventions. Ancient conventionalism focused on the question of justice, not merely because laws vary but, more basically, because even if – as the more discerning conventionalists knew – a common denominator among the cities' clashing views of justice could be found, that still did not prove that justice is natural. It could be that justice is simply a set of rules that are advantageous for any city to observe. By contrast, however, modern-day relativism does not think justice especially problematic or politics particularly important. Courage, moderation, wisdom, justice – it lumps all the virtues together as "value judgments." (The ancient conventionalists thought the other virtues, especially moderation and wisdom, to be according to nature, i.e., not conventional.) And politics, far from being the ruling element in culture, is regarded by most relativists today as being ruled by it: a country's politics is determined by its culture, not the other way around. The implication is that there is no exercise of choice that is not determined by culture – that behind every act that we regard as free there is imperious necessity in the form of a prior and sufficient cause termed "culture," a slippery determinism that lends itself to a kind of infinite regress.

The immoderate rejection of one's own that we identified earlier as characteristic of cultural relativism has, under the circumstances, a certain rationale. After all, if your "values" are no better than mine, why not insist on my own? Why not impose my own on you? All along relativism has been smuggling in the back door what it took such pains to toss out the front – namely, that from the "fact" that all values are equally unverifiable by reason a certain value judgment, in this case, toleration, must follow. But relativism stands or falls by the assumption that "values" cannot be derived from "facts," or vice versa. Facts are supposed to be objective and verifiable by reason or science; values are not. That the value allegedly derived in this case is mild and peaceable subtracts nothing from the impossibility of the derivation; in fact, it adds to the absurdity. Not only is a value magically derived from a fact, but the value is one that relativists just happen to like.

Given that the most intolerant jingoism may be as readily derived from relativist "values" as the most tolerant cosmopolitanism, it is understandable why cultural relativists are at such pains to try to suppress any preference for one's own. There is, in their view, no stopping place once one begins seriously to love one's own; and that is so because, admitting no connection between one's own and what is good in itself, they do not conceive that one can love both: that love of the good can help to discipline the love of one's own (e.g., though, or rather because, you love your child, you don't want him to grow up to be a brat).

In practice, then, cultural relativists refuse to countenance the moderate or proper love of one's own, because they believe it is indistinguishable from the extreme love of one's own. But then they rebound to the opposite extreme of the uncritical acceptance of all other cultures, because they refuse to follow the sensible middle path of seeking first what is good in their own country, in America. Value relativism thus presumes upon a certain American goodness or naïveté. In teaching Americans that there is no objective measure of right or wrong, the relativists presume that Americans will not draw the "wrong" conclusion, and seek to impose their own values on their fellow citizens or on other cultures. How long they will refrain from drawing the wrong conclusion is another question, insofar as the relativist doctrine is constantly undermining the self-restraint on which it relies. Thus arises a perceived need to find some outside confirmation of or support for the relativists' pacific worldview, a support that neither nature nor reason, as we have seen, can provide.

It is eventually to History that cultural relativism turns to find a ground for itself. That is why such relativists do not usually appear in American classrooms teaching the stern doctrine of the scientific transcendence of all "values," not even as tempered with some grudging acceptance of our all-too-human need to have values. Instead, the relativist doctrine seems to flow easily into the left-leaning, progressive orthodoxy of the modern academy; the same people who teach the relativity of all values may thus be found condemning Israel, Donald Trump, capitalism, and other causes unpopular among academics. But this contradiction is not regarded as embarrassing if it can be shown, or asserted, that history itself has condemned these forces; for then it can be claimed that history's verdict is not a value judgment but a *fact*, to which reasonable men (and women) must submit. At this point, cultural relativism reveals itself to be only a decadent form of the philosophy of history or of Social Darwinism.

If a culture or country or cause survives, according to relativism-cum-Darwinism, it must be not only hardy but good. If it does not survive, it was not worthy of living.

In practice, then, there seems to be no alternative to deriving value judgments from facts, even from the brute fact of historical survival. The nature of politics seems to require that facts and values be related, and it is only a secondary question whether those facts be drawn from history (revealing the mandate of heaven) or from nature. It does not take much reflection on the events of the past and present century, however, to see that the notion of inevitable or irreversible human progress is hardly to be believed. That the trends of history are beneficent, or that any regime that wins its wars is ipso facto just, is a thesis so blind to the real facts of morality – to the differences between good and bad regimes – as to be indistinguishable from nihilism. It represents the utter prostration of all values, of all moral considerations, before the altar of the most ignoble facts.

THE SEARCH FOR WISDOM

For all of its talk of openness, what is most characteristic of the contemporary academy is its unwillingness to hear of relativism's alternative. There is a constituency within American universities for "diversity" in virtually every area except this, the vital one. (Republicans also need not apply.) Yet the argument against the radical separation of facts and values must be heard if American education is ever to be able to recapture its self-respect and its purpose.

This calls for the reading of great books, as Allan Bloom has argued eloquently, but not merely for the reading of great books. It is too easy for such studies to degenerate into their own kind of cultural relativism, in which moral and political questions are condescended to from the Olympian heights of intellectual virtue – or rather of the caricature of intellectual virtue that remains when practical wisdom (*phronesis*) is denied its rightful place as part of the intellect's perfection. In Aristotle's account, one of the distinctions between theoretical wisdom and practical wisdom is that the latter is concerned with one's own good, that is, with the relation between one's own and the good. Plato, who did not make a thematic distinction between theoretical and practical knowledge, understood the quest for wisdom to begin with a question at once practical and theoretical: How should we live? In short, according to both Plato and Aristotle, the concern with the highest questions of theory ought to begin with, and ultimately to return to, reflection on one's own situation.

Thus the reading of great books, although necessary, is not sufficient. They must be read with a view to the students' own good as human beings and citizens; they must be read with an eye for something outside the texts. For the aim of education is not simply the imparting of facts or an appreciation of great books, but *wisdom* – uniting theory with practice, knowledge with character, ideas with consequences. The recognition that the pursuit of knowledge, shorn of its moral and political responsibilities, becomes a kind of spiritless game, lies behind the frequent calls in our time for schools to teach values. Facts are not enough. Students need something more. The demand has been taken up by both liberal and conservative candidates in the last few elections. A movement called "cultural conservatism" sprang up several years ago explicitly to fight cultural relativism by encouraging attention to values. But to speak of conserving cultural "values" is already to make a crucial, and disabling, concession to the relativist position. Values are not truths, because values are by definition subjective. To invoke "absolute values" is to do no more than to announce that one feels particularly strongly about them. That the distinction is not merely verbal may be gathered from cultural conservatism's answer to the pointed question, *Why* ought we to conserve the "values" of Western civilization? Because "they work," cultural conservatives often reply. To which the relativist may fairly rejoin, "What do you mean, *work*?" The values of cannibals work very well for them.

Suppose then that the conservative were to say, "Look, no sane man doubts that the West's traditional values *work*, inasmuch as they produce today's material prosperity, political freedom, and peace among nations." "But what of those who despise luxury, who hunger for power, who grumble at the peace imposed on them by the will of other nations?" the relativist will respond. "Why shouldn't their values count?" To call men like Robespierre, Lenin, Hitler, and Mao "insane," absent a major refinement in cultural conservatism's argument, is simply to say that conservatives do not like such men's values. It is not to say they are wrong. And if a skeptic were to add, "Suppose that tomorrow the stock market plunges and a deep depression begins, or that war with Russia or China breaks out," what then would become of those conservative values whose only justification was that they used to work?

Our forefathers did not claim that the United States was based on such cultural values. They declared that the new nation was founded on self-evident truths. A self-evident truth is one that contains its own evidence, that carries the evidence for itself within its own terms. The proposition "Man is a rational animal," for example, is such a truth, because he who says "man" has already said "rational animal." The predicate is contained in the idea of the subject. "That all men are created equal" is also such a truth, since he who says "men" says "a group of beings each of whom is equally a man." "Created equal" therefore adds nothing to the account of "all men," but draws attention to what men are *not* – created so *unequal* that one human being might legitimately rule another without his consent.

By knowing what men are, the Declaration argues, we may know how we ought to treat one another. The "is" – created equal and endowed with certain rights – implies the "ought" – that we should institute government, operating with the consent of the governed, to secure men's rights. So far removed from the radical separation of facts and values is the Declaration, in fact, that it does not feel obliged to use the language of "ought" or "should." It speaks, in its majestic opening section, in straightforward declarative sentences: "When in the course of human events, it becomes necessary … a decent respect to the opinions of mankind requires … We hold these truths to be self-evident, that all men are created equal, that they are endowed by the Creator with certain unalienable Rights, that among these are Life, Liberty, and the pursuit of Happiness. That to secure these rights, governments are instituted … That whenever any form of government becomes destructive of these ends …," and so forth.

The authors of the Declaration do not suggest that this is the way things ought to be, but that this is how things *are*. Men are created equal, endowed with rights, and government exists to secure those rights. I do not mean to imply that Jefferson and the others imagined that in most countries such principles and institutions already existed, nor yet that they had a duty to confer civil governments upon peoples other than their own. What I am saying is they understood that the rightness of their principles did not arise from any act of their, or for that matter of any man's, will. The moral imperative contained in those principles arises from nature itself. In sum, the Declaration is a document of natural right, which means that the "is" (nature) and "ought" (right) belong together as two aspects of the same reality.

Relativism is the thorough-going but unsuccessful attempt to sunder these two aspects. Its failure involves not only the self-contradictions explored above but also this most basic dilemma: it cannot distinguish consistently between facts and values. Consider the elementary question, What is a "value"? It is commonly said that values are preferences or desires; but this definition leads to a problem. A person's desires can conflict, and even a strong desire can be fought. It would appear, then, that not just any momentary desire is a "value," but only one that is chosen or resolutely willed. But is this criterion itself a judgment of fact or value? Is the definition of value not itself a value judgment? Though relativism stands or falls by the ability to distinguish "facts" from "values," it cannot consistently do so. Hence relativism refutes itself, and the way is opened back to the relation of facts and values implicit in the basic principles of Western civilization, and in the Declaration of Independence.

COMMONSENSE KNOWLEDGE

"But is it *true*?" Yes, though to understand that answer properly, one must say something about what reason can and cannot demonstrate.

A more colloquial translation of the question would be, "Prove it!" which usually means prove it to the satisfaction of the most obdurate soul in the room. Self-evident propositions are precisely those which are as evident as they can be: they cannot be proven in the sense of being deduced from some anterior principle. In carrying their own proof or evidence with them, they operate in the fashion of axioms in a geometric proof – as the starting point, not the finishing point, of reasoning. Publius elaborated this point memorably in *Federalist* 31:

> In disquisitions of every kind there are certain primary truths, or first principles, upon which all subsequent reasonings must depend. These contain an internal evidence which, antecedent to all reflection or combination, commands the assent of the mind …. Of this nature are the maxims in geometry that the whole is greater than its parts; that things equal to the same are equal to one another; that two straight lines cannot enclose a space; and that all right angles are equal to each other. Of the same nature are those other maxims in ethics and politics, that there cannot be an effect without a cause; that the means ought to be proportioned to the end; that every power ought to be commensurate with its object; that there ought to be no limitation of a power destined to effect a purpose which is itself incapable of limitation. And there are other truths in the two latter sciences which, if they cannot pretend to rank in the class of axioms, are yet such direct inferences from them, and so obvious in themselves, and so agreeable to the natural and unsophisticated dictates of common sense that they challenge the assent of a sound and unbiased mind with a degree of force and conviction almost equally irresistible.

The conditions of all demonstration cannot themselves be demonstrated. But self-evident propositions are not necessarily self-evident to everyone. If their terms are not understood or recognized, then their truth will not be grasped. And of course their truth may be denied, even if it is grasped. As Publius puts it in the same paragraph, "Where it [the self-evident truth] produces not this effect ["the assent of the mind"], it must proceed either from some disorder in the organs of perception, or from the influence of some strong interest, or passion, or prejudice."

The only kind of proof that can properly be offered, therefore, is the kind that no one, at least no one whose mind and senses are functioning normally, needs. He has it already, in the commonsense knowledge that allows him to distinguish a human being from a dog, or from a bird or even a birddog. All men belong to the same species (in Latin, *species* means the "look" of a thing), and as such they have a look or form that distinguishes them from other kinds of beings. Their form is related to their ends or capacities or characteristic activities. Implicit in this recognition of different kinds of beings, therefore, is the awareness that they ought to be treated according to their different natures or capacities. A rational animal should not be treated as if it were irrational; a man, as we say, should not be treated like a dog. Or as Thomas Jefferson expressed it in one of his last letters, meant to be read at the celebration of the fiftieth anniversary of American Independence: "the mass of mankind has not been born with saddles on their backs, nor a favored few booted and spurred, ready to ride them legitimately, by the grace of God."

John Adams, Jefferson's colleague on the committee responsible for writing the Declaration of Independence, gave a similar though more elaborate gloss on the self-evident meaning of equality in that document and in the Massachusetts Declaration of Rights, which he had drafted. In a remarkable series of letters to his son, Charles, written in early 1794 while serving as Washington's Vice President, Adams said that what some might call "the modern Doctrine of Equality" was actually "a fundamental elementary Principle of the Law of Nature." As such, it was, so to speak, older than modernity and even than Christianity. In fact, Christian faith itself was "founded on that eternal and fundamental Principle of the Law of Nature, Do as you would be done by: and love your Neighbor as yourself." This was "not a Physical but a moral Equality." (letter dated January 9, 1794)

In a subsequent letter (February 24, 1794), Adams explained the nature of that moral equality.

> It really means little more than that We are all of the same Species: made by the same God: possessed of Minds and Bodies alike in essence: having all the same Reason, Passions, Affections, and appetites. All Men are Men and not Beasts: Men and not Birds: Men and not Fishes. The Infant in the Womb is a Man, and not

a Lyon.... All these are Men and not Angells: Men and not Veg-
etables, etc.... The Equality of Nature is a moral Equality only:
an Equality of Rights and Obligations; nothing more.

"Common sense was sufficient to determine," he advised Charles,
"that it could not mean that all men were "equally tall, Strong, wise,
handsome, active: but equally Men ... all equally in the Same Cases
intitled to the same Justice."

Of course, it is quite possible for a stubborn debater to deny that
he knows he is a human being or that other men are not horses or
dogs. But such disclaimers are, quite literally, not to be believed.
That he is speaking and not barking is proof enough of his insincer-
ity. Philosophy requires only that one love and seek wisdom, which
means that one must have some knowledge or wisdom to begin with,
even if it is only the meager portion claimed by Socrates. To assume
away all knowledge of reality at the very beginning of one's inquiries
is not a necessary or legitimate demand of philosophy but only of the
modern stultification of philosophy. Relativism's absurd strictures
require students to deny in the classroom what they know and
would readily admit to knowing outside the classroom. In this sense,
relativism is only a game, albeit a peculiar one, inasmuch as it claims
to have no rules. In fact, its rules are set by whichever faction or sect
is the strongest or the trendiest.

It is of the utmost importance, then, to help raise our own and
our young people's sights from the dehumanized, and dehumaniz-
ing, world of relativism. In the quest for educational reform, we
would do well to turn not only to great books, but also to the great
exemplars of wisdom with which our own country is blessed. To
help reclaim our destiny as human beings and as citizens, we need to
rediscover the generation that really could claim to be the best and
brightest in American history, at least from the statesman's point of
view: the founders of the American republic.

CHAPTER THREE

FEDERALIST 10 AND AMERICAN REPUBLICANISM

I⊤ ʜᴀꜱ ʙᴇᴇɴ ꜱᴀɪᴅ that the oldest word in American politics is "new." Even the United States Constitution, by far the oldest written constitution in the world, was once new, and had to be defended against charges that it was an unnecessary and unrepublican innovation. *The Federalist* was keenly aware of the novelty of the Constitution's enterprise – the attempt to establish "good government from reflection and choice" – but boldly turned it to account. "Hearken not to the voice which petulantly tells you that the form of government recommended for your adoption is a novelty in the political world," Publius admonished. For why should "the experiment of an extended republic" be rejected "merely because it may comprise what is new?" If the "leaders of the Revolution" had blindly followed precedent and tradition, the American experiment might have failed ingloriously – and the American people might already be suffering under one of those forms of government "which have crushed the liberties of the rest of mankind." But "happily for America, happily we trust for the whole human race, they pursued a new and more noble course."[1]

Yet not a perfect course. New things are noble because they are difficult; so one should not be surprised that mistakes were made in the American people's first efforts at self-government, both in the state constitutions and "in the structure of the Union." To correct these was the object of the proposed Constitution, whose superiority to the state constitutions and to the Articles of Confederation was based not only on its framers' good fortune but on their superior knowledge of political science. For as Publius declared, "the science of politics ... like most other sciences, has received great improvement," even as measured against the high standard of the political science of the classics. "The efficacy of various principles is now well understood, which were either not known at all, or imperfectly known to the ancients," he claimed.[2]

It is as a product of this new science of politics, of the modern as opposed to the ancient understanding of man, that *The Federalist* is principally known today. Broadly speaking, we owe this view of Publius and of the Constitution to the political scientist Martin Diamond – and to a lesser extent, to the historian Douglass Adair – who in a series of remarkable essays spelled out the thesis of *The Federalist*'s thoroughgoing modernity. Publius himself named five ingredients of the improved science of politics in *Federalist* 9: "the regular distribution of power into distinct departments; the introduction of legislative balances and checks; the institution of courts composed of judges holding their offices during good behavior, the representation of the people in the legislature by deputies of their own election"; and, finally, "the ENLARGEMENT of the ORBIT within which such systems are to revolve."[3] But it was Diamond's achievement to expound the central importance of the last principle to the republicanism of *The Federalist*.[4]

INTERPRETING *THE FEDERALIST*

Without neglecting the importance of the separation of powers, legislative checks and balances, the independent judiciary, and the principle of representation, Diamond nonetheless insisted that the Constitution's success in curing the ills of republican government depended "utterly upon the last item in Publius's science" – upon his "most novel and important theoretical teaching" – the extended sphere.[5] The doctrine of *Federalist* 10 was therefore at the heart of the American regime. Seen in all its ramifications, it marked a decisive break between the theory and practice of classical, and the theory and practice of modern politics. For while *The Federalist* rejects "the chains of despotism, i.e., the Hobbesian solution to the problem of self-preservation," Diamond wrote, "it nevertheless seems to accept the Hobbesian statement of the problem." The novel solution to that problem contained in *Federalist* 10 does not issue in a liberalism and republicanism that are "the means by which men may ascend to a nobler life; rather they are simply instrumentalities which solve Hobbesian problems in a more moderate manner." To put it differently, Diamond showed that Publius's republicanism becomes merely a means to his liberalism, to the doctrine of individual rights and freedom bounded only by the dictates of (comfortable) self-preservation.[6]

To protect men's rights, it is necessary to design a republicanism that avoids the characteristic malady of republican government – majority faction. To do this, according to *The Federalist*, it is necessary to ensure that the government, with its elaborate structure of separated powers, a bicameral legislature, and so forth, can endure any siege that a factious majority might mount. But even the daunting parapets of the Constitution can be overrun by a majority that is sufficiently persistent. Therefore, the majority must be weakened before it can close the siege ring around the government. Publius proposed to accomplish this by dividing the majority – which in all hitherto existing societies had been, as Diamond noted, "the great mass of the little propertied and the unpropertied," i.e., "the many" – into many different and competing interests that would serve to check one another. To encompass this "saving multiplicity of factions," republican government must be extended over a large territory; and the territory must be rich and variegated enough to support a vigorous commercial society. The "first object of government" must therefore be the protection of the diverse faculties of men from which arise "the possession of different degrees and kinds of property."[7] The requirements of commercial society exact a moral and political price, however, by encouraging "the aggressive private pursuit by all of immediate personal interests." This emancipation of acquisitiveness risks "magnifying and multiplying in American life the selfish, the interested, the narrow, the vulgar, and the crassly

economic"; but this "is precisely the substratum," Diamond emphasized, "on which our political system was intended to rest and where
it rests still."[8]

The resulting society is "solid but low," that is, it offers an elementary "decency if not ... nobility." Accordingly, *The Federalist*'s
republicanism abstracts "from politics the broad ethical function of
character formation" that had been the chief concern of the ancient
science of politics. "Other political theories," Diamond declared,
"had ranked highly, as objects of government, the nurturing of a particular religion, education, military courage, civic-spiritedness,
moderation, individual excellence in the virtues, etc. On all of these
The Federalist is either silent, or has in mind only pallid versions of
the originals, or even seems to speak with contempt."[9] Insofar as
Publius shuns the traditional goal of character formation, he also
abandons the traditional emphasis on the teaching of political opinions – on the education of citizens' habits and tastes – as a part of the
shaping of character. While "from the classic perspective, the political task is to refine and improve a regime's opinion of what is advantageous and just," Diamond explained, "Madison instead turns away
almost in horror from the human 'zeal for different opinions concerning religion, concerning government.' " It is not that higher concerns
will not manifest themselves in America. The cultivation of virtue
and opinion will instead be left to society, which will by and large be
a realm of bourgeois virtue and even of a species of republican virtue.
But these virtues, however high they may soar, will not lose touch
with their base, which is self-interest, albeit enlightened self-interest or self-interest rightly understood, as Alexis de Tocqueville later
explained. In America, virtue will always be colored by its origins, by
the horizon established in the founding and perpetuated by the Constitution: the horizon set by the attempt to supply "by opposite and
rival interests, the defect of better motives." For even when "better
motives" can be found, when statesmen of virtue and wisdom are at
the helm, their virtue will not be regarded as *indispensable* – and so
their nobility will never command the awe and deference that it
deserves. Publius's system "has no necessary place and makes no
provision for men of the founding kind," Diamond concluded.[10]

This interpretation of *The Federalist* – and of America – has over the course of the past few decades come to prevail in most sectors of the academy, Left and Right, and has molded several generations of students who have gone on to employ it, as citizens and as scholars, in the making and criticism of American public policy.[11] But then the influence of Diamond's work is not in question. As an interpretation of *The Federalist*, it must be regarded as a stunning breakthrough – the starting point of all future inquiries – as revolutionary in its own way as the famous constitutional iconoclasm of Charles Beard. In fact, the scholarly lines through which Diamond broke had been marked out by Beard in 1913 in *An Economic Interpretation of the Constitution of the United States*. As Douglass Adair has shown, Beard was the first to realize that *Federalist* 10 is the key to *The Federalist* as a whole, the first to thrust *Federalist* 10 into the spotlight as an authoritative guide to the character of American politics.[12]

But Beard fastened upon the tenth *Federalist* not because of its argument for an extensive Union but because it appeared to be "a masterly statement of the theory of economic determinism in politics." Indeed, Beard lauded *The Federalist* as "the finest study in the economic interpretation of politics which exists in any language." In recapitulating Publius's argument in Number 10, Beard did not overlook the case for the extended sphere, but he regarded its true importance to be as a part of the larger argument on the role of economics in politics. The genius of Publius lay in his acknowledgment that "the chief business of government, from which, perforce, its essential nature must be derived, consists in the control and adjustment of conflicting economic interests."[13] Beard insisted in the original text and in his Introduction to the 1935 edition that he regarded this "theory of economic determinism" only as a hypothesis – though as the most powerful and successful one hitherto devised. That it was devised by him, however, he never claimed, always insisting that he was following in the footsteps of Madison, James Harrington. Aristotle, and, to be sure, Karl Marx.[14]

It was this connection between the theory of economic determinism and the history of political philosophy that Adair took up. While not rejecting Beard's focus on the role of economic interests, Adair understood the clash of these interests to be not a continuation of the class struggle between the rich and the poor, the few and the many, but an alternative to that struggle: the conflict of interest groups cut across class lines, thereby allowing prudent statesmen to craft a moderate politics based on an equilibrium of interests. But such an equilibrium was possible, Adair maintained, only in an extensive republic that embraced a multiplicity of factions and an intricate, layered system of representation. Publius's patronage of interest groups was therefore in the service of something more fundamental – his argument for the extended sphere, in particular, and the ability of political theory to guide political life, in general. Whereas Beard thought that abstract political ideas had little influence compared to economic factors – even the abstract idea of economic determinism was, after all, only a hypothesis – Adair sought to restore the independence and something of the dignity of political theory, even if it was only from the historical point of view. Republican government in a vast country – an idea that Adair traced back from Publius to David Hume – would produce the stable middle-class regime that had been the desideratum for thinkers on government since Aristotle. Thus Adair, too, saw Publius's argument as part of a tradition stemming from Aristotle; but he identified the extended sphere as Publius's special contribution to that tradition, and implicitly rejected Marx, an advocate of class war and economic determinism, as being altogether outside it.[15]

Diamond pursued this same connection between *The Federalist* and the tradition of political thought, but brought to his efforts a much wider and deeper acquaintance with the history of political philosophy. Like Adair, he rejected Beard's economic determinism but retained *Federalist* 10 as the centerpiece of his interpretation of the book. But now the doctrine of the extended sphere was not only *not* an anticipation of Marx, but emphatically a refutation of him. Diamond viewed *Federalist* 10 as the modern answer to the threat of class struggle and violent revolution: the politics of regulating the "various and interfering interests" of an extensive commercial society would defuse the war between the rich and the poor, and avoid the ideological fanaticism that in the past had led to religious tyranny, and in the twentieth century to totalitarianism. At the same time, Diamond argued that ancient political philosophy was in the decisive respect superior to the modern political philosophy on which Publius drew, for the ancients had been able (at least in theory, and Diamond acknowledged that their practice fell short of their theory) to aspire to political nobility without abandoning the solid ground of decent, constitutional politics.

But in the modern world, Diamond insisted, men had to choose either the nonideological, low-but-solid politics of interest groups, or the ideological fanaticism and tyranny of the Nazis and Communists. In this context, his interpretation of *The Federalist* made perfect sense not only as a gloss on the Constitution but as a guide to the fundamental tendencies of contemporary American politics: *The Federalist* (especially Nos. 10 and 51) helped to explain how Franklin D. Roosevelt had steered the country between the Scylla and Charybdis of right-wing reaction and incipient socialism, preserving the rights of property and of minorities along the way. For the genius of FDR's approach, in Diamond's view, was precisely his bravura use of interest-group politics to assemble a vast middle- and lower-class coalition in defense of American democracy. His incremental, pragmatic, nonideological approach was a perfect demonstration of the effective use of the political system described by Publius. And the soundness of Publius's "sober expectations" was driven home to Diamond again in the 1960s as he watched the New Left attempt to transform the system bequeathed by the New Deal and invented by *The Federalist*.[16]

Yet despite its influence, its helpful insights, and its intellectual and political provenance, Diamond's view of the founding – and of Publius in particular – is somewhat one-dimensional. His rejection of ideological politics is sound as far as it goes, but it does not properly distinguish between political ideology and political philosophy; it seems to imagine that all efforts to form citizens or to inform public opinion on the basis of abstract truths are (at least since the seventeenth century) pernicious; it does not acknowledge (to speak of the present case) that interest-group politics cannot be defended apart from the ends that it is intended to serve and that therefore legitimize it, which ends must exist in public *opinion*, the special care of the greatest statesmen. The articulation of these ends is a task of political philosophy, whether undertaken by public or private men, by politicians or by academics. In short, if modern American politics is not to be cut off completely from the wellsprings of the Western tradition and from the first principles of our own founding, the rejection of ideology must be accompanied by the reassertion of the authority of political philosophy; and the politics of interest groups must be justified by and incorporated into the larger politics of public opinion.[17]

What Diamond neglected was the prudent political science of the founding, the political science that left room for and indeed regarded as indispensable the virtue of prudence, in the old-fashioned sense of the term: the virtue of the man who is adept at deciding what is the best thing to be done under the circumstances, who can determine what is the best way to get from here to there (and who therefore must know where he is going, the goal for which to strive), who can instruct public opinion without either scorning its backwardness or inflaming its passions. This is prudence in the traditional sense, the virtue that crowns the political art and is an indispensable part of political science. It is not a virtue that is especially needful in a regime of interest-group politics, where sobriety, calculating realism, and skill in maneuver usually suffice. But in a republican regime in which (as Lincoln explained) public opinion is everything, it is the one virtue most needful.[18]

To put it differently, from the standpoint of the "new science of politics" – of the political philosophy of Machiavelli and Hobbes and, so Diamond asserted, *The Federalist* – prudence properly speaking is dethroned; and alongside that, republicanism is made into the valet of liberalism, the obedient and almost invisible servant of interest-group pluralism. Yet *The Federalist* says nothing of this "new science of politics." That term belongs to Tocqueville – and it is even a question how new is the science that he calls for to understand "a world altogether new."[19] *The Federalist* speaks only of an *improved* science of politics that will supply the "means" by which the "excellencies of republican government may be retained and its imperfections lessened or avoided." As readers of cereal boxes know, "new" and "improved" are not the same, and hence cereal companies like to use both terms to communicate the sheer magnificence of their work. Publius, on the other hand, claims only to have added new elements to an already existing science, to have improved but not remade it. His improvements relate only to "means" and not to ends – the ends of republicanism, whose "excellencies" he wishes to retain and whose imperfections he wishes to lessen or avoid.[20] One should not forget that the authors of *The Federalist* are not embarrassed to write under the pen name of an ancient Roman statesman, one of the founders of the Roman republic.[21]

Let us then have a fresh look at what has been regarded as the centerpiece of the new political science in America, the argument of *Federalist* 10.

THE PLAN OF *THE FEDERALIST*

The Federalist is divided into two main parts, corresponding to the two volumes in which the collected papers were first published. The first thirty-six papers are a discussion of the Union, or more precisely, as Publius lists the topics in *Federalist* 1, of "the utility of the UNION to your political prosperity," "the insufficiency of the present confederation to preserve that Union," and "the necessity of a government at least equally energetic with the one proposed, to the attainment of this object."[22] Following the discussion of the Union, Publius turns to the particular "merits of this Constitution." It is this part of the book (Nos. 37–85) that discloses "the conformity of the proposed Constitution to the true principles of republican government." We may say provisionally, then, that Publius discusses the matter of the new nation in the first part of *The Federalist*, and the form of the new nation in the second.[23]

It is not until the second volume of *The Federalist* that one hears much about what the framers have chosen in the new Constitution, not to mention why they have chosen it. The first volume concerns rather the inextirpable power of "accident and force" in America's affairs. Its argument ranges over the many necessities, domestic and foreign, that require Union. The qualities of "good government," and the relation between the ends of good government and the form of republican government, are topics that are not examined systematically in Papers 1–36. Instead, Publius turns first to the lowest and most solid basis for all government, the force of necessity.

"Nothing is more certain than the indispensable necessity of government," he declares in *Federalist* 2, and in the ensuing papers proves that in America necessity requires a government of the whole Union, not separate confederacies of states. The reason for this is not so much Providence or even deference to the judgment of the "wise and experienced men" of the Convention, but safety. "Among the many objects to which a wise and free people find it necessary to direct their attention, that of providing for their *safety* seems to be first."[24] The case for the Constitution seems to rest almost entirely on the case for the Union, and the latter depends upon the "natural course of things" or the "natural and necessary progress of human affairs," arising from man's consideration of his natural weakness and his need to make himself secure at all costs. This Hobbesian-style reasoning ignores the differences among forms of governments and reduces politics to the questions of self-preservation and sovereignty, which are really two sides of the same question. "Safety from external danger is the most powerful director of national conduct," Publius advises. "Even the ardent love of liberty will, after a time, give way to its dictates."[25]

The concluding paragraph of the first volume (i.e., of No. 36) promises that what is to follow will be different in character: Publius declares that "a further and more critical investigation of the system will serve to recommend it still more to every sincere and disinterested advocate for good government." This "more critical and thorough survey of the work of the convention," as he calls it in Number 37, occupies the rest of the book, and is addressed to "the candid and judicious part of the community," those who "add to a sincere zeal for the happiness of their country, a temper favorable to a just estimate of the means of promoting it." With the shift in subject matter comes a shift in rhetorical mode: rather than teaching men to understand their passions so that they may satisfy their fundamental passion for self-preservation – rather than using necessity as an effective substitute for moderation – Publius chooses to speak in moderate tones to moderate men. For the "sincere and disinterested advocate for good government" will not be satisfied with proofs of the necessity of the plan. Morality, and especially the supreme political morality of framing and ratifying a constitution, involves choice; and what "the candid and judicious part of the community" wants to know is whether the new Constitution is worthy of choice. Whereas in the first part Publius strives to show the American people that they have no choice (in any rational sense) but to preserve the Union by adopting the Constitution, in the second part he attempts the very different task of persuading moderate men not only of the "expediency" but of the "propriety" of choosing the Constitution. And so he exclaims, in the transition to the second part, "Happy will it be for ourselves, and most honorable for human nature, if we have wisdom and virtue enough to set so glorious an example to mankind!"[26]

The Union may be necessary for our "political prosperity," but as depicted in the first volume of *The Federalist*, i.e., when prescinded from the principles informing the Constitution, the Union is not "most honorable for human nature." It becomes honorable only in the light of the Constitution. By initially teaching his readers the limits that necessity places on human choice, Publius prepares them to choose wisely when "the merits of this Constitution" are finally presented in their own terms. For the fact that choice is not completely free means that men must respect its conditions and anticipate its consequences if they are to choose well. Publius shows his readers that the truly necessary choice is to choose well.[27]

THE IMPROVED SCIENCE OF POLITICS

If the two parts of *The Federalist* are thus united by a common intention, we should expect that the first part's argument from necessity would have to provide some account of or room for human freedom. The danger to freedom is obvious, as Publius explains in Number 8: "The violent destruction of life and property incident to war, the continual effort and alarm attendant on a state of continual danger, will compel nations the most attached to liberty to resort for repose and security to institutions which have a tendency to destroy their civil and political rights." But Publius does not draw the Hobbesian

conclusion of absolute monarchy from the continual perils of this
state of war. Instead, in Papers 9 and 10, he presents a defense of the
Union that rises above necessity, that prepares the way for the argument in the second part of the book: free or republican government
is possible based on the advantages of a "firm" (No. 9) and "well-
constructed" (No. 10) Union.

The Union is made "firm" by being a confederate or federal
republic, combining the "internal advantages" of a small republic
with the "external force" of a monarchical government. Publius's
authority for this argument is "that great man" Montesquieu, from
whom he quotes extensively to prove that the proposed government
of the United States would fulfill Montesquieu's recommendations,
and that the much-discussed distinction between a confederated
and a consolidated government is therefore "more subtle than accu-
rate." But Montesquieu is introduced only in response to the circumstance that "the opponents of the PLAN proposed here, with great
assiduity, cited and circulated" his observations: he is not presented
as an independent authority for the Constitution on his own terms,
despite the fact that in the preceding paragraph Publius had
remarked the "great improvement" that the science of politics, like
most other sciences, had achieved when compared to the ancients.
"It is impossible to read the history of the petty republics of Greece
and Italy," Publius remarks, "without feeling sensations of horror
and disgust at the distractions with which they were continually agitated, and at the rapid succession of revolutions by which they were
kept in a state of perpetual vibration between the extremes of tyranny and anarchy." It is from such accounts that the "advocates of
despotism" have drawn arguments not only against the republican
form of government but against "the very principles of civil liberty."
"If it had been found impracticable to have devised models of a more
perfect structure," Publius concludes, "the enlightened friends to
liberty would have been obliged to abandon the cause of that species
of government as indefensible."[28]

The improved science of politics is introduced in *Federalist* 9, in
short, as a means of persuading "the enlightened friends to liberty"
to become republicans. The lovers of "civil liberty" must be taught to
cherish political liberty or self-government, and to accomplish this

Publius appeals to their "enlightened" fondness for devising "models" and their confidence in "improvement," in "wholly new discoveries" or discoveries that "have made their principal progress towards perfection in modern times."[29] It is because the opponents of the Constitution have "cited and circulated" Montesquieu's views on confederacies that Publius considers it important to answer them in kind; but what is at stake is the allegiance of the "enlightened friends to liberty," who as such are inclined to regard that "enlightened civilian," Montesquieu, as an authority. On the merits of the question, it would apparently have been possible to pronounce without recourse to him. Publius admits that "the utility of a Confederacy, as well to suppress faction and to guard the internal tranquillity of States as to increase their external force and security, is in reality not a new idea"; and Montesquieu himself cites ancient Lycia as a worthy example.[30]

By his carefully hedged employment of the improved science of politics, which, after all, he invokes with some fanfare in the same number, Publius suggests the limitations of that science. However important it is for political science to devise "models of a more perfect structure" for the better securing of liberty – however useful are such devices as the separation of powers, legislative checks and balances, an independent judiciary, and so forth, for the sake of civil liberty – they must finally be understood to serve the purposes of republicanism. "They are means, and powerful means" – but only means – "by which the excellencies of republican government may be retained and its imperfections lessened or avoided." It is precisely the continued importance of republicanism that connects the political wisdom of *The Federalist* with that of the ancients, that connects the American Publius with the Roman Publius. Although our Publius endorses Montesquieu's description of a confederate republic as "a kind of constitution that has all the internal advantages of a republican, together with the external force of a monarchical government," Publius never specifies in Number 9 what those "internal advantages" are. To do so, following Montesquieu, would require him to distinguish between republicanism (whose principle is, according to Montesquieu, virtue) and honor. But as we learn only later, Publius's case for the Constitution depends crucially upon connecting honor and republicanism, upon vindicating "the honorable title of republic."[31]

This is the deeper reason why the new science of politics, the science of Machiavelli, Hobbes, and Montesquieu, quietly elides into the old science improved by prudence, experience, and new instrumentalities suited to modern conditions.

The most famous of these new means or instrumentalities is the "extended sphere" or "the ENLARGEMENT of the ORBIT" of republican governments. Publius introduces this topic in Number 9 and explicates it in Number 10. In the course of introducing it, he changes his description of the valuable improvements in the science of politics. From being virtually new principles or indeed "wholly new discoveries," they become a "catalogue of circumstances that tend to the amelioration of popular systems of civil government." As a consequence of their status as means, they become "circumstances" that are interesting only insofar as they are the conditions of something better or good in itself, only insofar as they "tend" to a certain end. To this "catalogue" Publius, now speaking in his own name, ventures "to add one more" circumstance, "however novel it may appear to some."[32] As "circumstances" these means or instrumentalities seemed to be almost beyond human choice, to be "givens" in the sense of the ineluctable conclusions of science. But as parts of a "catalogue" Publius reminds us that they are in fact subject to human choice, which he underscores by emphatically adding an item to the catalogue. The founders of "popular systems of civil government" must choose from this "catalogue" when trying to improve their regimes, but their choosing must adapt itself to the character and circumstances of particular peoples; they cannot simply apply or implement "models of a more perfect structure." So we are prepared when, after the long excursus on Montesquieu's view of confederations, Publius takes up the discussion of "the ENLARGEMENT of the ORBIT" in Number 10 in his own name and without any reference to Montesquieu or any other philosophical authority.

THE PROBLEM OF FACTION

"Among the numerous advantages promised by a well-constructed Union," Publius announces at the beginning of Number 10, "none deserves to be more accurately developed than its tendency to break and control the violence of faction." Whereas a "firm" Union will act "as a barrier against domestic faction and insurrection," apparently by its ability to "repress" such outbreaks, a "well-constructed" Union will tend to "break and control the violence of faction." That is to say, it will not put an end to faction but will control it by breaking its violence or perhaps breaking it of its violent habits; if the violence of faction can be controlled it will not be necessary to "repress" faction because it will not threaten to become an "insurrection." This is an advantage of Union, and so is properly discussed in the first part of *The Federalist*; but it is not a tendency of the Union simply, but only of a "well-constructed" Union, and so suggests the need to transcend the first part's terms of discussion. A well-constructed Union is a firm Union but also something more. Its parts are not only put together well, but are well interpreted and regulated by the Constitution and by Publius. The "well-constructed" Union, like a well-constructed or well-construed Constitution, is the product of wise interpretation.[33]

Montesquieu cannot be the basis of the argument for the extended sphere because, as Publius shows in Number 9, on Montesquieu's authority the larger American states were already too large to be proper republics. With some reduction in the extent of these states, his argument did not, *mutatis mutandis*, rule out a confederated republic for the United States; but it did place the opponents of the Constitution – the defenders of the existing states – in an embarrassing position. From this standpoint, Number 10's argument is as necessary to rescue them from their predicament as it is to defend the new Constitution. In short, by severing his opponents' political interest from their philosophical authority, Publius prepares and gradually encourages them to connect their interest to his authority, and to elevate their gaze to "the greatness or happiness of the people of America," rather than by "the multiplication of petty offices" to seek to extend their influence in "the narrow circles of personal intrigue.[34]

The problem of faction provides the leverage needed to pry the respectable part of the opposition away from their present convictions, because the "dangerous vice" of factionalism disturbs both "the friend of popular governments" who is "alarmed for their character and fate," and "our most considerate and virtuous citizens," who share with the former an anxiety over the state governments' instability and injustice but add to it a concern for the common good. Both those who love the form of popular government and those who love the end of all good government (the common good) will have reason to study *Federalist* 10, which goes as far toward reconciling the form of republican government and the end of good government as is possible in this part of the book. That the state governments cannot realize these hopes is implied in the fact that they have failed to cure the "mortal diseases" of popular governments; the implication is that they are dangerously close to expiring, despite the fact that their improvements on ancient and modern models, Publius says, "cannot certainly be too much admired." Of course, their failings could be excused if the extended sphere were necessary to solve the problem of faction. It is only in the discussion of the separation of powers in the second part of *The Federalist* that we discover that the state constitutions were inherently flawed – and, literally, "cannot certainly be too much admired." [35]

Publius must show his fellow republicans that justice, stability, and liberty can be at home in a large territory; and he must persuade his countrymen who are less concerned with popular government than with the common good that the good of the whole will be sought after and secured in the new regime. All of these considerations are provisionally united in the definition and remedy for faction proposed in Number 10. "By a faction," Publius writes, "I understand a number of citizens, whether amounting to a majority or minority of the whole, who are united and actuated by some common impulse of passion, or of interest, adverse to the rights of other citizens, or to the permanent and aggregate interests of the community." As if to emphasize his distance from Montesquieu and from previous republican theory, Publius states his definition in the first person ("I understand") and makes clear that unlike the older Latin use of the term (*factio*), a faction can consist not only of a few but of the majority. This will, in fact, turn out to be the danger above all to be feared. A certain parallelism might be inferred from his disjunctions: perhaps majority factions (which are mentioned first) are more often united and actuated by some passion that is "adverse to the rights of other citizens," whereas minority factions are usually the creatures of an interest directed against "the permanent and aggregate interests of the community." The inference does not of course preclude the existence of factions that cut across the categories; but the definition does make clear that factions must be "united and actuated," i.e., that to exist they must enjoy both "the impulse" and "the opportunity" provided by a common passion or interest. By the singular implication of this carefully wrought definition, a majority or minority united and actuated by a common *opinion* does not qualify as a faction. Nor does *Federalist* 10 ever propose a multiplicity of opinions as a solution to the problem of faction. It is true that Publius will soon establish the reciprocal relation between opinions and passions, thereby implying that a multiplicity of passions would breed a multiplicity of opinions, and vice versa. But he never explicitly connects this implication with his definition of faction, or with his later solution to the problem.[36]

REMOVING THE CAUSES OF FACTION

"There are two methods of curing the mischiefs of faction," Publius explains, "the one, by removing its causes; the other, by controlling its effects." Before, the "well-constructed" Union was said to have the tendency to break and control "the violence of faction." Now it seems possible to accomplish something else: not only to break and control faction's violence, but to cure its mischiefs as well. Perhaps the violence of faction is not its worst feature, though it may well be its most alarming. If the mischiefs of faction (understood in a comprehensive sense) can be cured, then the Union's restraint on faction's violence may be unnecessary or at least of only secondary importance, because the conditions that lead to the outbreak of violence will have ameliorated. In any case, Publius says that there are two methods of curing these mischiefs. He does not say (although he implies) that either the one or the other must be chosen; that is, he does not explicitly exclude the possibility that both may prove useful.[37]

"There are again two methods of removing the causes of faction,"

Publius continues, "the one, by destroying the liberty which is essential to its existence; the other, by giving to every citizen the same opinions, the same passions, and the same interests." Publius rejects the first method as a cure worse than the disease: to destroy liberty in order to abolish faction would be like wishing the annihilation of air in order to eliminate fire. The analogy is complicated by Publius's specification that liberty "is essential to political life" just as air "is essential to animal life." But liberty can be abolished, air cannot; men can only "wish the annihilation of air." "Political life" is in this crude sense weaker than "animal life," but only because political life is distinctively human, i.e., it involves the capacity for reflection and choice. Man can choose to abolish liberty; neither he nor the other animals can choose to annihilate air. Men who would choose to abolish liberty do not understand the distinctiveness of human life: they do not appreciate what they have in common with all mankind but not with the other animals. Publius's rejection of this first method of removing the causes of faction teaches those men – the few – who would be tempted to deny the human claim to liberty based on the equal rights of man (perhaps acting in the name of the common good), that they are but men, and cannot afford to dispense with the rights to which their humanity entitles them.[38]

Even as the first method was denounced as "unwise" – an apt rejoinder to those who think themselves wise – so the second is dismissed as "impracticable." To give every citizen "the same opinions, the same passions, and the same interests" is impracticable because no government is so powerful as to be able to blot out the natural inequalities among men, which inequalities take two forms. In the first place, there is the connection between men's opinions and their passions. "As long as the reason of man continues fallible, and he is at liberty to, exercise it, different opinions will be formed. As long as the connection subsists between his reason and his self-love, his opinions and his passions will have a reciprocal influence on each other; and the former will be objects to which the latter will attach themselves."[39] Despite the "reciprocal influence" of opinion and passion, Publius does not state that men's passions will be objects to which their opinions will be drawn, only that their opinions will furnish the objects of their passions. That is, he maintains a certain independence and even dignity for opinion: men are divided in their opinions not so much on account of the influence of passion but due to the fallibility of reason. To be sure, one cause of the fallibility of human reason may well be the obscurantism of the passions; but Publius emphasizes that fallible men typically make mistakes in their reasoning or cannot quite grasp the truth, not that they are biased or unjust. This refusal to reduce opinions or reason to the effect of prerational or subrational causes is characteristic of *Federalist* 10's argument, and lays the groundwork for the politics of public opinion – of republicanism – that *The Federalist* is constructing.

The second reason why giving to every citizen "the same opinions, the same passions, and the same interests" is "impracticable" reveals more fully the character of the argument. It is especially the democrats – the many – or at least their most vociferous partisans, who think that the inequalities among men can be erased. So even as Publius's argument to the few emphasized that abolishing liberty is "unwise," so this argument, directed particularly to the many, emphasizes that radical egalitarianism is "impracticable." He addresses each in terms that are dear to their own passions or interests (to the few: don't show your unwisdom; to the many: don't show that despite your number you are weak) but in so doing corrects the partial opinion of justice held by each. Without appealing directly to their opinions regarding who should rule, Publius teaches them that neither claim to rule is sufficient. What is true in the claims of the few and the many will be preserved and enhanced not in the regimes of aristocracy or direct democracy but in Publius's own federal republic, in the regime of the Constitution. But refuting the claim of the many takes longer, partly because in a regime based on the consent of the governed the majority deserves a full hearing; but also because in a republic the majority is the most powerful, hence the most dangerous, political group.

The proposed uniformity of opinion and passion is quickly disposed of, but Publius essentially devotes the rest of Number 10 to considering the proposed uniformity of interests. Democrats may easily be persuaded that the liberty to hold opinions should be protected, inasmuch as it is an aspect of their own claim to equal freedom. Interest is another matter; it smacks of wealth, the principle of the (oligarchical) few. But interest is not the same as wealth: it is a kind of combination of wealth and freedom, of the desire or right to get wealthy with the freedom or right of every man to choose his own path or to be judge in his own cause. Publius's discussion of interests is thus part of his effort to combine the few and the many: the discussion of interests is part of his education of public opinion or to public opinion, i.e., to the creation of an American public formed by the Constitution and its principles.

"The diversity in the faculties of men," Publius maintains, "from which the rights of property originate, is not less an insuperable obstacle to a uniformity of interests. The protection of these faculties is the first object of government." Publius had said in *Federalist* 3 that "safety" was the first object of a people's attention; later he will define the object of government as the higher and more comprehensive one of "the safety and happiness of society," "the common good of the society," and "the happiness of the people."[40] The protection of "the diversity in the faculties of men, from which the rights of property originate" lies in between protecting the safety and securing the happiness of society, between the alpha and the omega of political life. It corresponds to the place of *Federalist* 10 in the overall argument of *The Federalist*. To understand any part of that argument one must see it in relation to the structure of the book as a whole. This consideration would save many commentators on *The Federalist* from the mistake of identifying the "first object" with the final object of government, as well as the corollary mistake of identifying the purposes of the Union – e.g., as stated in *Federalist* 23, "the common defense of the members; the preservation of the public peace, as well against internal convulsions as external attacks, the regulation of commerce with other nations and between the States, the superintendence of our intercourse, political and commercial, with foreign countries" – with the purposes of government or of the Constitution.[41]

"From the protection of different and unequal faculties of acquiring property, the possession of different degrees and kinds of property immediately results; and from the influence of these on the sentiments and views of the respective proprietors ensues a division of the society into different interests and parties." If the acquisitive faculties are protected, then society will necessarily be divided into "different interests and parties. The relation between interest and opinion, which Publius had not mentioned in his discussion of passion and opinion, now comes to the fore. With the division of society into interests one gets "parties" or politics, and only then the invocation of "nature": "the latent causes of faction are thus sown in the nature of man; and we see them everywhere brought into different degrees of activity, according to the different circumstances of civil society." Politics arises from the differences in men's opinions and interests, not from the conflict of their passions per se. From the diversity in men's faculties and the consequent diversity of property – or, considering men as themselves a kind of property arising from their faculties, from the diversity in the degrees and kinds of men – arise certain "sentiments and views" that produce the division of society into interests and parties. Again Publius places opinions first: it is opinions that give rise to interests and to politics, opinions themselves arise from (fallible) reflection on unequal human conditions, broadly speaking. The "latent causes of faction" are thus sown in the liberty of man's reason, in his self-love, and in his diverse faculties, including particularly his faculty for holding opinions concerning what is rightly his or what is his due. For it is not so much man's "faculties of acquiring property" but "the diversity in the faculties of men" from which the "rights" of property originate that stimulates faction and political conflict.[42]

But not all politics is factious. The latent causes of faction become activated "according to the different circumstances of civil society." "A zeal for different opinions concerning religion, concerning government, and many other points, as well of speculation as of practice" is mentioned as the first of these "different circumstances." This use of the term "circumstances" perhaps recalls Number 9's "catalogue of circumstances that tend to the amelioration of popular systems of civil government." Perhaps the "circumstances" of political science can ameliorate the "circumstances of civil society." It is certainly true that until zealous opinions concerning religion and government are separated and moderated, it is unlikely that "the regulation of ... various and interfering interests" will be the "principal task of modern legislation": so mild a preoccupation presupposes that the prior and divisive question of *who should rule* has been decided and consented to. Publius's task is to answer that question in, and through, his exposition of the Constitution. His task is complicated by the fact that the Constitution is a means to an end, to the ends of government proclaimed in the Revolution, which means particularly in the Declaration of Independence; and complicated further by the fact that a constitutional form of government is essential to the realization of those ends, and so is itself a kind of end. In other words, Publius must persuade his readers not only that the people should rule but that the people's rule can – indeed must – be constitutional. If republican government is to be "rescued from the opprobrium under which it has so long labored and be recommended to the esteem and adoption of mankind," Publius must show that the rule of the people will take place only through the rule of law, rather than through force, sheer will, or the tyrannical passions of the greatest number.[43] Concretely, this means that the people must not only rule through the law, but be ruled by the law: they must come to love the law, and in particular the fundamental law, the Constitution, more than they love their own sovereign authority. Or, more precisely, they must come to identify their rule with the majestic authority of the Constitution.

So Publius cannot remedy the factions caused by "a zeal for different opinions concerning religion, concerning government" by attempting to multiply these contending opinions. While he does endorse a "multiplicity of interests" and "multiplicity of sects" to provide security for "civil rights" and "religious rights," he never advocates a multiplicity of opinions to protect political rights. There must be a uniformity of opinion underlying the multiplicity of interests and sects otherwise the result would not be pluralism but civil war or anarchy, not America but Lebanon. Pluralism, then, is not enough; before men can be divided by interests and sects they must be united by citizenship. Far from "turn[ing] away almost in horror from the human 'zeal for different opinions,'" Publius himself inculcates an opinion; far from eschewing zealous politics, Publius concludes Number 10 by declaring, "And according to the degree of pleasure and pride we feel in being republicans ought to be our zeal in cherishing the spirit and supporting the character of federalists.[44]

VIRTUE AND INTERESTS

To be sure, that zeal is restricted to a republicanism embodying the "spirit" and "character" of federalists, and presumably of the chief federalist, Publius. It is only when that zeal has replaced the factious zeal "for different opinions" that the pluralistic polities of interest groups becomes possible. For "the most common and durable source of factions," Publius explains, "has been the various and unequal distribution of property." The unequal distribution comprises "those who hold and those who are without property," as well as creditors and debtors; the various distribution includes the landed, manufacturing, mercantile, moneyed, and other lesser interests that "grow up of necessity in civilized nations." Civilized nations are those that protect the diverse faculties of men; they are to that extent commercial nations.

To the extent that the Constitution secures more than the diverse faculties that give rise to property – insofar as it secures the people's "safety and happiness" – it exists for the sake of more than a merely commercial nation.[45] One should not forget that in the thematic discussion of commerce in *Federalist* 6, Publius depicts it as a source of dissension and war: "Has commerce hitherto done anything more than change the objects of war? Is not the love of wealth as domineering and enterprising a passion as that of power and glory?" Against those "projectors in politics" who maintain that "the genius of republics … is pacific" and that "the spirit of commerce has a tendency to soften the manners of men" – against Montesquieu, Kant, and Hume, among others – Publius asks, "Have republics in practice been less addicted to war than monarchies? Are not the former administered by men as well as the latter?" To answer these questions, he appeals to experience, and cites examples ancient and modern. In Number 7 Publius affirms the "unbridled spirit" of commercial enterprise in America, and in Number 11 attests that the "adventurous spirit, which characterizes the commercial character of America," has already "excited uneasy sensations in several of the maritime powers of Europe." Plainly commerce does not promise "perpetual peace" between the United States and the rest of the world; why should it be the handmaid of civil harmony within the United States? The multiplicity of interests becomes conducive to peaceful, nonfactious government within the United States only when commerce itself has been tamed or shaped by Publius's constitutionalism, by the opinions taught in *The Federalist*. After the discussion of the extended republic in Number 10, the importance of the Union to commerce is said to be "one of those points about which there is least room to entertain a difference of opinion," inasmuch as "the prosperity of commerce is now perceived and acknowledged by all enlightened statesmen to be the most useful as well as the most productive source of national wealth." From this new point of view, even the "often-agitated question between agriculture and commerce" has "received a decision which has silenced the rivalship that once subsisted between them" and proved "that their interests are intimately blended and interwoven."[46]

But the harmony of interest that underlies the multiplicity of interests that "grow up of necessity in civilized nations" is not itself a necessity: it must be taught and it must be learned. *Federalist* 10 suggests a common opinion about the value of commerce or of commercial prosperity that justifies it not as an end in itself but as a means to the public good, and therefore allows the peaceful division of society into competing economic interests. This opinion is "perceived and acknowledged by all enlightened statesmen" and has "commanded the most general assent of men who have any acquaintance with the subject," but it must be taught to and enforced upon men whose "general assent" is not sufficient to moderate their own particular interest. "The regulation of these various and interfering interests forms the principal task of modern legislation," Publius continues, "and involves the spirit of party and faction in the necessary and ordinary operations of government." But the whole purpose of Publius's inquiry in Number 10 is to find a way to remedy "the unsteadiness and injustice with which a factious spirit has tainted our public administration."[47] If a factious spirit is necessarily involved in the ordinary operations of government, how can there be any cure for the "unsteadiness and injustice" of our politics?

One must pay careful attention to Publius's words. "The regulation of these various and interfering interests forms the principal task of modern legislation" – Publius says nothing about those aspects of government that are not particularly modern (even as he has said nothing concerning "wise" as opposed to "enlightened" statesmen), nor does he bring up modern execution or judgment. The discussion in *Federalist* 10 seems to take place entirely on the level of the legislative power, as if the legislature were the whole government. Publius has alluded to but not yet investigated the separation of powers. The solution to the problem of faction proposed in Number 10 is therefore a partial solution. If the legislature were to be tainted by the spirit of party and faction, then the importance of the executive and judiciary in preventing "unsteadiness and injustice" would be all the greater. What is more, *Federalist* 10's discussion proceeds without discriminating the legislature into two houses; the importance of the Senate would, *ceteris paribus*, also be enhanced by this analysis.

A closer consideration reveals, however, that the problem of faction in the legislature is the epitome of politics in general. "No man is allowed to be a judge in his own cause," Publius writes, "because his interest would certainly bias his judgment, and, not improbably, corrupt his integrity. With equal, nay with greater reason, a body of men are unfit to be both judges and parties at the same time; yet what are many of the most important acts of legislation but so many judicial determinations...?" Republican politics, after all, consists in self-government, and self-government implies that men can take responsibility for judging themselves as parties to their own causes. Indeed, men *are* their own causes, particularly in the state of nature, where the fact that each is the sole judge of himself leads to anarchy. The problem of judging one's own cause seems merely to have been transferred from the state of nature to civil society, from individuals to parties and factions of men. For as Publius comments in Number 51, "In a society under the forms of which the stronger faction can readily unite and oppress the weaker, anarchy may as truly be said to reign as in a state of nature, where the weaker individual is not secured against the violence of the stronger ...."[48]

With this thought we reach the heart of the problem: so long as factions exist in society, and in particular so long as a majority faction threatens, the state of nature has not been overcome. It is not just that rights are insecure, but that men still act as if their passions (or their reason acting, so to speak, on the orders of their passions) and not the law were the measure of right. These men are not yet citizens; they lack the virtues that make them worthy of citizenship. The studied ambiguity in Publius's language evinces the problem. He speaks in Number 51 of "the stronger faction" oppressing "the weaker," as if there were no nonfactious groups in society at all. Yet justice "ought to hold the balance between them," and justice is "the end of government" and of "civil society." Surely justice cannot be obtained by replacing the anarchy of the state of nature with the regulated anarchy (such paradoxical terms are necessary) of a civil society that does nothing for, or to, its members other than encouraging their appetites with a view to what has been called the "saving multiplicity of factions" – so many that no one faction (a majority faction) can consistently rule. The difficulty with this thesis, however, is that Publius never speaks of a "multiplicity of factions"; he speaks of a "multiplicity of interests."[49]

Now, it is true that a majority or minority united and actuated by an unjust interest is a faction. But not all interests are unjust. Publius plays on the ambiguities of the term "interest" by using it sometimes as almost a synonym for faction, sometimes as meaning a legitimate claim under the rules of justice. The problem, in brief, is to lift unjust interests up to justice, or at least to see to it that factious interests are not simply checked but so checked as to allow nonfactious interests to predominate, thus encouraging the former to become more reasonable if only in order to be more successful.[50]

Although self-government inevitably requires parties to judge their own causes, this is not fatal to good government if the parties are virtuous, and part of Publius's effort is to inculcate a certain kind of virtue in American citizens. In keeping with the respect for law and especially for the Constitution that he teaches them, Publius will elevate the status of the judiciary in the new government by confirming or inventing its power to review laws for their constitutionality. By separating the partisan or factious politics of the legislature from the judging of the Supreme Court, he reminds citizens of their obligation to be more than partisans of factions, and helps to insulate the government against the people's weaker moments. In the same manner, while deprecating the "vain" notion that "enlightened statesmen will be able to adjust these clashing interests and render them all subservient to the public good," for the sensible reason that "enlightened statesmen will not always be at the helm," he admonishes the people not to count on the intervention of others to save them – thus encouraging them to be mindful of their own responsibility. "Nor, in many cases, can such an adjustment be made at all without taking into view indirect and remote considerations, which will rarely prevail over the immediate interest" of the parties. Publius himself is the great tutor in the importance of "indirect and remote considerations," and in the second part of *The Federalist* readers learn the wisdom of having a senate, an energetic executive, and an independent judiciary precisely to emphasize these considerations to the people. The quick dismissal of statesmanship as an answer to the problem of faction is not Publius's final word on the subject, but it is an ironic depreciation of his own function that accords with the rhetorical needs of the whole work and his own pseudonymous character. The Roman Publius Valerius was renowned for renouncing his own power and emphasizing "the majesty of the democracy" – all the while increasing his own *authority* over the democrats, and providing bona fides for future republican magistrates.[51]

CONTROLLING THE EFFECTS OF FACTION

After canvassing the possible methods of eliminating the causes of faction, Publius turns to the second half of his argument. "The inference to which we are brought is that the causes of faction cannot be removed and that relief is only to be sought in the means of controlling its *effects*." If the faction is a minority, the republican principle of majority rule provides a remedy. If the faction is a majority, the problem is acute; the very "form of popular government...enables it to sacrifice to its ruling passion or interest both the public good and the rights of other citizens." The republican form – reduced to the principle of majority rule – is incapable of securing private rights and the public good. Accordingly, from the limiting assumption that the "first object of government" is the protection of men's diverse

faculties (some spirited and political, others acquisitive and economic), the ends of government in Number 10 appear to be discrete
and almost unattainable, "the public good and private rights." But
when the end of government is seen as the "safety and happiness of
society" (as later in *The Federalist*), then private rights and the public good may become two aspects of a single common good.[52]

Having been brought to the "inference" (not a demonstrated
conclusion) that the causes of majority faction cannot be removed,
Publius takes up the possibility of controlling its effects. Two means
present themselves: "Either the existence of the same passion or
interest in a majority at the same time must be prevented, or the
majority, having such coexistent passion or interest, must be rendered, by their number and local situation, unable to concert and
carry into effect their schemes of oppression." Either the "impulse"
or the "opportunity" must be prevented. But for all its familiarity
Publius's reasoning is genuinely puzzling: if "giving to every citizen
the same opinions, the same passions, and the same interests" is a
way of curing the causes of faction, would not preventing "the existence of the same passion or interest in a majority" amount to the
same thing? Does not preventing the "impulse" mean dealing with
the *causes* rather than the *effects* of faction? And is not preventing
the "opportunity" merely another way of treating the causes of faction by abolishing or restricting the liberty that is faction's precondition? Publius is careful again not to say that the existence of the
same opinion in a majority is to be prevented, nor that a majority's
opportunity to act on the basis of that opinion ought to be prevented.
Publius is teaching the majority (not necessarily "every citizen") a
common opinion that will check majority faction, and that is necessary even for the extended sphere to control factions based on interest. The majority should not attempt to rule in its own name; for the
sake of the success and honor of republican government, the many
must yield to the law – to the Constitution. This opinion will be cultivated in the course of the second volume of *The Federalist* until it
becomes clear that the people must not only acquiesce in but revere
or venerate the Constitution. In practice, therefore, the people must
also respect the offices established under it; they must try to select
the best men for the job, or, in the case of those officers selected indi-

rectly (the president, senators, and Supreme Court justices), the people must recognize the special virtues or functions of the offices that justify the indirect selection.[53] Thus the people's own impulses are recruited to the regime's assistance, and the majority is persuaded of the justice and advantage of representative rather than direct government.

Publius deals with *causes* while seeming to deal only with *effects*: he teaches informally, and shapes the character of American citizens indirectly. This is appropriate to his own status as a literary rather than (like the Roman Publius) an actual statesman, and as an unelected or unauthorized interpreter of the fundamental law, which (unlike Roman law) does not claim to be divine.[54] Insofar as Publius removes the causes of faction, the "efficacy" of the cure for the mischiefs of faction comes not from the Union but from the Constitution and its interpreter, Publius himself. Publius's respectful indirection thus leads to the topic of representation, and to his famous distinction between republican and democratic government. "From this view of the subject" he declares, "it may be concluded that a pure democracy, by which I mean a society consisting of a small number of citizens, who assemble and administer the government in person, can admit of no cure for the mischiefs of faction." "From this view of the subject," but perhaps not from a more capacious or constitutional view. In contrast to a "pure democracy," a republic is a popular government "in which a scheme of representation takes place." But this definition proves somewhat elusive. Publius had called the democracies of Greece and Italy "petty republics" in Number 9, and in Number 63 he repeats the error, calling Sparta, Rome, and Carthage republics, and noting that "the difference most relied on between the American and other republics consists in the principle of representation." He admits in that essay, however, that "the position concerning the ignorance of the ancient governments on the subject of representation is by no means precisely true in the latitude commonly given to it," i.e., in the latitude he had given to it. Even in "the most pure democracies of Greece," there was representation, and "similar instances might be traced in most, if not all, the popular governments of antiquity." Publius concludes, then, that "the true distinction between these and the American governments lies *in the total exclusion of the people in their collective capacity* from any share in the latter, and not in the *total exclusion of representatives of the people* from the administration of the *former*." (Emphasis in the original.)

He reveals the "true distinction" only much later in the book, after his account of the principle of separated powers. In Number 10 he obscures this distinction, preferring to "heighten the advantages" of the Union or of republicanism based upon the Union by setting up the straw man of "pure democracy." (He makes no mention of monarchy, the regime to which in the preceding number he had attributed the advantages of an extended territory; and he abandons the Montesquieuan account of the "confederate republic" as a means of "reconciling the advantages of monarchy with those of republicanism.") Once "pure democracy" is discredited as the standard for popular governments, Publius can defend the American republic as "wholly popular" despite the fact or rather because of the fact that it is exclusively representative. In Number 10, speaking especially to the "friend of popular governments," he confines himself to the distinction between the republican form and "pure democracy" – and it is the former alone that can admit of a cure for "the mischiefs of faction," because it alone derives an "efficacy" from the Union.[55]

REPRESENTATION AND THE EXTENDED SPHERE

The cure depends upon the two "great points of difference" between the two forms of popular government: in a republic the government is delegated to "a small number of citizens elected by the rest," and (therefore) a republic may extend to a "greater number of citizens and greater sphere of country." At first glance the differences seem to be entirely numerical, in keeping with the democratic or popular character of the distinction under discussion, and with the fact that in Number 10 representation turns out to be a derivative advantage. Representation will "refine and enlarge the public views by passing them through the medium of a chosen body of citizens, whose wisdom may best discern the true interest of their country and whose patriotism and love of justice will be least likely to sacrifice it to tem-

porary or partial considerations." When the "public voice" is passed
through the "medium" of the representatives, it "may well happen"
that it is "more consonant to the public good than if pronounced by
the people themselves, convened for the purpose." We thus see that
representation, working through the forms of the Constitution,
turns interests into "views" that can be shaped to the "public good."
Interests cease to be factious insofar as they become based on opinions of what is due to one within the limits of a common or ruling
opinion of justice. When interests adopt "public views" they have
been constitutionalized; and as part of the "public good" they can be
both represented and regulated. Thus the "public voice" is a rational
expression or set of expressions that can be harmonized; it is not a
tumult. It appears then that representation is especially for the sake
of the public good (rather than for the rights of individuals) and is a
kind of substitute for or rehabilitation of the "enlightened statesmen" dismissed earlier. It offers the few, who have already been
shown the insufficiency of their claim to rule, a place and a calling
under the Constitution, without injuring the equal rights of other
men. It therefore plays a role in preventing minority faction. But
representation also helps to prevent majority faction, insofar as it
prevents the "opportunity" by excluding the people from playing
any collective role in the administration of the government, and prevents the "impulse" by allowing the people to look to, and to heed,
their representatives' wisdom, patriotism, and love of justice.[56]

The aristocratic tones of the latter are too much for "the friend
of popular government" to bear, however, and so Publius quickly
retreats from representation to the extended sphere as the cure for
the mischiefs of faction. "On the other hand," he observes, "the effect
may be inverted." Rather than men of wisdom, patriotism, and justice, the people may find themselves saddled with "men of factious
tempers, of local prejudices, or of sinister designs." We note that faction appears, from the standpoint of representation, as a problem of
character or of the soul: "men of factious tempers" have usurped
men of wisdom. To ensure that the effect is not inverted, Publius
seeks the greatest probability of electing "proper guardians of the
public weal"; his question is "whether small or extensive republics
are more favorable" to this outcome. And the question is "clearly

decided in favor of the latter," he holds, "by two obvious considerations." Republics are now the only defensible kind of popular government. "Pure" democracy, which now appears not as pure but as
debased, as popular government without a constitution, is returned
to where Aristotle in his *Politics* had left it, a bad form of government; and the republic, or constitutional democracy, becomes the
standard of good popular government. The debate between "pure
democracy" and the republican form is thus transformed into one
between small and large republics, and the latter debate is settled on
the same basis as the former. In both cases, the question of representation, which is linked to the structure of government, is absorbed
into the question of size, which turns upon the Union. Whereas initially it had appeared that representation would prevent the
"impulse" to majority faction and the extended sphere would prevent the "opportunity," it is now up to the sphere to prevent both.

The two "obvious considerations" that decide in favor of the
large republic are, however, far from obvious. In the first place, Publius argues that in a large republic the probability of making a "fit
choice" for office will be greater because the people will choose,
other things being equal, from a greater pool of "fit characters." But
even if Publius's conditions are granted, his conclusion assumes that
the people will take advantage of the wider choice, that they will
choose well, for surely there is also a greater pool of *unfit* characters
in the competition. In the second place, Publius argues that with
larger electoral districts, it will be more difficult "for unworthy candidates to practice with success the vicious arts by which elections
are too often carried." But in larger districts new arts of advertising,
image making, and public relations may spring up to replace the
"vicious arts" of old. Nonetheless, Publius makes explicit his assumption that when the suffrage of the people is "more free," they are
more likely to pick men of "the most attractive merit and the most
diffusive and established characters." By collapsing the issue of representation into the question of size, Publius shows his readers the
democratic bent of the argument for the extended sphere, and
underlines the emphasis on the legislature that pervades Number 10.
He gives no hint of what he will later discourse on at length, the tendency of the *offices* established by the Constitution, particularly the

presidency and the Senate, to attract men "pre-eminent for ability and virtue."[57]

The other great difference between a democracy and a republic, then, is "the greater number of citizens and extent of territory" that the latter may encompass; "and it is this circumstance principally which renders factious combinations less to be dreaded in the former than in the latter." Publius's reasoning is brisk and impressive:

> The smaller the society, the fewer probably will be the distinct parties and interests composing it; the fewer the distinct parties and interests, the more frequently will a majority be found of the same party; and the smaller the number of individuals composing a majority, and the smaller the compass within which they are placed, the more easily will they concert and execute their plans of oppression. Extend the sphere and you take in a greater variety of parties and interests; you make it less probable that a majority of the whole will have a common motive to invade the rights of other citizens; or if such a common motive exists, it will be more difficult for all who feel it to discover their own strength and to act in unison with each other.[58]

This second solution to the problem of majority faction is Publius's way of revisiting and rehabilitating the second method of removing the causes of faction. Even as representation is, in one view, a way of restricting the people's liberty, so preventing the majority from having the same interest is a way of giving everyone a "common motive" to conceive of himself as a minority, as one whose rights are endangered. Through such an opinion, it is, as Publius remarks in Number 11 in a different connection, possible to "take away the motive to such combinations by inducing an impracticability of success." As presented by Publius, the extended sphere is an automatic governor that restrains our politics by nonpartisan or mechanical or indeed virtually quantitative means. That it raises no partisan claim – more precisely, that it checks democratic claims by democratic means, encouraging various interests to flourish freely – and that its operation seems automatic, only serves to commend it more highly to "the friend of popular government." Its seemingly ineluctable working becomes a kind of self-fulfilling prophecy, militating against both the ardor and the injustice of a potential majority faction.[59]

Still, thinking of oneself always as a threatened minority is as little suitable for decent republican politics as a faction's constant self-aggrandizement. It is, of course, necessary to ensure in a republic that majorities are moderate and just – are constitutional, in the profoundest sense of the term. But to the extent that majority rule is the republican principle, majorities must rule: the political life of the regime must be lived. "In the extended republic of the United States," Publius declares in Number 51, "… a coalition of a majority of the whole society could seldom take place on any other principles than those of justice and the general good." On the basis of the prevailing interpretation of *Federalist* 10, however, it is hard to see how any majority, especially a just one, could be formed athwart the various and interfering factions. When it is seen that Publius is contending not for a multiplicity of factions but of interests, and these informed by a common opinion, the way from *Federalist* 10 to republican politics (and to the rest of *The Federalist*) opens up. To indicate that the citizens of America are not to be regarded simply as members of factions or as legislative claimants, Publius speaks to his readers as fellow founders: "Extend the sphere and *you* take in a greater variety of interests and parties," he tells them; "*you* make it less probable that a majority of the whole will have a common motive to invade the rights of other citizens.…" (Emphasis added.) The "friend of popular governments" can join with "our most considerate and virtuous citizens" in the act of founding a republican government that is purged so far as possible of the danger of majority faction. But that partnership in founding becomes a common citizenship in the course of *The Federalist*'s argument as a whole.[60]

This common citizenship is based on common principles, on the principles of the Revolution especially as they are embodied in the Constitution. The veneration of the Constitution and its principles is the form that this citizenship takes in common opinion. For in the last analysis, the security of the people's rights depends "altogether … on public opinion, and on the general spirit of the people and of the government." But that public opinion is itself partially a

product of the "general spirit" of the Constitution that Publius urges
them to respect. Republican government cannot rest on opinion
alone, but it cannot be either safe or happy without having its ruling
public opinion anchored in the Constitution and keen on its perpetuation. Publius writes to "fortify" this opinion by inculcating certain
truths about republican constitutionalism that many previous
republicans and many of the opponents of the Constitution had
either denied or overlooked.[61]

This purpose is not fulfilled in *Federalist* 10 or in the first volume of *The Federalist*, but these papers prepare the way for the
actual discussion of the Constitution in the second volume (see
chapters Eight and Nine below for further remarks on Publius's
account of separation of powers and good government). The qualifications that the latter imposes on *Federalist* 10 have been indicated,
but they deserve to be restated plainly: Number 10 overstates the
case for the extended sphere. though for good rhetorical purposes.
In expounding the Senate in Number 63, Publius confesses what he
had refused to say in Number 10, that "the same extended situation
which will exempt the people of America from some of the dangers
incident to lesser republics will expose them to the inconveniency of
remaining for a longer time under the influence of those misrepresentations which the combined industry of interested men may succeed in distributing among them." The extended sphere does *not*
provide a fully effective "republican remedy for the diseases most
incident to republican government." Although a large republic is
necessary to alleviate faction, it is not only not sufficient to the purpose, but can actually make the problem worse.

The root of the problem is that Publius has not yet explained
what are "the true principles of republican government"; hence
the republican diseases have been inadequately diagnosed and the
"republican remedy" too easily prescribed. Publius reiterates the
importance of a large republic in Number 63, but he subordinates it
to the proper kind of representation – in this case, to a properly constructed Senate; and insofar as he describes the mischiefs of faction
now as "misrepresentations," he implies that their proper cure is
good representation. "It adds no small weight to all these considerations," he writes, "to recollect that history informs us of no long-

lived republic which had not a senate," and he proceeds to reconsider the examples of Sparta, Rome, and Carthage. Those "petty republics," whose "transient and fleeting brilliancy" had so engaged Publius's attention in Number 9, turn out (fifty-four papers later) to include "long-lived" republics whose examples, though in some respects "repugnant to the genius of America," had managed nonetheless to "blend stability with liberty."[62]

Whereas in Number 10 representation had been for the sake of the extended sphere, in Number 63 Publius reveals that the sphere is also, at least partly, for the sake of the right kind of representation – the kind that accustoms "the genius of America" to expect that republican government shall be good government, in which the reason of the public prevails over majority and minority factions alike. Candidly, he states that the size of the Union not only allows the exclusion of the people from the direct administration of the government (most visible in the most perduring parts of it: the senate, presidency, and supreme court), but allows this exclusion to have its full salutary effect. In *The Federalist*'s great exercise in civic education, then, the extended sphere plays a subordinate but still important role. It ministers to what Abraham Lincoln would call our political religion.

CHAPTER FOUR

CIVILITY AND CITIZENSHIP: GEORGE WASHINGTON ON CIVIL AND RELIGIOUS LIBERTY

To be "civil" in ordinary usage means to be polite, respectful, decent. It is a quality implying, in particular, the restraint of anger directed towards others, whether fellow passengers, siblings, or citizens. In this sense, it is not the same thing as warmth and indeed implies a certain coolness: civility helps to cool the too-hot passions of citizenship or of a certain kind of citizenship. From this thought, however, it is only a small step to a different and higher view of civility as something positive rather than negative. In this light, civility seems to correspond to that concord or *homonoia* that Aristotle identified as characteristic of political friendship.[1] When citizens are civil to one another despite their political disagreements, they reveal that these disagreements are less important than their resolution to remain fellow citizens. They agree – or, as Aristotle would put it, are of the same mind – on the fundamental political questions, even if they differ on secondary issues. Without this fundamental agreement reflected in civility, citizenship would be self-contradictory and finally self-destructive; it would be partisanship or, in the worst case, civil war by another name.

For the sake of its own perfection, citizenship requires civility, or more precisely, the concord of opinions underlying civility. The

French Revolution remains the unforgettable modern example of citizenship's self-destruction in the absence of such a harmony of views and affections. Citizen Brissot, Citizen Danton, Citizen Robespierre – one by one they fell victims to ever more radical and ever more exclusive definitions of the good citizen. Tyranny itself is the process of exclusion carried to its logical extreme. So far as the tyrant is concerned, he is the sole citizen: he is the state.

Still, it would be a great mistake to believe that the opposite of tyranny or of permanent civil war, whether explicit or implicit, is simply a concord of opinion. Political friendship can be based on better or worse opinions. The criteria for evaluating them must therefore be extrinsic to the opinions themselves. In other words, even as citizenship requires civility, so civility points beyond itself to certain permanent and objective moral standards – to the nature of "civil government," and, higher still, to the moral and theoretical concerns of what is rightly called civilization.

RULES OF CIVILITY

To look at civility and citizenship in the American founding is a rather different task from examining them in liberal democracy as a whole. The American founders spoke (*inter alia*) of popular government, democracy, republicanism, free government, and civil government, but not, so far as I know, of liberal democracy. This is a more recent term, applied to everything from Weimar Germany to contemporary India. Indeed it is a serious question whether thinking mainly in terms of the genus "liberal democracy" does not distract us from what is distinctive and valuable and, in truth, generally relevant about the American political experience – the sort of things that kept and continue to keep the United States from going the way of Weimar Germany. Let two examples suffice. The "veneration" or "reverence" for the law, above all for the Constitution, spoken of in *Federalist* 49 and confirmed by observers of America from Alexis de Tocqueville to the sociologist Robert Bellah, is not part of traditional liberal democratic theory, at least if Hobbes, Spinoza, and Locke are taken as representative. Similarly, the very notion of "founding" or

"Founding Fathers," in the American sense of those terms, is absent from the horizon of liberal democratic theory. The social contract, understood simply as the alternative to anarchy, or as a by-product of individual calculation or utility maximization, is almost the antithesis of a real founding, as Plato, Aristotle, and Cicero knew long before, and better than, Rousseau, whose treatment of the problem has become famous.

Given these and other reasons, I think it is sensible to look at the problem of civility and citizenship in the American founding primarily in the light of what is distinctive to the founding. This is not to deny that the United States was intended to be an example unto the nations. But it was intended to be an example of republicanism, purer and nobler than any previous incarnation, precisely because it was to be founded explicitly and proudly on the rights of man as man, rights whose title derived from the "laws of Nature and of Nature's God." Broadly speaking, the American founders thought of themselves as perfecting the tradition of republicanism, of rescuing liberty, equality, and the rule of law from their more or less imperfect embodiments in previous republics. Yet in invoking "nature's God" – who was also the living God, the "Supreme Judge of the world," to whom they appealed for the rectitude of their intentions – the founders acknowledged a world changed, in vital respects, by the presence of Christianity. In these circumstances, the republican cause had to be thought through again in light of the conflicts and potential harmony between reason and biblical revelation.

There is nothing more distinctive, nor more representative of the founders' largeness of soul on these difficult questions, nor, to come to the main point, is there a more reliable guide to civility and citizenship in the American founding, than the words and deeds of General and later President George Washington. Although I have no desire to out-parson Parson Weems, I do think it is impossible to understand the founding without coming to grips with the phenomenon of Washington, which is above all a moral phenomenon of the utmost gravity. In what follows, therefore, I will appeal primarily to his speeches and writings to illustrate my argument.[2]

Civility is in the first place a matter of moral education, involving the shaping of young people's character. The tools of this art include precepts, examples, exhortation, and shame liberally applied as the case permits or demands. It is not surprising, then, to find that one of the earliest writings of the young Washington, laboriously entered into his copybook, is a set of 110 "Rules of Civility and Decent Behavior in Company and Conversation." Thanks in large part to Richard Brookhiser's superlative "moral biography," *Founding Father: Rediscovering George Washington*, these rules have become well known.[3] For the most part the Rules of Civility comprehend lessons useful and necessary for reducing any adolescent to a civilized state: "Shake not the head, feet or legs; roll not the eyes; lift not one eyebrow higher than the other, wry not the mouth and bedew no man's face with your spittle by [approaching too near] him [when] you speak." These rules are a playful (though serious) reminder that civility consists first of all in good manners. "Every action done in company," reads the first rule, "ought to be with some sign of respect to those that are present." [All citations of Washington appearing in the text refer to W. B. Allen's excellent one-volume edition, *George Washington: A Collection* (Indianapolis: Liberty Classics, 1988), hereinafter *GW*. See *GW*, 6.] Of course, bad manners are not evil per se, but they can make one unwelcome, uncouth, and in the end unhappy. Good manners are a reminder that one's own interest and happiness are bound up with one's family and friends, and that the authority of such essential social groups is – practically speaking – more obvious than, and just as fundamental as, the liberty of their members.

Civility in this sense stands athwart the modern ethic of self-expression. Nevertheless, good manners aim not to crush but to form individual character. Washington's list begins with what might be dismissed today (in theory, though rarely in practice) as mere social conformity; but it ends with these words: "Labor to keep alive in your breast that little spark of celestial fire called conscience" (*GW*, 13). A certain conformity to social custom is part of good manners, but it is justified because we are social or political animals and because it frees us to cultivate the distinctions that matter. A serious man does not manifest his seriousness or his superiority by wearing his tennis shoes with a tuxedo or by eating spaghetti with his fingers (though serious men in previous ages have, of course, eaten without forks). Civility allows for, and at its best is, a kind of gentlemanship, the fanning and feeding of that "spark of celestial fire" in man to produce a steady blaze of moral seriousness.

Washington's civility is thus a species of honor or of concern with honor. Explaining to his wife why he had to accept command of the Continental army in 1775, for example, he wrote: "It was utterly out of my power to refuse this appointment, without exposing my character to such censures, as would have reflected dishonor upon myself, and given pain to my friends. This, I am sure, could not and ought not to be pleasing to you and must have lessened me considerably in my own esteem" (*GW*, 41; cf. 57–58, 65, 83). Washington set high standards for himself, and the consciousness of his own honor, reflected in and reflecting the honorableness of his friends, provided the touchstone of his conduct. At the highest level, his civility was thus a form of what Aristotle would call magnanimity. Such greatness of soul, the crown of the moral virtues, as Aristotle explained, accepts external honors as the highest tribute that can be paid it, but regards all such popular offerings as vastly inferior to its own internal sense of dignity and propriety.[4]

One of the most famous and instructive displays of Washington's magnanimity was his response to Colonel Lewis Nicola's letter (May 22, 1782) proposing that Washington seize power from Congress and make himself King of America. "With a mixture of great surprise and astonishment I have read with attention the Sentiments you have submitted to my perusal," he answered Nicola, a loyal and respected officer.

> I am much at loss to conceive what part of my conduct could have given encouragement to an address which to me seems big with the greatest mischiefs that can befall my Country. If l am not deceived in the knowledge of myself, you could not have found a person to whom your schemes are more disagreeable .... Let me conjure you then, if you have regard for your country, concern for yourself or posterity, or respect for me, to banish these thoughts from your mind and never communicate, as from yourself or anyone else, a sentiment of the like nature. (*GW*, 203–4).

What is remarkable is the letter's tone – not outraged or accusatory but profoundly surprised and disappointed. It was calculated to shame, not to condemn, and Nicola was so ashamed that he wrote three apologies in as many days. In this short missive Washington refused the honor of being king on the ground that it was beneath him! Honor, without principle, would be infamy. True honor, in Washington's eyes, lay in performing just and noble deeds for their own sake, not for the sake of extrinsic and tawdry rewards, no matter how glittering they might seem to many men. And in the most fundamental sense of the word, the letter's tone was "civil," that is, it was not the voice of a commander upbraiding his inferior officer, but of one gentleman remonstrating with another, one civilian to another. Civilian control of the military – the indispensable republican principle that Washington's resignation as commanding general and surrender of his sword in 1783 did so much to establish – was itself founded on the commanding general's civility – the perfect gentleman's civil or reasonable control of his militant passions.[5]

Thus did Washington's civility lay the basis and set the standard for republican citizenship and republican government in America. In a way, the crowning glory of the founding may therefore be said to be the fact that Washington was unanimously elected (by the Electoral College) America's first president. His virtues may be considered the final cause of the new regime, even as they played an indispensable role in its efficient causation, the victories won by the Continental army. Be that as it may, the formal cause of the new order was something different. This was the great principle proclaimed in the Declaration of Independence, "that all men are created equal." It is a matter of some academic and political dispute how this was understood at the time. Certainly, however, there should not be any dispute about how Washington understood it.

As over against those present-day commentators who emphasize the lowness of "unalienable rights," reducing them to expressions of the most elemental passions, to the desperate liberty of doing anything to appease one's fear of violent death, Washington esteemed them as high and dignified principles. Far from signifying the abandonment of virtue, man's natural rights required the virtues to sustain and justify them. As he put it in his general orders to the army on March 1, 1778, the fortitude of

> the virtuous officers and soldiery of this Army ... not only under the common hardships incident to a military life, but also under the additional sufferings to which the peculiar situation of these States have exposed them, clearly proves them worthy of the enviable privilege of contending for the rights of human nature, the freedom and independence of their country. (*GW*, 95; cf. 220, 222, 237)

These rights were not antipolitical or directed against political spiritedness. On the contrary, as Washington noted when explaining (in 1774) his opposition to the British government's policies, it was "an innate spirit of freedom" that first told him "that the measures, which the administration hath for some time been, and now are most violently pursuing, are repugnant to every principle of natural justice." He went on to say that "much abler heads than my own" had fully convinced him not only of the measures' repugnance "to natural right," but of their subversion "of the laws and Constitution of Great Britain itself" (*GW*, 38). "Abler heads" were needed not so much to describe natural justice as to expound the positive law of Great Britain: natural right was in harmony with the spiritedness of his own soul.

In addition to Washington's own "sacred honor," then, there is an honor due to human nature, which honor may be called the rights of man. It is an "enviable privilege" to contend for them because they are something special, that is, they are based on what is special to man – his rank in creation. The human species is implicitly distinguished from other species, man from non-man. Man's possession of reason distinguishes him from the beasts, but his imperfect possession of reason – that his faculties are fallible, and above all that his passions may cloud his reason – distinguishes him from the being or the kind of being whose rationality is perfect and unaffected by desire. Non-man includes, therefore, not only the subhuman but also the superhuman, the idea of the divine nature. As the in-between being, man's dignity derives from his place in this ordered universe; it does not result from the attempt to make himself the master and possessor of nature.

Writing to the inhabitants of Canada, Washington contrasted "the Blessings of Liberty" with "the Wretchedness of Slavery," warning the Canadians that to submit slavishly to Great Britain would show their "poverty of Soul and baseness of Spirit." Instead, he called upon them to prove "that you are enlightened, generous, and Virtuous; that you will not renounce your own Rights, or serve as Instruments to deprive your Fellow subjects of theirs" (*GW*, 47). In his understanding, the rights of man demand an unprecedented moralization (properly so called) of politics.

CIVIL AND RELIGIOUS LIBERTY

To grasp the significance of this for American citizenship, it is important to understand the relation between what the founders called civil and religious liberty. Indeed, Washington expressed the whole purpose of the Revolution in those words: "The establishment of Civil and Religious Liberty was the motive which induced me to the Field ..." (*GW*, 271).[6] This motive takes us to the heart of the problem – the theological–political problem, as Spinoza called it – confronting the founders.

In the ancient world, this problem did not exist because there was no divorce between the gods and the city. On the contrary, every city had its own gods and understood itself either to have been founded by these gods or to have been founded by mortals who were later taken up into heaven as gods (voluntarily or not: Romulus's promotion was said to have been the handiwork of assassins sent by the Senate).[7] The "constitutional" law of every ancient city was therefore a species of divine law. Consider the opening question of Plato's *Laws*, the Athenian Stranger speaking to the Cretan and the Spartan: "A god, is it, or some human being, who is credited with laying down your laws?" The Cretan responds (on behalf of the Spartan, too) "A god, stranger, a god."[8] Or consider the children of Israel, who, except for their monotheism, were a typical ancient people. They were emancipated, conducted out of Egypt, given their law, and led into battle to secure the Promised Land, all by their God.

The ancient city as such had no "religion." It had only its gods, law-giving gods, who were perforce jealous gods. To be sure, some cities held some gods in common, most notably the Olympian deities among the Greek cities, which is why, incidentally, the Greeks could hold the Olympic games. But these gods commanded different things to different *poleis*, and at any rate they were only part of the elaborate structure of local and ancestral gods that cumulatively distinguished each city. (Fustel de Coulanges has given the clearest picture of this in his classic book on the ancient city.[9]) The city was the work of its gods, who in return demanded not so much faith, or belief in particular doctrines, but obedience to the city's laws. Indeed, if the city was defeated in battle, its gods were also considered losers; and it was not thought craven or impious for the vanquished, if their lives were spared, to transfer their allegiance to the gods of their conquerors.

When Christianity conquered Rome, however, the nature of political life and of citizenship in the West was profoundly changed. Rome had already destroyed the independent civic life of its rival cities, but now the last and greatest of the ancient cities was itself cut off from its gods. In their place rose the Christian God, One and separate from the created world, knowable only through His revelations, the God of all men everywhere but of no city in particular. Now it was that the idea of "religion" was born, for men's civic and divine loyalties were no longer identical. However various the cities of men, the City of God was one. The children of Israel, like every ancient people, had believed *itself* to be the City of God or of the gods. Under the Christian dispensation, however, the City of God was not a human or earthly municipality. Divine law was no longer constitutive of particular polities, but offered the means of salvation to individual souls in every city. Hence the problem: If the principle of civic obligation was obedience to the divine law, and cities were no longer thought to have divine lawgivers, what principle was to oblige citizens to obedience? How would the various cities and their laws be justified?

If the whole world were Rome, then the problem might be

mitigated or dodged by identifying that city with the city of God –
the ancient city writ large. But citizenship in the far-flung Roman
empire was more a legal formality than a share in political rule; and
at any rate, a single political community, even for the corner of the
earth conquered by Rome, proved unsustainable. The political history of the West after the establishment of the Holy Roman Empire
consisted of a series of attempts to answer these fundamental questions – to find a new ground for political right. Each attempt
ultimately unraveled, partly because Christians fell to fighting
among themselves over the exact definition of Christianity, but more
profoundly because of the conflict between revelation as such and
reason. This conflict underlay the battles between theological and
secular authorities during the Holy Roman Empire and during and
after the Reformation.[10]

In the face of this theological-political problem, citizenship and
civility were both endangered. As a religion not so much of law but
of belief, Christianity, when established by temporal authorities, had
the distressing if somewhat paradoxical tendency both to sap obedience to civil laws and to invite civil coercion in matters of faith. By
virtue of the first tendency, membership or citizenship in a political
community became peculiarly problematic. By virtue of the second,
civility and gentlemanship became swamped by religious fanaticism
and hypocrisy. For gentlemen, according to Aristotle, are precisely
those who do not need extrinsic reasons to be moral; they act for the
sake of the virtues themselves, guided by practical wisdom. As a
political phenomenon, as a real force within the city, such gentlemanship is only possible where religion is civilized, i.e., friendly to
morality and the rule of gentlemanly virtues.

Restoring the foundations of gentlemanship, civility, and citizenship within the Christian West was a great accomplishment of
the American founding. It did this in the name of civil and religious
liberty, not of virtue *eo nomine*, inasmuch as the deepest cause of the
millennium-long civil war within the West might be said to be the
dispute over the ultimate or transpolitical meaning of virtue –
whether it consisted in following Athens or Jerusalem, in skeptical
questioning or faithful obedience. But this was a debate, Washington
and his American compatriots realized, that had precisely to be car-

ried on at the highest intellectual and spiritual levels. As a theoretical question, it called for conversation among friends disposed to seek the truth. It could not be conducted politically, and any attempt to resolve it politically was bound to be ignorant, presumptuous, and finally tyrannical. This had been the cause of the holocausts of the Old World during its wars of religion. In America, by contrast, men would have the liberty to carry on this transpolitical conversation while cultivating the civic and religious friendship that was its precondition and product.

Two principles were therefore required: a ground of citizenship and a ground for separating citizenship from church membership or religious belief. The Americans found both in the doctrine of natural rights. In the first place, they discovered the basis of political obligation in the consent of each individual, premised on the grounds of his natural freedom and equality. This individualism had to be as thorough-going as Christian individualism – recall the affecting scene of Christian's departure from his family and village (the City of Destruction) in search of the Celestial City in John Bunyan's *The Pilgrim's Progress* – in order to establish a common and unshakable foundation on which to build a doctrine of civil authority. The decision voluntarily to form a civil society thus involved the particular exercise of rights that are prescribed by the universal "laws of nature and of nature's God," eliminating any conflict between the particular and the universal. At the same time, religious liberty for all was secured by virtue of the limited nature of the social contract, which did not seek to dictate the conditions of eternal salvation in the world "which is to come," to invoke Bunyan's subtitle. Freedom of the mind cannot be alienated: it is impossible to grant to government the power or right to compel our mind to believe something of which it is not persuaded by the evidence and arguments presented to it. Especially is this true of religious questions, for faith above all cannot be forced or extorted.

By virtue of these principles, men could be good citizens of the City of God – and good citizens of their particular earthly city – without prejudice to either. "Civil government" and "civil liberties" are made possible precisely by excluding questions of revealed truth from determination by political majorities. Majority rule and minority rights can be made consistent only on this basis. The Americans saw that under modern conditions, limited government is essential to the rule of law. But the justice of limited or moderate government for all times and places depended upon a higher, indeed the highest consideration, namely, the limits of human knowledge, whether viewed in the merely human or Socratic light, on the one hand, or in the light of divine omniscience on the other. For the Christian West, the separation of church and state meant that revelation is not forced to overrule the protests of human reason, nor reason compelled to pass judgment on the claims of revelation. The limits of human wisdom from every point of view thus affirmed the justice of limited government and of citizenship governed by civility.

AMERICAN GREATNESS

Although church and state must be separated, Washington thought, this is not true for religion and politics in general, or for religion and morality in particular, which are distinguishable but in many respects mutually reinforcing.[11] Today, the separation of church and state is often regarded as the beginning of the divorce between morals and politics, or between values and facts.[12] What this interpretation overlooks is the fact that separation was intended not to divorce but to unite civic morality and the *moral* teaching of religion: disestablishment was meant to *establish* common standards of morality to guide political life. The point is well illustrated in the founders' use of the term "conscience." In general, conscience is the knowledge of right and wrong that men share with one another and with their Creator. It comprises the duties men owe to their Creator, especially the duty of worshipping Him according to the modes we think He finds agreeable – hence the "right of conscience." Writing in 1789 to a group of Quakers, Washington expressed the idea in these words:

> The liberty enjoyed by the people of these States, of worshipping Almighty God agreeably to their consciences, is not only among the choicest of their blessings, but also of their rights. (*GW*, 533)

That is, religious freedom is not only a dispensation of a loving God who abhors persecution, but also of the fallible human reason that admits it cannot penetrate the highest mysteries of faith.

But conscience comprises also the duties men owe more particularly to one another. The founders distinguished the commands of conscience *in this sphere* from the "right" of conscience grounded in the limits of human reason. Our duties to our fellow man depend not upon a right to interpret private or revealed wisdom, but upon our duty to acknowledge the "self-evident" truths of human nature and the special status of man in the universe, whether that universe is thought to be ordered by the inherent power of nature or by the will of the Living God. In short, because human knowledge of the highest things is limited does not mean that we know nothing at all, that we cannot tell the difference between a man and a pig. Such fundamental distinctions must be knowable if revelation itself is to make sense – in order to know, e.g., that "love thy neighbor as thyself" applies to neighboring human beings but not cows or horses (see the discussion in Chapter Two). The broad morality built on the commonsense *agreement* of revelation and reason – on "the laws of nature and of nature's God," properly so called – was what the founders meant to inculcate as America's common public morality. This morality was implied even in the title of Thomas Jefferson's famous bill "for Establishing Religious Freedom in Virginia": he intended to replace one establishment – the state's established Anglican Church – with another, religious freedom and its attendant morality, established partly by law and partly by public opinion. He painted the bounds of that morality in broad strokes, mentioning "honesty, truth, temperance, gratitude, and the love of man."[13]

One of Washington's most celebrated letters, composed during his first term as president, is to the Hebrew Congregation in Newport, Rhode Island. All Americans, he writes,

> possess alike the liberty of conscience and immunities of citizenship. It is now no more that toleration is spoken of as if it were [by] the indulgence of one class of people that another enjoyed the exercise of their inherent natural rights, for, happily, the

> Government of the United States, which gives to bigotry no sanc-
> tion, to persecution no assistance, requires only that they who live
> under its protection should demean themselves as good citizens
> in giving it on all occasions their effectual support. (*GW*, 548)

In America, the members of this esteemed Congregation could be
good citizens and faithful, observant Jews at the same time; for perhaps the first time in the history of the West, Jews could enjoy civil
and religious liberty not as a matter of toleration but as a result of
"their inherent natural rights." Good citizenship involves more than
simply a quid pro quo for the state's protection, however. To be worthy of the rights of self-government citizens must show themselves
capable of governing their own passions. Despite reason and revelation's disagreements about what is trans-moral – whether nature or
God is the highest principle – they agree substantially on the definition of morality, beginning more or less with the basics contained in
the Second Table of the Decalogue. The moral virtues provide a
touchstone to help distinguish good from bad citizenship, and true
from false prophecy. As Washington puts it in a letter to the General
Assembly of Presbyterian Churches:

> While all men within our territories are protected in worship-
> ping the deity according to the dictates of their consciences; it
> is rationally to be expected from them in return that they will
> be emulous of evincing the sanctity of their professions by the
> innocence of their own lives and the beneficence of their
> actions; for no man, who is profligate in his morals, or a bad
> member of the civil community, can possibly be a true Chris-
> tian, or a credit to his own religious society. (*GW*, 593)

Washington's point is that the "right of conscience" cannot command anything contrary to that conscience which monitors and
embodies the natural law. The right of conscience itself being one of
man's natural rights, it has to be exercised consistently with the rest
of them. The same point may be expressed in religious terms: new
revelations cannot repeal or contradict the basic moral command-
ments of the Bible.

It is common in the founders' writings to come across the distinction between public and private happiness. The innermost core of the distinction is the profoundly private relationship between the individual soul and its Creator. The blessings of this communion involve the destiny of the individual soul in the life to come. Within this world, however, public and private happiness are aspects of the same reality. Above all, both public and private happiness are connected to moral virtue. "The foundation of our national policy," Washington urged in his First Inaugural Speech, should be "laid in the pure and immutable principles of private morality" (*GW*, 462). In his Farewell Address he proclaimed, "Of all the dispositions and habits which lead to political prosperity, Religion and morality are indispensable supports. In vain would that man claim the tribute of Patriotism, who should labor to subvert these great Pillars of human happiness, these firmest props of the duties of Men and citizens." Religion and morality are not merely means to political prosperity, it should be emphasized. They are "these great Pillars of human happiness." Happiness is a condition or activity requiring morality and religion; without them, one cannot be genuinely happy, although he concedes that "the influence of refined education on minds of peculiar structure" may in a very few cases allow morality alone to suffice (*GW*, 521).

In his First Inaugural, Washington emphasized the same point: "… [T]here is no truth more thoroughly established," he declared, "than that there exists an indissoluble union between virtue and happiness…." (*GW*, 462). Morality, or morality and religion, were therefore indispensably necessary to the happiness of the American people. Accordingly, the line dividing church and state did not run, as John Locke had seemed to argue, between the soul and the body.[14] It ran *within the soul*, distinguishing the exercise of the right of conscience, with its concern for the suprarational doctrines of revealed religion, from the consciousness of moral right.[15] The political effects were striking. With the doctrines of speculative theology now free to be expounded and contested in the churches, uncontaminated by the secular pursuit of power, morality and the moral teachings of religion were free to wield an unprecedented influence over public and private opinion. This *moralization* of politics gave an unprecedented scope for gentlemanship and civility – for what might justly be called Christian gentlemanship.[16]

It was the statesmanship of the founders, and above all of Washington, that secured this realm of gentlemanly civility for the United States. "We are a young nation and have a character to establish," he wrote candidly in 1783 (*GW*, 246). To do justice to Washington's role would require a biography, not an essay; but the core of his genius was always to recognize the moral implications and consequences of human action. He knew when and how to conciliate opinions – on the democratic character of the House of Representatives (the subject of his sole intervention in the debates of the Constitutional Convention), on the Bill of Rights, even among party factions in his own cabinet – so that his countrymen might join hands as fellow citizens. Most importantly, he knew the power of his own example. During the ratification debates he wrote confidently of the historic role that the first officers elected under the Constitution would be called upon to play.

> I have no doubt but ... those persons who are chosen to administer it will have wisdom enough to discern the influence which their example as rulers and legislators may have on the body of the people, and will have virtue enough to pursue that line of conduct which will most conduce to the happiness of their Country; as the first transaction of a nation, like those of an individual upon his first entrance into life, make the deepest impression, and are to form the leading traits in his character. (*GW*, 387)

The means and ends of founding are great themes of classical political science. This science is indispensable to the proper understanding of the American founding, despite the fact that it was not an ancient city Washington and his allies were establishing. The United States might be a new Rome, but it would not be the old Rome nor a mere imitation of the old. Ancient Rome, it suffices to say, would never have described its reason for being as "protecting the rights of human nature and establishing an Asylum for the poor and oppressed of all nations and religions" (*GW*, 237). But this did form a great part of America's purpose. In the founders' view, American citizenship and civility were distinguished by their dedication to the common purposes of Western civilization, though "civilization" was a word only beginning to settle into dictionaries in those days. James Boswell, in fact, records in 1792 that Dr. Johnson "would not admit *civilization*, but only *civility*" to his Dictionary. "With great deference to him," said Boswell, "I thought *civilization*, from *to civilize*, better in the sense opposed to *barbarity*, than *civility*." Civilization is the opposite of barbarism, at least, but the word came to suggest, too, the high civility that resulted from the joint patrimony of reason and revelation. Neither the best regime of the Classics nor the holy city of the church was what the founders sought, but a polity that for the first time in history would seek to do justice to both without establishing either at the expense of the other. This was the *novus ordo seclorum* they proclaimed.

To Washington belongs perhaps the most striking statement of the founders' consciousness of the West as a civilization, and of America's place within the West. It occurs in his famous Circular Letter of June 14, 1783, and deserves to be quoted in full.

> The foundation of our empire was not laid in the gloomy age of Ignorance and Superstition, but at an Epocha in which the rights of mankind were better understood and more clearly defined, than at any former period; the researches of the human mind, after social happiness, have been carried to a great extent; the Treasures of knowledge, acquired through a long succession of years, by the labours of Philosophers, Sages and Legislatures, are laid open for our use, and their collected wisdom may be happily applied in the Establishment of our forms of Government; the free cultivation of Letters, the unbounded extension of Commerce, the progressive refinement of manners, the growing liberality of sentiment, and above all, the pure and benign light of Revelation, have had a meliorating influence on mankind and increased the blessings of Society. At this auspicious period, the United States came into being as a Nation, and if their Citizens should not be completely free and happy, the fault will be entirely their own. (*GW*, 240–41)

The auspices could not be more favorable, but the political lesson is that the freedom and happiness of the American people, and the destiny of the civilization they represent, depend on their conduct. "This is the time of their political probation," Washington adds in the next paragraph, "… the moment to establish or ruin their national Character forever.…" (*GW*, 241).

The civility of the American founding connects American citizenship to the civilization of which it is an illustrious part, but a part nonetheless. One might say that this civility looks to the other parts of the civilized world as a kind of community of like-minded nations. Thus the Declaration of Independence pays "a decent respect to the opinions of mankind," presupposing that those opinions are at least decent enough to merit respect. But Washington and the signers of the Declaration were well aware that "cruelty and perfidy scarcely paralleled in the most barbarous ages" could be committed by "the Head of a civilized nation" – were aware more generally that ages of science and commerce could be as barbarous, in some respect more barbarous, than ages of "Ignorance and Superstition." It was precisely such a threat from within that faced the United States less than seventy-five years later in the Civil War, when civility and citizenship were rent in two by the controversy over slavery. It was in the midst of this crisis that Abraham Lincoln, leaving Springfield for the nation's capital, declared somberly that he went "with a task before me greater than which rested upon Washington." In contemplating the future of American citizenship and civility, in contemplating the nature of American greatness, we ought to remember how he bore the task – and what he may have learned to help him bear it, as an avid young reader of Parson Weems's *Life of Washington*.

CHAPTER FIVE

PERPETUATING THE REPUBLIC: EDUCATION AND POLITICS

We are a young Nation and have a character to establish.
GEORGE WASHINGTON
Letter to John Augustine Washington,
June 15, 1783.[1]

EDUCATION AND POLITICS are inseparable, although not identical. They are inseparable because anything that is taught – even doctrines in physics or biology (for example, Darwinism) – may have political consequences, shaping the opinions of those who rule or will rule; and because what should be taught is therefore an eminently political question. They are inseparable, too, because political speeches and deeds are instructive to citizens, young and old, as well as to non-citizens. So it is not surprising that some of the greatest works of political philosophy take education as their principal theme – Plato's *Republic* and Rousseau's *Emile*, for example – and that many others treat education as the most important way to preserve governments – notably Aristotle's *Politics* and Montesquieu's *Spirit of the Laws*.

To be sure, not every bit of knowledge has immediate political relevance, and only a fool would maintain that the arts and sciences should simply have their conclusions dictated to them by politicians.

To that extent, politics and education remain distinguishable. In fact, the restriction of direct political control over the arts and sciences is itself one great mark of a free society. At the same time, however, another mark of a free society is that citizens have the right to contest and to protest, through the political process, what is being taught by teachers in the schools, politicians in office, and even artists whose works are displayed in public forums.

In the United States, these debates take place under the aegis of the Constitution and the Bill of Rights, whose interpretation, but not whose authority, is often disputed. That is to say, seldom does anyone openly question whether the Constitution itself should be "the supreme law of the land." The legitimacy of the Constitution and the laws made pursuant to it is generally assumed. What the proper relationship between democratic politics and education should be is therefore commonly regarded as ultimately, or in large part, a constitutional question. Whether state governments are obliged to equalize expenditures per pupil across school districts,[2] whether race, sex, and ethnicity should count in student admissions and faculty hiring,[3] whether bilingual instruction is a right guaranteed to every student who might need it[4] – these are questions that nowadays, for better or worse, look to the Equal Protection Clause of the Fourteenth Amendment for an answer.

But to see the relation of politics to education more comprehensively, we need to step back from the current legal controversies and examine the arguments out of which the Constitution itself emerged. We need to return to the guiding principles of the American Revolution. "There is nothing more common," the physician-patriot Benjamin Rush observed in January 1787, "than to confound the terms of *American Revolution* with those *of the late American war.*"

> The American war is over, but this is far from being the case with the American Revolution. On the contrary, nothing but the great drama is closed. It remains yet to establish and perfect our new forms of government, and to prepare the principles, morals, and manners of our citizens for these forms of government after they are established and brought to perfection .... To

conform the principles, morals and manners of our citizens, to our republican forms of government, it is absolutely necessary that knowledge of every kind should be disseminated through every part of the United States.[5]

The work of the Revolution was not merely the struggle against Great Britain or even the establishment of new forms of government, but the revolution in "the principles, morals, and manners of our citizens" that would be necessary to support and perfect the new republican forms. Indeed, the American founding properly so called is nothing other than this bold educational enterprise. A founding creates new political institutions for a new political community; but "institutions" are at bottom a form of *institutio*, of training or education. A regime or form of government cannot survive for long if it is not "instituted" in the hearts and minds of its citizens.

The American founding, therefore, may be said to provide the original and authoritative education in being an American. Today, that education is under attack on two main fronts. On the first, critics from both the Right and Left accuse the founders of neglecting civic education – of bequeathing us a regime of egoistic individuals absorbed in the pursuit of private gain at the expense of the common good.[6] From this point of view, the civic culture is weak and there is insufficient unity of opinions and affections. On the second front, critics, again from both the Right and Left but predominantly and most vocally from the Left, deprecate the founders and their view of education for paying insufficient attention to "diversity." Not its defective but its excessive unity is the complaint: the American founders attempted to impose a property-holding, white, male, cisgendered, Eurocentric culture upon the diverse cultures that then existed or would later spring up in America. This suppression of competing or alternative cultures is the root of our present ills, and multicultural education is the necessary remedy – so runs this second line of criticism.[7]

In this chapter I shall take up each criticism in turn, using it as the occasion to restate important elements of the founders' view of the proper relation among republican politics, law, and education.

CIVIC EDUCATION

That the founders failed to provide adequately for the education of future American citizens is today a common charge. Undergirding the charge is an implicit or explicit contrast between American republicanism and the civic-spiritedness of ancient republicanism. Rousseau is the past master of this kind of sweeping, Romantic dismissal of modern liberal arrangements. Writing on a more or less practical assignment and only a few years before the Declaration of Independence was penned, Rousseau, in his *Government of Poland*, wondered:

> As we read the history of the ancients, it seems to us that we have moved into another universe and are surrounded by beings of another species. Our Frenchmen, our Englishmen, our Russians – what have they in common with the Romans and the Greeks? Almost nothing except the shape of their bodies .... What prevents us from being the kind of men they were? The prejudices, the base philosophy, and the passions of narrow self-interest which, along with indifference to the welfare of others, have been inculcated in all our hearts by ill-devised institutions, in which we find no trace of the hand of genius.[8]

In this passage one can see something of the provenance of the contemporary criticism of the founding from both Right and Left. On the Right, for example, Rousseau's disdain for the "ill-devised institutions" of modern government echoes in George Will's claim (since retracted or greatly modified) that liberal democracies, including the United States, are "ill founded."[9] Following in the footsteps of such neoconservative scholars as Martin Diamond, Walter Berns, and Robert A. Goldwin, Will accuses the American founders of relying "almost exclusively" on institutional arrangements and the "sociology" of competing factions to substitute for public-spirited citizens and statesmen.[10] The charge was repeated and elaborated by Allan Bloom in *The Closing of the American Mind*.[11]

Whereas these critics on the Right tend to deplore the founding's alleged undermining of patriotism and the nobler virtues, the critics on the Left see the founders' original sin to be the neglect of "community." Deploying many of the same arguments used by the Right, the liberal critics come to a similar but more egalitarian conclusion. They reject the possessive or bourgeois individualism of the founding, including the founders' supposed view that, in Sheldon Wolin's words, "the aim of a political organization was not to educate men, but to deploy them; not to alter their moral character, but to arrange institutions in such a manner that human drives would cancel each other or, without conscious intent, be deflected towards the common good."[12] This reliance on laws and institutional arrangements led to the decay of political life and art, to what Benjamin Barber calls "public purposelessness."[13] The same regret over the eclipse of lively, communitarian politics permeates much of the historical scholarship of the so-called "civic humanist" or "classical republican" school.[14]

All these critics are correct, of course, in noticing that Washington, Jefferson, Madison, and the other great statesmen of the period were not intent on founding a *polis*. The founders knew they could not have built such a narrow, soaring structure because they lacked the keystone, the absolutely essential and binding part: the gods. Absent the civic and ancestral gods possessed by every ancient city, the comprehensive and intense political life of a *polis* was impossible. Consider Rousseau's description of the type of patriotism he wished to confer on Poland, modeled, needless to say, on the patriotism of the ancients:

> The newly-born infant, upon first opening his eyes, must gaze upon the fatherland, and until his dying day should behold nothing else. Your true republican is a man who imbibed love of the fatherland, which is to say love of the laws and of liberty, with his mother's milk. That love makes up his entire existence: he has eyes only for the fatherland, lives only for the fatherland; the moment he is alone, he is a mere cipher; the moment he has no fatherland, he is no more; if not dead, he is worse-off than if he were dead.[15]

As Rousseau well knew (though he did not let on while writing to the pious Poles), such dedication could be sustained only where religion and the city were one, where men's religious and familial passions were absorbed and defined by the city, where all non-citizens were infidels and all citizens brothers. To express it in the language of *The Social Contract*, civil religion is necessary in order to produce the general will.[16]

In the world transformed by the presence of universal religion, in the Christian West in particular, civil religion in the original sense of the term could not be re-established.[17] The intense and total loyalty of the *polis* could not be recreated even in the small city-states of Italy – as no one understood better than Machiavelli. How then could it be resurrected in the large American states or in the vast continental expanse of the United States? Beginning with the Virginia debate over the disestablishment of the Anglican Church, the American founders faced up to the revolution brought about by the advent of Christianity, and to the legacy of religious wars and other disorders that had developed in its wake. America would be a republic, but it would be a liberal republic, acknowledging the right of conscience as a fundamental human freedom, and thus limiting government for the sake of protecting man's relation to God.[18]

As a consequence, reason and revealed religion could now join hands in defense of morality, precisely because the theological dogmas of the different sects were prescinded from politics. On this basis, the American founders, far from abandoning education in moral and civic virtue, undertook an unprecedented campaign for public and private education.[19] These efforts took place mainly on the state level, and so are not mentioned in the Constitution or *The Federalist*.[20] Nevertheless, they were extremely significant for the American way of life. The schools founded in the late-eighteenth and early-nineteenth centuries were new kinds of schools, adapted to the task of inculcating the skills, habits, and virtues of republican self-government. Not common meals (as in Sparta) or common property (as in the Soviet Union), but common schools and a common dedication to republican principles would be the touchstones of American citizenship.[21]

Critics of the founders, however, seem to doubt not only the significance but even the existence of the founders' concern for moral and civic education. Walter Berns, for example, asserts that the Constitution was based on the "newly discovered principles" of modern political philosophy, and that these were "decidedly not principles having to do with the education of citizens, or the preparation of persons for their role as citizens."[22] Nor does it seem that the adepts of this new political science were keen on having the states take up the educational slack. Declares Berns, "[i]t is not possible to point to a single statement proving that the framers expected the states to provide the sort of civic or moral education required of Citizens in a republican regime," although he does admit, somewhat contradictorily, "there is ample evidence that they were aware of the requirement."[23] He attempts to resolve the contradiction by imputing it to the framers, arguing that their theory and practice were at odds – that the framers' new political science gradually eroded the "older and civilized politics" of the states, in which moral and civic education were important concerns.[24]

Yet the framers' concern for moral and civic education at both the state and national levels can easily be illustrated. "In every government, which is not altogether despotical," wrote James Wilson, one of the most active and influential framers, in his celebrated law lectures delivered in 1790–91, "the institution [that is, education] of youth is of some publick consequence. In a republican government, it is of the greatest."[25] The peculiar dependence of the republican form of government on popular enlightenment or on the education of the great body of the people is a constant theme in the books, pamphlets, newspaper articles, and letters of the day. George Washington put it this way in his Farewell Address:

> 'Tis substantially true, that virtue or morality is a necessary spring of popular government. The rule indeed extends with more or less force to every species of free Government. Who that is a sincere friend to it, can look with indifference upon attempts to shake the foundation of the fabric.
>
> Promote then as an object of primary importance, Institutions for the general diffusion of knowledge. In proportion as the structure of a government gives force to public opinion, it is essential that public opinion should be enlightened.[26]

Throughout his life, Washington was himself a discerning patron of public and private education, and he frequently urged both the state and national governments to support the provision of education so far as they were able. In 1784, he wrote to George Chapman, the author of a book on education:

> My sentiments are perfectly in unison with yours sir, that the best means of forming a manly, virtuous and happy people, will be found in the right education of youth. Without *this* foundation, every other means, in my opinion, must fail .... Of the importance of education our Assemblies, happily, seem fully impressed; they [are] establishing new, and giving further endowments to the old Seminaries of learning, and I persuade myself will leave nothing unessayed to cultivate literature and useful knowledge, for the purpose of qualifying the rising generation for patrons of good government, virtue, and happiness.[27]

Long before the Constitution had been written, most states, spurred on by the Continental Congress, had adopted new constitutions that addressed both the ends and means of moral education in a republic. The Virginia Declaration of Rights, composed by George Mason (later a participant in the Federal Convention), warned that "no free Government, or the blessing of liberty, can be preserved to any people but by a firm adherence to justice, moderation, temperance, frugality, and virtue, and by frequent recurrence to fundamental principles."[28] The Massachusetts Constitution, drafted by John Adams, commanded the Commonwealth's schools "to countenance and inculcate the principles of humanity and general benevolence, public and private charity, industry and frugality, honesty and punctuality in their dealings, sincerity, good humor, and all social affections and generous sentiments among the people."[29]

This solicitude for citizens' character extended even to the future states that would be formed out of the territories west of the Appalachians. Here the national government had perforce to play a direct role, inasmuch as it owned and administered the territories on behalf of the Union. And so the Northwest Ordinance, enacted by the Congress under the Articles of Confederation and re-passed by the First Congress, adjured that "Religion, Morality, and knowledge being necessary to good government and the happiness of mankind, Schools and the means of education shall forever be encouraged."[30] Under its provisions, the territories were divided into townships, and the federal government granted the sixteenth part of every township to the new state governments for the maintenance of schools. The same grant was made to almost every new state admitted thereafter; beginning with California's admission in 1850, it was increased to two sections per township; and with Utah, Arizona, and New Mexico, to four. By the 1930s, these grants, together with miscellaneous other National Land Grants for public education, amounted to 145 million acres, which at the traditional government price of $1.25 an acre, constituted an endowment for public education of at least $181,250,000 (unadjusted for inflation).[31] Not only did the federal government talk about citizen education, it put its money where its mouth is.

Before and after the Constitution's ratification, the states were (and in fact continued to be, at least until recently) the primary protectors of the public health, welfare, morals, and order; but in the eighteenth century they were not deeply involved in civic education, or for that matter in education of any kind. Only in New England – in Massachusetts, Connecticut, and New Hampshire – did state law establish common schools for all children, with compulsory attendance and public financing. In the middle states, parochial schools flourished; and in the South, private tutoring, private academies, apprenticeship training, and pauper schools predominated.[32] The great movement to institute public schools and to inculcate republican principles in students was not launched until the Constitution-making period, and did not take hold until the early nineteenth century, when American nationalism was firmer.[33]

What is more, this movement represented a change in emphasis within American education-away from the New England Puritans' sectarian apprehension over "that old deluder, Satan"[34] and toward a concern with the maintenance and perfection of republican government. The cultivation of this reverence for the laws and Constitution formed a chief goal of subsequent public education in America, both formal and informal, as the notable example of Abraham

Lincoln's Lyceum Address shows.[35] This speech, entitled "On the Perpetuation of Our Political Institutions," was delivered in 1838, before the Young Men's Lyceum of Springfield, Illinois, an offshoot of the American Lyceum movement that flourished in the early and mid-nineteenth century.[36] An adult education club featuring lectures, debates, and instruction in political, economic, and scientific subjects, the American Lyceum sought, in the words of its constitution, "to favor the advancement of education, especially in the common schools, and the general diffusion of knowledge."[37] The local, county, and state branches of the Lyceum lobbied for public financing of education and training for teachers, established libraries, and donated scientific equipment for the use of local schools and citizens.[38] Thus Lincoln's monitory call in the Lyceum Address for a "political religion" based on reverence for the laws and Constitution – his striking fusion of religious zeal and republican rationalism – can be seen as a kind of rhetorical culmination of the founders' and their successors' campaigns for civic education.[39]

If a nation is to be self-governing, it must be able to protect itself against the wiles of those eager to subvert a republican constitution; at a minimum, the people must be vigilant and well-informed enough to evaluate their own elected officials. James Madison, writing in 1822, approved of Kentucky's plan of public education for this reason. "A popular Government, without popular information, or the means of acquiring it," he wrote, "is but a Prologue to a Farce or a Tragedy; or, perhaps both. Knowledge will forever govern ignorance: And a people who mean to be their own Governors, must arm themselves with the power which knowledge gives."[40]

In the final analysis, however, the people would be unable to control their government if they were unable to control themselves. Virtually everyone who wrote on education in the founding era stressed, therefore, the central importance of moral education for republican government. Noah Webster's discussion is piquant and worth quoting at length:

Our legislators frame laws for the suppression of vice and immorality; our divines thunder from the pulpit the terrors of infinite wrath against the vices that stain the characters of men.

And do laws and preaching effect a reformation of manners? Experience would not give a very favorable answer to this inquiry. The reason is obvious: the attempts are directed to the wrong objects. Laws can only check the public effects of vicious principles but can never reach the principles themselves, and preaching is not very intelligible to people till they arrive at an age when their principles are rooted or their habits firmly established.... The great art of correcting mankind, therefore, consists in prepossessing the mind with good principles. For this reason society requires that the education of youth should be watched with the most scrupulous attention. Education, in a great measure, forms the moral characters of men, and morals are the basis of government. Education should therefore be the first care of a legislature .... A good system of education should be the first article in the code of political regulations.[41]

Surely the most well known and carefully worked out of the founders' educational plans was Jefferson's in Virginia. His system despised neither the utilitarian value of basic education nor the seemingly useless pursuit of the highest learning for its own sake. But his plans focused on the intermediate level, on the proper cultivation of men who love honor and "whom nature hath endowed with genius and virtue."[42] Although his proposals went through several revisions, their general outlines did not vary: every child would receive a free elementary education in the three R's, geography, and history.[43] From there, the most able would advance to the general schools, where languages, higher mathematics, and philosophy would be taught, also at public expense.[44] A third and final layer of schools for professional education would be provided so that students whose families were not wealthy would be able to acquire a means of supporting themselves in independence and dignity.[45] In this way civic and liberal education were blended in Jefferson's plan. The primary schools furnish the basic level of civic education, but the liberal learning confided to the better minds in the general schools (and deepened and refined at the University of Virginia) made this elite group "worthy to receive, and able to guard the sacred deposit of the rights and liberties of their fellow citizens."[46]

Republican morality suffused both the civic and liberal components of Jefferson's plans, and there was no doubt that from the history taught in elementary schools to the political science imparted at the University of Virginia, no relativism concerning the forms of government would be permitted. The merits of republicanism were everywhere to be stressed, but this was in keeping with its truth: republican government's superiority rested on its ability to secure the people's safety and happiness more fully than any other regime could. Indeed, a republican constitution was itself a great vehicle of public or civic education, instructing the people in their rights and duties and summoning the virtues necessary to fulfill both. John Adams, Jefferson's old friend and sometime political adversary, described his expectations of the educational benefit of republican constitutionalism in his *Thoughts on Government*:

> A constitution founded on these principles introduces knowledge among the people, and inspires them with a conscious dignity becoming freemen; a general emulation takes place, which causes good humor, sociability, good manners, and good morals to be general. That elevation of sentiment inspired by such a government, makes the common people brave and enterprising. That ambition which is inspired by it makes them sober, industrious, and frugal.[47]

The founders expected that the cultivation of republican opinions among the people would engender republican manners, and thus restrain and shape the role of passion and interest in the new regime. They looked, then, not merely to the fracturing of a majority faction into a multiplicity of interests, as in the pluralist reading of the famous *Federalist* 10, but to the formation of just majorities whose interests and passions would be in harmony with the Constitution and the common good.[48] Madison affirmed this when, for prudential reasons and after his vigorous opposition to adding a bill of rights to the Constitution during the ratification struggle, he reversed himself and sponsored the Bill of Rights in the First Congress. "The political truths declared in that solemn manner," he wrote at the time, "acquire by degrees the character of fundamental maxims of free Government, and as they become incorporated with the national sentiment, counteract the impulses of interest and passion."[49] What was true of the Bill of Rights was true of the Declaration of Independence and the whole constitutional structure of republicanism. The point of American politics was to educate American citizens.

UNITY AND DIVERSITY

The American founders were not silent on the question of diversity, if by diversity one means a variety of points of view.[50] "Difference of opinion is advantageous in religion," Jefferson wrote in *Notes on the State of Virginia*, comparing a governmental establishment of religion with the benighted efforts of tyrannical European governments to prescribe medical cures and fix systems of physics.[51] *The Federalist* also approved of a "multiplicity of sects" to guard religious freedom against the power of an overweening religious majority, even as it approved of a "multiplicity of interests" to safeguard civil rights.[52] Neither Jefferson nor Madison praised such diversity for its own sake, however.

A variety of interests and sects was useful, in their view, as a means to protect something on which differences of opinion would not be advantageous – mankind's civil and religious rights. For the basis of these rights was human nature itself: man was entitled to them not because of a particular culture or set of value judgments but because of what he *is*. Unity of opinion on this principle had to be zealously cultivated. It was, after all, chiefly this opinion that helped to encourage the great variety of peoples, religions, and classes to come together peaceably in America. This openness to humanity required the rejection of any attempt to derive political right from any accidental, as opposed to essential, characteristic of a human being. For that reason, claims based on race, sex, religion, ethnicity, class, and culture were excluded as the grounds of political right.[53] We should recall that the exaltation of race and class, of the diversity of local values and domestic institutions, was the hallmark of the antebellum defense of slavery as well as of post-Civil War Social Darwinism and Jim Crow.

Similarly, the present-day case for diversity or multiculturalism tends to trace the decisive differences among human beings to our bodies – to our race, sex, and ethnicity. Our minds are regarded as enslaved to our bodies; all thought is supposed to be conditioned or determined by something more fundamental, something subrational. Hence the emphasis on "cultures." A culture (*cultura*) is something that grows or is grown; yet, at least in current parlance, it is *not* something chosen by human minds that can deliberate rationally and consent freely. Under today's view, everyone is both a product and a victim of his own culture. The cure for this condition, promoters of this view argue, is not to seek the perfection of one's own culture in light of some permanent, transcultural standards, but to be exposed to as many other cultures as possible – multiculturalism.[54]

Why this exposure should breed appreciation rather than contempt is anybody's guess. For if all cultures are equally valid, why bother learning about new ones? Why not stick with the one that is rooted in your own race, sex, or ethnic group? But if all cultures are not equally valid, why not choose to concentrate on the better ones or indeed on the one that is best?

The founders did not speak of "cultures" in the modern sense because they believed in permanent standards of right and wrong that were valid for human beings as such, and that could – and should – be discerned by a free people. Thus they distinguished, in the Declaration of Independence, between "barbarous ages" and "civilized" ones, and even condemned "the merciless Indian Savages, whose known rule of warfare, is an undistinguished destruction of all ages, sexes and conditions." But the Indians were savage not because they were red-skinned but because in warfare they did not distinguish between combatants and non-combatants. Similarly, the white-skinned King of England was "totally unworthy the Head of a civilized nation" because he endeavored "works of death, desolation, and tyranny ... scarcely paralleled in the most barbarous ages."[55] Savagery and barbarism are thus permanent dangers confronting and underlying civilized life; they represent retreat from the civilized standards of equal natural rights and government by consent.

The diversity prized by the founders was rooted not in men's bodies but in their souls. Madison, writing as Publius, opposed the attempt to eliminate the causes of faction by giving everyone the same opinions, passions, and interests. He believed that as long as man's reason is fallible and free, different opinions would necessarily be formed and that "the diversity in the faculties of men, from which the rights of property originate" will naturally tend to obstruct any uniformity of interest.[56] Notice that it is from the diverse faculties of men, not (as for John Locke) from labor as such, that the rights of property stem. In order for labor to beget private property it must first be human labor, the product of distinctively human faculties. But these are diverse – that is, not existing as a simple unity – both within the individual soul and among men, who vary in talents, character, and intelligence. Madison believed that our knowledge of this diversity, however, is itself incomplete. "The faculties of the mind itself have never yet been distinguished and defined with satisfactory precision by all the efforts of the most acute and metaphysical philosophers," he writes. The exact boundaries of "sense, perception, judgment, desire, volition, memory, imagination" have "eluded the most subtle investigations, and remain a pregnant source of ingenious disquisition and controversy."[57]

The corollary to the mind's freedom is the uncertainty of much of our knowledge, including self-knowledge. The freedom of the mind is thus the foundation of the most important kind of human diversity: the diversity of opinions that gives rise to the pursuit of truth. To be sure, human beings are governed more by opinions than by wisdom; that is why politics and philosophy, or democracy and education, are always so near and yet so far. Still, that much of our knowledge is uncertain does not mean it is all uncertain, for some truths are self-evident and others are demonstrable. Among the former is the truth that all men are created equal, which rests on the mind's ability to recognize, for example, the difference between human beings and brute animals. The faculty that grasps such essential differences was traditionally called the intellect (*nous*) – a faculty unmentioned by Madison in his map of the doubtful provinces of the mind. Madison nonetheless demonstrated this faculty in his discussion of slavery in *The Federalist*, when, speaking through one of "our Southern brethren," he stated that "[t]he Federal Constitution, therefore, decides with great propriety on the case of our slaves, when it views them in the *mixed* character of persons and of property."[58] He could not label the slave's character as "mixed," however, if he could not first distinguish between the discrete characters of persons and property (like cattle) – that is, if he could not first differentiate between what is proper to the nature of human beings or "moral person[s]" as opposed to what is proper to the nature of "irrational animals."

Political freedom thus rests on the freedom of the mind to recognize the sameness and differences among men. Lincoln, in his speech on the *Dred Scott* decision, put it well: "I think the authors of that notable instrument [the Declaration of Independence] intended to include *all* men, but they did not intend to declare all men equal *in all respects*. They did not mean to say all were equal in color, size, intellect, moral developments, or social capacity. They defined with tolerable distinctness, in what respects they did consider all men created equal – equal in 'certain inalienable rights, among which are life, liberty, and the pursuit of happiness.'"[59] In Lincoln's and the founders' view, then, a free society could reflect the natural inequalities among men in terms of "color, size, intellect, moral developments, or social capacity,"[60] as well as the range of outcomes that a diversity of talents, ambitions, and virtues would produce in commerce and the arts. Republican politics and education could modify or ameliorate some of these inequalities, too. But in any case these inequalities would be less fundamental than the natural equality of human beings *qua* human beings, which gives rise to their rights.

Lincoln's "political religion" sought a unanimity of opinion on these natural rights that, in turn, supplied the condition for the rambunctious political diversity of the early republic. The party system in the United States could not have operated peacefully or respectably without an underlying agreement on the most important political questions. This is what Jefferson meant in his First Inaugural when, after the bitter partisan strife of the 1800 election, he declared that "every difference of opinion is not a difference of principle." The two parties were actually "brethren of the same principle" who were "called by different names"; hence his famous pronouncement, "[w]e are all republicans – we are [all] federalists."[61] In short, because

neither party doubted the fundamental equality of men, their disagreements over the role of executive power and the scope of federal
authority could be solved by the republican principle of majority
rule. Neither party was actually anti-republican, though it is perhaps closer to Jefferson's real meaning to say that the election of
1800 had decided that henceforth the Federalists would not and
could not be anti-republican – on account of the smashing victory of
his fellow Democratic-Republican partisans.[62]

It was the breakdown of this consensus, of course, that precipitated the Civil War. In one sense, that war stands as the gravest possible indictment of the educational efforts of the founders: so poor
was their handiwork that less than seventy-five years after the Constitution was ratified, it teetered on the brink of ruin. Yet in a more
profound sense, the war and Lincoln's preservation of the Union
confirmed the wisdom of the founders' views on education: without
citizens, no republic; without republican education, no citizens.

DEAD WHITE MALES

Lincoln's achievement was the culmination of the founders' goal of
republican education. His career is a reminder of the educational
value of republican politics itself, and especially of the lessons displayed in the speeches and deeds of the greatest statesmen. Theodore Roosevelt understood this lesson well, and expounded it
movingly in an essay he wrote in 1895:

> [E]very great nation owes to the men whose lives have formed
> part of its greatness not merely the material effect of what they
> did, not merely the laws they placed upon the statute books or
> the victories they won over armed foes, but also the immense but
> indefinable moral influence produced by their deeds and words
> themselves upon the national character …. Each of us who
> reads the Gettysburg speech or the second inaugural address of
> the greatest American of the nineteenth century, or who stud-
> ies the long campaigns and lofty statesmanship of that other

American who was even greater, cannot but feel within him that lift toward things higher and nobler which can never be bestowed by the enjoyment of mere material prosperity.[63]

In today's academy, Washington and Lincoln are dismissed as "dead white males," whose educational relevance to a multicultural world is nil. The truth, however, is very nearly the opposite. The true liberalism and genuine cosmopolitanism of these great men have never been more needed in American education and in American politics. But who will educate the educators?

CHAPTER SIX

A NEW BIRTH OF FREEDOM:
ABRAHAM LINCOLN, HARRY V. JAFFA,
AND THE FOUNDERS

Harry V. Jaffa is the political scientist about whom his long-time friend William F. Buckley, Jr., wrote memorably, "If you think Harry Jaffa is hard to argue with, try agreeing with him." This *bon mot*, the opening sentence of Buckley's warm Foreword to Jaffa's 1984 volume, *American Conservatism and the American Founding*, played off the evident assumption that it was "nearly impossible" to agree with this scholar whose passionate devotion to the integrity of the American political tradition led him into renowned, often acerbic, disputes with his closest philosophical and political friends, including many fellow students of Leo Strauss – Martin Diamond and Walter Berns, most notably. Yet Buckley's Foreword, a perceptive defense and explanation of Jaffa's ways, demonstrated that it *is* possible to agree with him and have him agree with you, temporarily, at least!

As exasperating as his arguments may be, however, one has to admit that it is almost impossible not to learn from them. His first book, *Thomism and Aristotelianism* (1952), was an interpretation of Thomas Aquinas's *Commentary on the Nicomachean Ethics* in which Jaffa set out to disentangle pagan from Christian ethics. His purpose was to determine whether Aristotle's investigations of moral phenomena, in all their richness, might cure the self-impoverishment of modern social science – its presumptions that reason could neither confirm nor deny the truth of any moral claim, and hence that science ought to be "value-free." The challenge was to meet modern social science on its own ground – reason alone, unassisted by divine revelation of any sort – and to show that Aristotle's observations were more empirical, more faithful to the facts of moral and political life than the so-called scientific accounts. Precisely in order to meet this challenge, Aquinas's appeal to reason "informed by faith" (*fide informata*) had to be radically distinguished from Aristotle's reliance on natural reason alone. The positivism and relativism of modern social science were deeply rooted in modern philosophy – in the revolt against Aristotelian science that began in the sixteenth and seventeenth centuries. Jaffa's *Thomism and Aristotelianism* thus contributed to the re-opening of an old question: whether Aristotle's *Ethics* might not be the true ethics.[1]

Jaffa's first book did not purport to answer this question directly, though it did provide its own penetrating interpretation of the *Nicomachean Ethics*. Instead, *Thomism and Aristotelianism* was a kind of propaedeutic, liberating Aristotle from Scholastic theology and not incidentally justifying the right of the Straussians rather than the neo-Thomists to speak on behalf of the Philosopher. With the way cleared to move from Thomism back to Aristotelianism, a real test of the latter's adequacy as a guide to understanding moral and political affairs was possible. This demonstration of classical political science's vitality, indeed of its indispensability for the understanding of modern politics, was a chief object of Jaffa's second book, *Crisis of the House Divided: An Interpretation of the Issues in the Lincoln-Douglas Debates*.[2]

Unlike his fellow students of Strauss, who commenced their study of America with the founding, Jaffa began his scholarship on America *in medias res*, with the great crisis over slavery that precipitated the Civil War. His consideration of the issues raised by Abraham Lincoln and Stephen Douglas required Jaffa to turn back to the Constitution and especially to the Declaration of Independence, of course, but he appealed to the founding in order to illuminate the 1858 debates, not vice versa. His focus was the statesmanship of Lincoln and Douglas, not the political thought of the founding per se. In pursuing this goal, he brought to the analysis of America several different themes of Strauss's scholarly project – the distinction between ancients and moderns, the interpretation of John Locke and his followers as decisively modern, the importance of statesmanship, the reciprocating dignity of reason and revelation, and even, to some extent, the significance of prophecy as a political format for philosophy.

The horizon of Jaffa's interpretation of America was thus much broader than that of his contemporaries, though in *Crisis* his view of the founding was very similar to theirs. For almost all of them, the founding was fundamentally Lockean, and as they had learned from Strauss, Locke was fundamentally Hobbesian. In the beginning was Strauss's chapter on John Locke in *Natural Right and History*, as it were; that, together with Strauss's thematic essays on the history of political philosophy (especially "What is Political Philosophy?") had taught his students that the significance of Locke lay not so much in his overt political teaching but in his philosophical underpinnings.[3] In *Natural Right and History*, the Locke of popular sovereignty, natural rights constitutionalism, and the right of revolution took a back seat to the Locke of private property and the state of nature. According to Strauss, Locke's account of property showed most clearly the true character of his state of nature doctrine – namely, that nature is a hostile, amoral, penurious condition from which man has to flee if he is to acquire knowledge, power, and comfortable security. Furthermore, Strauss showed that Locke's support for the liberation of acquisitiveness led to his solicitude for private property and for the bourgeois society dedicated to "the joyless quest for joy." In seeking primarily to understand the origins and character of modern natural rights, Strauss thus emphasized the similarities between Hobbes's and Locke's understanding of nature and society, not the conspicuous differences between their political teachings.

Strauss's students applied this view of Locke, in effect, to the study of America. In different ways, each started from the notion that the founders had created a nation and a Constitution dedicated to the "solid but low" principles of Lockean liberalism. Martin Diamond's interpretation of *The Federalist* was perhaps the clearest and most influential statement of this case.[4] Yet given the more or less inevitable declension that Strauss had discerned in modern thought, his students knew that Hobbesian–Lockean liberalism was, in the long run at least, more low than solid. In the course of their careers, each of the Straussians struggled with this implication, and many discovered elements in the founding that called for a higher or at least more complicated view of America. In some of his later essays for example, Diamond supplemented *The Federalist*'s account of American institutions with Alexis de Tocqueville's, in order to show that federalism and decentralized administration provided room for a certain republican virtue in our politics. Walter Berns wrote extensively on such pre-liberal or higher liberal components of the founding as the censorship of obscenity and pornography, tough libel laws, and nonpreferential assistance to religion. Herbert J. Storing limned the high statesmanship displayed in the founding's great deliberative moments – at the Federal Convention, and again in the debates between the Federalists and Anti-Federalists (in whom he found at least a few lingering elements of pre-modern republicanism). Paul Eidelberg found in the same materials the makings of a new version of the ancient idea of the mixed regime, which he argued, controversially, had been the founders' goal all along.[5]

Jaffa's first, and second, thoughts about America were different from any of these. In *Crisis of the House Divided*, he made one of his themes the distinction between the founders' liberalism, which he agreed was basically Lockean (understood as Strauss had understood him), and Lincoln's higher and more comprehensive view of politics.[6] In Jaffa's account, the founding was "modern" in the sense that it took its bearings by the egalitarian and "egotistic" view of natural rights, i.e., the Hobbesian–Lockean view. But the character of Abraham Lincoln was that of a proud or great-souled man, fiercely conscious of his own superlative virtue. Lincoln was an "ancient" or, more precisely, a classical exemplar of statesmanship, a magnanimous man whose character and activity became intelligible on the basis of Aristotle's *Ethics*, not on the basis of *Leviathan* or the *Second Treatise*.[7] Jaffa's America was not entirely "modern" then, for it contained, and indeed its survival as a free society depended on, the virtues of a great-souled statesman. Nor was Jaffa's America exclusively "modern" in the sense that Lincoln was an anachronism or a throwback to an earlier time – the startling appearance of a species previously thought extinct, as though America were the Jurassic Park of classical statesmanship. However modern were the principles of the American founding, and Jaffa emphasized their Lockean provenance, *Crisis of the House Divided* was Jaffa's demonstration of the thesis that nature was the ground of politics, that nature had not been eclipsed by history, and that the distinctions of nature, including virtues and vices, remained permanently relevant to the understanding of political life.

Through his interpretation of Lincoln's statesmanship, that is, he showed the permanent relevance of classical natural right even to the politics of the United States. Jaffa's focus on statesmanship throughout his writings was not a form of sentimental hero worship but rather an application of classical political science, which insisted that the low be seen in the light of the high, rather than the high in light of the low. The latter viewpoint distorted the noble words and deeds that politics at its best could display. By contrast, the high-minded viewpoint did not prevent the base elements of politics from revealing themselves in their fullness.[8] For example, Lincoln's magnanimity, his consciousness of his own excellence, was inseparable from his reasons for opposing slavery and defending the Union and the Constitution. Jaffa's interpretation of Lincoln's Lyceum Address built to the conclusion that the goodness of democracy itself depended on Lincoln's correctness in affirming that his own excellence and the proposition "that all men are created equal" were compatible – indeed, that each somehow implied the other. But how could magnanimity keep house with democracy?

It is easy to see how democracy might stand in need of magnanimity. American republicanism, Jaffa averred, is based on the equality of all men, but it depends in fact on founders and political saviors who were, to say the least, uncommon men. Other types of regimes depend on great men, too, of course, and aristocratic regimes reward them by elevating such men to the ruling class. Mixing nature with convention, these regimes then typically treat great virtues and talents as if they were heritable, and the natural aristocracy elides into a hereditary or artificial aristocracy. Republicanism stops short of rewarding such men by recognizing in them a right to rule, though often and especially in dire situations it will happily elect them to (temporary) office. In a strange way, however, American republicanism is more aristocratic than professed aristocratic regimes, inasmuch as it insists on recognizing and rewarding merit in non-hereditary ways. That is, it prefers its aristocracy straight, not mixed. It tries through elections to capture the talents and virtues of the natural aristocracy without letting it become an artificial one, though (under republican theory) even natural aristocrats' rule must be consented to by the people in order to be legitimate. All that is clear, and it explains why great men might occasionally be tapped, for utility's sake, by popular government. But it does not explain why *they* should choose *it* – why great souls should identify with the form and substance of popular government. After all, his people's neediness hardly mattered to Coriolanus.

Lincoln was an even more perfect example of the magnanimous man than Coriolanus, however, and Jaffa argued that it was this, paradoxically, that allowed Lincoln to embrace the cause of popular government. In *Crisis*, Jaffa developed the point through a comparison between Lincoln's position in the Lyceum Address and the argument of Callicles in Plato's *Gorgias*. Like Callicles, Lincoln admits that there are men who belong to "the family of the lion, or the tribe of the eagle" whose "genius for and will to domination," in Jaffa's words, "makes them virtually a species apart" from ordinary men. The natural superiority of these geniuses leads them to disdain the rule of law among equal citizens, for men like Alexander, Caesar, and Napoleon (Lincoln's examples) are radically unequal: they are a law unto themselves. That these great men were also destroyers of republican regimes is therefore not surprising. For "if their superiority is real," Jaffa commented, "as Lincoln no less than Callicles appears to affirm, then morality must in fact consist in whatever vindicates their superiority," however infamous that may appear to republicans and others deluded by "what is commonly called morality."[9]

What is it, however, that actually vindicates the superiority of such unequal men? By exploring this question, Jaffa threw new light on the sense in which Lincoln and the classics affirmed "a political role transcending that of Caesar and opposed to Caesar." Callicles had argued that the natural ruler's lust for domination would make him despise a regime of equal rights. "But the Calliclean thesis is not pushed far enough by its advocates," responded Jaffa. For the Caesar who one minute contemns the opinions of the weak (including their opinion of justice) in the next moment is seeking "the adulation of these selfsame weaklings." In other words, Callicles assumes "a qualitative similarity in the superior and inferior men, believing that the superior have the same pleasures as the inferior and differ only in their ability to gratify themselves." The "immortal" fame that stems from political success may be the highest good from the popular point of view, but it is not in fact the highest good; and in the best men, the appetite for political fame is therefore subordinated to the passion for genuine human excellence. The desire for this higher good makes the best men moderate or self-controlled in all their other appetites, which to inferior men is a wonderful phenomenon, for while the self-control of an Olympic athlete in respect of the pleasures of ordinary life is understandable, the moderation of a man who could (but refuses to) rule as a tyrant and thus gratify at a whim his every appetite – achieving immorality and immortality all at once! – is wondrous. The one who can act as if there were a good beyond political fame must therefore be more than a man. This man of godlike virtue, as Aristotle described him, who can look down on fame itself, is "the antithesis to the Caesarian destroyer of republics." He is "the savior of republics."[10]

In the best case, a political savior's actions will succeed, which combined with the mysteriousness (from the popular viewpoint) of his motives may well win for him an even greater political glory than Caesar's. But "the actual achievement of such glory is incidental or accidental," because "the true statesman in the highest sense" aims not at fame but at virtue. "He alone can save his country who can forgo the honors of his countrymen," Jaffa explained. "Like Aristotle's great-souled man ... he alone is worthy of the highest honor who holds honor itself in contempt, who prefers even to the voice of his countrymen the approving voice heard only by himself, 'Well done, thou good and faithful servant.'"[11] This is a striking formulation of the virtue of magnanimity, combining Aristotle's account with a quotation from the biblical parable of the talents, a part of Jesus's discourse with his disciples on the Mount of Olives. In the New Testament, these words are spoken by a master, back at his estate after a long trip, who praises the servants to whom much was given, from whom much was expected, and by whom much had been accomplished.[12] Jaffa converted the master's praises of his servant into the magnanimous man's praise of himself, in keeping, one might say, with Aristotle's own discussion of magnanimity as the proud self-consciousness of moral excellence. In *Thomism and Aristotelianism*, Jaffa had described the magnanimous man as "the highest *non-philosophic* human type" who desires to achieve a divine good insofar as he understands the divine to be a moral agent. That is, even as the gods are held to be great benefactors of men, so the magnanimous man desires to be a great benefactor.[13]

Yet to be a "good and faithful servant" is not quite the same thing as the magnanimous man's pride and pleasure in knowing that, compared to himself, "nothing is great." Strictly speaking, the magnanimous man does not conceive of himself as a servant to anyone or anything, not even virtue, which for him is inseparable from the actions and contemplation of his own greatness; like the gods, he is a benefactor, not a servant. To be sure, it is possible to understand the great-souled man's supreme moral virtue as being in the service of a higher virtue, what Aristotle would call intellectual virtue; but this would be to violate the horizon of the high-minded man's own self-understanding. "To explain to him that morality is good because it is a means to an end that is better than morality," argued Jaffa, "would be destructive of the motive that makes him concentrate all his energies in supreme actions of moral virtue, in which he thinks that he will attain a supreme good."[14] This does not mean that the magnanimous man may not "at the same time be something more than magnanimous," and Jaffa explicitly left open the possibility that the philosopher may also be magnanimous – though assuredly then his motives for great actions would not be the same as those of a non-philosophic magnanimous man.[15]

Still, by ascribing to Lincoln and to Aristotle the notion that the high-minded man may consider himself a "good and faithful servant," Jaffa stressed a pious side of the great-souled statesman that is not apparent in Aristotle's *Ethics*. This sort of piety or sense of duty has Platonic roots but is more obviously Christian.[16] In his study of Lincoln in *Crisis*, Jaffa put together again, at least partly, the threads of classical political philosophy and Christianity that he had taken pains to disentangle in his first book. Jaffa suggested, gently, that Lincoln's understanding of himself transcended that of a magnanimous man. Whether this transcendence was in the direction of the love of God, the love of the Good, or both is a difficult question that Jaffa did not explicitly answer. Certainly, the Biblical God is a god of particular providence and of moral actions, and so is a source of duties and a kind of model for statesmanship as well as salvation. Platonic political philosophy had blended with Biblical religion in many striking forms, however, throughout the history of Judaism, Islam, and Christianity. Perhaps the most relevant to the case at hand was the tradition, arising from Alfarabi and Maimonides, of understanding prophecy as the supreme form of rational or philosophic legislation. Although Strauss had written extensively on it, Jaffa did not appeal to this tradition in *Crisis*, even though he called attention to Lincoln's prophetic role in summoning the American people back to their "ancient faith." At any rate, in seeking to be a good shepherd to his flock, Lincoln looked explicitly to the Biblical tradition and invoked or alluded to God in explaining his own statesmanship and the Union's cause.[17] And Jaffa, in interpreting Lincoln, placed particular emphasis on his efforts to weave together revelation and reason in defense of American republicanism.

Tracing the many implicit connections in Lincoln's thought between political salvation and the salvation of individual souls, Jaffa argued that the Lyceum Address confirmed that "the qualifications of a savior ... require a temptation in the wilderness." Even the savior "of the political soul of a free nation" must know "all the attractions of becoming the destroyer before he can become the savior." Jaffa showed persuasively that Lincoln disclosed those attractions to the attentive listener or reader of the Lyceum Address, but that Lincoln revealed at the same time his utter rejection and "triumph" over them.[18] Insofar as Lincoln was a magnanimous man, there was no room in his character for such a temptation, which would imply the presence of bad or excessive desires that would have to be conquered by reason. The high-minded man, according to Aristotle, is truly moderate in his desires.[19] The role of the political savior seems then to require a more Christian view of virtue, in which what Aristotle would call continence – the triumph over temptation – would be nobler than the achievement of moral good without temptation. Or at the least, Lincoln's role as a political savior required acknowledgment of temptation, whether or not he had actually experienced it.[20]

Jaffa's emphasis on the political savior took off from Lincoln's sense of the dangers presented by a Caesar-figure. Elaborating on Lincoln's quiet suggestions, Jaffa cast Lincoln as the figure who could save the republic from Caesarism. In painting this dramatic confrontation, Jaffa was guided less by Aristotle than by Shakespeare, one of Jaffa's – and Lincoln's – favorite authors, whose profound combination of classical rationalism and Christianity provided another matrix against which to view the drama of Lincoln's life and statesmanship.[21] The epigraphs of *Crisis* are Shakespearean: a passage from *Measure for Measure* on the problem of magnanimity, as it were, and a passage from *Macbeth*, relevant to the injustice of slavery. "O, it is excellent to have a giant's strength," announces Isabella in *Measure for Measure*, "but it is tyrannous to use it like a giant." The giant's strength is not given for him alone, in other words, but also for the common good; or to put it in Christian context, in this world, for the sake of the weak, too. In Lincoln's character, Jaffa argued, both "the giant's strength" and an incredible moderation and justice in the use of it reached their consummation. He quoted with approval Clinton Rossiter's famous eulogy: "Lincoln is the supreme myth, the richest symbol in the American experience. He is, as someone has remarked neither irreverently nor sacrilegiously, the martyred Christ of democracy's passion play." To which Jaffa added: "Many things in Lincoln's life, like the accident of his death, may have been fortuitous – or providential – but the myth that came to life with his passing was neither." It was, instead, Lincoln's own Shakespearean achievement, "the finely wrought consummation, of philosophic insight and a poetic gift."[22]

Lincoln was more than a magnanimous man, then, but Jaffa emphasized his magnanimity in order to illustrate, in the clearest terms possible, the continuing relevance of classical political philosophy to modern social science and to the understanding of American politics. By discovering a strikingly "ancient" trait in the midst of a modern political crisis, Jaffa also demonstrated *ad oculos* that the history of politics was not determined utterly by the history of political philosophy. Politics was a human activity with natural roots; nature did not change, and the nature of politics did not change, though of course changing political ideas and circumstances had enormously affected the manifestation, in mid-nineteenth-century America, of man's political capacity.

Nonetheless, Jaffa did not conceal the fact that Lincoln's enterprise involved a reinterpretation of the political principles of the American founding. In fact, he advertised the novelty of Lincoln's interpretation and lauded it as a major feature of his greatness. Lincoln saw that the founders' political understanding was "incomplete," according to Jaffa, because it had neglected the high for the sake of the low or, rather, because it had tried to understand the high in light of the low. Jaffa centered his discussion of this issue, as had Lincoln, on the meaning of the equality clause of the Declaration of Independence. Jaffa addressed the issue first in the context of the Lyceum Address, and again and more extensively in his interpretation of the Lincoln–Douglas debates.

In the first case, Jaffa argued that the "irreducible meaning" of the Declaration was that "the government of man by man, unlike the government of beasts by man, is not founded in any natural difference between rulers and ruled." Moreover, he associated Lincoln's view with Jefferson's on this "irreducible" contention: "As Jefferson was fond of saying, and Lincoln sometimes echoed, some men are not born with saddles on their backs to be ridden and others with spurs to ride them." This argument became a staple of Jaffa's subsequent discussions of the Declaration.[23]

But Jaffa then raised an objection, posed by Lincoln in the Lyceum Address, to this equality: if some men belong to "the family of the lion, or the tribe of the eagle" and are by nature so superior as to be virtually a species apart, then would not their submission to their inferiors be "a violation of natural right"? Jaffa answered that the savior or preserver of republics, having undergone his temptation in the wilderness, had "no desire for those things with respect to which the law lays constraints" on the "grasping passions" of ordinary men. For such a man "to claim superior rights would be absurd because such a claim would imply an appetite for those political goods" for which he has no desire. "All men *are* created equal," Jaffa wrote, "because those who are really superior are in the decisive sense above humanity." Here, then, the argument is *not* that "the government of man by man ... is not founded in any natural difference between rulers and ruled," but rather that the natural differences are so great as to approximate the difference between god and man. The godlike political savior does not press his advantage, however, thus exhibiting the gentleness that in juxtaposition with his strength makes him so wondrous. Human equality remains "the decisive *political* truth," Jaffa concluded, "because those who might with justice deny it have no motive to deny it, while those who do deny it can only do so because of an unjust motive."[24]

Extreme human inequality and fundamental human equality were both true. This result may itself seem either too good to be true – a *"political* truth" is hardly the whole truth – or too true to be good, insofar as it appears to sideline all human virtue that fell short of the godlike. But Jaffa's point was that it was impossible to do justice to human equality and to human inequality at the same time in politics. On the one hand, the godlike man was not a god, after all, but only godlike, and hence had both to know his limitations and to acknowledge what was due him simply by virtue of his humanity.[25] On the other hand, it was natural to the superior man *not* to demand recognition of his superiority from those who might marvel at it but could never understand it. His "mastery" consisted not in exploiting other men but in "confirming and enhancing his fellow citizens' capacity for self-improvement" and chastening "any backsliding from the convictions that entitle them to be considered rational men."[26]

Jaffa tried further to moderate these tensions between equality and inequality in his second, extended discussion of the Declaration in *Crisis*, where the context was not magnanimity and political salvation but the debate over American slavery and American freedom. Lincoln proved, by his reinterpretation of the founders' precepts, that the equality of man was a higher principle than it might seem, that a more high-minded view of human equality was possible and desirable, according to Jaffa. To begin with, however, the founders "read the Declaration as an expression of the sentiments of Locke's

Second Treatise of Government, wherein many of them had read, almost from childhood" that all men are naturally in a pre-civil state of nature, a state of perfect freedom and equality, though also of insecurity. This state of nature was the primeval basis of human or natural rights, rights based on the indefeasible passion of self-pres-ervation. The right to life thus sprang from the passion for life, or rather from the passionate aversion to death, especially violent death. Given the "egotistical" quality of these rights, all duties in the state of nature were merely conditional. From "the strictly Lockean standpoint," no man was "under an obligation to respect any other man's unalienable rights until that other man is necessary to the security of his own rights." Equality was therefore a fact of human nature, an inconvenient and problematic fact because it led to a nat-ural condition of insecurity verging on a *bellum omnium contra omnes*. The insecurity could be overcome – the right to life could be secured – only by leaving the state of nature for civil society. For the founders, civil society was constituted by a movement away from nature, away from a highly undesirable condition under natural law and towards one in which minimal conditions of human welfare may be secured by positive law.[27]

By contrast, the idea of a pre-political state of nature "plays no significant role" in Lincoln's thought. For him, "all men are created equal" did not imply a condition from which men had a right to escape, but a condition "*toward* which men have a *duty* ever to strive." In the "predominantly Lockean interpretation" of the Declaration, civil society was constituted by the movement away "from the con-dition in which the equality of all men is actual"; but in Lincoln's subtle reinterpretation, civil society is constituted by "the move-ment *toward* a condition in which the equality of man is actual." The natural state of man, in short, was not pre-political but political – a good civil society, in which the equality of man was secured, to the extent possible, by wise laws. In the full sense, however, equality remained a "standard maxim for free society," as Lincoln called it, a lofty goal for both public and private life, which could only be approximated and therefore would engender a "striving for justice" that "must be an ever-present requirement of the human and politi-cal condition."[28]

Lincoln "transforms and transcends" the original meaning of "all men are created equal," treating the proposition "as a transcendental goal and not as the immanent and effective basis of actual political right." But he does not destroy the original meaning: "Lincoln's morality then extends the full length of Jefferson's, but it also goes further," Jaffa wrote. Jaffa's case rested on Lincoln's reinterpretation of human rights. Whereas Jefferson had taught Americans to claim and assert their natural rights, Lincoln instructed his countrymen to *respect* "what they had asserted." To be sure, Jefferson had warned his fellow citizens of the divine wrath that might befall them for the injustice of slavery. But "the Lockean root of Jefferson's conviction – the deepest root of Jefferson's generation – regarded this precept as pre-eminently a requirement of enlightened self-interest," according to Jaffa. Whereas Jefferson, influenced by Locke, saw "all commands to respect the rights of others as fundamentally hypothetical imperatives – i.e., "*if* you do not wish to be a slave, then refrain from being a master" – Lincoln saw them as "categorical" imperatives as well. "As I would not be a *slave*, so I would not be a *master*," he said famously. This implied that all men by nature have "an equal right to justice," not as an inference from their passions, but as a dictate of distributive justice or proportional equality – an acknowledgment by right reason of their status as rational animals, as *men*. Because all men have such a right to justice, they also have "a duty to do justice, wholly irrespective of calculations as to self-interest."[29]

The Kantian language was a bit misleading, because in this celebration of Lincoln's statesmanship Jaffa certainly did not mean to exclude prudence from the moral horizon. On strict Kantian terms, of course, prudence has no moral significance because the rules of morality brook no exceptions: "categorical" morality means that the circumstances and probable consequences of moral and political action do not matter. For the statesman, however, such prudential considerations are essential to wise moral and political action. What Jaffa meant to say, and did say at other points in his surrounding discussion, was that while man's duties were not derivative from his rights or self-interest, what his duties were in any particular circumstance would have to be decided with a view to justice and the common good. The fundamental point for Lincoln was that man's rights

and duties were correlative: each arose from man's status as an imperfect rational animal, as a being whose place was in between God and
the beasts. The law of man's nature reflected his place in nature, and
his rights were under the authority of that law: e.g., no human being
had a right to treat another like a dog, nor to rule like a god over his
fellows. To this extent, Lincoln resubordinated natural rights to natural law. But this was natural law with equality as its leading edge and
major precept – a new formulation not found in Aquinas, for instance,
nor even in Jefferson, at least as described by Jaffa in *Crisis*.

In the course of his debates with Douglas, Lincoln showed what
it meant to subordinate or incorporate natural rights under a natural
law standard. He denounced as an absurdity Douglas's celebrated
"don't care" policy – his value-neutral attitude toward the spread of
slavery, which he thought a local question that should be decided by
popular sovereignty in each territory. Douglas's prescription was
absurd, Lincoln argued, because slavery was wrong and the "don't
care" policy "tolerated the notion that there was such a thing as a
right to do wrong." Here, then, natural rights bumped up against
natural law. For the Lockean doctrine of an unalienable right to liberty, commented Jaffa, meant "that no one can consistently appeal
to *my* sense of right to give up *my* liberty, but it does not mean that a
man who enslaves another violates the enslaver's sense of *what is
right*." In other words Lincoln "confounds the meaning of a *right*,
meaning an indefeasible desire or passion, with *what is right*, meaning an objective state or condition in which justice is done." Lincoln
never rejected or attacked natural rights in the Lockean sense, but
he realized that "right conceived as subjective passion does *not* for-
bid us to do what is objectively wrong; it only directs us to do whatever we deem necessary for *our* lives and *our* liberty." And so he tried
to find a foundation for rights in objective reason, in "an objective
condition" discernible by reason, rather than in subjective passion.[30]

Lincoln's "reconstruction" of the founders' meaning provided a
higher and more consistent ground on which to be pro-freedom and
anti-slavery than the egotistical or Lockean view of rights, whose
objections to slavery were always in some sense conditional. Moreover, by condemning the enslavement of men who were by nature
capable of freedom, Lincoln made effective for the first time in

human history Aristotle's own distinction between natural and unnatural slavery, according to Jaffa.[31] But Lincoln's "creative interpretation" led also to a higher view of America. America was no longer based on a minimal social contract providing for mutual defense and prosperity, but was a regime or political community – in something like the classical sense – dedicated to, and constituted by, an opinion of justice.[32] Jefferson thought in terms of justice, too, but Jaffa maintained that for Jefferson the political association was more about preventing injustice than achieving justice; hence politics was essentially a necessary evil. Hence, too, "Jefferson was always more concerned to remind the people of their rights than of their duties. He emphasized what they should demand of their government rather than what they must demand of themselves."[33] For Lincoln, however, "the freedom of a free people resides above all in that consciousness of freedom which is also a consciousness of self-imposed restraints." But what was true of a free, and great, people was also true of "the highest ambition of the loftiest souls," whose ambition culminated not in domination but in the highest service they could render to others – namely, the perpetuation of the rule of law in democratic government.[34]

Since the publication of *Crisis of the House Divided*, Jaffa's principal research interest has been the American founding. As the result of almost four decades' inquiry, he has deepened and sharpened his understanding of that event and its principles. His second thoughts are summed up in *A New Birth of Freedom: Abraham Lincoln and the Coming of the Civil War*, the sequel to *Crisis of the House Divided*. The new book, published in 2000, followed Lincoln's statesmanship up to his July 4, 1861, Special Message to Congress, and featured dazzling commentaries on that message, the First Inaugural, and the Gettysburg Address, all in the context of the political–philosophical confrontation between natural right, on the one hand, and relativism, historicism, and nihilism, on the other. Jaffa admits in *New Birth* that in *Crisis* he failed to understand Lincoln completely because (to adapt Strauss's words on a similar occasion) he read Lincoln too literally, by not reading him literally enough. That is, Jaffa writes that he had been wrong in arguing that Lincoln's understanding of natural rights transformed and transcended that of the founders. Jaffa had thought that Lincoln's "Aristotelianizing," i.e., his high-minded view of human rights, was original, whereas Lincoln had been right all along in disclaiming originality and tracing his view of justice to the founding and particularly to the Declaration of Independence.[35]

Jaffa comes to this realization partly as a result of a re-examination of the founders' arguments for religious freedom. In *Crisis* he regarded the founders' arguments for the separation of church and state as a pure emanation of Enlightenment rationalism. Even in so pious a document as George Washington's Farewell Address, Jaffa detected only "the mingling, like oil and water, of the rationalism and religion of the eighteenth century." There was "no trace of reverence in Washington's discussion of the need for reverence," nor in *The Federalist*'s similar pleadings, nor in Jefferson's; for all of them, "the sacred is treated as a necessity of the profane." In Lincoln, however, "the profane is transformed into the sacred," and the Civil War, as interpreted by him, fused religious passion and secular rationalism into the canon of America's "political religion."[36] In re-thinking the founders' views on religious liberty, however, Jaffa discovers in them a profound meditation on, and response to, the changes that Christianity over many centuries had wrought in politics; in this context, even the most Enlightened of the founders' arguments glowed with a reasonableness and a true charity that bespoke a genuine love of man's highest ends.

To explore Jaffa's new view of religious freedom as the solution to a problem immanent in Western Civilization is beyond the scope of this chapter, but some brief comments, at least, would not be out of order. The starting point of his re-evaluation was probably the natural theology of the Declaration, which he increasingly featured in his accounts. Although natural reason may not be able to prove that God exists, it can prove that a divine nature would carry to perfection those incomplete perfections discoverable in man ("reason, justice, mercy") without the corresponding imperfections. At the Declaration's core as understood by the founders, Jaffa thus emphasizes, was an ontological doctrine of man's place in an intelligible universe, which reason and Revelation agreed in conceiving of as crowned by a perfect Being – the cause and end of the universe's intelligibility. Accordingly, both natural and revealed morality rests on the premise that man is neither beast nor God.[37] What had once been the Declaration's "irreducible meaning," a kind of least common denominator among interpretations of the document, now becomes for Jaffa its heart and soul; and the differences between Lincoln's and the founders' understanding of human equality begin to be elided or to seem less significant. This objective and even common-sensical account of man's place in a rationally structured universe – especially in contrast to the historicist and nihilistic arguments of later philosophers and their votaries – suggested more and more to Jaffa that the founders were not far from Lincoln's view of human rights as something high-minded or God-given: that natural rights are expressions not of a base but of a noble and lawful freedom.[38]

From Lincoln's point of view, of course, it was he who was fol-lowing the founders on this question. Jaffa has come to the conclu-sion that Lincoln was right about that. Lincoln *had* learned from the Declaration of Independence that human rights were the dispensa-tions of a just God or of an intelligible nature. But the founders had come to this conclusion as part of their general confrontation with the problem of political authority in Christendom. Before the advent of universal monotheism, Jaffa points out (following Fustel de Cou-langes' enduring analysis), each city had its own sheltering deities and the city's laws and its founding were in various ways the work of these gods. The ancient city's laws were, as far as its citizens were concerned, a species of divine law, an assumption that was shattered, however, by the rise of Christianity. The One God did not play favor-ites with earthly cities. His was a heavenly city. The various cities of men were then left to find a new reason why their citizens should obey them. Christianity's severing of the classical relation between God (or gods) and the Law led to a millennium-and-a-half of *stasis* in the West, of conflicts between Pope and Emperor, Emperor and Pope, culminating in the wars of the Reformation. Seeking to escape the holocausts of the Old World, argues Jaffa, the American found-ers found in the doctrine "all men are created equal" a solution to the hitherto insoluble problem of civil war within Christendom. The doctrine announced that God's authority was manifest not in kings, popes, or parliaments, but in the people, whose rule was for the first time to be understood as the collective expression of individual rights, imbued in each individual by the Creator. So, in popular government based on the social contract, divine authority was finally reunited with the rule of law.[39]

But the doctrine of rights *limited* even as it authorized popular sovereignty. The purpose of government was limited to the securing of men's rights, including above all the right of conscience, which was the individual and political liberty that resulted from men's duty to worship their Creator in the manner they thought most agreeable to Him. Liberty of conscience was protected even against the people themselves – a guarantee made explicit, for the first time in human history, in many of the state constitutions, in the prohibition of religious tests for office in the U.S. Constitution, and in the First Amendment. Purer, non-persecuting forms of Christianity could now thrive. The civil war in the Christian West had been waged partly over the definition of true religion, which meant over the true definition of theological and intellectual virtue; this warfare had been destructive of religious faith, moral virtue, and political decency, not to mention of the civic friendship that was practically a precondition of the more intimate friendships in which intellectual virtue could be pursued. Under these circumstances, the self-assertion of virtue had actually become inimical to political decency and moderation. For this reason, the founders did not make their revolutionary political reforms in the name of virtue itself, much less in the name of true religion, but in the name of human liberty. As a consequence of excluding direct claims to rule based on superior virtue, however, the founders opened a new avenue for moral virtue to reassert itself as a qualification for election to office and as an informal criterion of citizenship and statesmanship. With church separated from state – with the theological virtues prescinded from political rule, and vice versa – magnanimity was again free to show itself for what it was. George Washington became possible, as it were; and Abraham Lincoln, too.[40]

What becomes of Lincoln's greatness in Jaffa's new estimation? Lincoln was, Jaffa writes, less original but more profound than he had originally thought. Lincoln distilled the political thought of the founding to its purest, most concentrated form, and expressed it with supreme eloquence. By defining the issues of the Civil War, that "people's contest," in terms of the people's fidelity to their "ancient faith," he effectively joined with the founders in order to defend the Law against those who had abandoned it in order to worship the golden calf of slavery. In *Crisis*, Jaffa saw the Civil War as the greatest (and characteristic) drama of American politics, pitting equal natural rights against majoritarianism in a "modern" dispute that could be reconciled only by Lincoln's magnanimous statesmanship. In *A New Birth of Freedom*, however, Jaffa depicts the Civil War as a world-historical drama in which Lincoln personifies the classical prudence and high-toned natural rights teaching of the founders, in opposition to the Confederacy, whose most sophisticated apologists base their defense of it, and of slavery, on some of the most willful, historicist, and collectivist elements of modern political philosophy. For Jaffa, the "new birth of freedom" signifies more now than the nation's rebaptism in its Aristotelianized "political religion." While definitely including the nation's re-dedication to the principles of the Revolution, Lincoln's "new birth of freedom" means also America's baptism of fire, so to speak, as the model regime and exemplary empire of the modern world – as the best regime neither of the ancients, nor the Church, but of the civilization formed by the confluence of faith and reason. Jaffa calls the United States or, more precisely, its principles – for he is describing a regime in speech, as articulated by Lincoln and the founders – nothing less than "the best regime of Western civilization."[41]

Finally, a few words on Jaffa as a controversialist and avowed conservative. Like Strauss, Jaffa seldom wrote a theoretical work without adverting to the practical situation or crisis to which it might be related. The maladies of modern social science which Jaffa set out to cure or ameliorate in *Thomism and Aristotelianism*, for example, were not merely theoretical ills; they were intimately bound up with "present-day political problems," he wrote, meaning both the external confrontation with Communism and the internal weakness or demoralization of the Free World. In *Crisis*, he indicated that the issues of the Lincoln-Douglas debates lived on in the current struggles over civil rights (and over the Cold War), and that the academic dispute over the interpretation of the 1858 debates was itself a kind of continuation of those debates. Unlike Strauss, Jaffa forthrightly calls himself a conservative, and he made the founding and Lincoln central to his conservatism. Since he regarded the current academic and political debate over the meaning of the Civil War and the founding as a kind of continuation of those great contests, he freely adopts a polemical style in his many essays on contemporary politics, and especially in his many critiques of modern American conservatism.[42] But he is interested in conservatism mainly because he thinks it is the best means by which "the best regime of Western civilization" may be perpetuated.

In *How to Think About the American Revolution* (1978), *American Conservatism and the American Founding* (1984), and *Original Intent and the Framers of the Constitution: A Disputed Question* (1994),[43] Jaffa exposes, somewhat acerbically, the far-reaching alienation of modern conservatives – paleo, neo, originalist, libertarian, Straussian, traditionalist, populist, "doughfaced" Northern, and Southern – from their own political tradition. The American political tradition, he insists, had as its central idea the Lincolnian, and Jeffersonian, understanding of human equality. This equality of natural rights was not the enemy or even the opposite of freedom, but freedom's foundation or counterpart, inasmuch as men deserved to be free because they were equally human beings. Jaffa labors to reconstruct American conservatism along Lincolnian lines, and he disagrees with many of his friends' preference for Tocquevillian, Burkean, or Hayekian conservatism because he denies that any of these schools quite does justice to America. For that very reason, he deems the alternatives insufficiently attentive to the challenging demands of Aristotle's approach to natural and political right, which Jaffa has, for more than four decades, sought to apply to, or to elicit from, America. Martin Diamond put it nicely once, that in the beginning political philosophy consisted of the Socratic critique of the opinions of the Athenians – and for a long time it remained the study of the Socratic critique of the opinions of the Athenians. But Harry V. Jaffa has shown, said Diamond, that political philosophy may consist also of the Socratic critique of the opinions of the Americans.

PART II

THE PROGRESSIVES' CONSTITUTION

CHAPTER SEVEN

THREE WAVES OF LIBERALISM

The perception of modern American liberalism as something novel, audacious, and comprehensive has faded, lost in the enduring authority of its innovations and the familiarity of its boasts. Whatever else he accomplished, President Barack Obama reminded right- and left-wingers alike that liberalism can be an assertive doctrine aiming, in his famous words, at "fundamentally transforming" the United States of America. As if to underline the point, political correctness on and off campus bloomed during his time in office: to liberals today as in the 1960s and 1930s, the reconstruction of language, manners, and thought is at least as important as overhauling the national government.

This ambitiousness shouldn't surprise. The twentieth century was, as Thomas B. Silver called it, "the liberal century." Modern conservatism was a late arrival, debuting as a self-conscious intellectual movement only in the 1950s, and lacking significant political success until the 1980s. By contrast, the liberal storm was already gathering in the 1880s and broke upon the land in the new century's second decade. It had made decisive changes in American politics long before conservatism as we know it came on the scene. It's true that the conservative movement had precursors, beginning early in the century with some of the resistance to Progressive high-handedness. That resistance (which, to confuse things further, sometimes called itself liberal and sometimes conservative) centered on a defense of individual rights and the Constitution, and reached its high-water mark in the 1920s. During the Great Depression and the New Deal it declined rapidly.

Those who would like to limit or reverse liberalism's effects must face the fact that, over many generations, it has pervasively reshaped Americans' expectations of government and of life. Nevertheless, it didn't win its victories all at once. Liberalism spread across the century in three powerful waves, interrupted by wars and by visceral reactions to its excesses. This fact is encouraging, because it shows it can be stopped; and discouraging, because it hints it cannot be stopped for long. The three waves each exhibited a different facet or focus of the liberal critique of America, and brought with it a novel political agenda and rhetoric. Each targeted a different set of American institutions, political, economic, and cultural: the New Freedom and its version of Progressivism aimed squarely at the foundations of American politics, the constitutional system and its assumptions; the New Deal labored to introduce a welfare state with new kinds of rights – socio-economic or "entitlement" rights – in order to overawe the market economy with its rights of private property, enterprise, and contract and its assumption of self-reliance; and Sixties liberalism in most of its protean guises scorned the American way of life as bourgeois, inauthentic, and oppressive, but hoped, at least for a while, to make it great (not again but) at last. The targets overlapped, of course, as did the critiques. Although it wasn't inevitable that one wave would follow the next, a certain logic connected them. Each attempted not merely to reform but to *transform* the country into something altogether freer, fairer, and more fulfilling.

Previous reform movements in America aimed at ameliorating specific evils, like slavery, intemperance, or a prolonged agricultural depression, through specific measures, like abolition, Prohibition, or "free silver." Broader and deeper waves of political discontent tended to assume an overtly constitutional shape – like the Philadelphia Constitution itself, or the Bill of Rights, or the post-Civil War amendments. Modern liberalism is something else again. Over the twentieth century liberalism declared in favor of many specific reforms, some of them very sensible, but it was never *defined* by any of them.

Its goal was reform without end: a continual, guided progress into a better future. Though its second and third waves worked out or radicalized themes implicit in the first, they did not stop there, often subjecting their predecessors to bitter criticism for insufficient vision and zeal. *A fortiori* was this true of the third wave, which showed just how radical, and fratricidal, liberalism could become.

When liberals relate their own history, of course, they don't tell it this way. They tend to emphasize the improvisational character of it all, the way various reform movements came together, loosely, to form and reform "liberalism." Even their name seems haphazard. They answered to "Progressives" (with a capital P) at the turn of the century, before signing up as "liberals" in the 1930s and sticking with that proud sobriquet until both Hillary Clinton and Obama preferred being called "progressives" in 2008. Eric Alterman, a professor of English and journalism who likes to write books defending liberalism, explains the fluidity: "liberalism arose as a matter of pure pragmatism with next to no theory in the first place and was led by a politician [Franklin D. Roosevelt] who prided himself on his willingness to try almost anything."

This argument, repeated in countless mainstream histories, is a continuation of FDR's politics by other means. Though he was leading the Democratic Party in increasingly progressive directions, Roosevelt knew the party base was still the Solid South, the bastion of Democratic traditionalism. He pressed the party to call itself "liberal," defined as generous to the poor and middle class and open to pragmatic experimentation, in order to perpetuate his own New Deal coalition. As he made the case, liberal politics is or ought to be a kind of reaction to the problems spun off by modern life – an adjustment of governing institutions and policies to the unfolding realities of the American society and economy. In his telling, liberalism comes across as realistic and modest – in fact, almost conservative – but also inevitable. Political change can't lag behind social and economic change for long, you see, and what liberals do is mind that gap: they claim to prescribe the minimal adjustments necessary to keep the social organism healthy and whole, to cure emerging social problems. Sometimes the minimal adjustment may be quite jarring (e.g., national health care, the Green New Deal), but it is prescribed not in a radical but in an almost clinical spirit.

This narrative has the distinct political advantage of distracting attention from the reality of liberals' ambitious ideas and their role in the growth of the modern state. The same liberals who push this pragmatic account invariably speak at the same time, passionately, of their movement's "vision" or "dream," revealing that cautious adjustment cannot be the whole story. In fact, both pitches, for liberalism as modest adaptation and as idealistic transformation, were originally made by the same progressive statesmen – by FDR and his predecessor Woodrow Wilson.

Wilson endorsed liberalism's modest account of itself as politically useful and even true, up to a point. Ever since he was an undergraduate, however, he had been contemplating how to lead American politics away from its original, and still more or less prevailing, constitutional principles, which he disdained as both inefficient and unjust. The cover-up was thus coeval with the crime, you might say. Ever since its origins in the Progressive movement, and in the new political science taught in the new research universities where eminent Progressives had studied (like Wilson, B.A., Princeton, 1879; Ph.D., Johns Hopkins, 1886), liberalism had indulged a radicalism that dare not speak its name. Progressive liberalism could look moderate or even conservative sometimes, because it eschewed abstract ideas and permanent truths in favor of immanent concepts, evolutionary processes, pragmatic tests, and historical relativity. That, however, was the essence of its radicalism – its firm break with natural right, higher law, limited government, and constitutionalism, with the intellectual and political commonsense of Washington, Adams, Jefferson, Madison, and Lincoln. Liberalism was a choice, not a destiny, and its new moral and political ideas were in the forefront of its rise to respectability and power.

PROGRESSIVISM AND THE LIVING CONSTITUTION

Political liberalism began with a rejection of the Constitution and the morality underpinning it. Not every Progressive thinker early in the twentieth century took a jaundiced view of the document and its principles, but the ones who did became famous. Among these, the so-called "Progressive historians" – especially Charles A. Beard, Vernon Parrington, and J. Allen Smith – stand out. They interpreted the American Revolution as a nascent social uprising, the beginnings of a new, radically egalitarian social order. This slumbering social democracy awakened not upon hearing the theory of the Revolution as contained, say, in the Declaration of Independence and the colonists' earlier protests against the British parliament, but upon being called to perform the deeds and actions of the Revolution itself. As the majority discovered its power in street demonstrations, Tea Parties, militia service, and legislative halls, it discovered itself as a social force capable of standing against domestic as well as foreign elites. The innermost character of the Revolution revealed itself, therefore, in anti-Loyalist mobs, the seizure of Tory property, and the newly forged and unabashedly democratic state constitutions, with annual elections, strong populist legislatures, and weak courts and governors. Shay's Rebellion (1786–87) was, in this view, not a challenge to but a reaffirmation of the Revolution's vital spirit.

All this promising tumult ended, however, with the Constitution. Beard and his fellow historians regarded the Philadelphia Convention and the resulting frame of government as a decisive counterrevolution, which, unhappily, subordinated human rights to property rights, democracy to oligarchy, and continued to do so into the twentieth century. The new system weakened the state governments, protected the obligations of contract against popular interference, and erected a powerful, distant central government designed to limit the people's rule and to enhance rule by the rich, especially investors in bonds and stocks, i.e., capitalists. In his influential *An Economic Interpretation of the Constitution of the United States* (1913), Beard held, in fact, that the authors of *The Federalist* had explained the scheme forthrightly in *Federalist* Number 10: the

Constitution was designed to check "majority faction," meaning, Beard asserted, majority rule or democracy.

Most Progressive critics of the Constitution were not as quasi-Marxist as Beard, who hid neither his economic determinism nor his philosophical debt to the theorists of class conflict, including Aristotle and Karl Marx. The majority took a different line, more Hegelian than Marxist, and owing much as well to the German and English historical schools and various forms of evolutionary thought descending from Herbert Spencer and Charles Darwin. Despite their intellectual diversity, these Progressive political and social scientists mounted a common criticism of the Constitution as time-bound and anachronistic. They argued our political system rested on certain eighteenth-century fantasies like the state of nature, natural rights, and the social compact, already exposed as illusory by generations of nineteenth-century political and social scientists. But no eighteenth-century doctrine could possibly fit the needs of twentieth-century human beings and societies; the problem was not so much the injustice of the framers' ideas as their primitiveness and obsolescence. Above all, they didn't grasp the historical relativity of their own "truths." The old freedom had to be replaced, therefore, by a modern, up-to-date freedom – and here the Progressive political and social scientists joined hands with the Progressive historians – which had to be more collectivist or socialist in spirit.

As their new critics saw it, the American founders had held to an atomistic and egoistic view of man – a view that, at its best, reflected their world of individual proprietors, family farms carved out of the wilderness, and religion centered on the drama of individual salvation or damnation. That spirit needed to be corrected now by a more well-rounded or social view, made urgent by the changed conditions of life and labor in a new industrial century. But the new view was made possible or thinkable, in the most profound sense, by Hegel's and his disciples' philosophy of history, with its teachings that all thought is a child of its time, that history itself is a progressive or evolutionary process, and that later ages therefore enjoyed a fuller self-consciousness and a higher realization of freedom and morality than preceding ones. Though political rhetoric is often designed to mystify, blame, or distract, in this case it clarified: the

Progressives really did believe in progress, and not as something devoutly to be wished but as something *inevitable* over the long term, and comprising not merely scientific and technological improvement but moral and political betterment, too. Liberalism's first wave therefore announced itself as a doctrine of human progress, disclosing new truths for a new age. Unlike Hegel, however, the American Progressives did not think that progress had to have an end point, the "end of history." It could go on forever, infinitely approximating but never touching the axis of social justice.

In *The New Freedom*, as Wilson called his 1912 collection of campaign speeches, he argued human rights were not natural but historical, not unchanging but constantly evolving. Even as the founders' "natural rights" reflected an early or primitive stage in the development of *Recht*, so too did the U.S. Constitution exhibit the baleful effects of clinging to a premature and erroneous conclusion. If the rights to be secured were fixed and permanent, then the government charged with securing them ought to be as fixed and permanent as possible, too, and the Constitution did its best to freeze American government in the eighteenth century, as the Progressives diagnosed the problem. They rejected the premise, and therefore rejected the conclusion as well. Yet paradoxically Americans' reverence for the Constitution had grown with time. The first stage of the new freedom called, perforce, for the discrediting of the old: it is time to stop believing "in political witchcraft," Wilson wrote in his first book, *Congressional Government*. "The Constitution is not honored by blind worship." For the first time the nation must become "open-eyed" to the Constitution's "defects" and undertake "a fearless criticism" of the constitutional system.

According to Wilson, the founders' political science was guilty of several category mistakes. The master science of their age, he claimed, was Newtonian physics, and so they tended to see everything in its light: political science became a branch of mechanics, and they designed a Constitution that would go of itself, a perpetual-motion machine. Madison and Hamilton expected the system would be as regular and unchanging in its movements as the solar system, relying on human nature's unfailing law of motion – self-interest – to power the checks and balances of the Constitution and keep the branches in their proper orbits. Wilson referred to this as the framers' Newtonianism. But the master science of the modern world, he insisted, is Darwinism, which implied an evolutionary sociology to go along with the evolutionary biology. The State, as Wilson called it right down to the capital "S," is a social organism, not a machine. "Individual" humans do not exist by nature but are always found in families and in society, ultimately in a people with its own spirit or values and usually its own racial identity. (Almost the first question Wilson posed in his political science textbook, *The State*, was: what races shall we study? The short answer was the Aryans.)

Hence there were no individual or natural rights, strictly speaking, nor a social compact implying inviolable limits on government. Rights came from the group or groups to which one belonged, and from their stage of development. The State emerged from shared religious, cultural, ethnic, and linguistic identity, and necessarily expressed that identity. The State was the politically formed people – the whole, not a part. Far from being potentially opposed to the State, family and civil society were aspects of it. Rights-bearing individuals, too, formed parts in that organic whole. They were a late product of historical development, created by the State in several stages of diversification, at first casually and then purposely, after the Renaissance and the Reformation. Compared to the ancient state, the modern one is "largely de-socialized," observed Wilson, meaning it no longer absorbs the individual but "only serves him" by fostering his growth and self-realization. One could say (with some exaggeration) the State now existed for the individual, not the individual for the State. Yet these "state integers," as he called them, still had no existence, and no proper rights or liberties, outside of the fostering State. And in order to provide them with "the best and fullest opportunities" for "complete self-development," the modern State would have to be prepared to do, in Wilson's italics, *whatever experience permits or the times demand.* There was, in other words, much less to this de-socialization of the State than Wilson let on.

The rejection of natural-rights individualism was not unique to Wilson. On the contrary, it was a commonplace of the age's political thinking. Writers without a future political career in mind could discuss it more candidly than he. Here, for example, is the pioneering organizational theorist and management expert Mary Parker Follett from her 1918 book, *The New State*:

> Democracy has meant to many "natural" rights, "liberty," and "equality." The acceptance of the group principle defines for us in truer fashion those watchwords of the past. If my true self is the group-self, then my only rights are those which membership in a group gives me. The old idea of natural rights postulated the particularist individual; we know now that no such person exists. The group and the individual come into existence simultaneously: with this group-man appear group-rights. Thus man can have no rights apart from society or independent of society or against society.... The truth of the whole matter is that our only concern with "rights" is not to protect them but to create them. Our efforts are to be bent not upon guarding the rights which Heaven has showered upon us, but in creating all the rights we shall ever have.

From Hegelian idealism to Darwinian realism in a single bound, and then back again. It was a familiar journey, though Wilson's formulation of it was distinctive and influential. Throughout his career, whether in political science treatises or in popular speeches, Wilson stressed that government "was not a machine but a living thing" and "accountable to Darwin, not to Newton." The competition of life demanded cooperation within each State organism, so that the organism as a whole might successfully adapt to new socioeconomic and other external challenges. "No living thing can have its organs offset against each other as checks, and live," he declared. Checks and balances, separation of powers, federalism – the founders' renowned institutional safeguards – conduced not to political health but to a "fatal" stasis among the departments and levels of power. The branches needed, instead, to be woven together into an "intimate, almost instinctive cooperation" of power for good. "*Living political constitutions,*" he wrote emphatically, "*must be Darwinian in structure and in practice.*"

Though he may have borrowed the phrase from Walter Bagehot, and though other Progressive thinkers had similar thoughts,

Wilson was the foremost American expositor of the theory of the "living Constitution." Since the 1980s, the term has turned up mostly in the discussion of judicial rulings and confirmation fights. But Wilson applied it to the whole political system, and to the executive more than the other branches. He was the first President to criticize the Constitution, to call it timebound and incapable of meeting modern problems due to the very spirit and contrivances of government that had once been its proudest boast. He was also the first to propose pouring new wine into those old emptied bottles. Though the founders' Constitution and its three branches need not disappear, the government's lifeforce would flow increasingly through the new constitution overlaying the formal one. In polite company one might speak of a convergence between the two, but the spirit of the founders' Constitution was abating while that of the Progressives' constitution was rising. The whole point was to transfer the original Constitution's legitimacy to the new one.

A living constitution had to be able to evolve; to change quickly in structure and function; to expand its powers on command to confront society's novel problems; to bring expert knowledge from the research universities to bear on the design, execution, and evaluation of new social initiatives; and to coordinate and lead those initiatives via administrative agencies that straddled the separated branches of the old Constitution, combining powers legislative, executive, and judicial in ways and for purposes that might fulfill "the very definition of tyranny," according to *Federalist* No. 47. The framers' idea was that the Constitution ought to set the parameters of the government. The Progessives' idea was that the government – how we choose to govern ourselves now, to solve today's social problems – ought to set the parameters of the constitution.

REDISTRIBUTION AND THE SECOND BILL OF RIGHTS

Economic or "entitlement" liberalism, the second wave, had been discussed or anticipated by the Progressives, who made much of the closing of the American frontier and the rise of large-scale corporations and economic trusts, developments that had put an end, they charged, to traditional American equality of opportunity. They had only the beginnings of macroeconomic remedies, however, mostly anti-trust policies (concerning which Teddy Roosevelt and Wilson had a memorable disagreement in the 1912 election) and wages and hours laws. But the Wilson Administration's "war socialism" gave the next generation a sense of how to command and reorder the wider economy (and society) from the center, through the exercise of emergency powers.

Pregnant with even greater mischief than the New Deal's centralizations of administrative power – and integral to them – was its sweeping victory at adding a whole new category of rights to the American canon. In 1944 Franklin Roosevelt rolled these new social and economic rights into what he called a "second Bill of Rights," implying they wouldn't replace the first but were needed to supplement it, though the exact relation between the two was left unclear. Among the new additions he listed the right to "a useful and remunerative job," to a decent home, to adequate medical care, and to protection from "the economic fears of old age, sickness, accident, and unemployment." Not all of these new rights got enshrined in law, but most were eventually, in one form or another, by the entitlement and regulatory programs of the 1930s or of the 1960s and early 1970s. None was added as a formal amendment to the written Constitution. The point of the new programmatic rights was that they were joining the living constitution, the constitution defined by how the American people had decided – by majority vote, by the consent of the wise, and by structures that had passed the test of time, that had survived and were presumed fittest – to govern themselves now.

The new rights were needed for a new economic age. Although liberalism's second wave did not let the crisis of the Great Depression go to waste – and could not have happened without it, at least not in anything like the same way – the new age Franklin D. Roosevelt and his allies thought was dawning was an age of unprecedented abundance. Thanks to the industrial revolution and the factory system, economic scarcity would be a thing of the past. The present task, he said in 1932 to San Francisco's Commonwealth Club, is "not discovery or exploitation of natural resources, or necessarily producing more goods. It is the soberer, less dramatic business of

administering resources and plants already in hand," of reestablishing foreign markets and otherwise "meeting the problem of underconsumption, of adjusting production to consumption, of distributing
wealth and products more equitably." An economic "plenty" already
existed, the product of an "industrial and agricultural mechanism"
that "can produce enough and to spare." As Roosevelt put it rather
portentously, "The day of enlightened administration has come."
Consumption and redistribution, not production and innovation,
formed the principal agenda of the new day. The virtues associated
with entrepreneurship and competitive enterprise belonged to the
past, or at least could take a back seat in a regime concerned primarily with stimulating aggregate demand and distributing an econo-
my-wide surplus. The point was to beat the Depression, and to
prevent future ones, by transferring purchasing power from the rich,
who supposedly had too much, to the poor, who had too little. An
inflationary floor would be built under the economy, correcting the
systemic evil of "underconsumption." Enlightened administration
would correct at the same time both the moral and the economic
faults of the market economy. Capitalism had produced not its own
gravediggers but its own regulators and tutors.

Already in 1932 FDR called for "the development of an economic declaration of rights, an economic constitutional order" as
"the minimum requirement of a more permanently safe order of
things." The new order would rest on "economic truths" that in the
twentieth century "have become accepted as self-evident," such as
that "true individual freedom cannot exist without economic security and independence." Or, to borrow his favorite epigram, that
"necessitous men are not free men." He meant that hungry, jobless,
homeless men are the stuff of which dictatorships are made – a more
dubious historical correlation than it may sound. If necessitous men
are not free, then it is up to government to make them free by providing for their necessities when they cannot, enabling them to live comfortably and fearlessly, come what may. In that way, socio-economic
rights purported to make Americans secure, or at least feel secure, in
a new age dominated by economic insecurity and depression amid
the promise of plenty.

The immediate results were fairly innocuous – Social Security, unemployment insurance, and federal jobs programs, among other things, each a way to put cash into the hands of people who could use it. The more radically corporatist programs of the early New Deal (the National Recovery Administration, the Agricultural Adjustment Administration) were soon struck down by the Supreme Court, to the benefit of the New Deal's ultimate pragmatic reputation. But an important philosophical bridge had been crossed. No one ever doubted that good jobs, sturdy houses, and decent medical care were fine things, which might well be the objects of government solicitude in some way. A middle-class democracy needed to guard its middle class, as Aristotle had taught statesmen for several millennia. But the liberal alchemy that transformed these goods into *rights* was powerful magic; once unleashed, it proved increasingly uncontrollable. Such rights implied duties, after all, to provide the houses, jobs, and medical care now guaranteed to everyone. On whom did the duties fall? They fell in the first place onto government, which had to enact a program to vindicate each right. But where would the money to pay for such programs come from? Liberals never came clean on that. They alternately fingered the rich, who had more than they needed and so could spare to have some of it redistributed, and the middle class, who they presumed could afford to pay for social insurance. Once established – and given the progressive presumption that the future would be better than the present, now reinforced by the assurance that scarcity had been conquered – the new rights' future looked rosy.

Could the promised benefits be reduced or eliminated? Liberals breathed nary a word about such unhappy scenarios. They sold the new rights as though they were personal, indeed almost inalienable, not to mention virtually cost-free, like the old rights of free speech and free exercise of religion. But in fact entitlements are positive rights, to positive benefits like monthly disability checks and doctor's visits; such benefits are the fruit of legislative formulas that can be trimmed or repealed by simple majorities of Congress. In the end these benefits have to be paid for by *someone* – in reality, so far at least, primarily by the young and the middle class. So the two Bills of Rights conflicted much more than FDR cared to admit. Which should take precedence – Peter's right to health care or Paul's right to consent to taxes? Peter's right to a decent home, or Paul's right to property in his own home?

The moral hazard of these new rights went farther still. Virtue was the way people used to deal with their desires and necessities. For example, it took industry and responsibility to go to work every morning to provide for your family. It took courage to handle the fears that inevitably come with life, particularly in old age. Confronting these necessities on one's own or with the support of family, friends, church, and other institutions of civil society allowed for a certain pride in one's hard-won equality and independence. The new social and economic rights tended to undercut such virtues, subtly encouraging men and women to count on government to rescue them and then to celebrate that implicit dependency as true freedom. Though this was less a problem at the beginning and with the contributory programs like Social Security, it became in due course a problem for almost all the programs. In fact, by the 1960s the appetite for the stream of benefits (the effectual truth of these new rights) promised by entitlements soon proved, to many unfortunate Americans, more addictive than liberating.

Social and economic rights go to some individuals but not others – usually, only to that group whose corner of necessitousness a new program seeks to tidy up. From the beginning, entitlements went to organized interests – e.g., union members, farmers – or to needy people in the same boat with others. Little wonder that such rights encouraged citizens to think of themselves in terms of their necessities and to organize themselves politically to press for the satisfaction of their group needs. In this sense entitlement programs sprang from the first wave's re-definition of individual rights in terms of State or group rights, with the group always defined with reference to its material, cultural, and historical setting. The old natural and civil rights were bound up with duties. Your right to life meant others had a duty not to take your life from you, and that you had a duty not to take their life from them. The new group rights, however, carried no specific, corresponding obligations to other claimants. At best, one assertion of need might check another. Old persons' benefits had to coexist with school teachers' benefits, cattle farmers' right to high beef prices with poor families' right to buy beef cheap. The interest groups would fight it out among themselves, in effect, to establish a kind of equilibrium based on power, not right.

Behind entitlements stood a beguiling new version of the social contract offered by second-wave liberalism – the "new deal," in the broadest sense of the term. As FDR proclaimed in his Commonwealth Club Address, government is based on a contract in which "rulers were accorded power, and the people consented to that power on consideration that they be accorded certain rights. The task of statesmanship has always been the re-definition of these rights in terms of a changing and growing social order." True to his Wilsonian roots, this is not a contract into which people entered bearing inalienable or natural rights; their rights were a *product* of the contract negotiation. Nor was this a contract, like the Declaration, among the individuals who would constitute the body politic or civil society; it was a contract between the people, already formed as a collectivity, and their rulers, whose identity was already a historical fact, more or less. This social contract resembles Magna Carta more than it does the Declaration: rights do not belong to the individual; they come as liberties or dispensations from government. The people give government *power*, it gives them *rights*. It is up to statesmen like FDR to keep the bargain timely, to re-define rights in line with the new needs and priorities disclosed by history or by social developments.

This arrangement did not work out well in English history because the people often distrusted their rulers, and for good reason. Roosevelt and most liberals ever since have expected a happier outcome because modern government is thoroughly democratic, and they found it hard to imagine a powerful democratic government would do anything undemocratic, anything that over time would contradict the will or infringe the rights of the people. They lacked Madison's and Lincoln's undying suspicion of the dangers of majority faction. Political tyranny, at least in America, FDR concluded by contrast, was essentially a thing of the past. "Economic tyranny" (his term) was another matter. Clandestine oligarchy – i.e., rule by "economic royalists" and "the privileged princes of ... new economic dynasties" hidden behind the forms of the old Constitution – was a clear and present danger. To counter it, the formalities and limits of "horse-and-buggy" constitutionalism had to be laid aside in favor of a living constitution that would allow government to overawe the rich. Not only could government grow big without endangering liberty, it had to grow big in order to preserve the ordinary man's liberty, or more exactly, liberties. In fact, the more powerful the rulers became, the more rights, in the sense of entitlement programs, they could bestow on the people. The more generous they could be: the more *liberal*.

It was Franklin Roosevelt who insisted that American progressives rebaptize themselves as "liberals." Though he talked it up from the beginning, he made the effort thematic in his "purge" campaign against reactionary Democrats in the 1938 primaries. The Democrats must be the party of "militant liberalism," the "truly liberal party" in American political life, he declared. From a certain point of view (Herbert Hoover's, for instance) Roosevelt had stolen the name from the Republicans, who identified themselves in 1932 and thereafter with liberalism, in the sense which we now distinguish by calling it "classical liberalism." He liked to discomfit his enemies, who were left reluctantly to call themselves conservatives.

The move also allowed the new liberals to reconnect themselves to the American founding and to our tradition of "rights" doctrines, including the majestic language of the Declaration. FDR sounded much friendlier to the founders than Wilson did, and the new liberalism of socioeconomic rights seemed to promise something permanent – a welfare state – amid the evolutionary flux of the living constitution. That was part of the security Roosevelt offered. In reality, of course, it depended on the economy remaining sufficiently productive, and the people sufficiently uncorrupted, to enable them to enjoy the new rights they had promised themselves.

AUTHENTICITY AND ANTI-AMERICANISM

Multicultural or diversity liberalism hit America in the 1960s and 1970s, and hit it hard. It was only when this wave crashed into them that the radicalism, the boundlessness, of modern liberalism began to dawn on Americans, only then that conservatism became, temporarily, a majority movement, insofar as it stood for America against its cultured and uncultured despisers. Third-wave liberalism agreed with economic liberalism that government had to be prepared to provide for our necessities in order that we might live beyond necessitousness, in freedom. But the third wave denied that freedom from want and freedom from fear (alongside the other two of FDR's Four Freedoms, freedom of speech and expression, and freedom of worship, both derived from the first Bill of Rights) were sufficient for genuine human liberation. Freedom required living not merely comfortably but also creatively. America had to move beyond "soulless wealth" (Lyndon B. Johnson's phrase), beyond the "rich society" and the "powerful society" to the "Great Society" where "the desire for beauty and the hunger for community" could finally be satisfied. Beyond necessity, in other words, lay the politics of meaning.

Hillary Clinton spoke of "the politics of meaning" in a 1993 speech about health care reform, borrowing the phrase from Michael Lerner, who later wrote a book with that title. Lerner, a leftist rabbi, professor of psychology and philosophy, among other things, and one of the founders of *Tikkun* magazine, had in his youth been a leader in the University of California, Berkeley, Free Speech Movement and chairman of the Berkeley chapter of the Students for a Democratic Society (SDS). He then helped found the Seattle Liberation Front and became one of the "Seattle Seven," defendants charged with inciting a riot in one of the last notorious trials of the era. Clinton admired his argument that Americans were hungry for "a different kind of society," one that transcended capitalist self-interest and quested for "caring, ethic and spiritual sensitivity, and communal solidarity." That search for meaning was probably never so strikingly expressed as in Justice Anthony Kennedy's famous, or infamous, decision in the *Planned Parenthood v. Casey* case (1992), upholding *Roe v. Wade*'s permissive regime of legalized abortion, in language that could have come straight from the 1960s: "At the heart of liberty is the right to define one's own concept of existence, of meaning, of the universe, and of the mystery of human life."

It is harder to make sense of Sixties liberalism than of the preceding waves because it was so fraught, so divided. It emerged from a kind of double civil war, within liberalism itself (pitting the Great

Society against the New Left) and then between both factions of liberalism and what Richard Nixon would call in 1969 the silent majority, many of whom (like Ronald Reagan, who voted for FDR four times before turning Republican in 1962) had been or still were New Deal Democrats. In the Sixties the radicalism that had been latent all along in liberalism broke free of its faith in progress, in science, and in democracy itself. Mainstream liberalism found it hard to confront the radicals because so many of their premises were its, too. The very familiarity of the New Left's arguments astonished and silenced Lyndon Johnson and many of his supporters.

In the first place, the Great Society set out to complete the New Deal, to finish its agenda of what the historian and presidential counselor Arthur Schlesinger, Jr., called *quantitative* liberalism, guaranteeing economic security and health care through such new entitlements as Medicare, Medicaid, and food stamps. The "war on poverty" aimed not just to relieve poverty, however, "but to cure it and, above all, prevent it," in LBJ's words. A "lack of jobs and money" was but the "symptom" of poverty, not its cause. Poverty's stubborn persistence in the "affluent society" of postwar America (to borrow John Kenneth Galbraith's book title) suggested to midcentury liberals that the poor were victims of a deep spiritual problem with the affluent society itself. To put an end to poverty, society itself would have to move "upward to the Great Society," where "the quality of our American civilization" would soar. The age of *qualitative* liberalism had arrived, in which, as Johnson told the graduating class at the University of Michigan in May 1964, "an end to poverty and racial injustice" would be just the beginning. The Great Society would satisfy every person's desire for learning, work, material security, creativity, contact with nature, beauty, community, and meaning. "You have the chance never before afforded to any people in any age," he explained to the graduates. "You can build a society where the demands of morality, and the needs of the spirit, can be realized in the life of the nation." Johnson and the students were on the same page, he thought, condemning "soulless wealth" and seeking to realize a vision of "a new world" without poverty, racial injustice, and war – "a way of life beyond the realm of our experience, almost beyond the bounds of our imagination."

Poverty and racial injustice, though distinct conceptually, were linked. LBJ secured the passage of the Civil Rights Act in 1964 and the Voting Rights Act in 1965, redeeming some of the notoriously neglected promises of the Declaration of Independence, even as Martin Luther King had dreamed in his great speech at the Lincoln Memorial in 1963. "There is no more civil rights movement," King went so far as to say in August 1965. "President Johnson signed it out of existence when he signed the voting rights bill." Yet Johnson, the civil rights leaders, and young blacks in the cities quickly upped the ante. At Howard University, a historically all-black school, LBJ declared on Commencement Day 1965 that "freedom is not enough.... You do not take a person who for years has been hobbled by chains and liberate him, bring him up to the starting line of a race and then say, 'you are free to compete with all the others,' and still justly believe that you have been completely fair." To equalize rights was not enough. It would be necessary to equalize the exercise of rights, the outcomes. "This is the next and more profound stage of the battle for civil rights," LBJ revealed. We seek "not just freedom but opportunity," "not just equality as a right and theory but equality as a fact and equality as a result." The preceding hundred years' struggle for equality had been merely a "stage," and a less profound one, than the struggle for the new equality now beginning. Several months later he issued an executive order commanding federal agencies "to take affirmative action" to ensure that blacks were hired. He didn't specify goals and timetables but these followed soon enough under his successor. Equal opportunity, always a slippery translation of equal rights, was on the way to being transformed into equal results. Liberals had set out boldly to transcend quantitative for qualitative liberalism. Now it turned out that qualitative liberalism would require a strict, intrusive, and apparently unending regime of quantitative illiberalism.

The theory was that equal rights were too formal or formalistic, the same argument used by the Progressives against natural rights and even earlier by Marx against "bourgeois rights." The only freedom that counted was *effective* or realized freedom, the equal freedom confirmed by equal results, whatever that would mean exactly. "Negro poverty is not white poverty," LBJ explained at Howard. Due to slavery's legacy, blacks "just can not do it alone," as other American minorities had. He pointed in particular to the breakdown of the black family, for which, "most of all, white America must accept responsibility." Two months later came the Watts riots in Los Angeles. When King and other civil rights leaders visited after the fires died down, they were shocked at how excited and empowered many of the young men on the streets felt. The nonviolent strategy had gone up in flames along with the Watts neighborhood. Black Power would soon be the new watchword.

As for the poor generally (though more dramatically for blacks), Johnson believed the problem was less their material poverty than their poverty of spirit, and his Great Society had the cure for both. It offered the satisfaction, in principle, of all material and spiritual needs and desires, in that order. The spiritual needs were not higher and certainly not prior to the material; they were "postmaterialist," as social scientists began to call them. The right to a "complete self-development" (as Wilson had termed it) came to something like fruition in the Great Society's gauzy hopes for itself. LBJ suffered no lack of optimism: "These are the most hopeful times in all the years since Christ was born in Bethlehem," he said after his election in 1964. Once the wars on poverty, racism, and war itself had been won, he predicted, the central question of American politics, of life, would be what to do with the unimaginable freedom Americans would enjoy. What was it all *for*? All of liberalism's promises of positive freedom (freedom *for*) would have to be redeemed. Politics would have to focus on man's religious, aesthetic, cultural, moral, and spiritual quality of life, but in terms of diversity, development and freedom, not in terms of excellence, virtue, and responsibility. In his Inaugural Address, for example, Johnson defined the Great Society as "the excitement of becoming – always becoming, trying, probing, falling, resting, and trying again – but always trying and always gaining." "Always becoming" *what*?

That was a problem. Although the Dionysian Sixties might seem far removed from the Apollonian – or at any rate Teutonic and WASPy – consciousness of early twentieth-century American Progressivism, there is a connection. From the beginning liberalism had renounced, in effect, commonsense views of a permanent or essential human nature. In place of the old-fashioned view of man as an in-between being – between the beasts and the angels – progressivism substituted the view of man as an open-ended being, defined *not* by his unchanging nature but precisely by how his nature had changed, or evolved, over the years in reaction to history's challenges. The most important aspect of human nature, in fact, was its very openness to change, its freedom in the sense of indefinite, and perhaps even infinite, adaptability. What we have seen of man's nature in the past is therefore not a good guide to what we may expect of him in the future. A new kind of idealism, based not on summoning the better angels of our nature but on eventually transcending that nature entirely, could take wing, promising, as LBJ put it, "a way of life beyond the realm of our experience, almost beyond the bounds of our imagination." This was Lyndon Baines Johnson talking, not the kids, not the radicals. The distance between his Texas life and character, his affect, and theirs might seem every bit as great as that separating Wilson's pince-nez and three-piece suits from the Sixties kids' tie-dye and denim. But LBJ didn't see it that way. He imagined he was one of them, a radical, a nonconformist, and he craved their support.

The Vietnam War was the principal cause of the civil war within liberalism that erupted in the 1960s, but for the New Left's various constituencies – Students for a Democratic Society (SDS), the Black Panthers, and others – the war was a synecdoche, standing for a much larger set of American evils. For the radicals, the Great Society was part of "the System," thus part of the problem not the solution. The Old Left (both its Communist and anti-Communist parts) had promised the rising generation a better world, after all, and the young radicals did not see the world getting better. The New Left saw a world with increasing technological dominance and power, symbolized by the hydrogen Bomb that threatened to destroy it. They didn't consider two world wars, colonialism, poverty, the Holocaust, the Cold War, and now the prospect of an atomic holocaust to be heralds of inevitable progress. Though they began the decade as admirers of and (some of them) participants in the nonviolent civil rights movement, they ended the decade believing that American society was more or less hopelessly racist. Johnson was both right – real equality was a long way off – and completely wrong – to believe that Great Society programs could get America there peacefully. The young cadres of the New Left were the first liberals (though they renounced the name) to reject the inevitability of progress, of belief in history as an evolutionary path with a guaranteed happy ending. They wanted to make or change history, not to wait for it to change them. They turned to a *revolutionary* path, unclear at first what it would mean, but increasingly clear as the decade and the War went on that it involved violence.

First came the consciousness-raising, however. Many philosophical progressives earlier in the century had conceived of history as the process by which man came to greater and greater consciousness of his own freedom – his freedom *from* nature, in the sense of permanent capacities and bounds – to the point at which man realized that he is essentially not a natural or created being at all, but a progressive one, free now to take charge of his own evolution. That *taking charge* was a crucial step, which separated the left-wing, all-in Progressive Darwinists like Lester F. Ward from the right-wing evolutionists like William Graham Sumner, and also distinguished the more progressive Progressives from the more conservative Progressives. To take command of human biology (eugenics) and social evolution meant leaving behind self-government and even self-expression for the brave new world of self-creation. In this vision, culture, conceived of as a product of *human will*, replaced culture understood as the cultivation of man's moral and intellectual endowment. And politics became the means of *transforming* man into a more perfect, or at any rate a more fully self-developed, being. "Democracy," wrote the arch-Progressive Herbert Croly in *The Promise of American Life*, the 1909 book that caught Teddy Roosevelt's eye, "must stand or fall on a platform of possible human perfectibility." Both creature and Creator, man became his own experiment.

Beginning in the 1950s if not earlier, the social sciences in America and much of high culture with them made a crucial turn which had a great effect on American conceptions of morality: the embrace of "values," the notion that all moral judgments are subjective or relative, reflecting nothing more than one's emotions or preferences. To be scientific, social science would have to become "value-free," that is, neutral in its methods and conclusions as to values, though not necessarily neutral as to the questions it posed. Wholesale madness but retail sanity, as Leo Strauss described it witheringly. By the 1960s students were familiar with the notion that all values are expressions of underlying passions, preferences, or will, which meant that reason, tradition, religion, and even common sense were disqualified as guides to right conduct. Although this discovery brought a rush of liberation, it also threatened a literal demoralization. The young radicals, schooled by Heideggerian Marxists and post-Marxists like Herbert Marcuse, were sensitive to the danger. The SDS's 1962 manifesto, the *Port Huron Statement*, charged that mainstream scientific or "value-free" social science had refuted itself as a guide to politics and life. Where did that leave the SDS, who had assigned college students the job of leading whatever revolution was necessary or possible?

Two momentous changes for the future of liberalism followed from the New Left's grappling with such questions. America's first two waves of liberalism had put great stock in the new social sciences, regarding them as authoritative guides to understanding and changing modern society for the better. The living constitution, the science of public administration, leadership theory, national economic planning – these were some of the constituents of liberalism that it owed to the new sciences. The Progressives had helped to build, and bend to public use, the great system of research universities, including state universities like Michigan and Wisconsin. Confidence in an educational elite marched hand-in-hand with liberalism's confidence in a mass democracy led by educated leaders of vision and compassion, all following the promptings of progress. But the student radicals had learned to distrust the experts' disinterestedness, and their science of progress. The experts proved to be uninspired men – "specialists without spirit, sensualists without heart," as Max Weber called them – who had led the world to a dead end. To the SDS, the Great Society and the Vietnam War (with the larger Cold War) appeared as two sides of the same technocratic coin.

To the young radicals, value-free or bureaucratic reason led to "apathy," the lack of passion or passionate moralism they diagnosed and despised in university administrators and professors, and in the country at large. "If it feels good, do it" was one response. "If it feels *right*, do it" was another. Believing America needed revolutionary change, they were eager to volunteer for a new revolutionary elite to stimulate or inspire the masses, but this elite had to be full of passion and idealism. Having learned that all values are relative and that reason cannot by nature tell right from wrong, they leaped to the non sequitur that feelings were a better guide than reason. If morals were grounded in emotions, then emotions could be a guide to morals. This is a form of what you might call Sixties existentialism, in which the key to morality became the intensity of your feelings about the subject. The intensity of your feelings was in turn a measure of their authenticity, of the real *you* taking a stand for something or other – but at least for something rather than nothing. So the culture of the demonstration, of living for the excitement or the high of the protest itself, became a characteristic part of Sixties-style radicalism, and a sign of enlightened consciousness ever since. The "possible human perfectibility" that Progressivism sought could be found right away and on the cheap. You may not be able, by reason, to prove or demonstrate your morality, but you can demonstrate you have one: you can signal you are a very moral person. Passionate intensity became the criterion of goodness. The new elite would be cursed with that now-familiar, contradictory combination: relativism *and* fanatical moralism.

Not that the New Left had entirely abandoned theory or moral-political knowledge as a guide to revolutionary action. But from reading a peculiar combination of Nietzsche, Heidegger, Freud, and Marx's early writings, the radicals had learned to be suspicious of abstract or deterministic reason as a form of alienation from life or being. The types of theorizing they cottoned to brought theory and practice as close together as possible, with practice, understood as a kind of immanent disclosure of being or of will to power, in the lead. Some of the radicals were drawn eventually, therefore, to the Communist revolutionary leaders who were on the cutting edge of the struggle – men like Fidel Castro, Che Guevara, and Ho Chi Minh – or who resisted Soviet-style bureaucracy in favor of keeping the revolution bloody and churning, like Mao Tse Tung. Others were drawn to the search for the authentic self in their own bodies. Sixties feminism, the Black Power movement, gay liberation, and the drug culture had their own stories, but they were part of the New Left's narrative, too. They shared the idea of the authentic self, liberated from "conventional morality" and free to choose its own values and create its own lifestyle in opposition to the alienated and oppressive mainstream. Whether this authentic self emerged out of the vasty deep of one's race, ethnicity, sex, gender, or just getting stoned, its source was something bodily or subrational, however much it might ultimately affect reason and society. Twenty-first-century identity politics started from similar premises. Even the more personal of these liberation movements soon turned into a claim for group rights. The weakness of the abstract or individual self, a theme that modern liberalism had always emphasized, made that inevitable: cut off from nature or God, even the supposedly authentic self needed affirmation – recognition – from other, similar selves if it were to be resolute in its freedom.

The other major change the New Left brought to liberalism affected its attitude to the people, to the democratic majority. They were the first liberals to turn against the people. After all the SDS's talk of "participatory democracy" and "Power to the people!" this may seem startling. But it turned out the people didn't want to participate in the New Left's kind of democracy, nor wield power for its purposes. Although they weren't part of the power elite, most Americans proved, not entirely to the New Left's surprise, complicit with "the System." White people in the South, that is, those whites who resisted desegregation, provided the model. Overwhelmingly Democrats, they proved the moral bankruptcy of the "liberal" party perhaps even more clearly than the party's approval of the war in Vietnam. Nor was it merely the plutocrats who were to blame: it was the rank-and-file, the middle and working classes, the vast majority of white Americans whose values proved stubbornly "bourgeois" (even though, in classical Marxist terms, they were supposed to play the role of the proletariat). In liberalism's own theory, the masses were supposed to be putty in the hands of the impassioned and visionary leader, who was, however, supposed to be interpreting their own innermost but unarticulated longing for a better future. The New Left found the people's values much less tractable, and had to apply a new and growing vocabulary to condemn them: racist, sexist, conformist, colonialist, etc. As Lenin had argued long before, the workers were not worthy of, and certainly not ready for, the workers' revolution. In the young radicals' catalogue of the American people's sins, which grew longer and darker as the decade advanced, the emphasis was on the systemic quality of the majority's prejudices, the sickness, apparently ineradicable, of existing American society. Thus liberalism's third wave devolved into a thoroughgoing contempt for the American middle class and its whole way of life.

The New Left played at revolution rather than seriously attempting it, with a few exceptions like William Ayres and some of the Panthers. Their most serious political efforts went instead to overthrowing Lyndon Johnson and pro-Cold War Democrats; they celebrated victory with George McGovern's nomination for president in 1972. After the American people elected Richard Nixon as president in 1968 and again by far larger margins over McGovern, and after Reagan's big victories in 1980 and 1984 showed the people weren't kidding, the radicals turned to another revolution in which they enjoyed much greater success, the long march through Hollywood, non-profit foundations, the administrative state, and, especially, the American university. From those redoubts they set about reshaping American culture and government in their own image, while dreamily scanning the horizon for that killer fourth wave.

CHAPTER EIGHT

WOODROW WILSON AND THE STATESMANSHIP OF PROGRESS

THE YEARS AFTER THE CIVIL WAR saw not one but two new beginnings in American politics. The first was to some extent a working and living out of the principles of the founding, a resumption of old ways now elucidated and ennobled by the tragedy of the War and by the triumph over slavery – which looked less definitive as Reconstruction faded and Jim Crow took its place. But very quickly this halting perpetuation or rebirth of the Old Freedom began to give way to the advance of a New, whose theories and experiments would increasingly capture the country's imagination and produce far-reaching consequences.

To begin to identify these novel undertakings, it would help perhaps to ponder the vast changes in structure and function that the federal government has undergone in the years since Abraham Lincoln was President. A standard list of innovations might include: the nationalization of commerce under the aegis of the interstate Commerce Clause; the establishment of new federal bureaucracies and regulatory agencies; the progressive income tax; provision of unemployment benefits, welfare relief, medical and disability benefits, and social insurance for ever-growing numbers of citizens; the broad assumption of responsibility for the macroeconomic health of the nation; construction of huge federal highway systems and other large-scale public works; revenue sharing, urban renewal, and other programs for state and local governments; federal enforcement of civil and voting rights; and federal aid to lower and higher education. The list is by no means exhaustive, but it does suggest the new extent of the federal government's domestic responsibilities, and the way in which both Democrats and Republicans contributed to the expansion.

Nevertheless, none of these developments in itself – nor even several taken together – marks a *fundamental* change from the founders' or Lincoln's understanding of the proper functions of government. Internal improvements, regulation of interstate commerce, and governmental protection of selected industries were all part of the nationalizing program of the Federalists and the Whigs, which program was taken over by the Republican Party. Every President from George Washington to John Quincy Adams urged the federal government to set up a national university. The Northwest Ordinance mandated that provision be made for schools – and churches – throughout the Northwest Territory; and federal support for state governments was manifest in ways ranging from the national assumption of the states' Revolutionary War debts to the actual purchase of the lands from which the trans-Appalachian states were carved to the Morrill Act's land grants for state agricultural colleges. Public relief measures, while not specifically undertaken by the federal government, were common in the states; and Civil War pensions provided Washington its own growing experience with social welfare spending. In short, taken by themselves, there is nothing in these newer programs that could not be explained or defended as a continuation, *mutatis mutandis*, of the traditional practices of American government.

Which is not to deny that there has been a decisive change. What characterizes that change is the transformed understanding of the *purposes* of government: of the *reasons* given for these (and, to be sure, many other) programs and the *uses* to which they are put. (A similar interpretation might be given of salient Supreme Court decisions since the Civil War.) This new view of the ends of government is in turn based on a new view of the nature of man; and the significance of these changes can be seen most clearly in their effect on the understanding and practice of American statesmanship. The man more than any other who prepared this revolution in American politics is Woodrow Wilson. It was he who first asserted in a comprehensive way that the traditional definition of statesmanship as the highest form of practical wisdom had become untenable – and had to be reconstructed with a view to the new truths revealed by the philosophy of history, evolutionary biology, and the emergent social sciences.

Practical wisdom, as Aristotle described it, presumes the existence and authority of moral virtue, for prudence is the ability to deliberate well concerning the best means to the ends supplied by moral virtue. But moral virtue itself is the perfection of human being with regard to the governance of the passions, and presumes that human being is articulated in a more or less fixed and permanent way.[1] To put it differently, moral virtues such as courage, moderation, and justice are inseparable from the notion of human nature and its perfection in accordance with what America's founders called "the laws of nature and of nature's God." Wilson believed that the historical school of philosophy in England and Germany had succeeded in anachronizing – and so disproving – the idea of nature as a standard for moral and political life, opening the way for the introduction of a novel kind of statesmanship into American politics. The distinctive character of the "statesmanship of progress," as he called his new theory of leadership,[2] was the requirement of historical "vision" or "sympathetic insight" – the ability to see whither history is tending and to prepare the nation to move in that direction, to move with the current rather than to struggle against it or be caught in its eddies or be dashed by it against the rocks. Barack Obama was merely following Wilson's lead when he memorably distinguished between the right and the wrong side of history, and urged his countrymen to keep to the right (i.e., the left) side. Just how different the "statesmanship of progress" is from the statesmanship of natural right may be seen in Wilson's own analysis of the American situation, and in his recommendations for its improvement.

FROM NEWTON TO DARWIN

To many historians there is not one Woodrow Wilson but two – the conservative southern Democrat and dyed-in-the-wool Burkean, and, after about 1910, the more familiar progressive reformer and idealistic crusader. The charitable explanation of the switch is that he finally saw the light; his detractors maintain that what he saw was how to get elected. While it is undeniable that there were important changes in his political opinions and alliances, both his defenders and his critics fail to appreciate the more fundamental continuity between the "two" Wilsons.[3] To his mind, Burkeanism and progressivism were not in the slightest incompatible. "There is nothing so conservative of life as growth," he explained in an address on the occasion of Princeton University's sesquicentennial in 1896. "Progress is life, for the body politic as for the body natural. To stand still is to court death. Here then … you have the law of conservatism disclosed: it is a law of progress."[4]

It is not to be wondered, then, that a critique of the founding is central to Wilson's project both in his "conservative" and "progressive" phases. The problem with the American Constitution, according to the early *and* the mature Wilson, is that it was composed under the influence of a theory: in designing America's political institutions, the framers looked to "the Whig theory of political dynamics" for guidance. Drawing upon the doctrines and experience of the Whigs in their successful efforts to rein in the British King, to constitutionalize the executive power, the framers undertook to ring the American President with offsetting departments so as to secure the courts and legislature against executive encroachment. In so doing, however, the framers "made no clear analysis of the matter in their own thoughts," for they were "practical men," and English to boot; it was not their habit to be "clear theorists." They did what any practical man (not Aristotle's *phronemos*, however) would do in the same situation: they borrowed their theory, not exactly from the Whigs themselves (who being Englishmen were also not metaphysicians), but from the famous Frenchman who had explained to the Whigs what they had wrought. To Montesquieu the framers turned, and learning from him that "it was essential for the preservation of liberty to differentiate the executive, legislative, and judicial functions of government and not to suffer them to be united in the same hands," they saw to it that "all intimacy of aim and cooperation of effort" between the branches was rendered impossible.[5]

But if the American Constitution had a philosopher, it was not itself a work of philosophy. Being practical men, the framers were turned into "Whig theorists" only imperfectly; they did not follow Montesquieu as philosophers would have; they "had no thought of re-examining his principles to see if they really held good for all cases." Wilson may seem to be accusing the framers of a lack of prudence, indicting their statesmanship for inattention to the peculiar circumstances of the American case. A closer inspection will show that he regards their decisive failing to be an inability to appreciate *historical* circumstances. Hamilton, Madison, and the other authors of the Constitution did not understand that Montesquieu had written "in a time which did not know the people as an actual and active sovereign authority," and that consequently he had not "hit upon exactly the right devices" for ensuring successful popular government. The fear of the executive that the framers had absorbed from Montesquieu was characteristic of only one stage of English constitutional history, a stage even then fast receding. It would not be long before the British ministry would become a committee of the House of Commons – a committee constituting the "working executive of the country" over which the King would wield only the formal power of appointment. Not being able to foresee that "party government by the legislative leaders of the people" was on the horizon, the framers in effect froze our constitutional arrangements (particularly regarding the executive) "at the stage of constitutional development which England was leaving."[6]

It was not the inherent plausibility of Montesquieu's views, then, but their familiarity as part of a larger "system of thought" that accounted for their acceptance by the framers. Behind the "Whig theory of political dynamics" was "the Newtonian theory of the universe," the paradigm according to which men of that time reasoned about "the structure or development of anything, whether in nature or in society." The political theory of the founding was "a sort of

unconscious copy" of Newtonian physics – it was not a fully conscious copy because, as we shall see, the founders had not discovered
the principle of historical relativity, and so could not acknowledge
the timebound sovereignty of their own paradigm. To them politics
was a branch of mechanics, government a machine regulated by
"mechanically automatic balances" – the President against Congress,
Congress against the President, Congress against the Court, and so
forth. As the "nice poise and balance of forces" produce a universe of
"symmetry and perfect adjustment," so the checks and balances of
the Constitution result in good administration and liberty. In short,
the framers "constructed a government as they would have constructed an orrery – to display the laws of nature."[7]

Unhappily, from Wilson's point of view, the Newtonianism of
the Constitution long outlived its framers. Although American politics had never quite lived up to the "literary theory" of equilibrium
among the branches of the federal government, it had come close.
Most galling of all, even when a rather serious disequilibrium set in
shortly after the Civil War – which derangement he analyzed in his
first book, *Congressional Government* (1885) – the Newtonian balances had simply and arrestingly reasserted themselves in a new
guise. To be specific, in the twenty years between Lincoln's assassination and Grover Cleveland's election, the separation of powers
broke down: the executive and judiciary became subordinated to an
imperious if not imperial Congress. Congress, in turn, consigned its
business to a system of standing committees whose squabbles, vani-
ties, and pomposities precluded efficient legislating, distracted congressional oversight of the executive, and doomed all schemes of
party responsibility and public enlightenment. Despite these manifold departures from the writ of the Constitution, the essential spirit
of the document was preserved in the new arrangements: from a
system of balances between the powers of the federal government,
America's constitutional existence became a system of balanced and
mutually checking committees within the sovereign Congress. Newtonianism had been called down from the heavens, and transferred
from the branches of government to the committees of Congress,
but its laws of motions were the same.[8]

Yet the Newtonian universe was not a cosmos of perfect and

eternal spheres, not even of perfect and invariable ellipses, for it was understood that orbits would change as new bodies or forces acted upon them. Could not new or weightier congressmen – one thinks of men in the proportions of Speaker Joseph Cannon – or even the forces of public opinion, sufficiently concentrated, override or restructure the system of standing committees? Wilson was skeptical, for the reason that committee government reflected something more fundamental in the country. "Congress in its composition is the country in miniature," he wrote in an essay published in 1893: "It realizes Hobbes's definition of liberty as political power divided into small fragments. The standing committees typify the individuals of the nation."[9] Newtonianism penetrated American society as well as American government, and if its political agent or intermediary was Montesquieu, its social agent was Hobbes. The "individuals of the nation," as Wilson paradoxically says, are practically in a state of nature with one another. In the virtual absence or suspension of political power at the center, this is what Hobbes would expect to happen, but also what he would *want* to happen, at least if his absolutism is in the service of a more fundamental liberalism. Wilson's criticism is that Hobbes's prescription is akin to his diagnosis, that civil society on Hobbesian principles is so very similar to the state of nature that the true inconveniences of the latter are never overcome.[10] Foremost among these is that men are encouraged to be private individuals rather than public citizens, to live on the level of material interests rather than common ideals. As a result, statesmanship is rendered nugatory; and as a result of that, the potential for social progress and individual self-development lies fallow.

Wilson is the most influential academic and political figure ever to criticize the American regime for being Hobbesian, and to connect that criticism to a program for the nation's reformation. Perhaps his closest competitors for the honor (if that is what it is) are the antebellum defenders of the positive good of Negro slavery, and in particular George Fitzhugh, who saw the contest between free society and slave society to be a reflection of the question between the social contract theorists and Aristotle: was man born free and equal, or unfree and unequal? Apart from the staggering question of how unfaithful is his interpretation of Aristotle – Fitzhugh is in any case a glaring example of applying classical principles imprudently, without making the necessary changes for the novel character of modern society – it must be admitted that Fitzhugh's program for American salvation had a Lincolnian consistency to it. He held that slavery was beneficial not only for blacks but also for whites (at least for nineteen out of twenty whites), and hence that it should be extended to the whole Union. In the event, Lincoln's statesmanship extinguished Fitzhugh's hope. Wilson's indictment of America's Hobbesianism began where Fitzhugh's had languished – in the academy – but swiftly left it to become a transforming force in American politics and, in one form or another, a staple of Democratic party rhetoric ever since. But its most sophisticated expressions are still heard in the universities, often from the least Wilsonian of scholars. Indeed it has become a kind of *obbligato* behind both liberal and conservative academics, whose voices sound discordant but frequently may be harmonized rather easily.[11]

In criticizing American government's reliance on balancing ambitions and interests to "supply the defect of better motives," as well as American society's consuming individualism, Wilson did not intend to discriminate between the lower and higher parts of human nature, in order to direct the nation towards the noble and the common good. His was not so much a vertical as a horizontal strategy – to open America to the salutary influences of progress, after which nobility and the common good would take care of themselves.[12] He repaired to history, not to nature, as the standard by which America would ultimately be guided to a new moral and political dispensation. Contemporary liberals, whether in the academy or in politics, would find nothing objectionable in Wilson's undertaking, except perhaps the pedigree of his, i.e., their ideas. (Hence it was far easier for Princeton to drop his name from the Woodrow Wilson School of Public and International Affairs than to drop his ideas from its curriculum.) Some of today's conservatives – paleoconservatives like Paul Gottfried, for example – would also see nothing wrong with the resort to history to purge our politics of the rationalism born of natural right, although they might complain of the pace and direction of Wilson's reforms.

It is, however, surprising to find neoconservative or Straussian scholars (albeit Eastern Straussians, to use that somewhat hoary term) who echo Wilson's criticisms of the founding. This is not because they like him or his ideas, exactly, but because they sometimes let their love of classical political philosophy inspire a kind of nostalgia for the glories of the *polis* – when politics was really *politics* – which distorts their analysis of later political life. They end up studying not so much American politics as an American version of *modern* politics (cf. Chapter One, above), which tends to reduce everything to a reflection of modern political philosophy and "bourgeois values."[13] With such preconceptions it is easy to forget that the road to radical modernity is paved with well-intentioned longings for antiquity.[14] To avoid traveling down this road requires studying American politics prudently, or starting from the perspective of a good citizen. Insofar as the best or most loyal citizen is he who has had a choice – who, after contemplating the alternatives, has *chosen* his own regime or would choose it again if he had the chance – the perspective of the best citizen is that of a founder or of the regime's greatest perpetuators.

It was, however, precisely Wilson's intention to replace the natural horizon of statesmanship (the horizon of human nature) with the new and constantly changing horizon of progress. The problem with constructing a government "to display the laws of nature," Wilson argues, is that it results in nothing *but* display, for the laws of nature are not laws of human freedom. Insofar as the laws of nature are laws of motion, of mechanical cause and effect, they express a determinism that excludes human freedom. "Government is not a machine," he objects, but "a living thing," and as such it falls "not under the theory of the universe, but under the theory of organic life." Organic life is part of the universe, of course, but Wilson's point is that living organisms not only move through time and space but can change or evolve as they go. They have an open-endedness, an indeterminacy to them that is akin to freedom. This openness to change became central to biology after Darwin's *Origin of Species* (1859). Wilson wished to make it central to political science too: In short, government is "accountable to Darwin, not to Newton. It is modified by its environment, necessitated by its tasks, shaped to its functions by the sheer pressure of life."[15]

"Living political constitutions must be Darwinian in structure and practice," Wilson emphasizes again and again. In practice this means that it is impossible to have successful government "without leadership or without the intimate, almost instinctive, coordination of the organs of life and action." However organic it may be, the state does not possess instincts, so it must make do with "leadership." Statesmanship understood as leadership is thus "the art of bringing the several parts of government into effective cooperation for the accomplishment of particular common objects." Wilson's indictment of the framers may then be epitomized as follows, that they constructed a regime in which the exercise of statesmanship was direly necessary but peculiarly difficult. Having created their own political universe, they absconded like the god of the Newtonian universe, taking with them the need, and so they thought, the desirability, of any future acts of particular providence.[16] The legislative, executive, and judicial branches were left to ply their respective orbits, held in place by the forces of ambition and interest. But the system's very self-sufficiency cast doubt on the need for the executive power; its ordinary use came to be contemplated skeptically and its energetic use regarded as scarcely less than a miracle. It was the intrinsic weakness of the executive that led to the breakdown of the system, that allowed the legislature to overwhelm the other branches. Since the same forces obtained within as without the legislature, however, the display of standing committees, as we have seen, soon replaced the more magnificent display of separated powers.

In both cases Wilson thought the dimensions of the problem were life-threatening, because "no living thing can have its organs offset against each other as checks, and live." That the American regime was still alive suggested either that his grasp of the theory of separation of powers was faulty or that the practicality which made the founders bad philosophers may in the end have made them good statesmen. It is well to consider the one before moving on to the other. The framers were well aware of the folly of attempting a too strict separation of the powers of government, as any reader of *Federalist* No. 47 will recall.[17] There Publius defends the proposed Constitution against the Anti-Federalist charge that "the several departments of power are distributed and blended in such a manner as at once to destroy all symmetry and beauty of form, and to expose some of the essential parts of the edifice to the danger of being crushed by the disproportionate weight of other parts." By recurring to the sibylline teachings of Montesquieu, "the oracle who is always consulted and cited on this subject," Publius exploits the Anti-Federalists' propensity to rush to oracles for guidance only to misinterpret the vouchsafed wisdom. Montesquieu, after all, had found in the British Constitution not political liberty itself but "the mirror of political liberty," meaning something that reflects it perhaps along with other objects' shadowy images. Publius "infers" from the facts of British constitutional life that Montesquieu had not meant to say, and did not say, that the departments of government "ought to have no *partial agency* in, or no *control* over, the acts of each other." It is only when "the *whole* power of one department is exercised by the same hands which possess the *whole* power of another department" that "the fundamental principles of a free constitution are subverted."[18] The Anti-Federalists had read Montesquieu in light of an exaggerated or misplaced love of "symmetry and beauty of form," which, as Publius proceeds to show, their own practice in the state constitutions belied.

Publius agrees with Wilson that politics is not the realm in which to look for "symmetry and beauty of form," not, however, because the laws of nature are Newtonian laws of necessity (the thought that Wilson erroneously attributes to Publius), but because in politics forms must be combined with imperfect matter. In Newtonian science, all bodies are essentially the same, obeying the same laws of nature; form is reduced to the laws of motion that govern all bodies equally. But in politics, form is the distinctive character of a country, that which chiefly distinguishes it from other forms of government and ways of life. Publius's criticism of the Anti-Federalists is that they do not understand the intractability of matter and so do not see the problem posed for the form of republican government. They believe that politics can easily and completely live up to the "political maxim" of the separation of powers, forgetting the delicate and difficult relation between theory and practice, as well as the limitations of our theoretical wisdom. "Experience has instructed us," Publius had remarked ten papers before, "that no skill in the science of government has yet been able to discriminate and define, with sufficient certainty, its three great provinces – the legislative, executive, and judiciary."[19]

The Anti-Federalists' confident expectation that republican government could be secured by a "separate and distinct" division of powers committed to writing, with every "i" dotted and "t" crossed, is the sort of intellectual and political vanity that comes from admiring oneself in the mirror, without ever really seeing oneself. If their eyes were opened, they would see that to vindicate their claimed republicanism would require more than a formal display of the separation of powers (the theme of *Federalist* No. 48), even more than a separation secured by recurrent or regular appeals to the people · (*Federalist* Nos. 49–50). It becomes clear from *The Federalist*'s argument that the Anti-Federalists' superficial understanding of the separation of powers is of a piece with their too-easy republicanism: the "parchment barriers" in the state constitutions had quickly been overrun by the encroaching legislatures. These encroachments put an end to the "symmetry and beauty of form" that the foes of the federal Constitution so greatly admired, and proved that these critics did not understand the danger to republicanism posed by the people themselves.

In other words, the Anti-Federalists did not truly comprehend the *need* for the separation of powers in order to make republicanism respectable. Publius is able to show the inadequacy of simple, unrefined republicanism – rule by the whole people in name, but by the many in fact and in spirit, whether directly or through their representatives – without offending republican sensibilities by resorting to the same "mirror" or "standard" that Montesquieu had used – namely, the British Constitution. More precisely, Publius adopts the principle of separated powers that Montesquieu had extracted from that Constitution and incorporates it, with some modifications, into the American Constitution, which itself becomes a kind of mirror of political liberty. As Americans turned to Montesquieu to view the principles of the British Constitution, so they henceforth would open *The Federalist* to see the true principles of their own Constitution. In such manner the "honorable determination, which animates every votary of freedom, to rest all our political experiments on the capacity of mankind for self-government," may be vindicated, by showing that republican government is honorable and good.[20]

To *The Federalist*, the separation of powers was not a "display" of merry-go-round laws of nature but a qualification and refinement of republicanism. To effect this, the powers had to be mixed in order to be kept separate, the mechanism of the mixing being the same as the guardian of the separation – namely, the famous system of ambition counteracting ambition, so that "the interest of the man" may be connected with "the constitutional rights of the place." Wilson's objection to this system is that "government is not a body of blind forces; it is a body of men, with highly differentiated functions ... but with a common task and purpose. Their cooperation is indispensable, their warfare fatal."[21] But Wilson's criticism of public purposelessness – which is, to repeat, a refrain common to both the Left and the Right – is not true to the nature of each of the powers. It does not speak to the constitutional *duties* of the place, which are based on an understanding of these natures or functions. The lack of an extensive theoretical discussion of these specific natures is one of the chief mysteries of *The Federalist*, explained only partially by Publius's admonition, already mentioned, of the difficulty in distinguishing between them.[22]

His reticence may be due not so much to lack of knowledge as to a desire to conceal as much as possible the non-republican origins of the separation of powers: the British Constitution, though having one republican branch, is not a form of republican government.[23] Moreover, the distinctive nature of the powers is most visible in the least republican branches – the executive and especially the judiciary, with its indirect mode of selection and good behavior tenure. In the duties of these powers one does not see "blind forces" at work, however much ambition and self-interest may be counted upon to guard the independence that is the necessary condition of the faithful discharge of their duties. For the highest duty of these branches, though not always the most urgent, is to instruct the citizenry in that "veneration" for the Constitution which is necessary to ensure that the "reason of the public" will "control and regulate the government," and that the government will control and regulate the public passions.[24]

Through the separation of powers, which elevates the Constitution above the people's passions without vitiating its claim to be the highest expression of their (reasonable) will, the American regime makes provision for the formation of character in its citizens. "Veneration" of the Constitution means acknowledging that it is the "reason of the public" and not its passions that should "sit in judgment" and "control and regulate" the government. Citizens are encouraged to think of themselves as judges and executives – and since the highest embodiment of the public's reason is the Constitution, as *founders* – instead of merely as legislators who have or reflect passions and interests that must be checked and either neutralized or compromised. Respect for the Constitution translates into moderation or self-restraint and the justice that is expressed in faithfulness to founding principles. Finally, then, veneration of the Constitution and its "inventions of prudence," foremost among them the separation of powers, must be seen in light of the ends or principles to which prudence ministers. It may be true that these inventions make statesmanship slightly less necessary in ordinary times of the nation's life; but they also provide a place for statesmanship in ordinary and extraordinary seasons, and charge American statesmen with a duty to the principles of the Constitution that is neither ignoble nor light.[25]

FROM NATURAL RIGHTS TO HISTORY

So far as *The Federalist*'s view of the separation of powers has been sketched here, it is clear that Wilson's account of it as a deduction from Newtonianism is perverse. Separation of powers is pre-eminently a device for moderating and refining popular government, and can more truthfully be said to point the way to statesmanship than to displace or subvert it. That Wilson never undertook a serious examination of *The Federalist*'s doctrine on the point, despite many asseverations as to its teaching, suggests that he prejudged the work as a child of its times that accordingly neither invited nor deserved close scrutiny. To put it differently, he considered the separation of powers, however understood, to be epiphenomenal. The real or fundamental obstacle to statesmanship in the American regime is not the system of separated powers but the purpose the whole system is designed to serve. It is the sun at the center of the orbiting powers that is the cause of the problem – not the Constitution so much as the Declaration of Independence that threatens the political life of the nation. For it is here that the eighteenth-century ideas of natural right and natural law, those reflections of the Newtonian *Zeitgeist*, dwell and reach out maleficently to stay the hand of statesmanship. "Liberty fixed in unalterable law," Wilson writes, "would be no liberty at all." Natural law, which he regards as the most unalterable of laws, is inconsistent with human liberty and especially with the freedom of action of statesmen. To open the American regime to progress therefore requires of Wilson a critique of the Declaration that severs the connection between the ends ordained there by natural law or right, and the means adopted to secure these rights in the Constitution.[26]

Wilson's reading of the Declaration – like his political science as a whole – begins with de-radicalization but ends in ever-greater radicalization. "We think of it as a highly theoretical document," he writes ironically, "but except for its assertion that all men are equal it is not."[27] Except for that "assertion," the Declaration is a practical document. If Wilson means that the "theoretical" argument of the Declaration was in the service of a practical end, namely, declaring independence, that is one thing; it would be an inadequate account of the Declaration's purpose, but it would be at least partially faithful to the facts. But he means something very different. The Declaration "names as among the 'inalienable rights' of man the right to life, liberty, and the pursuit of happiness, as does … many another document of the time; but it expressly leaves to each generation of men the determination of what they will do with their lives, what they will prefer as the form and object of their liberty, in what they will seek their happiness." Search the text of the Declaration as one will, there are not words "expressly" saying this; nor do the words imply it. Wilson's interpretation can be reconciled with the language of the Declaration only by supposing the ideas of inalienable rights and happiness to have been emptied of all objective content, effectively disconnecting them from the self-evident truth of human equality.

"That all men are created equal" is accordingly reduced from a self-evident truth or a Lincolnian "proposition" to a mere "assertion," as Wilson says so carefully.[28]

In fact it is the kind of "assertion" that has no place in a living, growing, constitutional order. "If any one ask me what a free government is," Wilson quotes Burke as saying, "I reply, it is what the people think so." The governed's consent to the "just powers" (only) of government is undoubtedly important to securing a free people's safety and happiness, but consent alone cannot turn an unjust regime into a just one. For Wilson, however, Burke's statement goes "to the heart of the matter" precisely because it reveals why the American regime must be sundered from the tradition of natural right, and why political science should not be the study of human happiness or regimes, but the investigation of "constitutional government" and its development. With every generation, the ends of government or the substantial definitions of liberty and happiness change, according to Wilson; and since forms are related to ends, the forms of government change in some measure, too. It follows that forms of government "do not affect the essence of government" but merely "exhibit the stages of political development." Monarchy and tyranny are behind us; they are historical curiosities or dead-ends, not ever-present possibilities or dangers in political life. The Declaration can therefore have no teaching concerning the best regime or even ranking legitimate regimes; it teaches only the "conception" or "large image" of what liberty is. Free government is what the people think it is, which means not that they can acquiesce in any regime (though there is some truth to that) but that they have the right "to adjust government to their own needs and interests." In Wilson's words, "government is a part of life, and, with life, it must change, alike in its objects and practices; only this principle must remain unaltered … that there must be the freest right and opportunity of adjustment." While this right is not grounded in human nature, it does justify itself by the fullest self-development of the individual, which is Wilson's problematic (because open-ended) replacement for natural right. "Constitutional government" is therefore not government according to the forms of the American Constitution or the ends of the Declaration, but government that respects the right of the governed to strike whatever balance may suit them between "the power of the government and the privileges of the individual."[29]

In deciding on this balance, the people must be guided by *leaders*, but neither the people nor their leaders should be guided by an abstract theory of rights, especially not by what Jefferson called the inherent and inalienable rights of man. At best the rights enumerated in the Declaration amount to a sort of eighteenth-century checklist of the people's general right to adjust government to their own satisfaction. Properly understood, the rights to life, liberty, and the pursuit of happiness are not natural but prescriptive, growing out of the long tradition of English constitutional history and of the Teutonic or Anglo-Saxon race's anciently cultivated capacity for self-government. These rights do not have to be granted or asserted because they are "taken for granted," as if no one doubted that "men should be free" or "their interests righteously adjusted to the powers of government." That they can be taken for granted is testimony to the English-speaking peoples' self-control and moderation, which is not the result of the statesmanship of the American or of any other founders, nor of the singular way of life inculcated by a particular regime. The character of the Americans, as colonists and as revolutionaries and as citizens, is due to the historical development of their race or people. Wilson remarks the aphorism of Walter Bagehot, "that it was no proof of the excellence of the Constitution of the United States that the Americans had operated it with conspicuous success, because the Americans could run any constitution successfully." Indeed so exiguous is the influence of constitutionalism on the American character that it is possible to imagine both the Declaration and the Constitution swept away, without at all affecting the people's capacity for self-government.[30]

To state it differently, constitutional government depends upon "a definite understanding" between governors and governed, but such an understanding presupposes a *people* capable of agreement. It presupposes what Wilson calls a "community" that is self-conscious and to some extent self-directive. A community is the product of shared history and common interests and habits and standards: "We know that body of persons is not a community along whose blood the same events do not send the same thrill, upon whose purposes and upon whose consciousness the same events do not make the same impression" – and here is the Darwinian imperative – "and who are not capable, at every turn in their affairs, of forming resolutions and executing measures which will meet the exigency." The form of modern constitutional government fitted to such a community is a late fruit, indeed is the last fruit, or political development. It is the *terminus ad quem* of an evolutionary process that began with government as the absolute master, first by force and later by intelligence; that saw government challenged by awakening peoples; and that culminated when "the leaders of the people themselves became the government," at which moment "the development was complete."[31] Resorting to any abstract, i.e., unhistorical, theory of rights interferes with this long, slow process of growth and leads either to social frustration and governmental paralysis, as was partially the case in America, or to tyrannical attempts to new-model society, as happened in the French Revolution. The latter provides ample material for Wilson's *argumentum ad horrendum* on this point, and he draws freely on the contrast between the American and French Revolutions to show the superiority of "constitutional precedents" to "democratic precepts," of "organic growth" to "discontent" and "revolution."[32]

That American government has had "a vital and normal organic growth," that it has had a *history*, proves that the Whig theory, though imbibed deeply by the founders, never left them so light-headed as to lose their "experienced eye for affairs" and "quick practical sagacity." They were, after all or perhaps before all, practical statesmen as well as devotees of Montesquieu and Hobbes. This was crucial in sparing America the trauma inflicted upon France by a class of revolutionary leaders whose devotion to abstract principle was not moderated by habits of self-control and patience and by long experience in self-government. Nevertheless, the American founders *had* established a regime in which the people's right to adjust government to their own needs and interests – to the "felt necessities of the time," as Oliver Wendell Holmes, Jr., would later call it – was limited by the separation of powers (and committee government) in particular, and by government's duty to secure men's natural rights in general. On Wilson's analysis, it seems that government roped to the star of "abstract" natural rights must be either behind or ahead of the times, either lagging behind social and economic development or attempting to force progress upon an unready nation. Only constitutional government dedicated to the "freest right and opportunity of adjustment" can hope to keep pace with progress, to distribute its benefits evenly and efficiently. Political liberty in Wilson's definition is both the right to make this adjustment and "the best practicable adjustment." It is the gap between the two that creates the decisive need for the new statesmanship of progress.[33]

LEADERS OF MEN

Wilson explains his views in a remarkable lecture and essay he called "Leaders of Men," which is worthy of extended consideration. He begins by distinguishing the statesman from the man of thought, although both are in some sense "leaders of men." As it is "the estimate of the world" that gives words their signification, however, Wilson accepts the view that the leader of men is the statesman who acts, rather than the man who writes books. The distinction is not, as it may at first appear, between practice and theory. That "the true philosophy of government can be extracted only from the true history of government" means that the traditional effort to understand politics in light of permanent standards of right and wrong – that is, of natural right – must be abandoned, and with it the problem of mediating between what is always and everywhere right, and what is right or desirable here and now. Instead, the problem becomes to distinguish between the statesman and the "literary man," the man who writes novels, who cultivates "the nice fashions of literary dress," who adores "artistic completeness of thought and expression." Why does the problem take this form? History and poetry both advance claims to understand political things, and poetry was traditionally understood to have superior credentials, insofar as it could grasp "universals" in a way that history, being the chronicle of mortal men and perishable deeds, could not. But Wilson, denying the existence of universals (properly speaking), undercuts poetry's superiority: no longer can universals be captured in particulars, in the manner of poetry; rather, particulars *constitute* the only intelligible universal, which is the rational unfolding of history, or progress. This is the ground of Wilson's superordination of history, or the philosophy of history, over poetry; but precisely because both history and poetry deal with particulars, there remains a need to discriminate between the understandings of the man of action and the literary man.[34]

The activity of both types, Wilson writes, is a kind of "interpretation." What marks the interpretations of writers is a love of "proportion," whereas men of action are obliged to neglect proportion. The difference is not between contemplating and acting, but between having certain literary "sensibilities" and lacking them. The literary man is a "sensitive seer" whose imagination can bring to life a thousand characters with a thousand different motives not his own; this "subtle power of sympathy" affords him a "Shakespearean insight" into the hearts of individual men. By contrast, the leader of men has a "sympathetic and penetrative insight" not into individual secrets but into the motives that move men "in the mass." His sympathy is with what "lies waiting to be stirred" in the minds of "groups and masses," and is oriented to command, not to service.[35] Again, the literary mind or "temperament" is said by Wilson to conceive "images" that are "rounded, perfect, ideal," "instrumental to nothing, sufficient unto themselves." (Of course these images have no existence independent of their conceivers; they are "outlooks," "such stuff as dreams are made of.") The leader of men, on the contrary, conceives "principles," which are "threads to the labyrinth of circumstances" – not self-sufficient "unities" that could function as arbitrary ends, but indications of where he has already been, at once bearing with them the accumulated knowledge of the past and warning him not to attempt to return to the past or to retrace his steps beyond what is necessary to open a new vista.[36]

The significance of this for statesmanship is nicely elaborated in another of Wilson's metaphors:

> The captain of a Mississippi steamboat had made fast to the shore because of a thick fog lying upon the river. The fog lay low and dense upon the surface of the water, but overhead all

was clear. A cloudless sky showed a thousand points of starry light. An impatient passenger inquired the cause of the delay. "We can't see to steer," said the captain. "But all's clear overhead," suggested the passenger, "you can see the North Star." "Yes," replied the officer, "but we are not going that way."

The moral: "Politics must follow the actual windings of the channel: if it steer by the stars it will run aground."[37] In Wilson's hands, the familiar ship of state becomes a riverboat, and the great ocean which provided challenge – but also immense latitude of action – to the statesman, is reduced to a meandering but confined waterway. There is a definite current, a direction of flow to the river; the great stream of time has a destination, a meaning. To be sure, it may be necessary to outpace the current sometimes in order to avoid shoals and hazards; and these hazards, as well as the sinuous course of the river itself, will have to be scouted to guard against unhappy surprises. But celestial navigation is not only useless but positively harmful to the negotiating of a mighty river whose bed has been carved from the earth by slow, steady processes at work for ages. Abstract principles or proportioned images, to bring the moral home, cannot be a proper guide to political action for a social organism that lives and grows by slow evolutionary adaptation to changing historical conditions.[38]

The work of the statesman is accordingly a kind of compromise, even as "all growth is a process of compromise" between organic forces and environmental or physical forces. Compromise in politics need be no more "dishonest" than in the biological growth of an organism, so long as this single condition is met – "if only it be progressive." Wilson's political career, in particular his great fall in the battle over the Treaty of Versailles, does not need to be clarified by psychohistory, provided that this fundamental limitation on his willingness to compromise, along with the general bearing of his political thought, is understood in its full significance. In Wilson's words, the task of the statesman is to read and interpret the "common thought" with a view to ascertaining "very circumspectly the *preparation* of the nation for the next move in the progress of politics." The object of course is not to counsel "a timid standing still for fear of possible mistakes," but "to point out the way of progress." The statesman's virtue, in a comprehensive sense, is "that wise sort of boldness which can afford to make mistakes because it knows what is essential and guards that from risk while it ventures all else for the sake of liberty and a freer course for reform." When "advance or catastrophe" is the choice, the responsible statesman must insist on advance, all the while admonishing his people in the cardinal commandment of the new morality: "*political sin* is the transgression of the law of political progress (rightly understood)."[39]

For the most part, the law of progress ("rightly understood") mandates "slow modification and nice all-around adjustment." Society is an organism, and must be vital in all its parts or else be stunted and deformed; development must therefore touch all regions, classes, and interests as equally as possible. But since the social organism is composed of a multitude of actual human beings, it is the majority that must and should rule, if only in the limited sense "that no reform may succeed for which the major thought of the nation is not prepared." A society or people being held together by habit – really by a habit of thought, a *Volksgeist* – it behooves the statesman to see that legislation stays near it. "The ear of the leader must ring with the voices of the people." This does not mean that the leader must echo what he hears: legislation can advance and modify habit, but it must always harmonize with the "constituent habit." There is room for "initiative" but not "novelty," for "interpretation" but not "origination." The leader is adjured to "discern and strengthen the tendencies that make for development," to distinguish the permanent and progressive forces from the transitory and reactionary ones, and to encourage the former.[40]

Progress, however, does not always dictate that the leader should appear in the "harness of compromise." "Once and again one of those great Influences which we call a *Cause* arises in the midst of a nation." The unharnessed, the authentic leader of men is the champion of a cause, the reformer who stands for a "political or moral principle" that he demands to be recognized by the majority. The rallying point for reform, or the banner under which his principle marches, is a *vision of the future* – an understanding of the direction that history is about to take, at once an extrapolation from and transformation of present trends.[41] The term "reformer" is apt, for it is as spokesman for a cause that the leader exercises the highest kind of statesmanship – quickening the conscience of society and freeing it from the sluggishness of all self-interest and partial attachments, what Nietzsche called "the spirit of gravity." In the moment of freedom offered by political idealism, the leader is free to re-form the people in the image of his vision. At that moment "men are as clay in the hands of the consummate leader," writes Wilson, and his is the "*power* which dictates, dominates." But it is not a form as such that the leader impresses on the clay; it is only "the application of force," a kind of inertia, a way of *moving* masses of men at the same time and speed and direction, like a flock of geese. "Form" in Wilson's understanding emerges from or is reducible to matter in motion, that is, in historical motion. "Get the country *moving* again" is therefore the characteristic call for statesmanship understood as, and limited to, leadership of the Wilsonian kind. But precisely in Wilson's identification of form with a law of motion (albeit historical motion), we see, to paraphrase Lincoln, that there is not such a Newtonian in the nation as Wilson, after all.[42]

Since the "forces of public thought" tend to be blind forces, it is up to the leader to give them "vision" both in the sense of the ability to see and of the "vision" given them to be seen. He stimulates their ability to see by opening them to movement, to progress – by fostering a confidence in the beneficence of Hope and Change. What he presents to their view is the sharp demand for progress together with a vague description of the perfected arrangements to come, all of which is clinched by the concrete example of his own faith, and by the earnest of his moving, not to say transforming, rhetoric. Hence the leader becomes a kind of poet for a new society, the herald of a new age and freedom, whose poetry is concerned as much with himself as with the next stage in the advance, or is concerned with himself for the sake of the next stage. That is to say, the leader *qua* poet is indispensable to the leader *qua* politician: his poetry must create and sustain the "image" of leadership, for only by serving history can poetry now be justified. The leader therefore re-creates himself as an imagination-capturing avatar of the dawning spirit of the age, so that to believe in him is to have, if not eternal, at least evolutionary life. Broadly considered, leadership is thus a way to engage public passions through an appeal to the public imagination that seeks to lift men from the Hobbesian realm of interest and necessity, toward the realm of true human freedom that lies at the end of history. "That is the whole thing that we are constantly fighting with," Wilson told New York Democrats in his first presidential campaign, "to keep down, to ride down, to suppress our own ambitions and our own selfishness. In order to do what? In order to ride higher. In order to see more of the Empyrean. In order to make a longer flight."[43]

In the meantime, reform is kept from being revolution by its connection to the people. If "vision" is one of the characteristic virtues of the new progressive statesmanship as it was conceived by Wilson – and as it continues to be understood in our time – then we have arrived at another of these modern virtues, "compassion." Leadership is a matter of "sympathetic insight," really of "a sympathy which is insight" into the heart (not the mind) of a people. Such sympathy, whether conscious or unconscious, allows the leader to move with the common impulse and to feel the common feeling, without becoming common himself. It is the function of the political party as Wilson saw it to provide the mechanism to effect this sort of fellow feeling, to sum up the concerns and desires of a vast nation so that its leaders would not become alienated from it. At the same time, the party serves as a conduit for the organizing vision of the leader – as the extraconstitutional or informal form that organizes motion in the nation as a whole.[44]

But at bottom the leader's sympathy or compassion for the led is his way of staying grounded in the evolution of the community; it is what keeps Wilson's doctrine of leadership from becoming Leninism. Sympathy or "common counsel," as he also calls it, assures the *timeliness* of reform; it ensures that "no man thinking thoughts born out of time can succeed in leading his generation," by *binding* him to his generation. Compassionate leaders are therefore "the more sensitive organs of society," the men who pick up "some principle of equity or morality already *accepted* well-nigh universally," but not yet risen to consciousness. Their task is to unlock the hearts of the people, to "formulate and make explicit" what lies "inchoate and vague" in the general sense of the community. At first society will resent the leaders' intrusiveness, even as we resent "the start and irritation of a rude and sudden summons from sleep." But once awakened, society will adjust to the situation and meet the "necessities of conduct" revealed to it.[45]

Hence "no cause is born out of time," Wilson declares, and every reform is "the destruction of an anomaly" or "the wiping out of an anachronism." This holds great significance for the reformer himself, because however great he may be, in the final analysis his greatness has very little to do with himself. He is produced by the occasion, even if in his reforms he gives little thought to occasion. Great reformers are "early vehicles of the Spirit of the Age," but nothing more. Their particular virtues are vision and compassion, which make for excellence in interpreting the common thought, but not excellence in deliberating about the means most conducive to the common good. The words and deeds of Washington or Lincoln – or, for that matter, Wilson himself – cannot be clarified or made intelligible on the basis of prudence and greatness of soul; instead, they must be understood as a form of the people's self-expression through the personality of their leader.[46] To quote Wilson in his 1912 presidential campaign: "I have often thought that the only strength of a public man consisted in the number of persons who agreed with him; and that the only strength that any man can boast of and be proud of is that great bodies of his fellow citizens trust him and are ready to follow him." The leader cannot do without his followers, even as the followers cannot do without their leader. "For the business of every leader of government," he averred, "is to hear what the nation is saying and to know what the nation is enduring. It is not his business to judge *for* the nation, but to judge *through* the nation as its spokesman and voice."[47]

The democratic statesman's duty, then, is quite different from how Lincoln conceived it. The leader's duty is not to recall the people to the moral truth in virtue of which they live, move, and have their being, but to follow them as their habits and thoughts progressively adumbrate the judgments of history. Although great leaders are "born of the very times that oppose them," Wilson writes, "their success is the acknowledgment of their legitimacy." To triumph is to be right; or, at best, to be right guarantees that one will eventually triumph. The two formulations are in practice the same, since the ultimate test of justice remains success, i.e., historical vindication. As Wilson admitted before the election in which he would first become President, "I would a great deal rather lose in a cause that I know some day will triumph than triumph in a cause that I know some day will lose."

One might have expected a statesman to say he would rather lose in a just cause than triumph in an unjust one. But Wilson, the Hegelian Darwinist, trusts in the survival of the morally fittest. And who are the morally fittest? Why, those who survive, of course. There is implicit also in this desire for a final reckoning and a once-and-for-all vindication not a little Christian eschatology – except that the judgment which Christianity reserved for the next world, Wilson obtrudes into the petty pace of this world. Even when seeking to deny it, he admits it. "Practical leadership may not beckon to the slow masses of men from beyond some dim unexplored space or some intervening chasm; it must daily feel under its own feet the *road* that leads to the goal proposed, knowing that it is a slow, a very slow, evolution to wings, and that for the present, and for a very long future also, Society must *walk*...." Yes, society must walk, and for a very long time to come; but *someday it will fly*. The "evolution to wings" lies at the end of a long road, but society can walk that road, all the while preparing itself for the great metamorphosis. "The goal of political development" Wilson affirms, "is identical with the goal of individual development. Both singly and collectively man's nature draws him away from that which is brutish towards that which is human – away from his kinship with beasts toward a fuller realization of his kinship with God." Translated into political terms, the peaceful rule of common counsel "is an earnest of the ascendancy of reason over passion."[48]

Political development will be completed when this earnest is made good, when reason *is* finally ascendant over passion. At that moment, when the final and irreversible victory over passion has been won, the political problem, the human problem, will be solved. But with such exalted and providential goals comes the inevitable temptation to embrace immoderate means to immoderate ends. Or to put the shoe on the other foot, to defer and surrender to the stronger immoderation of some other group, regime, or cause. Just how bitter is this fruit of the tree of historicist "knowledge" we are only now learning. Far from containing or fulfilling the knowledge of good and evil, it turns out to hold only confusion and a kind of moral nescience. If we are not to add to this bitterness the cup of our own degradation, we must be prepared to face the worst in a spirit of noble defiance.[49] But first it is necessary to reclaim the principles that make possible and intelligible that defiance – to return from the statesmanship of progress to the statesmanship of natural right.

CHAPTER NINE

CONSTITUTIONAL DECLINE
AND THE ADMINISTRATIVE STATE

IN THE FINAL THREE DECADES of the twentieth century, a great wave of democratization (the third one, by political scientist Samuel Huntington's count) swept over the world. In one unlikely country after another, old tyrannies or oligarchies expired and new popular constitutions were established. Russia, Turkey, Mongolia, South Korea, the Philippines, Nigeria, Chile, Brazil, Hungary, Poland, and scores of others turned into democracies with free elections and guarantees of human rights. Francis Fukuyama, in a renowned article in *National Interest* in 1989 and later in book form, pronounced this extraordinary moment "the end of history." He borrowed the term from the philosopher G. W. F. Hegel but gave it an updated meaning: the end of history implied not only the end of philosophy – that the fundamental questions about justice, freedom, and nature had been answered – but also the end of politics, insofar as the worldwide triumph of liberal democracy confirmed that the "final form of human government" had arrived. Though Fukuyama allowed for some temporary retreat at the margins, he seemed sure that aristocracy, monarchy, oligarchy, and tyranny had no future: the future belonged to liberal democracy. Political scientists who specialized in comparative politics turned this confidence into a theory called "democratic consolidation," which purported to explain how these new democracies would mature, through several stages and numerous difficulties, into stable, prosperous, liberal regimes even as had the old, mostly Anglophone democracies in previous centuries.

In the first decades of the twenty-first century, however, the democratic tide went out. Young liberal democracies lost their bloom – Russia and Turkey became conspicuous backsliders, and all the hopes invested in Communist China's liberal evolution came a cropper. Political scientists discerned a powerful new wave of populism or "authoritarian populism" surging in to replace the former democratic currents. In his book with the revealing title *The People vs. Democracy* (2018), Yascha Mounk writes of the process of "democratic deconsolidation" – of formerly solid or at least solid-looking democracies slipping away in Turkey, Hungary, Poland, India, the Philippines, and around the globe. He and many other observers point to ominous "populist" developments – Brexit in Great Britain, Marine la Pen's rise in France, and above all Donald J. Trump's ascension to the White House – posing a clear and present danger even to some of the world's oldest democracies.[1]

From Plato to the American Publius, the older political science would not have been surprised by the need to measure decline as well as advance, to treat disease as well as political health. They faced squarely the unpleasant truth that everything that comes into being passes sooner or later out of being. "If Sparta and Rome perished," asked Rousseau, "what state can hope to survive?" They taught that forms of government are a kind of partnership in justice, distinguished by who gets to rule and for what purposes – both the rulers' identity and the rulers' goals being aspects of justice. Different regimes have different opinions about justice, whether one, few, or many should rule, and whether they should rule for the rulers' good alone or for the common good. Such differences give rise to a variety of forms of government with a corresponding variety of strengths and weaknesses. Often their greatest weakness is the flip side of their greatest strength or of their most emphatic and obvious characteristic – the partial or narrow view of justice they hold and incorporate into their laws and customs.

A great legislator's or founder's task was in part to correct his society's bias, to enlarge or moderate its too partial and therefore partisan opinion of justice, into something more complete, more reasonable, and more stable. The hope, too, was that a more stable and well-balanced form of government would make for a more enduring country. Aristotle and Cicero sought for this saving prescription in the ideas and institutions of the "mixed regime," mixing the few and many, rich and poor, as well as their respective opinions of justice, into one form of government. They called this form of government a republic. America's founders sought a similar republican outcome not by explicitly mixing social classes and claims to rule but by moderating the claims of the few and the many indirectly, incorporating them into a common opinion of justice based on equal natural rights, the consent of the governed, and a limited social compact. As the means to secure those ends, the founders devised a republican Constitution with free elections and the rule of law, and with such auxiliary precautions as federalism, checks and balances, and, above all, the separation of powers.

Neither that Constitution nor that opinion of justice is particularly healthy today. The intense and increasing polarization of our politics is only the most obvious sign of that, and the process of polarization began decades before President Trump's election. American government suffers wider and deeper dysfunctions, too, which suggest that the health of the constitutional system as a whole ought to be an urgent concern of citizens, statesmen, and political scientists. It used to be expected that the Congress would pass laws, the president would execute them, and the Supreme Court would interpret them in individual cases. It used to be expected that the national government would stick to the great and pressing objects of the nation's business, and leave state and local governments to handle the rest of the people's business. In the early nineteenth century, Alexis de Tocqueville painted in *Democracy in America* the classic picture of American politics as combining centralized (national) government with decentralized (state and local) administration. Later in that century, James Bryce in *The American Commonwealth* (1888) took a more minute view of American political institutions, dilating on new problems like big-city government and the flourishing, and in some respects corrupting, system of political parties. Yet more than a century after its founding and a generation after its great testing in the Civil War, the constitutional system in its lineaments, particularly federalism and separation of powers, Bryce found to be stronger than ever. Most twenty-first-century political science textbooks present the Constitution's broad framework as though it were still thriving, however modified or improved by its encounter with modern problems. (This obliviousness is one reason such books are so sterile and lifeless.) It is obvious to even a casual observer, however, that this is not the way the federal government operates anymore.

Congress rarely rouses itself to legislate in the grand, deliberative sense of old. Plenty of laws or rather "regulations" are added to the Federal Register every year, but not by Congress deliberating more or less in the open (including in committees), but by unelected civil servants whose presumptive wisdom apparently would be compromised if brought into too close contact with the governed and their representatives. Congressmen and senators spend their time raising money for reelection, acting as ombudsmen for their long-suffering constituents, harassing the executive branch's political appointees, and conducting oversight hearings of the rule-making agencies, a pastime that justifies renewed attention to the dictionary's first definition of oversight, "failure by omission." Serious lawmaking, the kind involving large moral and political questions, is increasingly the province of the judiciary. Forget constitutional amendments – they went out when the living constitution came in. America's abortion laws (so to speak, for the point is they aren't *laws*) are created and policed by the Supreme Court, actually by a changing majority of five justices, which is to say, by the decisive vote of a single justice, for a long time Anthony Kennedy, now apparently Chief Justice John Roberts. He manages voting rights and free speech, too. We owe our affirmative action regime to the credulity of Lewis Powell (who believed Harvard's account of its admissions process), faithfully channeled for another quarter-century by Sandra Day O'Connor. The president is left with two difficult tasks: to execute "the laws," that enormous, continually expanding, and ill-digested mass; and to speak and act for the nation by claiming his elusive "mandate," i.e., by leading public sentiment, a task often indistinguishable from following public sentiment. No wonder that modern presidents turn increasingly to foreign policy, where they have greater independence, and to the "pen and phone," in President Obama's oddly pathetic boast, that is, to the use of executive orders and presidential cajolery.

The balance of power between the branches has been thrown off, to the advantage of the unelected parts of government, the judiciary and the bureaucracy. But just as striking is the *maldistribution of powers*, the mixing and confusing of governmental functions, which has resulted. Together, the two disorders amount to an operational definition of "the administrative state," an ugly and unedifying term referring to the centralized administrative power that modern American liberalism has intentionally added to the national government over the past century, particularly in the 1930s and again in the 1960s and 1970s. Republicans are not innocent in this matter – Eisenhower and certainly Nixon have much to answer for – but they had the excuse of trying to compete politically with the liberals, who came up with the idea and pushed it repeatedly to novel extremes. Of course, not all accretions of power to the federal government were unwise or ill-intended. For example, as interstate commerce came to involve railroads and airplanes, not to mention radio, television, and the internet, some increases in national regulatory capacities were necessary and prudent. So long as whether and how to make these accommodations with modern life remained statesmanlike judgments, the new regulatory authority effectively remained within the horizon of the limited government established by the founders' Constitution. When "administration" became the object of a new science divorced from politics and practical wisdom, however, it effectively became part of a new constitution – the "living" or progressive constitution – striving to supplant the old one. At the point when the ambition to regulate in detail the social and economic life of the nation – the ambition to establish full-blown "centralized administration," which Alexis de Tocqueville had denounced as tyrannical – came to the fore, one could say the administrative state was born.[2]

Liberal politicians rarely defend "the administrative state," however, in those words. The term suggests a locus of power independent of the people's control. Resorting therefore to euphemisms, they laud the "experts" in the agencies and exhort public opinion to "follow the science." In their own way, these euphemisms remind us that the original philosopher of such a political order – featuring the key role of an unelected and expert civil service, advising the prince (for this was a constitutional monarchy, not a democracy) and constraining and guiding the legislature – was Hegel, who called this regime "the rational state." For Hegel and his disciples, the rational state was the culmination of the science of the state (*Staatswissenschaft*); it was the first fully rational or scientific form of government. It was also the last form of government, the stopping point of constitutional development.

Here we return to Fukuyama's and modern political science's enthusiasm for liberal democracy and its inevitable spread. They effectively inherited their historical optimism from the Progressives who flourished three-quarters of a century before them, who in turn borrowed it (in a much democratized form) from Hegel and German political science. What they all had in common was the notion that the inevitability of progress had freed politics from an active interest in political and constitutional decline. What the ancients called the "cycle of regimes," the alternation of good and bad constitutions (or, in another version, the decline from the best to the worst regime), was at best ancient history, at worst a needless worry sure to mislead modern statesmen. Genuine political science, what one could call progressive or liberal political science, was concerned only with reform, that is, mopping up the last vestiges of corruption or imperfection on the way to a necessarily better, and more just, future regime. The living constitution would, or should, never die; it was guaranteed to overcome every political disease or disorder. The living constitution would gradually nullify and transcend the founders' Constitution, for example, amputating or curing the bad parts and incorporating any good parts. It should not have been surprising, then, that such a political science would be surprised by signs of decay among the world's liberal democratic regimes. Nor should it surprise that progressive thinkers have failed to discern the decay within the American constitutional order itself.

Addicted to reform, they presumed that every change, certainly every change that lasted, would be an improvement. Hostile to definite or permanent forms, they embraced "growth" as the goal of political development – the constant evolution of forms that amounted to more or less permanent transformation. They never worried about de-formation, the consequences of sapping and under-mining the founders' Constitution based on natural rights, with its statesmanlike attention to stability, energy, and liberty, and to the formal institutions of federalism and separation of powers. But it is clear that the administrative state's evolving practices and protean institutions have put severe pressure on our original Constitutional order, without having vouchsafed us a better one. After all, "the administrative state" is quite a come-down from "the rational state," suggesting that something has gone wrong somewhere, somehow. The former term's bleakness owes much to the great sociologist Max Weber's analysis of bureaucracy as a form of rational-legal "domina-tion" (*Herrschaft*), the rationality of which is merely technical or instrumental. Writing several generations after Hegel, Weber regarded Hegel's confidence in the ultimate rationality of History as a tragic blunder. The only rationality science could verify arose from the efficient application of means to ends, which ends were them-selves arbitrary, value-relative, and unverifiable by reason. Rather than in a triumph of freedom and rationality, History appeared to end with modern man imprisoned in an "iron cage" of cold, inhu-man, bureaucratic authority.

Believers in the living constitution never quite registered Weber's critique. They remained optimistic that "growth" would deliver America to a more complex, diverse, and interrelated place, which somewhat mysteriously would be a better, freer, more inclu-sive, and more just democracy. They averted their eyes from the ele-mentary fact that cancer cells grow, too; that it is necessary, therefore, to distinguish between healthy and unhealthy growth. To distinguish healthy from unhealthy growth they would need to understand the natural form and functions of the organism and its organs, and how to tell the difference between a flourishing and a diseased or dying democracy. In that spirit, we need to appraise the constitutional deformations wrought by modern progressive government, even as our statesmen have a duty to deliberate on how those injuries might be repaired and a healthy constitutional order restored. Here we con-sider one central problem, the status of the separation of powers.

SEPARATED POWERS
AND THE FOUNDERS' CONSTITUTION

Separation of powers was an idea accepted by all sides in the American founding, though its precise meaning remained unclear – at least until its famous exposition in *The Federalist*. The confusion over the meaning of separation of powers arose mainly from the status of the executive power: if the executive were subordinate to the legislature, as its name implies it should be, would not the legislature quickly overpower the executive? And in that event, how could the powers long remain separated? The initial context of this problem was the English Civil War, when the idea of separated powers first appeared in the pamphlets and essays of parliamentary writers who distinguished between legislative and executive powers in order to subordinate the executive to the legislative. The aim of such republicans as John Milton and Philip Hunton was to establish the rule of law by guaranteeing that those who made the law could not execute it, and that those who executed it could not make it. In effect, of course, the doctrine was anti-monarchical, inasmuch as it reduced the King to the status of an "executive" (that is, someone who carries out the will of another).[3]

Such a weak executive could hardly balance the power of the legislature, however. John Locke, addressing himself to this difficulty in his *Second Treatise of Government* (*ca.* 1688), added a third power to the balance to strengthen the executive. The "federative" power, as he called it, concerned foreign relations (the ability to federate or ally with other countries). Circumstances would frequently demand that these two powers be exercised for the common good, but in the absence of a standing law and sometimes even against the law. The justification for such extra-legal but prudent action Locke described as the "prerogative" power, yet another dimension of the executive. In this fashion, Locke acknowledged what was reasonable in the claims of each side in the English Civil War – the rule of law for the Whigs and of prerogative for the Tories. But he combined them along novel lines, freeing the former from excessive jealousy of the executive power and the latter from any pretensions of divine right.[4]

His doctrines lived on in the thought of the so-called "Commonwealthmen," a circle of eighteenth-century republican radicals who resisted the "corruption" of the House of Commons by the King and his ministers. Through their patronage power, the ministers could confer pensions and sinecures on complaisant members of Parliament, compromising the legislature's independence. The practice was denounced on this side of the Atlantic as well, and figured prominently in the Americans' criticisms of the British in the 1770s and in their distrust of the colonial governors appointed by the crown. Thus the separation of powers as Americans thought of it in the early 1780s harked back to the Commonwealthmen's fear of corruption and the seventeenth-century republicans' preference for a weak executive.

The framers of the Constitution of 1787 solved the problem of reconciling a strong, durable separation of powers with republican government by means of a new doctrine of constitutionalism. The most authoritative account of their achievement, *The Federalist*, provides two justifications for the separation of powers – liberty and good government.

PRESERVING LIBERTY

The liberty argument held that separation is needed in order to prevent tyranny. According to Publius's famous definition, "The accumulation of all powers legislative, executive, and judiciary, in the same hands, whether of one, a few, or many, and whether hereditary, self-appointed, or elective, may justly be pronounced the very definition of tyranny."[5] Tyranny is a danger because man's passions and reason are not perfectly harmonious; his reason may be distorted by desire. Although each man has by nature the rights to life, liberty, and the pursuit of happiness, he cannot secure these rights without joining together with other men to form a civil society, a people. Despite the legal unity of this people, it is composed of individuals whose impassioned opinions and interests divide them into majorities and minorities. As a precaution against injustice, therefore, the powers of government must be so divided that no man or group of men may wield all of them at once. This precaution would not be necessary if reason and passion *were* utterly harmonious, and if the whole comprising such reason and passion were *a priori* unitary rather than synthetic. These conditions, however, are unique to God, who alone justly unites the legislative, judicial, and executive powers in the same hands. The Declaration of Independence affirms this by appealing at once to "the laws of Nature and of Nature's God," "the Supreme Judge of the world," and "the Protection of Divine Providence."[6]

But men are prone to seek power, which has an "encroaching" nature, and *The Federalist* insisted that if the people's liberty is to be secure, they must take precautions against the oppressions of their governors. The republican form of government, the elective principle itself, is the main defense. But Publius also proposes "auxiliary precautions," chief among which is the separation of powers. This separation will be enforced not by "parchment barriers" but by reciprocal checks – the president's veto, for example, and the Senate's confirmation power – requiring that the powers (here, the executive and legislative) be partially mixed in order to be kept independent. "Ambition must be made to counteract ambition," in the words of *Federalist* 51. This "policy of supplying, by opposite and rival interests, the defect of better motives," is designed to reinforce the people's distrust of their representatives, but to increase the people's confidence in the Constitution.[7]

The last step is crucial. In every form of government, cautioned *The Federalist*, whichever branch is most powerful is, by definition, most dangerous to the people's freedom. In a monarchy, the executive ought to be feared. But in a republic, it is the legislature that ought to be distrusted, precisely because it is the branch ostensibly closest to the people. In the state governments, for example, with their weak executives, it was the legislative department that was "everywhere extending the sphere of its activity and drawing all power into its impetuous vortex." Therefore, Publius admonishes, "it is against the enterprising ambition of this department that the people ought to indulge all their jealousy and exhaust all their precautions." To protect their liberty the American people must insist on a limited national government, but that means the people must limit Congress, in particular; and *The Federalist* argues that the Constitution's improved separation of powers (along with bicameralism) will do just that.[8]

PROMOTING GOOD GOVERNMENT

The people should feel, then, not that the Congress is peculiarly theirs, as if the other branches belonged to someone else or to another class; but that what is theirs is the Constitution. In the course of *The Federalist*'s argument, this opinion that the Constitution is good because it is theirs is gradually transformed into the opinion that it is theirs because it is good. Publius's second, positive argument for the separation of powers is responsible for this transformation. For in addition to the negative function of preventing tyranny, the separation of powers actively promotes good government. That is to say, it allows the branches of the federal government to perform their respective functions well or at least better than they otherwise could. In the first argument, "power" is treated as a generic thing, abstracted from any ends for which it might be used, and regarded as a dangerous end in itself (hence its "encroaching" nature). But in the second, "power" is divided into "powers," acknowledging that each has a "nature" that aims at the excellent performance of certain definite functions.[9]

Contrary to Woodrow Wilson and later critics of the separation of powers such as James MacGregor Burns and Robert Dahl, the purpose of separation was not to produce governmental "deadlock" but to produce good government, which is not the same thing as simply popular or majoritarian government. These critics reduce the separation of powers to its negative role, equating separation with "checks and balances." Though it does help to check governmental tyranny and to balance the Constitution, separation is also designed to elicit sound and deliberate legislation, a firm and energetic executive, and an independent judiciary faithful to the Constitution.[10]

Publius treats these qualities as the consequences of certain carefully ordered quantities. He traces the national legislature's ability to deliberate well to the relatively small size and two-year term of the House of Representatives (allowing congressmen to learn their job and to discover the common interests that make general legislation possible) and to the smaller size and longer term of the Senate (making it a force for stability, moderation, and wisdom). He expects the executive to be "energetic" because it is unitary (i.e., filled by one ambitious person at a time) rather than plural; and it will have a "moral certainty" or at least a "constant probability" of being occupied by "characters preeminent for ability and virtue" because of the president's mode of appointment (the Electoral College), his four-year term of office, and his indefinite eligibility for reelection.[11] The independence and fidelity of the judiciary (the crucial third power of government hailed by Montesquieu) are guaranteed by the judiciary's indirect mode of appointment and good behavior tenure.

In each case, "fit characters" are summoned to the office by virtue of its formal characteristics – its job description, if you will – and the task of the people or their representatives is to select the best person for the job. If the negative function of the separation of powers depends on connecting "the interest of the man" with "the constitutional rights of the place," as Publius argues in *Federalist* 51, then the positive function requires that the *virtue* of the man be linked to the constitutional *duties* of the place. As *The Federalist* discusses each of the branches, it gradually brings the virtuous function of each power to the fore, describing the special contribution that each can make to good government. From this viewpoint, even the negative or checking function of separation is reinterpreted as something positive: for example, the president's veto is shown to be not merely a defensive tool but a means of improving the deliberations of the legislature by slowing, moderating, and correcting them.[12]

THE CONSTITUTION AS HIGHER LAW

Although "parchment barriers" are unreliable, the Constitution can be relied on because the people's – and in a different way, their representatives' – passions and interests will be tied to their opinion of the Constitution's importance for good government. As such, the

Constitution underlies both the positive and negative functions of the separation of powers. For without some idea of what the branches' duties are, it is impossible to know when and how to defend their rights and their independence.

This argument is not disproven by subsequent developments in American politics, in particular the rise of political parties. It is true that the Constitution of 1787 had to be amended to accommodate the practice of presidential and vice-presidential candidates running for office on the same party ticket. The Twelfth Amendment, ratified in 1804, changed the method of voting in the Electoral College by requiring the electors to cast separate ballots for president and vice-president. (Originally, the electors voted for two candidates for president, with the runner-up becoming vice-president.) But the point of the amendment was to make party competition compatible with the separation of powers by securing the president's independence from Congress. Without that change in the Constitution, the power of electing the president would effectively have devolved from the people (represented indirectly in the Electoral College) to the House of Representatives, where tie votes between presidential and vice-presidential candidates would be decided (as in the election of 1800), and where electoral mischief of all sorts was possible.

Present-day progressives, again following the lead of Wilson and the early Progressive political scientists, argue that political parties evolved in America in order to *overcome* the separation of powers, to bring the executive and legislative together in a parliamentary-style party program. Undoubtedly, political parties did foster more cooperation between the branches on questions of public policy and appointments. But the overriding consideration for Jefferson and his contemporaries was to ensure that the system of party government could operate safely and benignly in conformity with the general principles of the Constitution.[13]

The existence of parties showed that the constitutionality (not to mention the wisdom) of specific policies was disputable. But the condition of their civil disputation was, of course, that the overall goodness of the Constitution was considered indisputable. Here, too, the party system was dependent on the constitutionalism most clearly articulated in *The Federalist*, which held not only that the people's rights are best secured in a written constitution structured around the separation of powers (and around bicameralism and federalism), but that the people have correlative duties to (and under) that constitution. The supreme achievement of the framers' constitutionalism was to elicit what Publius in *Federalist* 49 calls "veneration" or "reverence" for the Constitution. By identifying the people's sovereign will not with its latest but with its *oldest* expression, the framers succeeded in identifying the people's authority with the Constitution, vintage 1789 (and as amended), not with the statutory law made yesterday by their representatives. In this manner, republicanism in America came to enshrine the rule of law and of the higher law of the Constitution; and the people whose choice had authorized the Constitution in the first place came to regard *it* as the lofty authority that should help guide their own choices and those of their posterity.[14]

THE ADMINISTRATIVE STATE

Nothing could be further removed from the reverence for the Constitution recommended by the framers and encouraged by the separation of powers than the tone adopted by the chief American theorist of the administrative state, Woodrow Wilson. In his first book, *Congressional Government*, published in 1885, he acknowledged that "opposition to the Constitution as a constitution, and even hostile criticisms of its provisions, ceased almost immediately upon its adoption; and not only ceased, but gave place to an undiscriminating and almost blind worship of its principles...." Reverence for the Constitution would be "blind worship" only if reason's possible sway in political life had been gravely underestimated by the framers, and the Constitution's goodness greatly overestimated. This was exactly Wilson's position. He advised his countrymen to undertake an unsentimental and "fearless criticism" of the Constitution. "The more open-eyed we become, as a nation, to its defects, and the prompter we grow in applying with the unhesitating courage of conviction all thoroughly tested or well-considered expedients necessary to make self-government among us a straightforward thing of simple method, single, unstinted power, and clear responsibility," he counseled, "the better."[15]

Wilson and progressives ever since have rejected the separation of powers in favor of the allegedly more scientific and up-to-date separation between politics and administration. "No living thing can have its organs offset against each other as checks, and live," he declared. "There can be no successful government without leadership or without the intimate, almost instinctive, coordination of the organs of life and action."[16] Concerning the specific reforms that would be necessary to achieve this coordination, his own thoughts underwent an evolution. As a young man, he favored a series of constitutional amendments designed to make congressmen, senators, and the president serve roughly concurrent terms, so as to increase the probability that one political party would gain control of the whole elective part of the government. In addition, he proposed that the president be required to choose his cabinet from the leaders of the majority party in Congress, who would be authorized to introduce legislation on the Hill, thus obviating the congressional committee system. Later in his career Wilson decided there was an easier way. Strong presidential leadership, combined with a highly developed and expert administrative apparatus, could succeed in liberating the national government from the straitjacket of separated powers.

THE TURN TO LEADERSHIP

In rejecting separation of powers in favor of the separation of politics and administration, Wilson reformulated the terms of political debate. As he saw it, living constitutions would need to eschew the former and embrace the latter separation. To follow the old scheme would be to invite politics with all its confusion, compromises, and corruption to invade the pristine laboratories of administration, dooming all hope of transformative change. By contrast, the new scheme would yield both "democracy and efficiency," as Wilson had redefined them. "Democracy" now meant the last and most perfect stage in the evolution of the State, in which the people's will was directly responsible for setting public policy. This new democracy would combine, as he said, "single, unstinted power" with "clear responsibility." "Efficiency," on the other hand, meant bringing "simple method" or the spirit of the new social sciences to bear on social problems old and new. He admitted that the countries with the most advanced and efficient administrative systems, Germany and France, happened not to be democracies. But he insisted that we could separate their autocratic politics from their scientific administrations, and safely learn from the latter without risking contamination from the former.

To be sure, the Progressive understanding of democracy already had its own suspiciously autocratic innovations. Although Wilson, Teddy Roosevelt, and other major figures talked a lot about "direct democracy" and argued for direct election of U.S. senators, direct primary elections, and other reforms, they found it hard to conceive of a truly progressive democracy that didn't somehow guide the *demos*. The immediate expression of popular will could be whimsical, after all, even from a people like the Americans who had racial and historical experience in self-government. Besides, the common man had to be guarded against manipulation by the rich and reactionary. To assure that the people's will was authentic and conveyed its permanent instinct for progress, therefore, it had to be mediated by *leadership*, a word that the Progressives assigned a new prominence and respectability in the vocabulary of American politics. As compared to "the masses," leaders were more closely attuned to the Spirit of the Age; they were able to distinguish the faint but swelling notes of progress from history's background noise. Their task was to prepare the people for the march into the future, to act as interpreters and spokesmen for the *Zeitgeist*; and, of course, actually to lead the way. But they went only where the "common thought" and "common impulse" were destined eventually to take the people. The founders' Constitution, with all its representative and deliberative processes, had sought to "refine and enlarge the public views." Progressive leadership declined that invitation. The leader's function was to mediate between the people and the future, to discern and follow their real historical vectors; to govern *through* the people's will, not to educate or elevate the people's will to a rational or a constitutional standard.[17]

In seeking "fit characters" to hold office in each of the three branches, the framers had sought statesmen whose virtues and talents would mesh with the duties of their office. What Publius calls "energy in the executive," for example, would issue mainly from the president's position in the constitutional order. *Leadership* in the executive, however, would depend almost entirely on the president's personal traits – his charisma, as we say today. Around his personal appeal to the voters and his "vision" of their future, he could build a political movement that would enable him to lead public opinion, and thus Congress, and thus the bureaucracy. Separated powers would at last be overcome. His principal role in office would be the same as in campaigning for office: he would be first and foremost a political or party *leader*, not a statesman concerned with his constitutional duties.

The reason for this, in Wilson's blunt words, is that the president "cannot execute laws." In practice, it now takes a dozen or so departments, many more executive (and a few independent) agencies, and millions of executive branch employees to execute the laws. "It is therefore becoming more and more true, as the business of the government becomes more and more complex and extended," Wilson wrote, "that the President is becoming more and more a political and less and less an executive officer." His executive powers drain away into the bureaucracy while "his political powers more and more center and accumulate upon him and are in their very nature personal and inalienable."[18] (In the new dispensation, it is not our rights but our charisma that is inalienable!) Even as, in Wilson's considered view, it is inevitable for society to become more complex and in need of governmental regulation, so it is inevitable that the president must take more and more of the responsibility for leading the country into the future, and less and less for executing the laws.

Presidential leadership has therefore a certain hollow ring to it, of which Wilson was well aware. The president is the only truly national leader, chosen by the whole people; and if he rightly interprets the people's inchoate desire for progress, "he is irresistible," for the people's "instinct is for unified action, and it craves a single leader." Therefore, in Wilson's famous phrase, the president's office "is anything he has the sagacity and force to make it."[19] But this means that in ordinary times, with ordinary men in the Oval Office, the presidency will not be the center of affairs and the dictator of events. Largely bereft of constitutional powers and duties, the office will be as small as the man who occupies it. And even on those occasions when the president is a man of great "personal force," his leadership will depend absolutely on his connection to the people, on his ability to read their passions and sentiments and stir them to action. Far from being the energetic and independent executive the framers sought, the president in the routine operations of his office will probably be a hostage to popular opinion.[20]

THE RISE OF ADMINISTRATION

Perhaps the deeper reason why the president cannot execute the laws, however, is that few laws in the old sense – general rules and settled measures directing action toward the common good – will be necessary. The progressives' assumption is that History ultimately will direct human action toward the common good. The task of law, in the progressive view, is to see to it that the inevitable growth of society is *managed* – that it be as evenly distributed as possible among classes and sections of the nation. In short, law is not based essentially on a choice or a compromise between rival opinions of the common good, clashing views of justice, or competing interests: law is less political than administrative. Its function is to help the administrative state. "Legislation is but the oil of government," as Wilson put it. "It is that which lubricates its channels and speeds its wheels; that which lessens the friction and so eases the movement."[21] What is important, then, about law is its effect on the efficient working of government.

Such law or regulation is necessary because progress brings with it problems, and more importantly, progress exposes as "problems" what had once been regarded as unhappy aspects of the human condition. Selfishness, poverty, war, as well as many lesser evils – these became social problems in the modern sense when the assumption was made that man had power and will sufficient to solve them, that man did not have to content himself with alleviating or enduring them. What made their designation as social problems plausible, in turn, was the assumption that the future would be very different from, and much better than, the past. (In fact, once these assumptions had been granted, it became *imperative* to solve these problems: people had a *right* to the abolition of poverty, war, pandemics, etc.) From that tenet it was easy to conclude that the distinction between "progressive" and "reactionary" ought to replace the distinction between good and evil, because the former distinction was not only the functional equivalent of the latter but was historically demonstrable, hence beyond doubt.

The dichotomy between politics and administration, which Wilson did as much as anyone to popularize, meant ostensibly that the *ends* of government (politics) ought to change easily with the changing sentiment of the majority, and that the *means* to those ends (administration) ought to be efficiently and equitably determined by the disinterested class of well-educated civil servants. "The predictable and very much intended effect of this division," writes Jeremy Rabkin in a perceptive essay, "was to narrow the range of political debate and limit the opportunities for political compromise, while elevating the authority of the ostensibly impartial administrative expert."[22] Both politics and administration served the cause of progress – the one through leadership, sounding the trumpet of advance; the other through pacifying and reordering the newly conquered territory. For that reason, administration could not be as "value-free" or "value-neutral" as the reformers sometimes let on: the administrative class was intrinsically hostile to anyone who did not accept the rationale of its own existence, namely, the progressive faith in History, and with it the experts' own expertness.

Hegel had explained in *The Philosophy of Right* that the civil servants would form the "universal class," that is, the only class whose object was the common good rather than its selfish class interest, or perhaps the only class whose particular interest consisted in dedication to the common good. In any case, the administrators asserted a twofold claim to expertness: a special or pure morality that only they could inject into a commercial or egoistic society, and a technical or scientific mastery of a particular subject matter. The two claims reinforced each other, and doubt about one usually implied, or was taken as implying, doubt about the other. (The first claim was doubtful on its face. The second on consideration that not every claim of expertness is backed up by an expertise, that is, by the existence of a genuine body of knowledge or skill. There are genuine experts in civil or aeronautical engineering. But does an expertise really exist in erecting "model cities" or winning the war on poverty or in exorcising "implicit bias"?)

Publius states, with Alexander Pope's aid, in *Federalist* 68: "Though we cannot acquiesce in the political heresy of the poet who says: 'For forms of government let fools contest – That which is best administered is best,' – yet we may safely pronounce that the true test of a good government is its aptitude and tendency to produce a good administration."[23] For Publius, the poet utters a heresy because there *is* a connection between a properly constituted republic and good administration: republican government under the Constitution will have a greater "aptitude and tendency" to produce good administration than would other forms of government. The crucial point, however, is that politics and administration, ends and means, cannot be strictly separated, especially in a democratic republic dependent on the consent of the governed. Whereas Wilson treats public policies abstractly, as experiments by well-meaning experts and reformers upon a malleable and progressive people, Publius emphasizes that public policies have to pass muster with a spirited people jealous of their rights and interests under "a limited Constitution." As Publius writes, "It is a just observation that the people commonly *intend* the PUBLIC GOOD. This often applies to their very errors. But their good sense would despise the adulator who should pretend that they always *reason right* about the *means* of promoting it." The people can err, and the powers of government ought to be separated both to protect against governmental – including legislative, that is, popular – tyranny, and to provide the time and institutions necessary to decoct "the cool and deliberate sense of the community" from its "transient impulse[s]" and "temporary delusion[s]."[24]

For Wilson, however, the people always (not "commonly") express the historical forces working for good, and the leader's task is only sifting the timely from the untimely impulses at work in them.

In the long run this means that all popular impulses are regarded as ultimately rational, that neither popular nor governmental tyranny is seen as a fundamental danger anymore, that separation of powers may safely be dispensed with, and in particular that the Congress may be – must be – entrusted with "complete and convenient" authority over the executive agencies.[25] "Complete" is not the same as "exclusive," of course, and Wilson did not envision the executive surrendering all executive authority. But with the advent of the administrative state, whatever power the executive retained over the agencies was bound to atrophy.

The administrative state was invented as part of the effort to replace an outmoded constitution with a new one, organized around a powerful centralized government retaining, at most, only the independent judiciary as a holdover from a principled separation of powers. The new government would feature a closely integrated executive and legislative, dominated in political or partisan matters by a president who could influence Congress through his leadership of public opinion, and on the administrative side by an elite of nominal experts nominally overseen by congressional committees and subcommittees. On many levels, this is a description of American national government today. From the framers' point of view, this picture represents an unhealthy breakdown in the separation of powers, among other grievous constitutional deformations. From the viewpoint of the advocates of the administrative state, it represents a stupendous breakthrough for enlightened political theory and practice.

The Constitution, as defended in *The Federalist*, presumed that in order to be respectable, republican government had to be good government. It had, that is, to secure private rights and the public good, rather than simply obey the majority's will. Furthermore, it presumed that man, as a creature of passions as well as reason, would often act rashly and unjustly if he were not taught or habituated to respect the moral law superior to his own will, the law he revered and venerated in the Constitution. But the progressive architects of the new order assumed that History itself guaranteed the victory of reason in politics. Granted, this victory would not be direct but dialectical, employing men's passions or will as the vehicle by which reason would progress, and assigning rationality, in the instrumental sense, to the administrative class. Actually, however, the doctrine encouraged the belief that in ordinary political life there was no compelling need for self-restraint, for the moderation of political passions, for the reasonable accommodation of prejudices. Practically speaking, no respect was owed to anything except the future – that dark source of a new enlightenment, in whose name and by whose light leaders and experts of all sorts were encouraged, in effect, to rule ordinary citizens.

The success of the politics of progress was, in Wilsonian terms, a token of reason's ascendancy over passion. Man seemed, so to speak, to be reducing the distance between himself and God, as his reason worked itself out in the life of the administrative state. This is a strange, unholy justification for bureaucratic rule, but perhaps, in the final analysis, it is the only plausible one.

CHAPTER TEN

FROM CITIZENSHIP TO MULTICULTURALISM

The citizens of the United States of America have the right to applaud themselves for having given to mankind examples of an enlarged and liberal policy – a policy worthy of imitation. All possess alike liberty of conscience and immunities of citizenship. It is now no more that toleration is spoken of as if it were [by] the indulgence of one class of citizens that another enjoyed the exercise of their inherent natural rights, for, happily, the Government of the United States, which gives to bigotry no sanction, to persecution no assistance, requires only that they who live under its protection should demean themselves as good citizens in giving it on all occasions their effectual support.

GEORGE WASHINGTON
letter to the Hebrew congregation
in Newport, 1790[1]

THIS BEAUTIFUL STATEMENT, part of George Washington's response to a letter from the Hebrew congregation of Newport, Rhode Island, congratulating him on his election as the nation's first president, reveals much that is distinctive, and noble, about American citizenship. Grounded in the natural rights of mankind and guarded by a written constitution, U.S. citizenship marked a new beginning in the world's long experience with civic membership.

218

The American revolutionaries' self-proclaimed *novus ordo seclorum*, a new order of the ages, was in fact largely an implication of their novel understanding of citizenship; for the Jewish community in Newport, as well as for many other Jews, Catholics, and Protestant dissenters who had fled the Old World for the New, an invaluable emblem of the new, American view of citizenship was the Constitution's simple but emphatic declaration that "no religious Test shall ever be required as a Qualification to any Office or public Trust under the United States."

Thus, George Washington, celebrating in 1783 the official end of hostilities with Great Britain, thanked his soldiers for accomplishing "the glorious task for which we first flew to arms," namely, "erecting this stupendous *fabrick* of *Freedom* and *Empire* on the broad basis of Independency" and "protecting the rights of human nature and establishing an Asylum for the poor and oppressed of all nations and religions." Later that year, he addressed a similar sentiment to new immigrants from Ireland. "The bosom of America is open to receive not only the opulent and respectable stranger," he wrote, "but the oppressed and persecuted of all nations and religions."[2] In the subsequent two centuries, the United States lived up to Washington's words, admitting a larger number of immigrants from a greater variety of nations and religions than any other country in the world's history, and generously extending – to some sooner, to others later, but eventually to all new Americans – the privileges of citizenship on an equal basis with the original inhabitants.

Living up to the promise of American citizenship, however, has not been easy or without struggle. In 1790, the same year that Washington corresponded with the Hebrew congregation of Newport, he signed the country's first naturalization law, which provided that any alien who was "a free white person" might apply for citizenship after two years' residence in the United States. Naturalization remained limited to whites until 1870. Slavery was not abolished in the United States until the Thirteenth Amendment was added to the Constitution (1865); blacks en masse were not recognized as citizens until the Fourteenth Amendment (1868) and were not guaranteed the right to vote until the Fifteenth Amendment (1870) – and their right of suffrage proved unenforceable in most Southern states for most of the twentieth century.[3] The first federal immigration law, which followed hard upon these constitutional victories on behalf of black Americans, was the Chinese Exclusion Act, passed in 1882 in order to prevent a further influx from China. Immigrant Chinese (as distinguished from their American-born children, who became citizens by virtue of the Fourteenth Amendment) were not made eligible for naturalization until 1943. White American women (and black women too, after the Fourteenth Amendment) were certainly citizens, but most were denied the right to vote and gained constitutional recognition of this right only with the passage of the Nineteenth Amendment in 1920.[4]

Other examples could be cited. The salient question, however, is not so much whether the United States ever fell short of its moral and political principles – it did, of course, many times – but what those principles were in the first place, and whether they are worthy of respect and allegiance today. For the contemporary controversies that rage over the meaning of American citizenship turn, to a greater or lesser extent, on the interpretation of those first principles; they turn in particular on the question of whether those original principles are so disfigured by racism, ethnocentrism, and other ills as to be unworthy or obsolete guides to our contemporary immigration and citizenship dilemmas. Many scholars argue, for example, that America's failures to live up to its formal principles of liberalism and republicanism are endemic, proving that the "failures" are not historical lapses or exceptions but are themselves the rule – or at least a rule: an alternative, competing vision of American citizenship, every bit as authentic and "American" as equality and liberty, perhaps more so. These "illiberal, undemocratic traditions of ascriptive Americanism," as Rogers M. Smith calls them, therefore do not represent unfortunate frustrations of American citizenship's logic, much less imperfect stages of its development, but instead are essential to it. As confirmation of their intrinsic role, Smith reports that these ugly traditions live on in contemporary efforts "to maintain white supremacy, to preserve old gender roles, to uphold Protestantism in public life," and in general "to resist many egalitarian demands in liberal and democratic ideologies."[5]

The same kind of critique inspires *The New York Times*'s 1619

Project, named after the year in which the first black slaves arrived in British North America, at Jamestown. Announced in the August 19, 2019, issue of the Sunday *New York Times Magazine*, memorializing the four-hundredth anniversary of the beginning of American slavery, this "major initiative" intended to "reframe American history by considering what it would mean to regard 1619 as our nation's birth year," as the magazine's editor, Jake Silverstein, wrote. The project was the idea of Nikole Hannah-Jones, a *Times* reporter, who in the opening essay ventured that "the year 1619 is as important to the American story as 1776." A few pages later she bluntly explained that importance: "Anti-black racism runs in the very DNA of this country...." If anything, her editor went further. In a rhetorical question he implied that the "unanimously celebrated" belief that July 4, 1776, is the nation's birthday is "wrong, and that the country's true birth date" was in August 1619. Chattel slavery "is sometimes referred to as the country's original sin," he asserted, "but it is more than that: It is the country's very origin. Out of slavery – and the anti-black racism it required – grew nearly everything that has truly made America exceptional...." In other words, 1619 is not "as important" as 1776; it is far more important and revealing. American slavery is the effectual truth of American freedom.

If the old principles are inherently flawed, then we need new ones – friendlier to participatory democracy, socialism, feminism ("maternal citizenship"), or multiculturalism ("heterogeneous citizenship"), to mention only a few of the leading contenders.[6] At the end of this chapter, I shall take up for criticism the last of these alternative theories, which is probably the most influential and carefully worked out of the lot. But first, the threshold objection – that, in theory and in practice, the country's professions of equal rights were shams or, at best, half-truths – needs to be met.

HISTORY AND THEORY

Although this style of objection comes today from the Left, its political origins in America go back to the antebellum defense of slavery, when Stephen A. Douglas, for instance, argued that the human equality proclaimed in the Declaration of Independence did not apply to all men, but only to white men. This was how the signers of the Declaration had understood it, he claimed, against considerable, indeed massive, evidence to the contrary. Nonetheless, he insisted that "this Government was established on the white basis. It was made by white men, for the benefit of white men and their posterity forever, and never should be administered by any except white men."[7] This was the real thing: white supremacy. Why the contemporary Left, or important parts of it, should be embracing (as historically correct though repugnant) a view of the Constitution originally propounded by the defenders of black slavery is an interesting question. It has much to do with the historicist temptation, the tendency to believe that everyone is a child of his times and that, for the children of any given time and culture, "whatever is, is good." How could eighteenth-century Americans, living amid many "illiberal, undemocratic traditions of ascriptive Americanism," including Negro slavery, not believe wholeheartedly in these traditions?

This is a temptation shared by some on the traditionalist Right as well. Willmoore Kendall, for example, the Yale political scientist who served as an original senior editor of *National Review*, delighted in arguing that equality, as an abstract political principle, had little to do with American life as it had actually been lived from the Mayflower Compact up to the Civil War, when, in his view, Abraham Lincoln "derailed" the American political tradition by turning abstract equality into its goal. Here is Kendall on the real meaning of equality in America:

> "Every Frenchman," Charles de Gaulle has written somewhere, "wants a special privilege or two; that is how he expresses his passion for Equality." "Every American," I suppose an equally cynical observer here in the United States might say, "wants a right or two that he is by no means willing to concede to everybody else; that is how the American expresses *his* passion for Equality."[8]

American life as it had actually been lived, Kendall insisted, was a tradition rife with *inequality*, expressed in racial segregation, denial of voting rights, malapportioned legislative districts, local mixtures of church and state, and the like. Whereas the Left despised these "Illiberal, undemocratic traditions," Kendall liked or at least defended them as examples of good, old-fashioned American constitutionalism, which he defined as "deliberative" but otherwise unprincipled majoritarianism.

On the Left and Right, then, one can find important thinkers prepared (albeit for different reasons) to baptize racist and other unsavory American traditions as authoritative expressions of American principles. One difficulty with so readily turning history into theory – identifying historical practice with organic political principle – is that it underestimates the permeability of tradition, or in other words, the ability of human beings to use their reason in order to change a tradition. Tradition itself, after all, is not a static thing; its greatest defenders have always emphasized that living traditions must slowly adapt to life's changing circumstances. What's more, tradition is never a unitary thing: Every vital tradition contains diverse, competing strands. Such diversity is necessary, in fact, in order that the tradition may survive, may adapt.[9] Diversity and changeability provide the openings for reason's critique – as well as its use – of tradition. For in order to choose among the conflicting strands of tradition, in order to decide which are worthy to survive, reason must have resort to some standard that transcends tradition as such.

In American life as it has actually been lived, racist and antiracist traditions (to take one example, and to simplify a bit) have coexisted and battled over many generations, but this does not make them equally legitimate, authoritative, or good. For example, the presence in the Constitution of certain compromises over slavery does not, ipso facto, turn slavery into a constitutional principle or the Constitution into a proslavery document. That these are "compromises," of course, can be known only by looking at them in the light of the Constitution's principles – of the regime principles that are more fundamental than statute or even constitutional law, because they set the ends or purposes of all such law. The brute fact of slavery's continued existence under the Constitution, in other words, does not settle the crucial question of whether slavery was regarded by the Constitution's framers as a necessary evil or a positive good, which can be approached only by looking at the moral principles – the ends or aspirations – incorporated in the government they founded.

Consider the Constitution's treatment of the slave trade. The Northern and Southern delegates to the Constitutional Convention could not agree to ban the slave trade immediately, but they compromised on a provision of the Constitution (Article I, Section 9) that would give Congress the power to prohibit the slave trade beginning twenty years later, and they guaranteed the deal by making that provision unamendable (Article V). Even the Southern delegates, notice, were prepared to see this international traffic in human beings come to an end eventually, as indeed it did when Congress banned it two decades later, in 1808. This was an important compromise precisely because a vital principle was involved. James Madison, himself a Southerner and a slaveholder, made this clear in *The Federalist* in his defense of the compromise:

> It were doubtless to be wished that the power of prohibiting the importation of slaves had not been postponed until the year 1808, or rather that it had been suffered to have immediate operation. But it is not difficult to account either for this restriction on the general government, or for the manner in which the whole clause is expressed. It ought to be considered as a great point gained in favor of humanity that a period of twenty years may terminate forever, within these States, a traffic which has so long and so loudly upbraided the barbarism of modern policy.[10]

This "unnatural traffic," as Madison went on to call it, ought to be prohibited for the same reason that slavery itself was reprehensible and unnatural: Slavery treated a "moral person" as a "mere article of property."[11] America's prohibition of the slave trade showed how decisively the principles of the Revolution – the basis of the new account of American citizenship – were able to abrogate or abridge old traditions and institute new ones.

The difficulty, to be sure, is that slavery and racism were not ended by the founders' actions. This consideration raises a second general reason why historical practice cannot simply be equated with a regime's principles, namely, that it is sometimes very difficult to live up to those principles. With republican government this is especially true. Now, with some exaggeration – never admitted by the 1619 Project, by the way – one might say that America began as a nation of slaveholders. Slavery was eventually made legal in each of the thirteen colonies. By the 1780s, however, slavery had been abolished in three states; by 1804, five others had adopted laws for gradual emancipation, and the Northwest Ordinance had forbidden slavery to spread into the trans-Appalachian territory from which five more states would eventually be formed. So considerable progress had been made. But the Union was left half-slave and half-free, and so it would remain until the Civil War. From a certain point of view, America's inability to live up to its principles of equality and freedom could be – often is – condemned as hypocrisy. This opinion was held by many abolitionists at the time, is held by many historians today, and could be said to be quasi-Kantian in character: If you allow your interests and circumstances to prevent you from doing what it is your categorical duty to do, the critics reason, then you are acting immorally.[12] In the case at hand, if the founders did not abolish slavery immediately, they must not really have been against slavery. QED.

Yet political life is not Kantian. Its morality is prudential, always pitted against the weakness of human nature and mindful of the circumstances (and consequences) of human choice, and therefore usually measured by slow progress toward the good. For this very reason, hypocrisy is not the worst of all moral conditions: hypocrisy is the tribute that vice pays to virtue, as La Rochefoucauld said famously, and thus is a recognition that virtue deserves honor. Besides, hypocrisy is not the best and certainly not the only explanation for slavery's persistence. Stephen Douglas raised the charge of hypocrisy in his campaign for the U.S. Senate in 1858. If the founders really did believe that blacks were "created equal" and had natural rights that white men were bound to respect, why did these statesmen not immediately abolish slavery in the United States? His Republican opponent, Abraham Lincoln, responded:

They [the signers of the Declaration of Independence] did not mean to assert the obvious untruth, that all were then actually enjoying that equality, or yet, that they were about to confer it immediately upon them. In fact they had no power to confer such a boon. They meant simply to declare the right, so that the enforcement of it might follow as fast as circumstances should permit.[13]

Once the moral end or goal was clear, the means to realize that goal could be found and employed "as fast as circumstances should permit." Prudence, not hypocrisy, governed the founders' thoughts as they attempted to put slavery on the course of what Lincoln called "ultimate extinction" – but without extinguishing the Union and the Constitution along the way.[14]

Yet taking the founders seriously means trying to understand their principles not simply in light of historical circumstances, but also as reasoned conclusions about the proper ends or purposes of political life. What were the moral ends or goals intrinsic to the Americans' new understanding of citizenship, and how were they justified? What was so novel about their precepts? To answer these questions, we need to begin with the ideas that served as the American founders' own point of departure.

CITIZENSHIP AND ITS DISCONTENTS

Who should be a citizen? This practical question, which in moments of political founding and revolution is extremely urgent, depends for a reflective answer upon a prior, more speculative question: What is a citizen? The English word is cognate with "city," a relation that is constant throughout the term's backward etymological journey through Anglo-French and Old French to the Latin *civis* (citizen) and *civitas* (city), and finally to the Greek *polites* (citizen) and *polis* (city). The citizen is part of the city, a partner or member in the political association or community. The city, which seems to have been a Greek invention (at any rate, the Greeks were the first to celebrate and study it), was distinct from other forms of human association then prevailing – families, villages, tribes, and empires. The city came to sight as an alternative to the primitive tribes or nations then ruling northern Europe, on the one hand, and to the cultured but despotic empires of the East, especially Persia, on the other.[15]

The city or *polis* came into being as a unification or completion of the smaller kinship associations of families and villages. These kinship associations shared not only bloodlines, as we would commonly understand them today, but also ancestral gods who presided over and consecrated the bloodlines. From the standpoint of the citizens themselves, then, a standpoint brilliantly captured in Fustel de Coulanges' enduring study, *The Ancient City*, the *polis* was an elaborate religious cult: a complex structure of civic, local, and ancestral gods, centering on the sacred fire in the family hearth and forming a pantheon peculiar to each city.[16] In the ancient world, every city had its own gods, and its citizens thought of the city as the special handiwork and protectorate of those gods. More specifically, they thought their city had been founded by a divine lawgiver or by a mortal ancestor who was later promoted to godhood (as discussed in Chapter Four). The constitutional law of every ancient city was therefore a species of divine law, vouchsafed not to mankind but to a particular people who became a people – as opposed to a mere alliance of families or villages – precisely by acknowledging common gods and receiving the same (divine) law. Every ancient people was therefore a kind of chosen people, whose deities demanded not faith or belief in particular doctrines but obedience to the city's laws. The citizen was a part of the chosen people, a sharer in the divine rites, a child and servant of the laws.

This is how citizenship looked to the citizens of ancient cities, but not how it looked to Aristotle, the first political philosopher to give a thematic account of citizenship. To be sure, Aristotle preserves a place for the gods in his discussion by holding that although man is by nature a political animal – an animal suited to live in a city or *polis* – cities do not exist by nature. They must be founded, and "the one who first constituted" a city, whether "the one" was a god or a man, "is responsible for the greatest of goods."[17] Moreover, priests were a necessary part of every city, and honoring the gods was a public or political function that should be carried out by citizen-priests, preferably chosen from those citizens "worn out with age."[18] In general, however, Aristotle regards the city not as something divine but

as something natural to man, even though it must always be instituted by one or more men using certain conventions, laws, and
customs.

The necessity of conventions in politics means that the definition of citizenship is disputable; someone who is a citizen under a
democracy would often not be a citizen under an oligarchical regime.
The disputability of citizenship tells us, however, something important about it: that the citizen must speak up for his definition of citizenship, that he must defend his own partisan view of it in terms of
the qualities or virtues that he can contribute to the whole city.[19]
Citizenship does not mean merely living or working in the city, then,
nor even possessing legal rights, and it cannot be defined simply as a
birthright, because though children may in one sense be citizens,
Aristotle observes, they are "incomplete" because of their inability
to share in "decision and office." Accordingly, citizenship means participation in ruling the city. For all practical purposes, then, the city
is its citizens or its citizen-body; the city of Athens was always called,
in Greek, "the Athenians." But "ruling" the city, especially in antiquity, implied not only the right or duty to own land, to vote, and to
hold office, but also to fight for the city as a citizen-soldier. Even
today, the citizen's right or duty to fight for his or her country can
color or influence the debate over citizenship, if only as an implicit
contrast between the motives of the citizen and the mercenary
soldier.

In democracies, which tend to have relaxed definitions of citizenship, children are still regarded as "incomplete" citizens because
they cannot adjudicate and deliberate well. In other words, there is
still a tension between being born a citizen and being able to be one,
and the more virtues that are required of the democratic citizen, the
more acute is the tension. This is a key admission, say the oligarchs,
the partisans of the few; for if being a citizen means being able to
rule well, then only those few who rule well should be citizens. But
if this oligarchical (more precisely, aristocratic) element in citizenship were carried to its logical conclusion, Aristotle warns, then a
man of truly outstanding virtue, so preeminently good and wise that
he deserves to rule like a god among men, would be entitled to rule

over the city as though it were his own household; and politics – and citizenship – would be altogether at an end.[20]

Aristotle moderates and improves the partisan definitions of citizenship by showing that neither being free-born (the democratic standard) nor being rich or virtuous (the oligarchic standard) can, taken by itself, secure the city's common good. In other words, citizenship must necessarily be based on a mixture of claims of freedom and claims of ability or virtue; the proportions of the mix will vary from city to city, depending on the quantity and quality of the potential citizens. Within a particular city, individual citizens will possess different skills or virtues, even as among sailors one is a pilot, another a lookout, and so forth. Still, the sailors' overall purpose is to preserve the ship, and similarly the citizens' purpose is to preserve the city, or more exactly, the regime or constitution (*politeia*) that makes them citizens and orders the city.

As there are many forms of regime (aristocracy, republic, etc.), so there are many forms of civic virtue. But the virtue of a good man (as opposed to a good citizen) is unchanging, and it is the good man's virtue that serves as the standard by which Aristotle judges the goodness of particular regimes and their definitions of citizenship. In light of this he urges founders and lawgivers to reform the "mix" of citizen qualities characterizing their own regime. Even in modern times, how a regime treats a good man – for example, how the Soviet Union treated Alexander Solzhenitsyn – tells us much about that regime. The great difficulty in politics, needless to say, is that good men are hard to find! And so Aristotle emphasizes that, in most cases, regimes should aim not at unfettered rule by the best men but at the rule of good laws. In turn, wise laws will be able to educate or form citizens, enabling them to rule and to be ruled in turn in the spirit of obedience to the laws.[21]

Politics among citizens consists precisely in this alternation of ruling and being ruled, under law. Mere subjects, as opposed to citizens, experience being ruled but never the activity of ruling, certainly not in the exalted sense of free self-government. Thus active citizenship among a free and relatively equal body of citizens – the phenomenon described by Aristotle – is quite different from the perpetual subjectship that obtained under the absolute monarchies of early modern Europe, and even under the moderate monarchy of Great Britain in the eighteenth century. In practice, of course, most regimes with citizen-rulers (whether few or many – whether oligarchies or democracies) tend to agree that citizenship is inherited, that a citizen is born of citizen-parents. Such is, one might say, the citizen's view, *qua* citizen. He views the world of his city, whether oligarchy or democracy, as though it were *the* world.[22] The U.S. Constitution requires, for instance, that the president be a "natural born Citizen," and we speak of immigrants undergoing "naturalization," as though they were being made citizens not by law, but by nature – as though they were about to be born again as native citizens. But the principle of birthright citizenship, if traced back far enough, contradicts itself; eventually one arrives at the very first generation of citizens, who perforce were made, not born.[23] Consider the case at hand: George Washington and the other members of the founding generation were not born U.S. citizens. They made themselves citizens by throwing off their "perpetual" allegiance to Great Britain and making, that is, founding, the United States.

THE INNOVATION OF AMERICAN CITIZENSHIP

In one sense, Washington sought to establish a very different kind of citizenship, a very different kind of regime, from the types Aristotle had evaluated in his *Politics,* not to mention from the contemporaneous monarchies of Europe, each with its established church. Washington once explained why he took part in the Revolution: "The establishment of Civil and Religious Liberty," he wrote, "was the motive which induced me to the Field."[24] Civil liberty required finding a new ground for law and citizenship that would protect decent politics from arbitrary claims of divine right. Religious liberty meant separating church membership from citizenship in order to protect the conscientious pursuit of true religion from civil or ecclesiastical tyranny.[25] Civil liberty and religious liberty have the same root, a theoretical or philosophical insight, as we argued at length in Chapters Four and Six: the doctrine of natural rights, which Americans embraced forthrightly in the Declaration of Independence.

To get the gist of that argument, consider once again the striking image of equality that Thomas Jefferson adapted from Algernon Sidney: "the mass of mankind has not been born with saddles on their backs, nor a favored few booted and spurred, ready to ride them legitimately, by the grace of God."[26] In other words, no human being is by nature the ruler of another, in the way that any human being is by nature the ruler of a horse. Horses are suited by nature to be ridden by human beings, but no human being is suited by nature to be ridden – or owned, bred, and sold – by another human being. Nor are any humans born "booted and spurred," ready to govern "by the grace of God" or by divine right. Members of the human species stand in a natural equality with one another, which means that each is naturally free of any other human's authority. From this natural equality arise natural rights to life and liberty, and to the enjoyment of life and liberty in "the pursuit of Happiness." Life, liberty, and the pursuit of happiness are nature's gifts to the human species, not merely to white males: blacks and women can ride horses, too.[27]

As a consequence of humans' natural equality and freedom – the lack of natural or divinely appointed rulers within the human race – we must choose our own rulers. And so "to secure these rights," the Declaration affirms, "Governments are instituted among Men, deriving their just powers from the consent of the governed." The new basis of political obligation among people is thus found in the consent of each individual, in the social contract that arises when a multitude of human beings consent to form a society and be governed together. On the basis of rights shared universally with other humans, these particular men erect a government for themselves; the universal and the particular are reconciled through an act of human choice, not through the problematic legal establishment of a universal religion, that is, Christianity, in a particular society. In fact, the social contract's ground in the doctrine of natural rights requires that the contract be for limited government – a government that secures our natural gifts of life and liberty – not an unlimited one that pursues the supernatural gift of salvation in the next world.

By building government on the basis of natural rights and the social contract, the American founders showed how men could be both good citizens of the City of God and good citizens of their earthly city.[28] The key to the solution was the formal insistence that questions of revealed truth be excluded from determination by the political sovereign or by political majorities. Indeed, majority rule and minority rights could be made consistent only on this basis. Under modern conditions, limited government thus becomes essential to the rule of law. For Aristotle, government was essentially unlimited, in the sense that it had no formal or doctrinal limits extrinsic to the regime, and the regime itself (whatever the type) claimed to rule in the name of its view of the good life as a whole.

And for the actual citizens of ancient cities, the rule of law was anchored directly in divine, not merely human, authority. American citizenship departs from the classical models on these important points. But it does so, at least in part, for reasons that Aristotle would well understand: in order to restore to citizenship a moderation, civility, and responsibility that the amalgamation of church and state had threatened to destroy.

IMMIGRATION AND AMERICANIZATION

How, then, did the American understanding of citizenship affect questions of immigration and naturalization? On the American doctrine, rights inhere in individuals, who may exercise them by combining to form a body politic, a people. A people is not defined by preexisting ties of race, ethnicity, religion, culture, or language, though a people usually has such ties in common. In fact, the British and the American peoples shared most, if not all, of these traits in 1776, but nonetheless the Americans decided to "dissolve the political bands" that had connected them to the British. A people is defined, rather, by the unanimous consent of its members.[29] After a people has been formed by unanimous consent, "Governments are instituted" by majority consent to secure the people's rights against external and internal threats. But government is not charged with securing the rights of individuals who do not choose to join the body politic, much less the rights of foreign peoples. Political scientist Thomas G. West makes the point archly: "'We the People of the United States,'" he writes, "established the Constitution of 1787 to 'secure the blessings of liberty to *ourselves* and *our posterity.* '"[30]

The moral process at work here is vividly described in the preamble to the Massachusetts Constitution of 1780, drafted by John Adams: "The body-politic is formed by the voluntary association of individuals: It is a social compact, by which the whole people covenants with each citizen, and each citizen with the whole people, that all shall be governed by certain laws for the common good."[31] If the people do not wish to covenant or contract with a particular individual, or if he does not wish to covenant with them, then the contract fails and the conditions of citizenship are not met.[32] Consent is thus a two-way street: No one may justly be compelled to join a society, but society cannot justly be compelled to accept anyone, either. There must be mutual consent on the individual's and on society's part. Gouverneur Morris brought the point home at the Constitutional Convention, commenting that "every society from a great nation down to a club had the right of declaring the conditions on which new members should be admitted."[33] It may be objected that this process is ideal and that both the law and the history of American citizenship have been based on *jus soli* (citizenship by birth within the borders of the United States) and *jus sanguinis* (by inheriting the parents' nationality) much more than on the free consent of individual men and women. But this objection overlooks the importance of America's consciousness of itself as a founded (indeed, a revolutionary) society and an immigrant or settler society – features that neither territoriality nor "blood" inheritance can explain. To put it differently, what is puzzling is not the fact that most American citizens are birthright citizens, and so never have to consent explicitly to being American. What needs explaining is why, despite that, most Americans regard their citizenship as consensual.[34]

Every society has the right to exclude whomever it wishes from immigrating; and every society has the right to regulate its naturalization laws in accordance with the common good. To be sure, this does not give any country the right to harm noncitizens' life, liberty, or property. And indeed every society has the obligation to allow

members to emigrate, if they so choose, inasmuch as this is an implication of the natural right to liberty. Pennsylvania's Declaration of
Rights, issued in 1776, states this explicitly: "All men have a natural
inherent right to emigrate from one state to another that will receive
them, or to form a new state in vacant countries, or in such countries
as they can purchase, whenever they think that thereby they may
promote their own happiness."[35] But note that if they emigrate to an
already existing state, it must be one "that will receive them."

And if none *will* receive them? This is not an empty question, as
we are reminded by the painful spectacle of the many German Jews
who tried to flee Hitler in the 1930s but found no state willing to
admit them. There are present-day examples of the dilemma, too. In
some ways the problem is more acute than it was in the founders'
time, when "vacant countries" and vast amounts of frontier land
were available and international land swaps and purchases were
common. Despite the changed circumstances, however, the founders' general account of the morality of a world of "separate and
equal" peoples, to use the language of the Declaration again, remains
valid. What is everyone's business is no one's business. It strains the
limits of human affection and self-interest to imagine that a world
government, or regional and transnational governments, or even a
federation of governments like the United Nations, would care as
much about the private rights and public good of a people as would
this people themselves. What's more, the competence of such cosmopolitan governments would be in inverse proportion to their distance from the people whose affairs they were to administer. Less
care plus less competence is not a recipe for good government. On
the contrary, it is a prescription for maladministration, perhaps for
despotism. Despite its imperfections, then, a world of "separate and
equal" peoples is more liberal and more republican than any available alternative. And to the extent that such governments multiply
in the world, there is reason to hope that the worst kinds of emigra-
tion dilemmas will diminish.[36]

That every society has a right to regulate immigration does not
imply that any particular regulation is needful or wise, of course. In
the era of the American founding, the main lines of discussion over

immigration and naturalization contain some lessons on this score. To Washington, James Madison, Alexander Hamilton, and other founders, the chief concern was to "cement" the Union, to overcome the centrifugal forces that had almost shattered the Union during the war and again in the 1780s, and to bolster and deepen the young country's sense of nationhood. In Washington's words, "We are a young Nation and have a character to establish."[37] This meant that the most urgent task facing the founders was not to Americanize the immigrants but to Americanize the Americans. "The name of AMERICAN," Washington adjured his countrymen in his Farewell Address, "which belongs to you, in your national capacity, must always exalt the just pride of Patriotism, more than any appellation derived from local discriminations." It is "of infinite moment," he counseled, "that you should properly estimate the immense value of your national Union to your collective and individual happiness," and "that you should cherish a cordial, habitual, and immoveable attachment to it."[38]

Hamilton, Madison, and John Jay pursued a similar strategy in *The Federalist*, attacking the Anti-Federalists' preference for the simpler, smaller, more direct republicanism of the states by suggesting that the extended republic of the Union would be a better safeguard for republican liberty. Publius sought not only to fracture majority factions into a multiplicity of interests that would check one another, but also to elicit a healthy majority opinion among his readers in favor of a firm Union and the proposed Constitution. A sound majority opinion would help, in turn, to enlist the people's interests and passions on behalf of the new Constitution.[39] The point is often misunderstood: the manipulation of individual self-interest through the Union's extended structure and through the Constitution's clashing institutions was *necessary*, Publius argued, but not *sufficient* for securing republican government. In the end, republican government needed republican citizens who had a certain "veneration" or "reverence" – quasi-religious respect tinged with awe – for the laws and the Constitution.[40] Under republican doctrine, the people's will was the source of all legitimate authority, and America's new Constitution and laws were creatures of that will. But why and how should the people learn to look up to, to *revere*, what they had themselves created?

Publius's great contribution to American citizenship was to center it on the Constitution. He exhibited in *The Federalist* the wisdom inherent in the Convention's lawmaking, and so taught generations of Americans to revere the Constitution's framers and thus to respect the Constitution not simply as a creation of popular will but as a rare and precious achievement of reason. He brought consent and wisdom together in support of the Constitution, which he defended as the embodiment of "the reason ... of the public."[41] Furthermore, Publius interpreted the new plan of government in a manner designed to encourage the American people to regard the Constitution as peculiarly their own (hence not to be changed frivolously), whereas statute law was merely the work of their representatives. One of his masterstrokes was to show that, because the Constitution is uniquely the people's law, the people should mainly entrust its interpretation to a Supreme Court of independent, unelected justices, rather than to their own elected lawmakers.[42] By these and many other powerful arguments, Publius helped to ensure that American liberty would be under law, and that American citizenship would involve a deep emotional attachment and habitual deference to the Constitution.

Republican government had failed much more often than it had succeeded in the world, so the founders were not embarrassed to admit that it needed all the help it could get in America. This help included recruiting or attracting the right kind of immigrants to the new land. Efforts had been under way for a long time. One of the charges against King George III in the Declaration of Independence claimed that "He has endeavored to prevent the population of these States; for that purpose obstructing the Laws for Naturalization of Foreigners; refusing to pass others to encourage their migration hither." Benjamin Franklin, while serving as minister to France in 1784, warned potential immigrants to America that "America is the Land of Labour, and by no means what the English call *Lubberland*, and the French *Pays de Cocagne*, where the Streets are said to be pav'd with half-peck Loaves, the Houses til'd with Pancakes, and where the Fowls fly about ready roasted, crying, *Come eat me!*" Franklin advised skilled artisans, "hearty young Labouring Men,"

"Persons of moderate Fortunes and Capitals," and anyone who was prepared to work and to learn, to consider emigrating.[43]

The work ethic was important even then – "Industry and constant Employment are great Preservatives of the Morals and Virtue of a Nation," Franklin commented."[44] But even more important in evaluating potential immigrants, the founders maintained, were the political habits and principles they might bring with them. To be sure, the United States was a vast, sparsely populated country, eager to attract more inhabitants; but it was also a fledgling republic in a world of powerful and corrupt monarchies, and Americans were keen to retain and purify their republican morals. Jefferson was especially concerned about the fate of republicanism in America, and it is to him that we owe the most sustained reflections on immigration in the founding era. In *Notes on the State of Virginia*, Jefferson began to address the topic from general principles:

> It is for the happiness of those united in society to harmonize as much as possible in matters which they must of necessity transact together. Civil government being the sole object of forming societies, its administration must be conducted by common consent.

Living together in society is not an easy task, and the republican insistence that societies must be able to govern themselves by "common consent" makes the task harder still. Jefferson was therefore not embarrassed to try to find ways to make the enterprise easier and happier – by seeking for a certain homogeneity among immigrants, particularly in their political habits. This was also a purpose of the country's first naturalization law, though it, like almost every subsequent naturalization law, settled for residency requirements as the most practicable guarantee of good political habits. The 1790 act left immigration and permanent residence open to all, but restricted citizenship to any "free white person" who had resided in the United States for two years and in his state for one, and who could prove his "good character" and swear to "support the Constitution of the United States." There is no record of congressional debate on the racial restriction, and though racism or dislike of blacks undoubtedly played a part – as the 1619 Project insists – it was also likely that, impressed with the difficulty of maintaining republican government, many congressmen voted for the restriction on the grounds that a biracial or multiracial society would only make the republican task harder by raising additional obstacles to "common consent."[45] In a country already cursed with a system of black chattel slavery, this worry took on added dimensions.[46]

But let us return to Jefferson's extended discussion of immigration, which he composed in the mid-1780s:

> Every species of government has its specific principles. Ours perhaps are more peculiar than those of any other in the universe. It is a composition of the freest principles of the English constitution, with others derived from natural right and natural reason. To these nothing can be more opposed than the maxims of absolute monarchies. Yet, from such, we are to expect the greatest number of emigrants. They will bring with them the principles of the governments they leave, imbibed in their early youth; or, if able to throw them off, it will be in exchange for an unbounded licentiousness, passing, as is usual, from one extreme to another. It would be a miracle were they to stop precisely at the point of temperate liberty.

Jefferson acknowledged that emigrants from absolute monarchies may, probably will be, fleeing absolutism as much as poverty, and hence may well be eager to throw off their monarchical principles in favor of republican ones, But his doubts embraced habits (or character) as well as principle; it is far harder to change someone's character than his principles, because character is formed gradually over a long time. Hence Jefferson's reservation that the new immigrants' embrace of liberty, while sincere, might not be "temperate." Several years later, the French people's embrace of liberty, inexperienced and immoderate, proved his point; though for political reasons at the time, he would have been loath to admit it!

At any rate, Jefferson was not against immigration, particularly of "useful artificers," but he was hostile to offering bounties or "extraordinary encouragements" to lure unskilled laborers and farmers from Europe, bearing with them monarchical principles and habits. And like many of the founders, he worried not only about the political but also about what we would today call the cultural effects of immigration. Again, from Query 8 of *Notes on the State of Virginia*:

> These [monarchical] principles, with their language, they will transmit to their children. In proportion to their numbers, they will share with us the legislation. They will infuse into it their spirit, warp and bias its direction, and render it a heterogeneous, incoherent, and distracted mass.

American government would be "more homogeneous, more peaceable, more durable" without so many erstwhile monarchists speaking foreign tongues.[47]

When, more than a decade later, Jefferson and his Democratic-Republican Party triumphed over the Federalist Party in the election of 1800, President Jefferson reversed himself and proposed the immediate naturalization of foreigners, instead of the fourteen-year residency that the Federalists had put in place in 1798.[48] The new policy had much to do with Jefferson's sympathy for the French Revolution and with recent immigrants' support for the Democratic party at the polls in 1800.[49] Alexander Hamilton, his political archrival, took him to task, appealing to Jefferson's own words in *Notes on the State of Virginia*. Hamilton, himself an immigrant and a strong proponent of immigration, criticized the dropping of any residency requirements as extreme, and cautioned against too-rapid immigration:

> The safety of a republic depends essentially on the energy of a common national sentiment; on a uniformity of principles and habits; on the exemption of the citizens from foreign bias and prejudice; and on the love of country which will almost invariably be found to be closely connected with birth, education, and family. The opinion advanced in *Notes on Virginia* is undoubtedly correct, that foreigners will generally be apt to bring with them attachments to the persons they have left behind; to the country of their nativity; and to its particular customs and

manners. They will also entertain opinions on government congenial with those under which they have lived; or if they should be led hither from a preference to ours, how extremely unlikely is it that they will bring with them that temperate love of liberty, so essential to real republicanism?

The success of republicanism, Hamilton concluded, depended on "the preservation of a national spirit and a national character," and indiscriminate naturalization threatened both.[50]

In the end, despite their partisan differences, Hamilton and Jefferson agreed on the basic principles of American citizenship, and together with other members of the founding generation they agreed that there was no necessary conflict or contradiction between the universal precepts underlying that citizenship and the cultivation of "a national spirit and a national character" for this particular people.[51] Jefferson and Hamilton did part company, of course, on the exact character of that "national spirit" and the means to implement it – whether agrarian virtues or entrepreneurial and manufacturing skills would better serve republican liberty, whether states' rights or federal judicial review was a better guardian of American liberty, and so forth. But on the general principles of natural rights, the social contract, and the cultivation of republican and constitutional fidelity, there was a remarkable consensus among the founders. And on the specific question of immigration and naturalization, most of the founders also thought alike – that their society had, in principle, the right to admit new members or citizens only on the basis of mutual consent, and had the responsibility to exclude new members or citizens who would endanger the preservation of republican government in America.

DILEMMAS OF AMERICAN CITIZENSHIP

Having staked American citizenship on universal principles, however, every failure to live up to those principles, every concession to particular interests or prejudices, and every apostasy in favor of competing principles looks all the more glaring. The persistence of black slavery in the midst of a regime pledged to human freedom involved the worst and most obvious of these failures, concessions, and apostasies. But because it was in the name of equality, liberty, Union, and republicanism that slavery was condemned and over-turned in the Civil War and in the Thirteenth, Fourteenth, and Fif-teenth Amendments, it hardly seems fair to blame the principles for its persistence. And yet in one sense, there is blame to be assigned or at least understood. From the Declaration of Independence's truth "that all men are created equal," at least two conclusions followed: One was that governments exist to secure the equal rights of the governed, the other that governments must be instituted, and oper-ated, with the consent of the governed. The bifurcation of these goals makes possible and necessary the drama of self-government: A free people, according to American principles, possesses the right and duty to govern itself. But part of drama is tragedy, and with the necessity of self-government comes the possibility that the people, or a significant part of them, will govern incompetently or unjustly. The tragedy lurking in American principles is that the two com-mandments of the Declaration may contradict each other if the peo-ple cannot be persuaded to govern in accordance with the common good and the equal rights of all. Despite all the "auxiliary precau-tions" erected by the Constitution to prevent majority and minority tyranny, tyranny is still possible if a popular faction is sufficiently strong, wily, and long-lasting.

Popular tyranny is the bastard child of self-government, but its illegitimacy must be proven over and over, time and again, case by case. This is a requirement of self-government's own legitimacy and honor. In this light, the supreme task of American citizenship is to live up to its own best principles – to consolidate public opinion behind those principles, to persuade popular majorities to govern in the interest of minorities too, to encourage citizens to strive for the common good. So the cultivation of a virtuous or responsible "national spirit" and "national character" is essential precisely in order to live up to the universal principles animating that citizen-ship. To put it differently, American self-government not only pre-supposes a national "self" but must help to shape and refine it.

So American citizenship helps to form American culture; it is not just a by-product of a preexisting or somehow more fundamental culture. In fact, there has always been something peculiarly political – call it republican or democratic – about American culture. Our first national forms of literature were the sermon and the political pamphlet, and many of the sermons, especially in the later eighteenth century, were about politics. Our novels, poetry, painting, and so forth came later, after the founding had stamped us "American." These later forms of art deepened and broadened American culture but did not change its main lines. Religion, an important part of what used to be meant, at least, by culture, is in its ultimate concerns transpolitical, and thus in most respects is properly off-limits to American politics. But even on religion, the principles of American citizenship have had a formative influence. The precepts of non-establishment (the separation of church and state) and religious freedom are deeply ingrained in every American denomination. The Latter-Day Saints are only a well-known recent example of a church that, for whatever inspired reasons, has gradually conformed its teachings to the moral and legal precepts of American republicanism.

So the founders labored to shape the "national spirit" and "national character" of a people who could live together as republican citizens. This demanded much more than a simple, ritual assent to formal political principles. It demanded, as we have seen, among citizens and immigrants alike, the encouragement of a common language, of the work ethic, of republican habits of mind and conduct, of a spreading affection for the Constitution and Union.[52] And after the Constitution-framing and lawmaking of the early founding period, Americans increasingly turned their attention to education – establishing in state after state a system of free "common" or public schools (see Chapter Five) in which reading, writing, 'rithmetic, and republicanism could be inculcated.[53] By means of formal education, but also through civic festivals and oratory, public buildings and monuments, jury charges, biographies, histories, and the practice of self-government itself, the founding generation sought to perpetuate a republican regime. And of course the founders' own lives and character – more impressive and capacious than any list of virtues – exhibited to their fellow citizens what it meant to be an American.

From the citizens' point of view, however, what it means to be a good American elides, almost imperceptibly, into what it means to be a good, or the best, human being. This identification is, as Aristotle realized long ago, inherent in citizenship, though it can be elicited in better or worse forms in better or worse regimes; but it is one reason why many contemporary critics reject so thoroughly the founders' view of the matter. The closed character of even the most open and liberal society, the citizens' stubborn preference for their own and their willingness to fight for it, the inescapable limitations of public opinion itself – these are anathema to many progressive critics of American citizenship. The most radical, and interesting, of these critics are the so-called "cultural pluralists," who argue that many groups feel excluded from American culture despite having American citizenship, and who conclude therefore that U.S. citizenship needs to be reconstructed along cultural – that is, multicultural – lines.

MULTICULTURAL CITIZENSHIP

In the classic article of this genre, Iris Marion Young advocates what she calls "heterogeneous" or "differentiated" citizenship. Young (1949–2006) was a professor of political science at the University of Chicago, one of the most important political theorists working at the intersection of feminism, postmodernism, and global and social justice. To see what multicultural citizenship means, it will be necessary to follow her argument for a while. In the first place, this new kind of citizenship arises from a critique of rights, of individual or natural rights as we find them in the central documents of the American Revolution. At one time, Young writes, individual rights were championed by "emancipatory groups" who wished to show that "some groups" stigmatized as naturally inferior to "white male citizens" were in fact their equals and deserving of equal citizenship. At that time, "equal rights that were blind to group differences" were "the only sensible way to combat exclusion and degradation." But that was then; today, "equal rights for all groups," that is, for "all persons" (she does not seem to think that persons really exist apart from groups) has basically been achieved, but "group inequalities nevertheless remain." In short, individual or universal rights were fine so long as they were progressive; in today's circumstances, however, they are, to use Herbert Marcuse's term, "repressive." Once liberating and leveling, equal rights now must be overcome.[54]

Why did "equal citizenship rights" not lead to "social justice and equality"? Part of the answer, she explains, is "straightforwardly Marxist." The right to acquire and own property, Marx argued, is in bourgeois society supposedly held by every man equally; but this formal equality masks the real inequality that results when men actually exercise that right. The equality of rights does not yield an equality of results. And so, Young concludes along with Marx, equal rights are deceptive, spurious, oppressive – a disguise for the rule of the rich over the poor; or in Young's vocabulary, for the rule of privileged groups over oppressed groups.[55] As a consequence of his analysis, Marx abandoned the discussion of rights altogether. But Young, following a different strand of twentieth-century social criticism, takes the opportunity to correct bourgeois rights by a new kind of rights. Because equal civil and political rights only reinforce and perpetuate socioeconomic inequality, any attempt to find "neutral" principles of law will be unavailing. So "instead of always formulating rights and rules in universal terms that are blind to difference," declares Young, "some groups sometimes deserve special rights."[56]

Young recognizes that her pronouncement might sound a bit ominous, so she takes pains to reassure her readers that "special" just means "specific," as opposed to the "general" rights that "all persons" should have. But "special" rights are not just added to "general" rights; the special rights that some persons or rather groups receive seem to come at the expense of the general rights of the not-so-special groups. In other words, "special" rights may well subtract from "general" rights. One of her examples is "'affirmative action" or what she calls "'preference to race or gender," which she defends on the grounds that "the development of truly neutral standards and evaluations is difficult or impossible" for females, blacks, and Latinos who are required, for example, to take college entrance tests designed by white males. This argument proves too much (will there have to be a caste system for teaching and grading once the female, black, and Latino students are at college?), but let's leave it aside. The main point is that "preference to race or gender" can only come at the expense of those who don't possess the preferred qualities; she acknowledges this when she defends affirmative action programs "whether they involve quotas or not." So specific rights are special, after all. But not to worry, Young assures us: we're all special! She writes in a footnote: "in certain contexts and at certain levels of abstraction everyone has 'special' rights."[57]

In the end, everyone may have to have special rights because no one will be left with general ones. At least this is the tendency of some of her own examples and lines of argument. Young argues in favor of special rights for linguistic and cultural minorities, for instance, because cultural assimilation would require "a person to transform his or her sense of identity." Despite this statement, she confines language and cultural rights to "sizeable ... minorities living in distinct" communities; she appears to deny them to individual "persons who do not identify with majority language or culture."[58] But if the evil to be prevented is the forcible transforming of personal identity, why should only sizeable groups have their identities protected?

The answer has everything to do with the prominence of groups in her theory of citizenship. Young distinguishes groups from "aggregates" and "associations." An aggregate is "any classification of persons according to some attribute," like blue-eyed people. An association is "a collectivity of persons who come together voluntarily," like a bridge club or a political party. A "social group," by contrast, has a "sense of identity" based on an "affinity" that persons feel with one another and that outsiders recognize in the group. Now, an affinity can either be a resemblance or a liking. Do group members merely resemble one another, or just happen to like one another, or do they like one another because they resemble one another? Young comments that a light-skinned person may still "identify as black," but she then adds that certain "objective attributes" are "sometimes" a necessary condition for group membership. These attributes, generally speaking, are a shared "social status," a common history based on that status, and a "self-identification" with the group.[59]

It is the latter quality that lies at the heart of the social group. Like Marx's economic classes, Young's social groups depend on combining objective class or social position with the subjective consciousness of that position. That is, a person must not only belong to an oppressed group, he must be conscious of his oppression and prepared to do something about it. For Young, one might say, it is the difference between being a woman and being a feminist. At any rate, it is the subjective factor that distinguishes groups from associations. Associations are formed by individuals – "already formed persons," in Young's telling phrase – who come together voluntarily, who are capable of making and keeping contracts, including the social contract. Tocqueville spoke of the art and science of associations that could lead men to freedom and dignity, not to mention responsible citizenship.[60] Young prefers groups to associations because groups "define one's very identity"; they provide the sense of belonging and of purpose that humanity itself – that nature itself – cannot afford. "Group affinity," Young writes, "has the character of what Heidegger calls 'thrownness': one finds oneself as a member of a group, whose existence and relations one experiences as always already having been.[61]

Social groups impart meaning or "identity" to their members, who are definitely not "already formed men"; their identity depends decisively on "how others identify" them. Yet the "objective attributes" of group membership reside in race, sex, ethnicity, age – bodily characteristics that particularize persons, that invite stereotyping, but that are made the basis of group "culture" and hence of "differentiated" citizenship in this theory. For social groups do have "capacities, values," and even "cognitive and behavioral styles" unique to them, Young avers; that would mean, to use philosophical language, that the subrational parts of the soul reach all the way up to the rational, and shape or control reason itself.[62] "Heterogeneous" citizenship would then be the variety of citizenships corresponding to the willful and passionate "values" of social groups; or more precisely, it would be the attempt to manage or accommodate these largely incommensurable worldviews.

Young tries to avoid this problem by retreating from the

"thrownness," the givenness of group identity. At one point, she compares the defining quality of group identity to what "being Navajo might" be like. A few sentences later, however, she announces that "from the thrownness of group affinity it does not follow that one cannot leave groups and enter new ones. Many women become lesbian after identifying as heterosexual, and anyone who lives long enough becomes old."[63] If group loyalties are fluctuating, evolving, and crosscutting, then one may not have to worry so much about the passionate commitments or, in some cases, fanatical resentments underlying identity politics. But then identity politics and bourgeois interest-group politics would not be so far apart, a state of affairs that would likely lead to an identity crisis for identity politics: it has staked too much on its German philosophical borrowings to be unmasked as just another form of utilitarianism.

At any rate, the goal of respect or recognition marches hand in hand with the goal of greater socioeconomic equality in Young's group theory of citizenship. Greater economic equality implies the redistribution of wealth and power from privileged to oppressed groups, and this is the task not of revolution but of group representation in her scheme. She proposes that "a democratic public, however that is constituted," should provide mechanisms and resources to promote "effective representation and recognition" of its "oppressed or disadvantaged" groups ("disadvantaged" is now virtually the same as "oppressed"). Effective representation requires three things: "self-organization" of group members so that they may feel empowered and fully conscious of themselves as oppressed; "voicing" a group's perspective on policy proposals and aiding them in generating new proposals; and "having veto power regarding specific policies that affect a group directly."[64] It is characteristic of Young's argument that she calls for the "democratic public" to provide or foster the "self-organization" of groups; the groups are too diffuse, needy, or spiritless actually to organize themselves and make political or policy claims on their own. Their demand for recognition becomes truly self-confident only after the public or its representatives have validated it by reassuring the (potential) group members that, yes, they are oppressed. In fact, they are so oppressed or oblivious that they cannot or will not demand freedom and equality for themselves, without government's blessing – and without the leadership of vanguard intellectuals like Young.

A new form of group participation in political deliberation, conjoined to a veto power for each group over policies directly affecting it – these then are the specific political reforms she is advancing. "Reproductive rights for women" is one of Young's examples of a policy over which the veto power would extend, though it is unclear exactly at what level, for what reasons, in what manner, and by whom such a veto would be cast. Are the internal politics of the groups, e.g., women, based on majority rule (and of all women, or only those enrolled in feminist organizations?) or on some form of centralized decision-making among the leaders of the existing organizations? Young does not say, but she does emphasize that the purpose of representation for disadvantaged groups (privileged groups do not need it and do not get such a veto) is "to undermine oppression," to weaken or overthrow the advantaged groups and their policies.[65] This political goal could perhaps be achieved through a radical rehabilitation of all citizens or of citizenship itself, however, and it is to this less partisan purpose that most of her arguments are ostensibly directed.

REDEEMING AMERICAN CITIZENSHIP?

The new "responsible" citizen, Young explains, will be "concerned not merely with interests but with justice," and this means "acknowledging that each other person's interest and point of view is as good as his or her own," and furthermore that "the needs and interests of everyone must be voiced and be heard by the others, who must acknowledge, respect, and address those needs and interests." Yet Young admits that "persons from one perspective or history can never completely understand and adopt the point of view of those with other group-based perspectives and histories." If no one can finally understand another person's point of view, however, why regard it as "as good as his or her own"? Perhaps the answer is that no one can ever understand his own or his own group's point of view, either, because that view is grounded so firmly in the mysterious fate ("thrownness") of race, ethnicity, and gender – bodily or subrational factors, all. Young cautions that she does not think "cultural differences" arise from "natural, unalterable, biological attributes," but instead from "the relationship of bodies to conventional rules and practices." But "bodies" are biological, and hence "cultural differences" turn out to include such items as "body comportment," "gesture," "biological sex difference" (only women get pregnant), and "bodily difference" (including "persons with physical and mental disabilities," thus incidentally tracing mind back to body, again).[66]

If the culture of social groups is rooted in race, ethnicity, gender, and other bodily differences, then culture shares the privateness or the privatizing quality of bodily things. If I prick my finger, no one else actually feels my pain, however much others may sympathize with me. Reason, by contrast, allows human beings to transcend their bodily differences: when I think 2 + 2 = 4 or "all men are created equal," others (regardless of race, etc.) may think the same thought along with me. Thought is color-blind, because the objects of reason in the highest sense are universals: the idea of man, qua man, for example, is devoid of accidental attributes of color, height, weight, and so forth. Culture is more like the former than the latter, according to Young, except that culture does not have a natural standard of pleasure and pain by which to guide it. Hence social groups based on cultures really do have unique points of view – which cannot be known to be good and thus are regarded as "good" only insofar as they are authentic or truly one's own.

Citizenship based on group cultures must therefore be "heterogeneous" in the precise sense that each group's "interest and point of view" is "as good" as any other's. In Young's words, "a general perspective does not exist ... from which all experiences and perspectives can be understood and taken into account," and therefore "no one can claim to speak in the general interest, because no one of the groups can speak for another, and certainly no one can speak for them all." The "public" as a particular community sharing a universal or general view of justice does not exist; the "general will" is an illusion, and an oppressive one to boot. No one can even "claim" to speak in the general interest, then. Instead of "self-deceiving self-interest masked as an impartial or general interest," every group will assert plainly its own self-interest and point of view.[67]

Young's theory rests on two enormous non-sequiturs. The first is that because any group's point of view is "as good" as any other's, every group should be heard and represented. But this does not follow: If no group's point of view is better than your own, why not insist on your own? To put it differently, if politics is not about the clash of claims over justice – which claims might, in principle at least, be adjudicated by reason – but instead is about the clash of identities backed up by particularistic assertions of group will, then a democratic regime of equality and easygoing tolerance will hardly be the inevitable or logical outcome. Heidegger's own politics of group authenticity led him to be a resolute Nazi. Young herself spares no effort to be inclusive. In fact, her list of "oppressed social groups" in America comprises "women, blacks, Native Americans, Chicanos, Puerto Ricans and other Spanish-speaking Americans, Asian Americans, gay men, lesbians, working-class people, poor people, old people, and mentally and physically disabled people."[68] In sum, the vast majority of Americans. But one should not forget that group representation is not extended to the oppressors, to the privileged groups who "behave as though they have a right to speak and be heard." She never says that they do have a right to speak and be heard.[69]

Young's second non-sequitur is to assume that, because every group has a unique interest and point of view, justice will result from the full airing of this diversity. "Group representation is the best means to promote just outcomes to democratic decision-making processes," she declares. For justification, she resorts to "Habermas's conception of communicative ethics." Absent "a Philosopher King who reads transcendent normative verities," Young explains, "the only ground for a claim that a policy or decision is just is that it has been arrived at by a public which has truly promoted free expression of all needs and points of view."[70] Yet the claim that the "free expression" of needs and values yields justice is itself an assertion of a transcendent or at least an immanent normative verity. And besides, what ensures that the result of group representation and free expression is justice as opposed to, say, cacophony and stalemate?

Assume, for the sake of argument, that free expression and representation for all oppressed groups were a necessary condition for justice; would it be a sufficient condition? Yes, if whatever policy emerges from such a forum is, by definition, just, which seems to be Young's contention. In fact, according to her, free expression guarantees not only justice but wisdom: "group representation also maximizes knowledge expressed in discussion, and thus promotes practical wisdom." Members of social groups know "different things about the structure of social relations" and "have different ways of understanding the meaning of social events." For example, "many Native Americans argue that their traditional religion and relation to the land gives them a unique and important understanding of environmental problems."[71] Knowledge is not wisdom, alas, and even if group representation added to social knowledge, it would not necessarily add to the wise use of knowledge. The effect of the "free expression of all needs and points of view" would be more communication among groups, but not better deliberation, which presupposes shared goals and a shared inclination to act in pursuit of those goals. Young's "communicative ethic" promotes the "expression" of group needs and values, not action to secure them.

Thus a failed political movement is her example of group representation in action. Jesse Jackson's "Rainbow Coalition" in his 1984 presidential race fell short of "the promise of group representation," but it pointed the way. In "traditional coalitions," Young writes, diverse groups work together for common ends, suppressing their differences, especially in public. Not in a rainbow coalition, however, in which each group "affirms the presence of the others and affirms the specificity of its experience and perspective on social issues." According to the rainbow ideal, blacks, gays, labor activists, peace movement veterans, and feminists will not only work together but learn to like each other by expressing and affirming their differences – though Young notes that each group must maintain "autonomy in relating to its constituency" and all coalition decisions are to be made by group representation.[72]

Heterogeneous citizenship will be the rainbow coalition writ large. Despite the appeals to Habermas and to his complicated vision of the just society as a vast dialogic community, the basic political features of Young's project are straightforward. The philosophical problems involved in extracting justice from the group dynamics of a rainbow coalition may be insurmountable, but they are also irrelevant, for the fact is that the coalition members already agree on the most important political purpose of their association. They have come together in order to "undermine oppression," to wring some social justice from an unjust society. The pot of gold at the end of the rainbow coalition is the redistribution of wealth and power sought by coalition members and dictated by their new understanding of rights. In consideration of that common goal, the constituent groups will endure – and maybe learn to like, or at least profess to like – large quantities of self-expression and group affirmation. The ideological differences among coalition members are narrow to begin with, then.[73]

Yet a rainbow coalition is not merely a redistributionist ploy. Young's theory of citizenship is based not on the working class but on racial, ethnic, and other sorts of social and cultural groups, and it depends for its implementation not on workers abandoning their chains but on individuals forging new meaning in their lives through group membership. Young's project thus encourages individuals to think of themselves primarily as members of one or more groups, and it provides material as well as psychological incentives to do so. The internal danger in heterogeneous citizenship is that it may immure citizens in their group, making them not civic participants but only group-citizens, as it were. Encouraging this tendency is the other major political feature of Young's proposal, the veto that each group would wield over its own special policy areas. This is a weapon to be used against the oppressors, against the privileged groups: by clogging society's wheels, the disadvantaged groups will prevent injustice to themselves and persuade the powerful to respect the oppressed as fellow citizens. But the veto is also a weapon in internal coalition politics, reminding the other members of the rainbow coalition of the "autonomy" that each group wields on behalf of its own membership.

So the most potent political threat in Young's reformed polity would be the threat of inaction. To understand the orientation of this threat, it helps to know that insofar as there are "heterogeneous publics operating according to the principles of group representation in contemporary politics, they exist only in organizations and movements resisting the majority politics." The overall effect of the group-based veto is to subtract from the political, and moral, authority of constitutional majorities. Young's proposal moves the country away from majority rule, counting each citizen-voter as one, and towards a polity in which political authority resides in organized and favored (privileged?) groups, counting each group, regardless of its size, as one, and empowering each with an absolute negative on the actions of society. "Such structures of group representation should not replace structures of regional or party representation but should exist alongside them," Young explains.[74] But the insertion of group recognition and veto power into the traditional structures would quickly change them, and besides, the larger purpose of the reform is to open a fundamental debate on the nature of representation, rights, and good government in America.

Young might respond that she is proposing merely a shift from one form of majority rule, based on abstract or egoistic individuals, to another, based on man as a social being, who finds his or her identity primarily through affinity with one or more groups. A similar thought was expressed in the nineteenth century in these terms: the United States needs to move away from rule by the "numerical majority" – which is tyrannical because it threatens to override the most cherished affinities and disrupt the deepest sources of identity among oppressed minorities – and toward rule by the "concurrent majority," in which each threatened group would enjoy a salutary veto power over legislation directly affecting it. In the nineteenth-century case, the oppressed minorities were the citizens of the slave-holding states, whose cultural identity and political rights, they felt, were threatened by Northern abolitionists, politicians, capitalists, and immigrants. John C. Calhoun grounded his argument against the "numerical majority" on the forthright denunciation of the notion "that all men are created equal": rights, he insisted, varied with the group or race to which one belonged, and equality belonged not to human beings per se but to the groups or states in which they organized themselves. His proposal for a "concurrent majority" would have given a veto power to each state to defend itself against obnoxious laws, such as ones restricting the spread of slavery. And like Young, he thought that the brinkmanship produced by the use or promised use of vetoes would, paradoxically, lead to a rebirth of civic spirit.[75] Young's objectives are certainly not Calhoun's, but by their patronage of group representation and the group veto, both critics move away from republican government based on individual rights and the rule of constitutional majorities. For "the vital principle of republican government," as James Madison wrote in refutation of Calhoun, is *"lex majoris partis,* the will of the majority," properly qualified by constitutional protections for personal rights; and anyone who does not admit this, Madison declared, must "either join the avowed disciples of aristocracy, oligarchy, or monarchy, or look for a Utopia."[76]

How, finally, would Young implement her plan for a new kind of citizenship? Whether in national politics or in "factories, offices, universities, churches, and social service agencies," there are "no models" to follow in establishing principles of group representation, Young comments, though she adds immediately that some of the experiments in "publicly institutionalized self-organization" among "women, indigenous peoples, workers, peasants, and students" in Sandinista-ruled Nicaragua come close to the conception she has in mind. Again, the contradiction in terms – "publicly institutionalized self-organization" – this time presided over by the Nicaraguan Communists, suggests the extent to which implementation of the new citizenship has to be top-down, to say the least. Young eschews, however, all specifics as to "which groups" are to be represented initially and "by what procedures" that decision might be made, other than to observe that "a public must be constituted" to make such decisions and that "the principles guiding the composition of such a 'constitutional convention'" must somehow be found through the process of politics itself. Despite her uncharacteristic reticence, she confirms that the addition of group representation amounts to a kind of regime change or refounding, requiring a "constitutional convention" to authorize the emergence of a new public. And as for the "mechanisms" of group representation itself, they will take many evenings, for citizens must constantly "meet together in democratic forums" in order to "discuss issues and formulate group positions and proposals" as well as take part in "democratized decision-making processes" in "neighborhood or district assemblies" and in the "group assemblies" of oppressed groups.[77]

Young's elaborate scheme of group meetings is dedicated to turning American constitutionalism into something like, in T. Alexander Aleinikoff's approving words, "a contract under constant renegotiation."[78] Neither individual natural rights nor majority rule under the Constitution is a "privileged" part of the social contract, in her view, and she admits that even her program of group representation may have to give way if "in some utopian future there will be a society without group oppression and disadvantage."[79] In the meantime, however, some form of group representation is needed in order to bind the American public to its groups, and the groups to the public. Lost in the middle is the original American idea of a self-governing people, instituted and operated by the consent of the governed, who are citizens bearing God-given or natural rights. Lost, also, is the love of country – of its Constitution, laws, statesmen, history, and promise – that once bound citizens together and that was so zealously cultivated by the founders, who knew that citizens would have to be prepared to fight and, if necessary, to die for America. Young says nothing about national defense or the need for "heterogeneous" citizens to defend their country.

Young's proposal tends to replace these ideas with the concept of a nation of groups, even as today's cosmopolitan critics of citizenship urge that national sovereignty be reconsidered in light of what groups of nations might do for world peace and justice. Either sort of proposal threatens the unity of a self-governing people like the Americans, and seems to promise, in order to keep watch over fractious and unnatural groups, only a further bleak centralization of administrative power. This is why, to say the least, none of Young's arguments for "heterogeneous" citizenship is persuasive enough to justify abandoning American citizenship as the founders conceived it. Especially given the tendency of group representation to blur the meaning of rights and enhance the role of power, it is impossible that her style of multicultural citizenship would be compatible, over the long run, with limited government and the rule of law.

Far better to reflect on how Abraham Lincoln sought to fulfill the promise of American citizenship amid the Republic's gravest crisis, when millions of Americans set out deliberately to renounce their citizenship and tear the Union asunder. Two years before the crisis came, he described the promise of American citizenship in words that may serve as our conclusion. Anticipating, in a way, the claims of our citizens today who do not yet feel a part of the American nation, Lincoln spoke of the many Americans who were not blood descendants of the founders, but who nevertheless had something infinitely more important in common with the revolutionaries of 1776:

> If they look back through this history to trace their connection with those days by blood, they find they have none, they cannot carry themselves back into that glorious epoch and make themselves feel that they are part of us, but when they look through that old Declaration of Independence they find that those old men say that "We hold these truths to be self-evident, that all men are created equal," and then they feel that that moral sentiment taught in that day evidences their relation to those men, that it is the father of all moral principle in them, and that they have a right to claim it as though they were blood of the blood, and flesh of the flesh, of the men who wrote that Declaration – and so they are. That is the electric cord in that Declaration that links the hearts of patriotic and liberty-loving men together, that will link those patriotic hearts as long as the love of freedom exists in the minds of men throughout the world.[80]

CHAPTER ELEVEN

BARACK OBAMA
AND THE FUTURE OF LIBERALISM

In the late innings of the health care fight, President Barack Obama told a joint session of Congress in September 2009, "we did not come here just to clean up crises," even one as big as the Great Recession. "We came to build a future," to do the "great things" that "will meet history's test." He concluded, "This is our calling. This is our character." And that had been his ambition all along. "Let us transform this nation," he implored in 2007 when he announced his candidacy for president. As Election Day 2008 approached, he promised, "We are five days away from fundamentally transforming the United States of America."

Those words mean *this will be a different country* when he's finished with it. If, Rip Van Winkle–style, one had slept through the Obama Administration, one would awaken, as it were, in a new land. The old word for such a profound change was *revolution*. As a self-proclaimed progressive, however, he reckons his revolution will be one in a series, an unending series generated by social progress or history itself. His reforms will connect to Woodrow Wilson's, Franklin Roosevelt's, and Lyndon Johnson's before him, and others yet to come, and all these together will constitute a continual upward evolution. That sounds reassuring, insofar as it promises to take the sting and surprise out of change; but such inevitability comes at the expense of liberty, because there is no choice about the whole of liberal-style progress. In the old days, one could choose to make a revolution or not. A revolution could be defeated or reversed. But you cannot deliberate about the *inevitable*, which is how progressives think of history. As we've been told for generations now, *ad nauseam*: You can't turn back the clock.

HISTORY'S TEST

By the same token, however, you can't turn the clock ahead, either. What Obama invokes as "history's test" is a stern one: success or irrelevance, "power or nothingness," to borrow Michael Tomasky's suggestive language. Either you're on the right side of history or the wrong side, where the right side is necessarily understood to mean the winning side, and the wrong side the losing one. Otherwise this would not be a *historical* test but an abstract moral or philosophical one. The obvious moral difficulty – does the right side always win its wars? – can be finessed for a while by distinguishing between wars and mere battles. It's possible to lose many battles and still win the war, eventually. But history's test is of necessity a final examination; it can't be postponed indefinitely without the whole idea of historical validation becoming a laughingstock or an otherworldly stalking horse, neither of which liberalism fancies itself to be. Meeting history's test, as Obama sees it, means recognizing that the "moment" has come for bold, new reforms; but if these prove untimely and unattainable, if the moment comes and goes fruitlessly, then it casts doubt not only on the prophecy and the prophet but on the whole prophecy business. It was embarrassing enough to be succeeded by Donald J. Trump. What if Obamacare, his signature initiative that has survived two major Supreme Court cases and a thousand Republican cuts, were finally, definitively to be repealed and replaced? Then Obama's legacy and his claim to leadership would be in pieces.

Even so, American liberals would try to overcome their embarrassment by insisting that poor Obama was too far ahead of his time. Desperate as it is, that argument is neither unprecedented nor implausible, and it has the great advantage of being unfalsifiable. But it would certainly be a stretch, because it would highlight, by trying to ignore, the dispiriting truth that Obama had it *won* – had Obamacare enacted and written into law, its implementation under way – only to suffer the ignominy of defeat. After the repeal of Prohibition, for example, how many observers concluded that the problem with the Eighteenth Amendment was that it had been ahead of its time? After the dissolution of the USSR, how many Russians, or even Communists, defended the extinct Soviet Union as too good for this world, or tragically in advance of its age? It's one thing to claim grandiloquently to represent the future, to *be* the future, ever glorious and ever distant. It's quite another to *have been* the future. The former trades in utopian speculation, however scientific the speculation claims to be. The latter forces one, wearily, to confront a history of failure and disillusionment – to confess "the god that failed," to borrow that ever resonant term from the Cold War.

American progressives' favorite tense is future perfect; they hate like hell to wrestle with past imperfect. So President Obama faces, by his own standards, a crucial test. The election of 2008 proved, as that of 1992 had as well, that post-Reagan Democrats could win control of all three elected branches of the national government. In his first two years in office Obama further demonstrated that the Reagan legacy, both ideological and institutional, had not rendered impracticable an aggressive agenda of liberal social reform and government expansion. Obama in effect doubled down on the Left's bet on big government, and it is too late to take the chips off the table now.

But his bet came just when the political economy of the welfare state seemed to be reaching a turning point, both in the United States and Europe. Everyone knew, vaguely, that with Baby Boomers beginning to collect benefits and fewer young workers available to pay taxes, the welfare state would hit a demographic wall eventually – a decade or two or three down the road. That crisis, of unfunded liabilities and revenue shortfalls, is still to come, in fact. The near-term crisis is related, but different in origin. The wall that Europe is hitting, and that we are coming up on fast, is a wall of deficits and debt. Although chronic unrestrained entitlement spending is a part of it, the acute problem was precipitated by the financial crisis of 2007–08, the ensuing Great Recession, and governments' reaction to these shocks. And now we can add the West's expert-driven reaction to the COVID-19 pandemic, which has sent deficits and debt soaring.

Even as Greece proved insolvent and many other European countries teetered on the brink, Obama's policies on health care, taxation, and regulation pushed America further toward the European model of social democracy. In effect, his audacity made the problems of the American welfare state worse and more urgent. His policies made the chronic inability of big government to "make payroll," as William Voegeli dubs it, that much more acute. The advent of the true crisis of the welfare state has been accelerated, the hole into which it will plunge the economy dug deeper, and the options for dealing with the chronic shortfalls made worse. The Marxists call this policy of speeding up the social and political reckoning "heightening the contradictions." It's possible that Obama wanted to heighten the contradictions in order to hasten a crisis of the American welfare state that would be solved by its engorging another 10 or 20 percent of the American economy: social democracy, American-style. More likely, he was content to win the moral battle – a historic expansion of the welfare and regulatory state – and leave it to future administrations to wage the fiscal one.

What history confronts him with, therefore, is not merely a test of his own leadership but also a test of liberalism's credibility as the once-and-future American public philosophy. More and more, the blue-state social model, as Walter Russell Mead calls it, looks anachronistic and unimaginative – behind rather than ahead of the times. A health care reform bill, to take the central example, that stretched to three thousand pages and created 159 new boards, commissions, and agencies hardly betrays the nimbleness, efficiency, transparency, reliability, and personalization that Americans expect from new companies, products, and services at their best. Liberalism seems about to succumb to the very critique it once leveled disdainfully at the old American constitutional and political order: the failure to evolve. Beyond its bureaucratic shortcomings, however, looms a deeper problem with liberalism's understanding of human nature and the purposes of government, which led it to presume to lead and administer a free society and concoct rights to health care, housing, and a job in the first place. Heightening the contradictions could soon produce a kind of revolution all right, but not the one Obama hopes for.

The president had a century of modern American liberalism to draw on, and in a strange way his administration recapitulated that history. He campaigned on Hope and Change, attempting through his soaring speechmaking to awaken the idealism of a generation and resume the forward march of progressive politics, even as Woodrow Wilson and John F. Kennedy had done. Like FDR, Obama exploited an ongoing economic collapse to pass far-reaching regulatory reforms, boost federal stimulus spending, and enact a major new entitlement program that, not incidentally, attempted to secure the right to adequate medical care Roosevelt had proclaimed in 1944. And like Lyndon Johnson's administration, only much sooner, Obama faced an electoral rebellion against his signature policies that threatened to eject him and his party from power and to discredit liberalism itself. Though he won reelection, his party's fortunes sank to depths not seen since the 1920s. The acceleration and compression of events were remarkable. His administration launched a fourth wave of liberal reform to add to the storied greatness, in liberals' eyes, of the first three. But the wave crested so abruptly that it raised questions about its very existence, much less its significance. The wave was real enough in policy terms, and coming after almost thirty years of domestic politics (and foreign policy, though that's a more complicated story) conducted in the shadow of Ronald Reagan, it surprised liberals as well as conservatives. Whether it changed liberalism, and if so, how that change will affect liberal hopes and conservative fears, are now pressing questions. President Obama's tenure thus posed the test of history in concentrated form: is liberalism on its last legs, or about to be reborn?

PRAGMATIC POSTMODERNISM

Liberals like crises, and one shouldn't spoil them by handing them another on a silver salver. The kind of crisis that is approaching, however, is probably not their favorite kind – an emergency that presents an opportunity to enlarge government – but one that will find liberalism at a crossroads, a turning point. Unless it turns back, it faces difficulties both philosophical and fiscal that will compel it either to become something shamelessly illiberal and undemocratic, or to go out of business.

For most of the past century, liberalism was happy to use relativism as an argument against conservatism. Those self-evident truths that the American constitutional order rested on were neither logically self-evident nor true, Woodrow Wilson and his followers argued, but merely rationalizations for an immature, subjective form of right that enshrined selfishness as national morality. What was truly evident was the relativity of all past views of morality, each a reflection of its society's stage of development. But there was a final stage of development, when true morality would be actualized and its inevitability made abundantly clear, that is, self-evident. Disillusionment came in the 1960s when the purported end or near-end of history coincided not with idealism justified and realized, but with what many liberals, especially the young, despaired of as the infinite immorality of poverty, racial injustice, Vietnam, the System, and the threat of nuclear annihilation. Relativism rounded on liberalism. Having promised so much, liberalism was peculiarly vulnerable to the charge that the complete spiritual fulfillment it once promised was neither complete nor fulfilling. "History's test" was postponed indefinitely, or cancelled rather, because there were no final and true standards by which to judge it.

As Obama's own example shows, intelligent and morally sensitive liberals may try to suppress or deflect the problem of postmodern relativism but it cannot be forgotten. In a revealing section of *The Audacity of Hope* (2006), he wrestles with the question:

> Implicit in [the Constitution's] structure, in the very idea of ordered liberty, was a rejection of absolute truth, the infallibility of any idea or ideology or theology or 'ism,' any tyrannical consistency that might lock future generations into a single, unalterable course, or drive both majorities and minorities into the cruelties of the Inquisition, the pogrom, the gulag, or the jihad. (p. 93)

There is no absolute truth – and that's the absolute truth, he argues! Tyranny and extremism everywhere arise, it seems, from a belief in absolute truth. He doesn't apparently recognize any danger of "cruelties" stemming from the wholesale abandonment of truth-seeking, from relativism or historicism carried too far. Although it's certainly a good thing that America avoided religious and political tyranny, no previous president ever credited America's achievement of constitutional and ordered liberty to the rejection of absolute truth, previously known as "truth."

Two pages later Obama blames the founders for supposedly excluding black Americans from all constitutional protection, yet balances that criticism with praise of the founders' "realism, their practicality and flexibility and curiosity, that ensured the Union's survival." He can't decide whether to criticize them as racists or congratulate them as realists. He then plunges into deeper and murkier waters.

> The best I can do in the face of our history is remind myself that it has not always been the pragmatist, the voice of reason, or the force of compromise, that has created the conditions for liberty. The hard, cold facts remind me that it was unbending idealists like William Lloyd Garrison who first sounded the clarion call for justice.... It was the wild-eyed prophecies of John Brown, his willingness to spill blood and not just words on behalf of his visions, that helped force the issue of a nation half slave and half free. I'm reminded that deliberation and the constitutional order may sometimes be the luxury of the powerful, and that it has been the cranks, the zealots, the prophets, the agitators, and the unreasonable – in other words, the absolutists – that have fought for a new order. (p. 97)

He has a soft spot "for those possessed of similar certainty today," for example, the "antiabortion activist" or the "animal rights activist" who's willing to break the law. He seems to envy their certainty, and he certainly admires the passionate intensity of their commitment. He focuses on their subjective certainty, not, say, the objective difference between saving human beings and saving rabbits.

Though he may disagree with their views, he admits in his perplex-ity, "I am robbed even of the certainty of uncertainty – for some-times absolute truths may well be absolute."

Not true, necessarily, but *absolute*. It's hard to know what he means, exactly. That the "truths" are fit for the times, are destined to win out and forge "a new order"? That in any case they are willed absolutely, not pragmatically or contingently? Even his rejection of absolute truth is now uncertain. Despite his rhetorical investment in "deliberative democracy" and pragmatic progressivism, Obama is willing to throw it all aside at the moment of decision because it doesn't satisfy his love of justice – or rather his love of a certain kind of courage or of resolute action. "The blood of slaves reminds us that our pragmatism can sometimes be moral cowardice. Lincoln, and those buried at Gettysburg," he concludes, "remind us that we should pursue our own absolute truths only if we acknowledge that there may be a terrible price to pay." (p. 98) In a moment like that, he argues, a great man must follow his *own* absolute truth, and the rest of us are left hoping it is Abraham Lincoln and not John Brown, much less Jefferson Davis, who will get to enjoy his triumph of the will. The great man doesn't anticipate or follow or approximate his-tory's course then; he creates it, *wills* it (so far as he can) according to his own absolute will, not absolute knowledge.

When combined with liberalism's lust for strong leaders, this openness to Nietzschean creativity looms dangerously over the lib-eral future. If we are lucky, if liberalism is lucky, no one will ever apply for the position of liberal superman, and the role will remain vacant. But as Lincoln asked in the Lyceum speech,

> Is it unreasonable then to expect, that some man possessed of the loftiest genius, coupled with ambition sufficient to push it to its utmost stretch, will at some time, spring up among us? And when such a one does, it will require the people to be united with each other, attached to the government and laws, and generally intelligent, to successfully frustrate his designs. Distinction will be his paramount object; and although he would as willingly, perhaps more so, acquire it by doing good as harm; yet, that opportunity being past, and nothing left to be done in the way

of building up, he would set boldly to the task of pulling down.

More worrisome even than this danger of an *Übermensch* able to promise that everything desirable will soon be possible is a people unattached to its constitution and laws; and for that, liberalism has much to answer. By its encouragement of an easy multiculturalism, now hardened into the politics of identity and enforced by political correctness, liberalism has gone a long way toward "the disuniting of America," as Arthur Schlesinger, Jr., an impeccable liberal, warned in a book of that title thirty years ago.

In one crucial respect, our situation might seem more perilous than the danger Lincoln sketched, insofar as the very definitions of political "good" and "harm" are now uncertain. Richard Rorty, the late postmodern philosopher, specialized in trying to think through this liberal dilemma, which could not be resolved but could be expressed in sharp terms. He called himself a "liberal ironist." Liberals, he said, adopting the political theorist Judith Shklar's definition, are "people who think cruelty is the worst thing we do"; an "ironist," in his own definition, faces up to "the contingency of his or her most central beliefs and desires," including the "belief that cruelty is horrible." Unflinching liberals understand that liberalism consists in the revulsion to human cruelty, combined with the knowledge that hatred of cruelty is no more objectively moral, nor rational, than love of it. (Conservatives are lovers of cruelty, he implies.) In short, thoughtful liberals recognize that liberalism is a value judgment, with no ground in truth or science or Being or anything else supposedly "out there." Its central value judgment is not even a view of justice or of nobility, exactly, or an affirmation of something good; it stands merely for the negation of cruelty. Real liberalism *is* relativism, colored by a Rousseauian pity for the suffering animal (don't forget the rabbits) who is sensitive to humiliation. That suffering now comes in as many different varieties as there are races, genders, and identity groups. But in every case, according to Rorty, the demand for redress is driven not only by the will to truth or justice, but by the will to power.

To Rorty's disappointment, most actual liberals are not relativists, of course, but he thought they may eventually fall in line and at any rate could not refute postmodernism. They cannot even change the subject, though as a practical matter he recommends this, urging liberals to resume fighting for continual political and socioeconomic reforms as in the glory days, rather than listening to the siren calls of the academic and cultural Left with its endless criticisms of America and of the hopeless efforts to reform her. As president, Obama tried to take Rorty's practical advice, and to revive liberals' hope in progressive change. That seemed to be working, until Trump succeeded him. Obama's tactical successes, no matter how impressive, did not solve the strategic problem.

Avant-garde liberalism used to be about progress; now it's about nothingness. Perhaps, paradoxically, that's why Obama prefers to be called a progressive rather than a liberal. It's better to believe in something than in nothing, even if the something, Progress, is not as believable as it used to be before the 1960s. His residual progressivism helps insure him against his instinctual postmodernism. Still, liberalism is in a bad way when it has lost confidence in its own truth, and it's an odd sort of "progress" to go back to a name it surrendered eighty years ago.

THE BEST AND THE BRIGHTEST

Adding to liberal self-doubt is that its monopoly on the social sciences, long since broken, has been supplanted by a multiple-front argument with conservative scholars in economics, political science, and other fields. In the beginning, Progressivism commanded all the social sciences because it had invented, or imported, them all. Wilson, Franklin Roosevelt, and Lyndon Johnson could be confident in the inevitability of progress, despite temporary setbacks, because the social sciences backed them up. An expertise in administering progress existed, and experts in public administration, Keynesian economics, national planning, urban affairs, modernization theory, development studies, and a half-dozen other specialties beavered away at bringing the future to life.

What a difference a half century makes. The vogue for national planning disappeared under the pressure of ideas and events. Friedrich Hayek demonstrated why socialist economic planning, lacking free-market pricing information, could not succeed. In a side-by-side experiment, West Germany far outpaced East Germany in economic development, and all the people escaping across the Wall traveled from East to West, leaving their workers' paradise behind. Keynesianism flunked the test of the 1970s' stagflation. The Reagan boom, with its repeated tax cuts, flew in the face of the orthodoxy at the Harvard Department of Economics, but was cheered by the Chicago School. Milton Friedman's advice to Chile proved far sounder than Jeffrey Sachs's to Russia. Monetarism, rational choice economics, supply-side, "government failure," "regulatory capture," "incentive effects" – the intellectual discoveries were predominantly on the Right. Conservative and libertarian think tanks multiplied, carrying the new insights directly into the fray.

The scholarly counterattack proceeded in political science and the law, too. Rational choice and "law and economics" changed the agenda to some degree. Both politics and the law became increasingly "originalist" in bearing, enriched by a new appreciation for eighteenth-century sources and for the original intent of the founders and the framers of the Constitution. Above all, the Progressives' attempt to replace political philosophy with social science foundered. After World War II, an unanticipated and unsung revival of political philosophy began, associated above all with Leo Strauss, questioning historicism and nihilism in the name of a broadly Socratic understanding of nature and natural right. New studies of the tradition yielded some very untraditional results. Though there were left-wing as well as right-wing aspects to this revival, the latter proved more influential and liberating. The *unquestionability* of both progress and relativism died quietly in select classrooms around the country. Economics is an instrumental science, studying means not ends, and so much of the successes of free-market economics could be swallowed, pragmatically, by liberalism's maw. The developments in political philosophy challenged the *ends* of progressivism, proving far more damaging to it. In sheer numbers the academy remained safely, overwhelmingly in the hands of the Left, whose members in fact grew more radical, with some notable exceptions, in these years. But they gradually lost the unchallenged intellectual ascendancy, though not the prestige, they once had enjoyed.

Thanks to this intellectual rebirth, the case against Progressivism and in favor of the Constitution is stronger and deeper than it has ever been. Progressivism has never been in a fair fight, an equal fight, until now, because its political opponents had largely been educated in the same ideas, had lost touch, like Antaeus, with the ground of the Constitution in natural right, and so tended to offer only Progressivism Lite as an alternative. The superficiality of Progressive scholarship is now evident. They could never take the ideas of the Declaration and Constitution seriously, for many of the same reasons that Obama cannot ultimately take them seriously. Wilson never demonstrated that the Constitution was inadequate to the problems of his age – he asserted it, or rather assumed it. His references to *The Federalist* are shallow and general, and willfully ignorant of the separation of powers as an instrument to energize and hone, not merely limit, the national government. Like many of his contemporaries, his criticisms of the national government are based on an exaggeratedly negative reading of constitutional theory and practice. Though he thought of himself as picking up where Alexander Hamilton, Daniel Webster, and Lincoln had left off, Wilson never investigated where they left off and why. Neither he nor his main contemporaries asked how far *The Federalist*'s or Lincoln's reading of national powers and duties might take them, because they assumed it would not take them very far, that it reflected the political forces of its age and had to be superseded by new doctrines for a new age. They weren't interested in Lincoln's reasons, only in his results. Not right but historical might was the Progressives' true focus.

Today, liberalism looks increasingly, well, elderly. Hard of hearing, irascible, enamored of past glories, forgetful of mistakes and promises, prone to repeat the same stories over and over – it isn't the youthful voice of tomorrow it once imagined itself to be. Among the septuagenarian contenders for the Democratic presidential nomination in 2020, only one could win. Joe Biden, the frailest of them all, got the nod, but there was no Generation Gap (for good or ill) between his policies and Pete Buttigieg's. They were virtually indistinguishable. And now, with a century-old track record, liberalism will find it harder than ever to paint itself as the disinterested champion of the public good. Long ago it became an establishment, one of the estates of the realm, with its court party of notoriously self-interested constituencies, the public employee unions, the trial lawyers, the feminists, the environmentalists, and the big corporate executives aching to be social justice warriors with Fortune 500 salaries. Not visions of the future, but visions of plunder come to mind. This is one side of what Mead means when he criticizes the blue state social model as outmoded and heavy-handed. The Patient Protection and Affordable Care Act could have been written by the faculty of the Rexford G. Tugwell School of Public Administration in 1933. In fact, it resembles Roosevelt's NIRA (the National Industrial Recovery Act) in its attempt to control a huge swath of the economy through collusive price-fixing, restraints on production, aversion to competition, and corporatist partnerships between industry and government. It remains exhibit A in the case for the intellectual obsolescence of liberalism.

BANKRUPTCY

Finally, we come to the fiscal embarrassments confronting contemporary liberals. Again, Obamacare is wonderfully emblematic. President Obama's solution to the problem of two health care entitlement programs quickly going bankrupt – Medicare and Medicaid – was *to add a third*? Perhaps it was a stratagem. More likely it was simply the reflexive liberal solution to any social problem: spend more. From Karl Marx to John Rawls, if you'll excuse the juxtaposition, left-wing critics of capitalism have often paid it the supreme compliment of presuming it so productive an economic system that it has overcome permanently the problem of scarcity in human life. Capitalism has generated a "plenty." It has distributional problems, which produce intolerable social and economic instability; but eliminate or control those inconveniences and it could produce wealth enough not only to provide for every man's necessities but also to lift him comfortably into the realm of freedom. To many liberals, that premise implied that socioeconomic rights could be paid for without severe damage to the economy, and without oppressive taxation at least of the majority. Obama was among the first liberals to suggest that even capitalism cannot pay for all the benefits promised by the American welfare state, particularly regarding health care. Granted, his solution was counterintuitive in the extreme, which makes one wonder if he was sincere. To the extent that liberalism is the welfare state, and the welfare state is entitlement spending, and entitlements are mostly spent effecting the right to health care, the insolvency of the health care entitlement programs is rightly regarded as a major part of the economic, and moral, crisis of liberalism. "Simply put," Yuval Levin writes, "we cannot afford to preserve our welfare state in anything like its present form."

If something can't go on forever, the economist Herbert Stein noted sagely, it won't. It would be possible to increase federal revenues by raising taxes, but the kind of money that's needed could only be raised by taxing the middle class (defined, let us say, as all those families making less than $250,000 a year) very heavily. Like every Democratic candidate since Walter Mondale, who made the mistake of confessing to the American people that he was going to raise their taxes, Obama swore not to do that. Even supporters of Obamacare, like Clive Crook, a commentator for the *Atlantic* and the *Financial Times*, regretted the decision.

> It is right to provide guaranteed health insurance, but wrong to claim this great prize could be had, in effect, for nothing. Broadly based tax increases and fundamental reform to health care delivery will be needed to balance the books. Denying this was a mistake. What was worse – an insult to one's intelligence, really – was to argue as Obama has ... that this reform was, first and foremost, a cost-reducing initiative, and a way to drive down premiums.

If the bankruptcy of the entitlement programs were handled just the right way, however, with world-class cynicism and opportunism, in an emergency demanding quick, painful action lest grandma descend into an irreversible diabetic coma, then liberalism might succeed in maneuvering America into a European-style über-welfare state, fueled by massive and regressive taxes cheerfully accepted by the citizenry. That was Bernie Sanders's not-so-hidden agenda, which attracted fewer votes in 2020, however, than in 2016. Nonetheless, one path forward for liberalism would be to declare bankruptcy, as it were, and reorganize itself as an honest-to-God (perhaps the wrong term) socialist movement.

THE END OF LIBERALISM?

Few things in politics are permanent. Conservatism versus liberalism didn't become the central division in our politics until the middle of the twentieth century. Before that American politics revolved around such issues as states' rights, territorial expansion, war, slavery, the tariff, and suffrage. Parties have come and gone in our history. You won't find many Federalists or Whigs lining up at the polls these days. Britain's Liberal Party faded from power in the 1920s. The Canadian Liberal Party collapsed in 2011. Recently, within a decade of its maximum empire at home and abroad, a combined intellectual movement, political party, and form of government crumbled away, to be swept up and consigned to the dustbin of history. Communism, which in a very different way from American liberalism traced its roots to Hegelianism, Social Darwinism, and leadership by a vanguard group of intellectuals, vanished before our eyes, though not without an abortive coup or two. If Communism, armed with millions of troops and thousands of megatons of nuclear weapons, could collapse of its own deadweight and implausibility, why not American liberalism? The parallel is imperfect, of course, because liberalism and its vehicle, the Democratic Party, remain profoundly popular, resilient, and changeable. Elections matter to them. What's more, the egalitarian impulse, populist democracy, and the Democratic Party itself have deep roots in the American political tradition.

Some elements of liberalism are inherent to American democracy, as Tocqueville confirms, but the compound, the peculiar combination that is contemporary liberalism, is not. Compounded of the philosophy of history, Social Darwinism, the living constitution, leadership, the cult of the State, the rule of administrative experts, entitlements and group rights, and moral creativity, modern liberalism is something new and distinctive, despite the presence in it, too, of certain American constants like the love of equality and democratic individualism. Under the pressure of ideas and events, that compound could come apart. Liberals' confidence in being on the right, the winning side of history could crumble, perhaps has already begun to crumble. Trust in government, which really means in the State, is at or near all-time lows.

What might persuade American liberals that they have failed history's test? A series of epic political defeats and painful repudiations of their impossible dreams might do the trick. At the least, liberalism would then have to downsize its ambitions and get back in touch with political, moral, and fiscal reality. It would have to – all together now – *turn back the clock*. But in the meantime – and for what looks like a long time – post-Obama liberalism seems determined to radicalize itself in the direction of socialism, or nihilism, or both.

CHAPTER TWELVE

THE OLD NEW LEFT
AND THE NEW NEW LEFT

In 2017, the "Summer of Love" turned fifty. The hippies who flocked to San Francisco with flowers in their hair are now aging boomers who have long given up LSD for statins and blood pressure pills. Today's youth couldn't tell a hippie from a Yippie, though they may have heard, vaguely at least, of the yuppies, a later species from whom they are more directly descended.

Will the Sixties ever end? Ever since the 1960s we've been debating the 1960s. With the recent bursts of rioting and student activism at Berkeley, Yale, Middlebury, Claremont McKenna, and colleges across the country, followed hard by the Black Lives Matter wave of protests sparked by the death of George Floyd, even today's millennials and post-millennials (Generation Z, as they're called, perched on the alphabetic cliff) find themselves drafted into comparisons with their grandparents' generation.

Cuba, Selma, Watts, Vietnam, assassinations, the Beatles, the pill, the moon landing – the '60s seemed to have it all, including some diversions so bizarre at the time that they can scarcely be believed now. The world's first "Human Be-In," for example, was held at Golden Gate Park, San Francisco, in January 1967, a sort of prelude to the summer's love-in. Its sponsors predicted it would initiate a "new epoch" in human history. "In unity we shall shower the country with waves of ecstasy and purification," they told the

Berkeley Barb. "Fear will be washed away; ignorance will be exposed to sunlight; profits and empire will lie drying on deserted beaches." Twenty thousand turned out for what *Newsweek*, in a lavish photo spread, called "a love feast, a psychedelic picnic, a hippie happening."

Yet already a serpent of discord had crept into the stoners' Eden. Among the stars at the Be-In was Timothy Leary, celebrated for his experiments with LSD and for spreading the countercultural gospel of "turn on, tune in, and drop out," meaning drop out of high school, college, graduate school, and the corporate rat race, to follow him in search of your bliss. Also present was Jerry Rubin, a gadfly leader of the New Left, fresh out of jail, who at a press conference proclaimed a rather different message: "Tune-In, Drop-Out, Take-Over." For better or worse, mostly worse, the future lay with the take-over artists.

THE SIXTIES

The very idea of the '60s is, of course, very '60s. It presupposes a generational consciousness, defined against hapless parents and forebears – "Bliss was it in that dawn to be alive, / But to be young was very heaven!" – and marked by the enlightened superiority of those "strong in love," to borrow again from William Wordsworth. As a concept, the '60s is, and always was, less about the decade than the generation that took possession of it.

One often reads, accordingly, that the '60s began in 1963 with John F. Kennedy's assassination and ended in the early '70s with Watergate, the energy crisis, the fall of Vietnam, and *Roe v. Wade*. That certainly captures the '60s as a tale of lost innocence or disappointed idealism. But as a storyline it shortchanges the determined cultivation of all that innocence, the peculiar roots and character of that generation's self-proclaimed idealism. To understand those one has to glance back at the 1950s. Elvis, the Beat poets, *Brown v. Board of Education*, massive resistance in the South – many points are relevant; too many – but for our purposes the startling changes in American higher education demand attention.

Charles Murray and Richard Herrnstein put their finger on

these developments, using Harvard as their leading example, in the opening pages of *The Bell Curve* (1994), and David Brooks gave a classic account of them in *Bobos in Paradise: The New Upper Class and How They Got There* (2000), a work that has lost none of its charm and bite. At the beginning of the 1950s, Harvard was a bastion of the WASP aristocracy. "Two-thirds of all applicants were admitted," Brooks notes. "Legacy" applicants, i.e., sons of alumni, had a 90% admission rate. The average verbal SAT score for freshmen was 583, higher than the Ivy League average of around 500.

In a single decade the school was transformed. By 1960 the freshman verbal SAT had soared to 678. "The average Harvard freshman in 1952," observes Brooks, "would have placed in the bottom 10 percent" of the freshman class of 1960. Harvard and almost all of the elite schools around the country became meritocratic hothouses, open to Jews, Catholics, non-mainline Protestants, women (eventually), and other "brainy strivers." In absolute and relative numbers, Americans going to college rose to unprecedented, by previous standards perhaps unimaginable, levels.

The story of the boomers triggering a boom in higher education is familiar. What's less well known, however, is the connection with the upheavals to come. Here, Brooks is illuminating:

> Imagine now you are a young meritocrat, the child of, say, a pharmacist and an elementary school teacher, accepted to a prestigious university in the mid-sixties. You are part of a huge cohort of education arrivistes. Your campus still has some of the aristocratic trappings of the WASP culture, though it is by now a little embarrassed by them. And as you look out into the world, you see the last generation of the Old Guard ... still holding key jobs and social authority. They are in the positions of power and prestige you hope to occupy. But they are still living by an ethos you consider obsolete, stifling, and prejudiced.... Naturally, you and your many peers, even if you do not think about it deliberately, are going to try to finish off the old regime.

The ascent of the "meritocrats," in Brooks's and Murray's analysis, produced a revolution of rising expectations that made the culture wars of the 1960s almost inevitable: as barriers and inequalities fell, the remaining ones seemed all the more hateful and intolerable. And because their scores really were higher than the old elite's, the '60s' kids felt they had *earned* the right to be listened to by the world, to dictate to the world the terms of its remaking.

This was their "bubble," to use Murray's favorite word, a bubble that was self-inflated, though many adults who ought to have known better contributed to the students' premature self-regard. To begin with, it was the WASP elites who had embraced the Scholastic Aptitude Test and opened the university's doors to the high scorers. It was not quite educational suicide – the WASPs survived as a much smaller part of the new meritocracy. But it came close enough, as Nicholas Lemann emphasized in his history of the SAT, *The Big Test* (1999), to make one wonder at the old elite's dutiful willingness to supplant itself for what it believed was the country's, and the academy's, benefit. It got no credit for its devotion to duty from the student protestors then or now, to be sure. But the old WASPs (Harvard's president James Bryant Conant was a crucial figure) should have known that verbal and mathematical skills, laudable in themselves, do not guarantee wisdom or the moral credentials for leadership.

Then there was Lyndon Johnson, no part of any pre-existing elite, but a poignant example of feeding the tiger that would soon eat him. Announcing the Great Society at the University of Michigan commencement in May 1964, he flattered the graduates in the standard modern mode. "Your imagination, your initiative, and your indignation will determine whether we build a society where progress is the servant of our needs, or a society where old values and new visions are buried under unbridled growth."

After the Great Recession and the longest, flattest economic recovery in American history, it may take some imagination to recall the startling prosperity of the 1950s, and the Sixties liberals' anxieties over the downsides of "unbridled growth." It is equally remarkable that President Johnson and the students shared those fears. He was wrong, of course, to assume that he and the kids would remain on the same page. He praised particularly their capacity for "indignation" – not dreaming that it would soon be turned against him.

THE OLD NEW LEFT

Although the hippies played an important part in the '60s, promoting free sex, drugs, and other groovy alternatives to virtue, they did not lead the way politically. In the political vanguard stood the self-described New Left (in uneasy conjunction with the emerging Black Power movement), and at its head marched not flower-children or dropouts but serious student activists.

As the name suggested, the New Left defined itself against the old Left, meaning both dogmatic Marxists and mainstream American liberals. In his 1961 "Letter to the New (Young) Left," Tom Hayden, then a twenty-one-year-old Michigan graduate, explained, "Marx, especially Marx the humanist, has much to tell us but his conceptual tools are outmoded and his final vision implausible." He rejected Marx's economic determinism and its corollary, an inevitable workers' revolution that would issue in a stateless society. But he hinted at appreciating Marx's early writings (then much in vogue) and their critique of religion, private property, and the state as forms of alienation. For Hayden and many young radicals, Fidel Castro and especially Che Guevara would prove more attractive examples of *praxis*, of Marxism as a living revolutionary faith. The New Left would come to admire a version of Marxist *struggle* at its most Nietzschean, or with the most resemblance to Nietzsche.

Concerning American liberals Hayden had more to say, scorning the "inhibiting, dangerous conservative temperament behind the façade of liberal realism which is so current." He criticized virtually the whole roster of 1950s liberal intellectuals:

[Reinhold] Niebuhr in theology; [William] Kornhauser, [Seymour Martin] Lipset, and [Daniel] Bell in political science and sociology; the neo-Freudians in psychology; [Richard] Hofstadter in history; [Arthur] Schlesinger and others of the ADA mind in the Democratic Party. Their themes purport to be different but always the same impressions emerge: Man is inherently incapable of building a good society; man's passionate causes are nothing more than dangerous psychic sprees (the issues of this period too complex and sensitive to be colored by emotionalism or moral conviction); ideals have little place in politics – we should instead design effective, responsible programs which will produce the most that is realistically possible.

Hayden identified himself with the radicals against the liberals. The "false liberals" had abandoned their "youthful dreams" and "the great optimistic tradition of liberalism," he charged, betraying morality and, more important, passionate idealism as such. Man could not thrive, he insisted, without "emotion, dissent, outrage" and the other resolute "wellsprings of life itself."

After graduation Hayden went to work for Students for a Democratic Society (SDS), originally the youth arm of the League for Industrial Democracy, a socialist group on the old Left. But under new leadership (its founder and first president was Robert "Al" Haber, a twenty-four-year-old Michigan graduate student) and with a new name, the SDS was keen to shed that skin and emerge as the authentic voice of campus radicals.

In 1962 Hayden put SDS on the map by writing a manifesto for its annual meeting, held at a United Auto Workers' retreat on Lake Huron. Extensively debated and revised by the five-dozen attendees over five days, the *Port Huron Statement* caught on immediately as the best account of student grievances at the beginning of the '60s. It sold sixty thousand copies in four years, and put SDS at the forefront of the radical movement, but not just of the radical movement. Richard Goodwin, LBJ's aide and speechwriter, credited the *Statement* as part of his inspiration for the Great Society speech.

"We are people of this generation," the *Statement* began, "bred in at least modest comfort, housed now in universities, looking uncomfortably to the world we inherit." The traditional Democratic constituencies like union members, Southerners, and poor people were in no position to lead the way to a new age. That task fell to students and intellectuals (in, or fleeing, the universities) who, looking around them, saw a country suffering from "[t]he decline of utopia and hope." Only the student Left knew, or could learn, what this diagnosis meant and how to treat the underlying malady so as to spare Americans a life of "apathetic absurdity."

"Utopia and hope" – it sounded like a road picture, coming to a screen near you: "Road to Utopia," starring Bob Hope, Bing Crosby, and Dorothy Lamour. But the SDS wasn't known for its sense of humor, certainly not about itself. It was always in deadly earnest. Barack Obama's 2008 presidential campaign speeches could almost have been transcribed from the youthful imaginings of the *Port Huron Statement*, except that he had the political sense to confine himself to hope and change, and leave utopia for the sequel.

PROTEST, THEN AND NOW

Yet there was something ingenuous and almost admirable about the SDS's early manifesto that is lacking in post-Obama radicalism. Tom Hayden had spent fall 1961 as a Freedom Rider, getting beaten up by the KKK in Mississippi and jailed in Georgia. He and his comrades were appalled by the racial bigotry of the American South (and North), and they revered, at least in the beginning, the non-violent civil rights movement of the 1950s and early 1960s. They longed, in a way, to emulate the heroes of that movement, who like Martin Luther King drew explicitly from Christian sources, among others, and insisted on strenuous "self-purification" as an essential stage of non-violent consciousness. Indeed, the *Port Huron Statement* quoted the Declaration of Independence and Abraham Lincoln, even as the civil rights leaders did, accusing the country of not living up to its own principles. It assailed American hypocrisy, and the apathy and alienation that went with it.

No such Americanism, however vestigial, remains in today's campus protestors, who celebrate only victims, not martyrs, and who have been taught to believe that America, and the West as a whole, are oppressors and nothing but oppressors, six ways from Sunday – racists, sexists, imperialists, homophobes, xenophobes, transphobes, etc.

The early SDS wanted to overcome "[t]he decline of utopia and hope" by showing that young people, on the New Left as in the civil rights movement, could *make* history rather than wait patiently for progress to find them, or for the millennium to arrive in God's good time. Real hope was not passive but active, indeed transformative. For Marx, "utopian socialism" was a contradiction in terms, the opposite of his own "scientific socialism." For the New Left, social-ism *without utopianism* was the contradiction, because change came not through an inevitable dialectic but through hope, that is, hope in man's own ability to *will* a different or more humane future, where all latent or self-created human potential could be realized. That was the utopia, the no-where land that had never been found because it had never been truly lost. In the words of the *Statement*, "We regard men as infinitely precious and possessed of unfulfilled capacities for reason, freedom, and love," where freedom meant "finding a meaning in life that is personally authentic." The object was not "to have one's way so much as it is to have a way that is one's own." Such individualism rejected the old "egoistic individualism" in favor of an open-ended "humanism": making oneself by choosing or willing one's own values.

The crucible of the New Left's individualism – where "do your own thing," "justice now," and "participatory democracy" were thought to be reconciled – was the universities. It was from there that the SDS vowed to "reinsert theory and idealism" in politics. The idealism depended on the theory, as we've seen, and thus on theo-rists, but the idealism was for everyone, at least in theory. Thus the '60s New Left launched sharp critiques of the prevailing theories in the university. The *Statement* condemned, in particular, value-free social science and the conformist premises of the military-industri-al-collegiate complex.

Nonetheless, the SDS still regarded the university as the essen-tial locus of the new politics, because despite its faults it stood as the "only mainstream institution ... open to participation by individuals of nearly any viewpoint." The radicals honored the university as "a community of controversy" – no safe spaces or trigger warnings for them – and championed "the personal cultivation of the mind" as over against the rampant, neurotic specialization of the bureaucra-tized academy.

The "old" New Left hated being treated as children by profes-sors and deans who claimed to stand *in loco parentis*. Nothing offended Tom Hayden more, as he remarked in his 1961 Letter, than American universities' "endless repressions of free speech and thought, the stifling paternalism that infects the student's whole perception of what is real and possible and enforces a parent-child relationship until the youth is suddenly transplanted into 'the world.'" When the Free Speech Movement (FSM) formed at Berkeley in 1964, its analysis of frustrated, alienated students, as Allen J. Matusow writes in his fine *The Unraveling of America: A History of Liberalism in the 1960s* (1984), "came straight out of the *Port Huron Statement*." "In our free-speech fight," said one of FSM's leaders, Mario Savio, "we have come up against what may emerge as the greatest problem of our nation – depersonalized, unresponsive bureaucracy."

Nowadays, student protestors demand in effect, and sometimes literally, that colleges protect them from adulthood – from humanistic debates and political disagreements. "It is not about creating an intellectual space!" a Yale student shouted in 2015 at Professor Nicholas Christakis, then master (the title has since been officially retired) of Silliman College, one of Yale's residential colleges. "It is not! Do you understand that? It's about creating a home here!" She added, not exactly maturely, "You should not sleep at night. You are disgusting!"

Authentic or strong individualism seems far from what today's protestors are seeking. They raise their voices almost always as members of groups, whose relevant identity is more collective than personal: students of color, the marginalized, victims of microaggressions, who seek protection by and from the white power structure, and compensation to boot.

On their own, apart from the group, they often seem emotionally fragile. As another Silliman resident, Jencey Paz, wrote in her *Yale Herald* article "Hurt at Home," "I don't want to debate. I want to talk about my pain." The journal removed her article from its website after it attracted unflattering attention – thus confirming Paz's preferences.

THE NEW NEW LEFT

No one would have called Hayden or Jerry Rubin or the other leaders of the old radicals "snowflakes." They wanted to oppose the macroagressions of a society that, in their view, had lost its way amid racism and the existential threats of the Bomb and the Cold War. They wanted to change society, not retreat from it. What happened to the New Left's passionate idealism?

It hasn't disappeared entirely, but the theory embraced by today's campus Left is far different from that of the '60s New Left. The *Port Huron Statement* reflected deep intellectual engagement, if not exactly seriousness. Its contemporary influences included Herbert Marcuse's *Eros and Civilization* (1955), C. Wright Mills's *The Power Elite* (1956), and Frantz Fanon's *The Wretched of the Earth* (1963). Marcuse, a student of Martin Heidegger's, had perhaps the primary philosophical influence on the movement, and along with other writers helped to connect it, however tendentiously, to Freud, Nietzsche, Marx, Hegel, and Rousseau.

The "new" New Left has no comparable philosophical grounding or intellectual foundation. A widely adopted primer of its thought, *Critical Race Theory: An Introduction* (2001) by Richard Delgado and Jean Stefancic, now in its third edition, nods in the direction of Antonio Gramsci, Michel Foucault, and Jacques Derrida, but these are dusty portraits on the wall rather than active intellectual interests. The book presumes the truth of an easy-going and politically convenient postmodernism without ever establishing it, or reflecting on the alternative. But that's what's so handy about postmodernism, isn't it? It lets you *get on with it* – skip past the questions of truth and justice, and get right to the delicious matter of power.

In the present case, that means cue the law professors and radical feminists. So far as I can tell, the ideology of the new campus Left – centered on identity politics, or what has come to be called identitarianism – was born from a shotgun marriage of critical legal studies, a postmodern enthusiasm at elite law schools (particularly Harvard, just when Barack Obama was studying there) in the late 1970s and 1980s, and radical feminism. What drew them together was the discovery that formal or legal equality, by then essentially achieved for blacks and women, did not guarantee equality of results, and above all did not guarantee the most essential aspect of equality of results, the *feeling* of equal recognition and respect. They joined together in pursuit of that comprehensive equality, and of the high that only that *feeling* could give, and dared any man to put asunder what Harvard Law School had brought together.

More particularly, *Critical Race Theory* acknowledges the late Derrick Bell, one of the "Crit" (critical legal studies) professors at Harvard Law and later New York University Law School, as the movement's "intellectual father figure." Father figure – so much for dismantling the patriarchy! The book lists many other minor scholars – usually by race or gender or ethnicity, but including "a number of fellow travelers and writers who are white" – as having contributed to the intellectual heritage of today's radicals. From the Crits they drew the notion that legal texts have indeterminate meanings, hence are playthings of the powerful. From the feminists they learned of "the relationship between power and the construction of social roles, as well as the unseen, largely invisible ... patterns and habits that make up patriarchy and other types of domination."

Consider the "basic tenets" of the position.

First, in America (and the theory seems to be purpose-built for this country) racism is pervasive, inescapable, "ordinary" and "not aberrational" – the "common, everyday experience of most people of color in this country." Only "most"? But the bigger problem is the refusal to define "racism." Does discriminating against people on the basis of race mean denying them equal rights, or objecting to the imposition of equal results?

The second principle is "material determinism" or "interest convergence," meaning that whites (but not other races?) are guaranteed to pursue their own economic interests as a race, thus ensuring and perpetuating "white supremacy."

Third, the "social construction" thesis, which holds that race and races are not "objective, inherent, or fixed" and correspond to no "biological or genetic reality," but are social inventions. But how can there be "material determinism" if races are immaterial? You begin to see the problem.

The fourth tenet, "differential racialization," presumes "that each race has its own origins and ever-evolving history," which the powers-that-be exploit and manipulate. But now races are the real substratum under the constantly changing interpretations of society, not mere artifacts of those interpretations.

Fifth, "intersectionality and antiessentialism." Identity politics has to recognize that "no person has a single, easily stated, unitary identity," the authors declare. This notion traces to black feminism's big discovery, that you can be black and a woman (and gay, Democrat, Episcopal) at the same time, and have to deal with the potential conflicts lest there be a nasty crash at the intersection. Notice that the ugly new terms contribute nothing to the solution of the problem of who should yield to whom.

Finally, the "unique voice of color." "Coexisting in somewhat uneasy tension with anti-essentialism," the authors admit, "the voice-of-color thesis holds that because of their different histories and experiences with oppression," minorities have "a presumed competence to speak about race and racism" that whites are "unlikely" to have. Check your white privilege at the door, in other words, because whiteness implies a presumed *incompetence* in matters of justice, at least regarding anyone who is non-white. This is passed off as a matter of history and experience, but the (acknowledged) tension arises precisely because, as the name suggests and everyone realizes, the "voice-of-color" thesis keys off the color of your skin, not the content of your character or experiences.

It is hard to believe how many contradictions are papered over in this catalogue of "basic tenets." To take the most obvious example, for something that calls itself "critical race theory," it has no consistent theory of race and no critical distance from its political agenda. Is race something real, indelible, and fundamental, which shapes the soul itself and commands opinions, passions, and interests across society? Or is it all in our heads, a social construction that we could do without? It is as if Marxism proclaimed both that the history of the world is the history of class struggle, and that it isn't. Or that the Communist revolution is inevitable, or maybe not.

The new New Left can live with its contradictions because of its postmodernism. It finds each part of the contradiction politically useful, and that is the standard that matters. Sometimes it is useful to say that whites are objectively privileged and therefore oppressors, and that blacks, say, cannot be racist because they objectively lack power and are the oppressed. But other times it is useful to deny this, and to say that anyone can be a racist because racism is a state of mind. Sometimes it is useful to claim, as Justice Harry Blackmun did (adopted as one of the volume's epigraphs), "In order to get beyond racism, we must first take account of race." At other times it is useful to insist that in America it is never possible to get beyond racism.

Is it any wonder that liberal idealism, or any sort of idealism, is in short supply on today's campuses? Postmodernism isn't about justice – because there is no justice "out there" – it's about the will to power. Add that to an invidious, fine-grained racial consciousness that might have made the antebellum South proud, and you have an ugly combination. Having run that banner up their flagpole, it's clear why young people who salute it can be vicious and violent in packs on and off campus, while despondent and fragile at heart. Idealism depends on transcending self-interest, and today's protestors expect every ethnic, racial, class, and gender group to follow its interest, and the most powerful to win. The Black Lives Matter protestors appeared to be a partial exception, insofar as they seemed to want to revive some notes of idealism. But the mutual hopefulness soon eroded amid a long series of riots. We are a long way from utopia and hope.

FROM OLD TO NEW

Most college students have nothing to do with campus radicals, of course. They don't want to transgress the thorny thickets of political correctness, however, and so they let the radicals do their thing and set much of the campus agenda and climate. In enforcing political correctness, the radical students usually command immense assistance from the college administration and faculty, where the original New Left went to die, or rather to rule.

For the contrasts so far between the old and the new New Left are only part of the story. The *Port Huron Statement* caught the SDS at its most thoughtful and idealistic, in 1962. The rest of the '60s saw its descent into violence and anti-American extremism, and its defeat as a political force. The SDS's campaign against the Vietnam War, which became its focus from 1965 on, did not halt the war but did help to elect President Richard Nixon, twice. From a too-soaring or unnatural idealism, the radicals plunged into a deep, cynical hatred of the country they had once hoped to lead and redeem.

Speaking at an antiwar march in Washington, D.C., in late 1965, SDS president Carl Oglesby explained that the leaders who had taken America into Vietnam "are not moral monsters. They are all honorable men. They are all liberals." They had rationalized their folly with the ideology of "anti-Communism," a word that Hayden and the early SDSers had always loathed as part of the "fascist" political vocabulary. For Oglesby, the mainstream liberals, whether they knew it or not, stood for "corporate liberalism," or what his predecessor, Paul Potter, had called "the System," unjust and oppressive in its operations at home and abroad, always putting "national values before human values."

Liberals were the enemy, but in a more urgent and comprehensive way than in the *Statement*. Marcuse's influence was growing among the radicals, and his essay "Repressive Tolerance," published in 1965, pointed them away from their old free speech idealism and towards a more ruthless, revolutionary consciousness. Toleration was once a great progressive cause, he argued, when liberals adopted it as a weapon against authoritarian societies. But now it risked becoming silently repressive: toleration in a liberal society like America was a means of neutralizing and coopting all opposition to the power structure or the power elite. It was a means of preventing a liberal society from being replaced by a revolutionary one. Marcuse urged the students to treat tolerance as a proud double standard or partisan tool, i.e., to show no tolerance for "affluence," the war, or the Right in general. Tolerance for me, but not for thee. His argument laid the groundwork for political correctness.

By late 1966 the SDS had denounced the war as "genocidal." The students' fight was therefore for the Vietnamese people, as well as for themselves. Opposing ROTC, the draft, and black Americans' conditions of life at home, the radicals increasingly saw all of their protests connected by the tyrannical nature of American society. It was only logical to move "From Protest to Resistance," the title of a celebrated piece in *New Left Notes*, the SDS journal, in early 1967. (So student-led were these developments that Matusow, whose account I follow here, switches in his history at some point from regular years to academic years.) America's besetting sin, said the SDS, was "imperialism," an old Left (Leninist) indictment now endorsed by the New Left, which echoed as well the black power movement's charge that inner city ghettos constituted "internal colonies."

"Once the new left determined that America was the villain," writes Matusow, "it shifted from an antiwar movement to a movement favoring victory for the Vietcong." Hayden and friends began to meet with Vietnamese Communists. Bigger, more violent demonstrations followed, designed, among other things, to shut down the "war machine" and in early 1968 to seize Columbia University. As the New Left came more and more to resemble the old, cheering Marx and Mao, it turned its back on the *Port Huron Statement*'s hope for "participatory democracy" and adopted Lenin's principle of democratic centralism, concentrating control at the top, finally in 1969 in the so-called "Weatherman" faction.

Outnumbered at the 1969 SDS national convention in Chicago, that faction tried to stage a coup, bringing in the Black Panthers to ring the meeting hall and chanting "Smash racism!" when their opponents tried to speak. The coup failed. Next, the Weathermen's call for "Days of Rage" in Chicago, designed ultimately to stop the imperialists' war by starting a civil war at home, failed miserably, too. Afterwards, keen to sow terror, they went underground to plant bombs, which later blew up several of their own as well as a few innocent victims. From Summer of Love to Days of Rage – the descent had taken a little more than two years.

But all was not lost. The Weatherman manifesto, published in the June 18, 1969, issue of *New Left Notes*, came close to being the birth announcement of identity politics. "You Don't Need a Weatherman to Know Which Way the Wind Blows" counted among its authors William Ayres and Bernadette Dohrn, later friends of Barack Obama. They argued that black Americans would be the new revolutionary vanguard, but that their Leninist captains, mostly white student radicals, would determine the direction of advance and who – black, white, or Latino – truly represented the oppressed of the earth. Any white who does not support the black revolutionaries is "objectively racist," the manifesto proclaimed, in words that still echo.

Students for a Democratic Society collapsed in 1969, paralyzed by schism and by its own decadent principles. But its spirit and many of its leaders moved into the academy. Bill Ayres became a tenured professor of education. Why bother seizing university buildings if you can move in and run the whole university? A vast effort began to counter false consciousness by the endless indoctrination of correct consciousness – political correctness – in the American mind. Though in some ways out of sympathy with today's P.C. radicals, most of the old New Left and its successors find it difficult to oppose them, on or off campus. The old radicals still find it hard to recognize an enemy to their left.

PART III

CONSERVATIVES AND THE TWO CONSTITUTIONS

CHAPTER THIRTEEN

REAGAN'S UNFINISHED REVOLUTION

Serious students of American politics ought to be thinking about Ronald Reagan, studying his speeches and decisions, reflecting on his successes and failures. Today's questions differ from those he confronted in the 1980s, and so it is less his specific policies than the reasoning behind them – and his leadership on behalf of them – that matter. The crisis of the two constitutions has much to do with the confrontation, still occurring in many ways, between the "Reagan Revolution" and Barack Obama's (and his progressive predecessors' and successors') long-sought "transformation" of the United States.

TRANSFORMERS

Candidate Obama implied as much in his famous comment in 2008: "I think Ronald Reagan changed the trajectory of America in a way that Richard Nixon did not and in a way that Bill Clinton did not. He put us on a fundamentally different path because the country was ready for it." If Americans were ready for another path – up from Reagan – Obama was offering himself as the guide. He would be the Democratic Reagan; perhaps, if he were lucky or audacious enough, as he freely insinuated elsewhere, the Democratic Lincoln. The "fundamentally different path" Obama called us to follow was not altogether new, but neither was it altogether old. It was the path of "transformation" itself, of constant self-reinvention, endless becoming, unceasing adjustment to new social conditions, challenges, and ideals. This was the road modern American liberalism had been on for a long time. This was the line of march Reagan himself had been on when he was a Democrat – from New Freedom to New Deal to the Great Society, each meant as a transformation of the existing America. Together these promised the *Aufhebung* (the absorption, nullification, and transcendence) of the old freedom of the Declaration of Independence, the agreed deal of the original Constitution, and the not-so-great society (as liberals saw it) of selfish or repressed individualism. Reagan abandoned this path before the Great Society, having realized where it was heading. Obama's threatened transformation, the fourth in a series, would not have surprised him.

Reagan expressed his objections to this project in one of his earliest political addresses, a televised speech in 1962 (the year he became a Republican) on behalf of Richard Nixon's ill-fated campaign for California governor.

> Senator Fulbright, speaking at Stanford University, referred to the President as "our moral teacher and our leader," and he said "he is hobbled in his task by the restrictions of power imposed on him by a constitutional system designed for eighteenth-century agrarian society," and we've been told that the talk of taking the country back to the Constitution is talk of taking it back to the days of McKinley. Well, I for one, don't think that's a bad idea. Under McKinley we freed Cuba.

For a president (John F. Kennedy in this case, who had "lost" Cuba in the Bay of Pigs fiasco and the later missile crisis) to be hailed as "our moral teacher and our leader" struck Reagan as sycophantic, even un-American – and as repugnant to the genius of the U.S. Constitution. He took Senator J. William Fulbright, the liberal Democrat from Arkansas, to be implying that an *unhobbled* president, the kind of leader and moral teacher that the times really demanded, would have to escape "the restrictions of power imposed on him" by America's obsolete Constitution.

Once free of those restrictions, the president would be free to be "as big a man as he can," in an office that could be "anything he has the sagacity and force to make it." Those rather ominous phrases come not from Reagan or Fulbright but from Woodrow Wilson, who devised our modern and highly favorable view of leadership, and who was elected president the year after Reagan was born. By coincidence or perhaps by design, Reagan asserted that to find a well-functioning, constitutional presidency it was not necessary to go all the way back to the eighteenth century or its agrarian aftermath (as Senator Fulbright had insinuated). It was sufficient to return to a point just before the Progressive Era, to the presidency of William McKinley (elected in 1896 and 1900, and liberator of Cuba in the Spanish-American War of 1898). The Constitution had been alive and well in the early twentieth century.

A leader-president untethered from the Constitution might be ambitious or unambitious, progressive or reactionary; Reagan's objection was that, regardless, such a figure could not be *safe* for a free people. The very idea smacked of "Kaiserism" and "Hitlerism," he said elsewhere. So, quoting Daniel Webster, he urged his fellow Californians in 1962 to "hold on" to the "Constitution of the United States of America and to the Republic for which it stands. Miracles do not cluster. What has happened once in six thousand years may never happen again."

Wilson's complaint against the old Constitution and its principles lay behind Senator Fulbright's condemnation of it. In Wilson's striking phrase, the old system amounted to "leaderless government," which he regarded as a contradiction in terms. The Constitution, with its separation of powers, checks and balances, federalism, and tortuous amendment process – the very eighteenth-century impediments Senator Fulbright regretted – had divided authority and rendered leadership by a Big Man of "sagacity and force" peculiarly difficult. And without such leadership, rational and continual political progress – transformation – was impossible. "Leadership and control must be lodged somewhere," Wilson insisted. "No living thing can have its organs offset against each other as checks, and live." The frame of government suitable for "leadership and control" was not George Washington's or William McKinley's Constitution

but a new one, what Obama, following Wilson, calls "the living constitution." The term implies, none too subtly, that the old Constitution is dead or on life support, and that the new one, to remain alive
and healthy, must be coordinated or overseen by a leader. To sugar
coat this shocking news, the advocates tell a soothing tale to friend
and foe alike, that the new constitution is nothing more than an
extension, an updating, a gradual, unthreatening, and altogether
necessary evolution from the old. "Darwinian," Wilson liked to call
it. He meant that human rights, governments, and constitutions, just
like biological species, have their "natural evolution and are one
thing in one age, another in another." Transformation is all.

As a Progressive, Wilson thought the times could be counted on
to be gradually but inevitably improving, so much so that mankind
in the twentieth century could for the first time recognize the difference between, as Obama likes to say, the right side and the wrong
side of history. Although "leadership" had a reputation as undemocratic (try saying it in German), so long as leaders follow the permanent path of progress – keep to the right side of history – democrats
need not fear. The danger is further reduced because true leadership,
combining Darwinian ethics with Darwinian efficiency, summons
people into a better and more or less inevitable future where they
would want to go anyway, if only they knew how.

To help the people overcome their blindness – to persuade the
people to follow them – leaders like Obama need two novel qualities,
now grown familiar: vision and compassion. The leader lends the
people *vision* by appealing to them to imagine a much better future
that is closer than they think, e.g., a world in which health care is
universally available, dirt cheap, and surpassingly excellent. Imagine that! Why would anyone want to deny your right to *that*? Visionary politics relies primarily on imaginative appeals, not syllogisms or
enthymemes, as anyone who has listened to recent presidential campaigns will recognize. The leader must feel a lively *compassion* or
sympathy for the people in order to keep these dreams of the future
tethered to some present-day reality. He must move with the common impulse and interpret the common feeling. Bill Clinton summed
up the qualifications in one sentence: "I feel your pain."

Leadership opened the royal road that modern liberalism took into American politics. Rather than separating and checking governmental powers, liberals sought a way to combine and concentrate them. Needless to say, such accumulated power would be safe only in the hands of selfless experts devoted to the people's good, i.e., liberals. Rather than an embarrassing case of self-delusion fanned by self-interest, they regarded this arrangement as a great ethical advance, because these powers were to be spent in the continual emission of a new class of social and economic rights for the people. Each right denied was the kernel of a social problem. Each social problem demanded a social program. Every social program constituted a solemn promise, in conjunction with all the other programs, to bring unprecedented material well-being and unimaginable spiritual fulfillment to the people.

In this way American government, once limited by natural rights and a written Constitution, became perpetually engaged in the reconstruction of society itself, of the people themselves. Rather than the government representing *us,* we came to represent them, our rulers. It's hard not to be reminded of Bertolt Brecht's 1953 poem "The Solution," which was about a workers' riot in Communist East Germany. "[T]he people," Brecht wrote,

Had forfeited the confidence of the government
And could win it back only
By redoubled efforts. Would it not be easier
In that case for the government
To dissolve the people
And elect another?

Gradually, a people with the capacity to govern themselves were tempted to become a people addicted to transforming themselves – or rather to *being* transformed – into whatever the times demanded, down whatever path "our moral teacher and our leader" beckoned. Hope and change became the coin of the realm.

THE REAGAN REVOLUTION

Beginning in the 1960s, Reagan's political ambition forced him to face an unusual set of questions. Could a conservative be a leader in the new and now established sense, without succumbing to the concept's implicit progressivism? Furthermore, could a conservative chief executive actually turn the conventions and expectations of leadership to conservative policy ends – and still more important, to the end of somehow leading the country back to the Constitution and limited government? As his political career took off, Reagan confronted the Obama Transformation in advance, as it were, and tried to redefine leadership in a populist, conservative, and at least partly constitutionalist direction.

Wilson had distinguished leadership from old-fashioned rulership. Rulers thought themselves superior, and used their unequal power to impose their opinions and interests on the ruled; leaders were of the people, though slightly in advance of them. Rulership involved looking down; leadership involved looking forward. Ruling implied ordering the souls and bodies of the ruled. Leadership implied opening up individuals to "self-development," which would proceed hand in hand with the performance of their social duties, in constant adjustment to the spirit of the age.

In effect, Reagan tried to turn this distinction against liberalism. It was the living constitution, he argued, the sprawling, evolving Big Government produced by modern progressivism, that desired to *rule* Americans. It did so through a new kind of ruling class, a mixture of leaders and experts, whose rule could hardly be resented because it was justified, in theory at least, by the solution of the people's problems, the alleviation of their needs, and the recognition of their lifestyles. By contrast, Reagan and the conservative movement sought to remind Americans that they were not needy victims whose freedom, dignity, and happiness depended on the State, but citizens capable of ruling themselves, and capable therefore of returning to a smaller, more limited government. He wanted to lead them back to the Constitution as it had stood earlier in the century, still more or less in the full vigor of its founding principles.

His starting point was, invariably, American exceptionalism. "This idea," as he put it in 1964, speaking on behalf of Barry Goldwater, "that government was beholden to the people, that it had no other source of power except the sovereign people, is still the newest, most unique idea in all the long history of man's relation to man." Twenty-five years later, in his Farewell Address, he expanded on the point.

> Ours was the first revolution in the history of mankind that truly reversed the course of government, and with three little words: "We the People."... Almost all the world's constitutions are documents in which governments tell the people what their privileges are. Our Constitution is a document in which "We the People" tell the government what it is allowed to do. "We the People" are free.

"This belief," he continued, "has been the underlying basis for everything I've tried to do these past 8 years." Reagan spoke of *reversing* the course of government, that is, returning it to first principles. That's what a "revolution" means in one of its basic senses, a complete circular turn, a return to the beginning. Reagan's three little words are, to be sure, a derived truth. "'We the People' are free" because each human being who consents to form this people is himself, or herself, by nature equal and free. That self-evident truth stands opposed to what he called in the Goldwater speech the latter-day "perversion" which presumes that "our natural unalienable rights are ... a dispensation of government, divisible by a vote of the majority." Reagan was clear that "we have certain rights which cannot be infringed upon, even if the individual stands outvoted by all of his fellow citizens. Without this recognition, majority rule is nothing more than mob rule."

Although the Declaration of Independence supplied the basic principles, Reagan emphasized the Constitution, and especially the Preamble's opening words, which he called "probably the most meaningful words" in the whole document. This focus on "We the People" lent a democratic or populist tone to his interpretation, which has been noted but not sufficiently emphasized. Like the latter-day Tea Party's, his was a populism dedicated ultimately to restoring, not supplanting, the Constitution. Before the people could take significant steps in that direction, however, Reagan thought they needed first to regain confidence in their own capacity – and right – of self-government. Americans' self-confidence had been shaken by the political and moral beating they had endured in the long decade of the 1960s, when liberalism's vanguard turned for the first time openly anti-American. In 1972 he remarked to the American Legion, "Some of our young people find little to love or defend in this country.... [T]here is an increasing tendency to believe the system has failed." In that and many other speeches he emphatically rejected the notion that America was a democracy in name only, or that it was (and some said, always had been) a force for evil in the world.

> It is time for us to quit being apologetic, especially to our own children. Even more important, it is time to challenge some of their most cherished notions by presenting facts about their world as it really is – facts that will expose the sorry myth that ours is a sick, racist, materialistic society.

Reagan rejected easy talk of "the masses" and so of the kind of leadership necessary to deal with the masses. Here is another choice passage from "the Speech," Reagan's televised address on behalf of Goldwater's presidential campaign.

> Another articulate spokesman for the welfare state defends liberalism as "meeting the material needs of the masses through the full power of centralized government." I for one find it disturbing when a representative refers to the free men and women of this country as "the masses," but beyond this "the full power of centralized government" was the very thing the Founding Fathers sought to minimize. They knew you can't control *things*; you can't control the economy without controlling *people*. So we have come to a time for choosing. Either we accept the responsibility for our own destiny, or we abandon the American Revolution and confess that an intellectual elite in a far-distant capital can plan our lives for us better than we can plan them ourselves.

This so-called elite presumes that Americans must be ruled for their own good because they are incapable of ruling themselves, at least justly. And the elite presumes that the common people must be ruled by a *different* law than applies to their rulers, for the very reason that the ruling class is far ahead of the masses. The new would-be ruling class comprised not only the political leaders at the top but also "powerful academics, fashionable left-revolutionaries, some economic illiterates who happen to hold elective office, and the social engineers who dominate the dialogue and set the format in political and social affairs," Reagan argued.

As opposed to the would-be ruling class, he championed the "common sense and common decency of ordinary men and women, working out their own lives in their own way." "In my own mind," he often said, "I was a citizen representing my fellow citizens against the institution of government." When he became governor, he asked citizens to volunteer for a "recruiting committee" to staff his administration with "men and women who did not want government careers and who would be the first to tell me if their government job was unnecessary." He asked for "expert people" in many fields to volunteer for task forces to audit and apply "modern business practices" to every department and agency of California government. He summed up his premise: "I believe in the people."

That was what President Reagan was getting at in the famous words of his First Inaugural: "In this present crisis, government is not the solution to our problem; government is the problem." He underlined the point by distinguishing, in the same paragraph, between the contrary forms of government implicitly battling it out in American politics.

> From time to time we've been tempted to believe that society has become too complex to be managed by self-rule, that government by an elite group is superior to government for, by, and of the people. Well, if no one among us is capable of governing himself, then who among us has the capacity to govern someone else?

In the struggle between the oligarchy of leaders and experts (ruling a nation of victims) and the republican government of old, he was clearly on the side of "government for, by, and of the people," his rearrangement of Lincoln's triad at Gettysburg, followed immediately by a paraphrase of a famous quotation from Thomas Jefferson's First Inaugural Address.

Nonetheless, Reagan's emphatic focus on the quarrel between "the people" and "the institution of government" tended to overwhelm his own insight that this was also an epic struggle between two very different forms of government – between republicanism and oligarchy, the Constitution and the living constitution. Though he didn't neglect this dimension of the conflict, he sided more often and more passionately with "the people" than with the form of government they had solemnly chosen. Where one would have expected to find a defense of the founders' Constitution (as amended) – an interpretation of it and its powers and duties – one found instead, all too often, a sidestep to "We the People." Where Thomas Jefferson, Andrew Jackson, Lincoln, and in their own way even Wilson and Franklin Roosevelt argued boldly for their own interpretation of the document, Reagan deferred to popular "values," not so much in a majoritarian as in a unitarian, or consensus, sense, claiming these embodied "the collective wisdom and genius of the people." When he did speak up for a constitutional provision or doctrine, it was usually federalism, in sweeping Tenth Amendment (and for that matter, in Barry Goldwater) style.

Why didn't he make a sharper, more sustained constitutionalist case? It is hard to know precisely, but several considerations occur. He was not a lawyer. He had seen Goldwater's unbending campaign to roll back modern government lose by a landslide. One of the highlights of Reagan's administration, of course, was Attorney General Edwin Meese's bold campaign for a return to "original intent" in interpreting the Constitution. Though almost all conservatives supported the idea, what exactly was being returned to and why remained a little unclear. Originalists split over the relative authority of constitutional text, tradition, who counted as ratifiers, legislative intent, and especially over whether the ratification of the Constitution was an act of pure popular will or of will informed by natural reason and law. Politically, originalists disagreed over civil rights (including the legitimacy of Brown v. Board of Education) and whether judicial deference to democratic laws and to administrative agencies' regulations was a virtue. These fault lines, still active today, did not make things easier. And when the Left turned against the American middle class and its morality, a gifted politician could hardly avoid returning the favor on behalf of the American people and its "traditional values," as Reagan called them.

Still, it wasn't as though the Constitution was irrelevant to the defense of American morality, or to the defeat of liberalism. Reagan's appeals to the people would have been stronger, more coherent, and more republican had he tied them consistently to the people's Constitution, which demands a degree of virtue from the people and of statesmanship from the people's representatives. In separating the healthy from the diseased parts of modern government, "modern business practices" and "common sense" could only go so far; these needed to be supplemented by a discerning application of the founders' own political science and art. After all, the point, as Reagan well knew, was not to get the public simply to laugh at or curse the follies of government as such. The people had to remember why, and how, to govern themselves in a constitutional way. Sensible and decent though they may be, Americans needed to be led back to the habit of self-government, but in a manner that did not vitiate the conditions of self-government. That was the essence of his dilemma.

Here we arrive, perhaps, at the deepest reason for Reagan's populist sensibility. He believed in the people *not* because he thought a leader or an elite could bring vision and order to their disjointed stirrings, but because he trusted their good principles and their good character – their values. It was not so much their inchoate perception of the future but of the past, the living past, from which Reagan-style leadership took its orientation. In a strange way, the people were for Reagan the vital, that is, the living link with the cause of the American founding, and with the heroic pursuit of its principles over the centuries. "We the people" *embodied* the cause of American constitutionalism, forming both its substratum and its living expression. This was a conservative version of living-constitution theory, dispensing with social science experts and progressive leaders in favor of business experts and grass-roots leaders who appreciated Americans' practical genius for freedom. The people and their values formed the kind of living constitution that Reagan could favor and, indeed, follow, insofar as this vision of the past implied a vision of the future – of choosing anew the path the people had taken before the advent of big government and the administrative state.

Accepting the nomination in 1980, he said, "My view of government places trust not in one person or one party, but in those values that transcend persons and parties. The trust is where it belongs – in the people. The responsibility to live up to that trust is where it belongs, in their elected leaders. That kind of relationship, between the people and their elected leaders, is a special kind of compact." He restated that compact in his Farewell Address. "I wasn't a great communicator," he demurred, "but I communicated great things, and they didn't spring full blown from my brow, they came from the heart of a great nation – from our experience, our wisdom, and our belief in the principles that have guided us for two centuries." He called what his administration had accomplished over the past eight years "the great rediscovery, a rediscovery of our values and our common sense."

VALUES, PROGRESS, AND THE MAYFLOWER COMPACT

In the end, however, this populist path did not lead where Reagan really wanted to go, or at least where he thought the country needed to go. And it came with costs and consequences he had not anticipated.

To begin with, at some point the tension between trusting the people's values and honoring the Constitution's principles (those principles that "have guided us for two centuries") could, and did, become acute. The problem had arisen in the 1960s and earlier, according to Reagan, who in his Second Inaugural admitted that our "system has never failed us, but, for a time, we failed the system. We asked things of government that government was not equipped to give." What options are left to a leader, then, who says "trust the people" and "I believe in the people," if the people, or a substantial fraction of them, cease to trust or even understand, at least as fully as they once did, those fundamental values?

The term itself pointed to problems ahead. "Values," in the sense of the standards or beliefs of a person or group, is not a word that Washington or Lincoln used. Its new meaning came into general use in America around the middle of the twentieth century, though it had been around for decades as a specialty word introduced by philosophers, principally Nietzsche, and social scientists, especially Max Weber. Its implications are relativist: "values" are no more and no less than the standards which someone happens to "value." Valuing things differently, other people will have different values. Strictly speaking, all values are therefore relative, as Nietzsche and Weber emphasized. As the banner for Reagan's effort to "renew our faith," it was an odd choice. Earlier generations of Americans, trying to make a point similar to Reagan's, would have put it differently, as the state of Virginia did in its famous Declaration of Rights (June 12, 1776), drafted by George Mason. Its Fifteenth article reads:

> That no free Government, or the blessings of liberty, can be preserved to any people but by a firm adherence to justice, moderation, temperance, frugality, and virtue, and by frequent recurrence to fundamental principles.

Where Reagan urged a return to the people's values, Mason called for a recurrence to virtues and fundamental principles. What's the difference? Values are what the people value; virtues and principles are what they *should* value. And they should value them because the principles are true (some of them self-evidently so) and the virtues are good, not only for Americans but (as Reagan often emphasized) for human beings as such.

By invoking "values," Reagan did not mean, of course, to traffic in relativism. He did not for a moment imagine he was seconding the worst tendencies of postmodern liberalism, and he sometimes spoke of values and virtues in the same breath. But the language he used had a logic of its own, and it quietly left the arguments in favor of those traditional American "values" in worse shape than he had found them, and employed them, in some of his better speeches.

Though he never abandoned the argument that Americans had

embraced these values because they are true, he was increasingly drawn to the argument that the values are true because Americans had embraced them – for a long time, and very successfully. If the symbol of the first argument may be said to be the Declaration and the spirit of the American Revolution, the symbol of the second, in Reagan's mind, was the Mayflower Compact. In his speech accepting the Republican presidential nomination in 1980, Reagan gave pride of place to the families who in 1620 "dared to cross a mighty ocean to build a future for themselves in a new world." When the Pilgrims arrived "at Plymouth, Massachusetts, they formed what they called a 'compact,' an agreement among themselves to build a community and abide by its laws." He emphasized, "This single act – the voluntary binding together of free people to live under the law – set the pattern for what was to come." He traced that pattern forward to the Declaration of Independence a century and a half later, to Lincoln at Gettysburg, and to his own moment. "Isn't it time once again," he asked, "to renew our compact of freedom, to pledge to each other all that is best in our lives, all that gives meaning to them – for the sake of this, our beloved and blessed land?"

It was an eloquent and urgent question. By taking the Mayflower Compact as the model, however, Reagan seemed to presuppose that Americans were already of one mind about the terms of the community and the goals of the law to which they were asked to renew their allegiance. The Pilgrims were a small, fervent community of Calvinists (though accompanied by other passengers, grown restive on a voyage that was supposed to have ended in Virginia, not New England), and they were shrewd enough to persuade everyone to sign the Compact before the *Mayflower* made landfall. Still, the beginning "pattern" relied on an effective unanimity that did not fit the circumstances of the Revolutionary War and the Civil War, Reagan's other historical examples. In 1776 and 1863 Americans had to win a war to ensure the validity and meaning of their renewed compact. The unanimity came later, so to speak. And the cause of both wars was a deep disagreement about the truth and implications of the Declaration's claims, especially "that all men are created equal." Did he think Americans in 1980 had a viable political compact that needed only to be remembered to be renewed, or did he think he had to win an argument as part of a (non-shooting) political war in order to reestablish, to reconsecrate "our compact of freedom"? Toward the end of his 1980 Acceptance Speech, he indicated his awareness of the problem. He asked Americans "to trust your values – our values – and to hold me responsible for living up to them. I ask you to trust the American spirit, which knows no ethnic, religious,... or economic boundaries," the spirit that millions of immigrants brought with them to the country. But he pointedly acknowledged, "Some say that spirit no longer exists."

Years later he took credit, as mentioned, for "the great rediscovery ... of our values and our common sense." In that project, the language of values offered two advantages. First, it bridged the differences between the traditionalist and the libertarian wings of modern American conservatism. Reagan's juxtaposition between "the people" and "the institutions of government" sounded at once populist and libertarian. His repeated call for a return to "traditional American values" sounded populist and traditionalist. But the openness of "values" invited both types of conservatives to see themselves on Reagan's side: traditionalists got tradition, with religion as an important if vague part of it, and libertarians got values, meaning the freedom to choose lifestyles as well as investments. They both got America, positioned somewhere in the middle. And behind America, as it were, stood the authority of the people, who got to choose or recognize in practice what is traditional and what will be valued. Values provided the formula, in short, for the continued coexistence and competition of the main conservative factions – and not for a resolution of their differences in light of what they *should* value.

Second, by implication, "American values" would be defined not so much by "frequent recurrence to fundamental principles" as by the American people's timely reading of history's writ. "The choices this year are not just between two different personalities, or between two political parties," Reagan told the 1984 Republican National Convention. "They are between two different visions of the future, two fundamentally different ways of governing – their government of pessimism, fear, and limits, and ours of hope, confidence, and growth." Reagan cast the central issue of the election as the choice between hope and fear, optimism and pessimism, the future and the past. The Democrats too thought progress was the issue, but in their 1984 platform insisted on progress with "social decency" as opposed to "Social Darwinism." In a way, neither party questioned that the fundamental choice confronting the voters was which party would get, or keep, the country moving forward – a difference over the *means* to progress toward the future. Even the Pilgrims, according to Reagan, had sought "to build a future for themselves" in this new land. The debate over values or justice (within and between the parties) was still present and often lively, as in the Democrats' swipe at the GOP's alleged Social Darwinism, but it tended to become part of the debate over the means to "growth."

In accepting his 1984 nomination Reagan declared, as he had in several speeches over the preceding two decades, "Isn't our choice really not one of Left or Right, but of up or down: down through the welfare state to statism … and ultimately totalitarianism, always advanced as for our own good. The alternative is the dream conceived by our Founding Fathers, up to the ultimate in individual freedom consistent with an orderly society." Not Left and Right but freedom and order were therefore the relevant categories. With the right mixture of freedom and order society will evolve upwards, which would satisfy progressives, libertarians, and traditionalists alike, not to mention the Founding Fathers, apparently. This formula for orderly progress would appear to be reducible to a sort of Laffer Curve relating freedom to order – a scientific solution to the problem of value relativism. It is all a fantasy, of course, to the extent it escapes the platitudinous. What *kind* of ordered freedom are we charting? Spartan ordered freedom? Jefferson Davis's ordered freedom? Lincoln's? And how would one choose between the varieties on offer? Everything depends on what counts as good order and what figures as wholesome freedom, and for that one needs precisely the kind of moral and political knowledge that the whole exercise is designed to avoid or deny. Reagan did not dwell on such depoliticized visions, but they may have influenced his hope that progress or historical success would provide a secular confirmation of the divine blessings invoked by the Pilgrims, and later by John Winthrop on this "shining city on a hill."

COMMUNITY AND CONSENSUS

In any case, he focused his campaigns in 1980 and 1984 on the American people as they recovered their moral and political health. The immediate enemy was the sense of paralysis and drift that had set in under the Carter Administration. "For those who have abandoned hope, we'll restore hope," he promised the 1980 GOP convention, "and we'll welcome them into a great national crusade to make America great again!" "We must act today in order to preserve tomorrow," he declared in the First Inaugural, and he stressed the people's *capacity* to save themselves. "[W]e as Americans have the capacity now, as we've had in the past, to do whatever needs to be done to preserve this last and greatest bastion of freedom." He urged the people "to believe in ourselves and to believe in our capacity to perform great deeds...." The "citizens of this blessed land" are "heroes."

Reagan mentioned the Constitution once in his First Inaugural, in a beginning salute to the "orderly transfer of authority" between administrations "as called for in the Constitution." His single reference was to an instance when the Constitution was being obeyed. Though the speech contained many criticisms of the "unnecessary and excessive growth of government," he chalked that problem up to violations of "the consent of the governed" more than to violations of the letter or spirit of the Constitution. Both his diagnosis of the problems afflicting the country and his prescriptions for them remained strikingly populist, not in an angry but in a flattering sense, albeit with a constitutionalist accent. Everything depended on the people acting "worthy of ourselves." "'We the people,' this breed called Americans," as he hailed them, had to reassert our authority over government, and in so doing rediscover our heroic past and future, our heroic *selves*.

His arguments were less about the form of government and its principles than about the small-C constitution, in the sense of the health, of the American people's own opinions, habits, and values. Because public opinion was so important, the leadership of public sentiment remained essential to his conservatism. In his 1980 Acceptance Speech, he called for "a new consensus with all those across the land who share a community of values embodied in these words: family, work, neighborhood, peace, and freedom." Justice, moderation, virtue, and principles like natural rights and checks and balances were not among those words. Reagan thought these and other aspects of our form of government and way of life valuable, as many passages in his writings and speeches attest. But he seemed to think them derivative from or entailed in the people's own recovery of self-confidence. Once president he began to feature at the State of the Union address ordinary citizens who had done extraordinary things, later ordinary citizens who had done less extraordinary things – "heroes for the eighties," the 1980s, he once called them revealingly. He pointed them out in the gallery, driving home the moral that "the heroes are our people, not government."

These heroes were picked as representatives of that "community of values embodied in these words: family, work, neighborhood, peace, and freedom." That community already existed; it did not need to be created or won. He had appealed to this community in his unsuccessful run against President Gerald Ford in the 1976 GOP primaries, and he discussed it in his important speech the following year to the Conservative Political Action Conference. "[W]e who are proud to call ourselves 'conservative' are not a minority of a minority party," he told CPAC; "we are part of the great majority of Americans of both major parties and of most of the independents as well." Three years later, in his Acceptance Speech at the GOP national convention, he restated the point: "Everywhere we have met thousands of Democrats, Independents, and Republicans from all economic conditions and walks of life bound together in that community of shared values of family, work, neighborhood, peace, and freedom." These were the values that "transcend persons and parties," the ones that Reagan as a political leader asked to be held responsible for living up to. The political task he set himself and the Republican party was "to build a new consensus" with all those Democrats and Independents who already shared those values. At the CPAC convention, he had described this as bringing together social conservatives and economic conservatives. The former – "blue-collar, ethnic, and religious groups ... traditionally associated with the Democratic Party" – were concerned about issues like "law and order, abortion, busing, quota systems." The latter comprised Republicans and Independents concerned about "inflation, deficit spending, and big government." Isn't it possible, he asked, "to combine the two major segments of contemporary American conservatism into one politically effective whole?"

Reagan called in that Acceptance Speech for bold measures to correct "a disintegrating economy, a weakened defense, and an energy policy based on the sharing of scarcity," and he made no bones about who deserved the blame: "The major issue of this campaign is the direct political, personal, and moral responsibility of Democratic party leadership – in the White House and in Congress – for this unprecedented calamity which has befallen us." President Jimmy Carter had attributed the country's crisis to a malaise (though he never used the word), a spiritual failing or lack of self-confidence and faith in the future, among the American people themselves. Reagan rejected that analysis as blame-shifting. "I will not stand by and watch this great country destroy itself under mediocre leadership that drifts from one crisis to the next, eroding our national will and purpose." The remedy for a crisis of failed leadership was a change in leadership, one that would restore Americans' national will, trust in their values, and faith in their future. That is what he meant by his pledge, "Together, let us make this a new beginning." His explanation of that new beginning was somewhat anti-climactic: "Let us make a commitment to care for the needy, to teach our children the values and virtues handed down to us by our families, to have the courage to defend those values and the willingness to sacrifice for them."

Here was the problem of conservative leadership in a nutshell. How could a conservative make a new beginning? More precisely, what kind of new beginning could a people be led conservatively to embrace? Reagan in 1980 and 1984 diagnosed America's problem in surprisingly Wilsonian terms: the country was suffering from leaderless government, which could be solved only by new leadership that would reconnect our politics to the optimistic spirit of progress. To succeed in textbook fashion, the Wilsonian leader needed to deploy a vision of the future, grounded in a deep sympathy with the people's strivings and desires, but expressing new values for a new age; and the leader needed to organize the forward march through a political movement, and ultimately a political party, dominated by his transformative vision. The leader and his party would then overcome the separation of powers and unite the departments of government in a national agenda of progressive reform. Reagan agreed with much of the Wilsonian-style diagnosis but – as a conservative – could hardly follow the Wilsonian prescriptions. For his part, Jimmy Carter had basically abandoned the Wilsonian diagnosis, in effect ceding the future, or the right to conjure the future, to his Republican opponent. (And supplying Senator Edward Kennedy with the grounds for his challenge to Carter in the Democratic primaries: "the hope still lives, and the dream shall never die.")

To be specific, Reagan rejected the notion of new values for a new age, insisting that Americans' old values were themselves up-to-date, that the winnowing process of history had confirmed these as the best values, precisely because they had endured so long and brought such success to our country. He rejected "abstract theorizing" and "ideological purity" in favor of the lessons of "experience," drawn not merely from "one generation or a dozen" but from "the combined experience of mankind." Conservatism, he told CPAC, means "principles evolving from experience and a belief in change when necessary, but not just for the sake of change." The Declaration and the Constitution were therefore not eighteenth-century anachronisms but proven examples of political principle in action. He rejected as well the progressive insistence on a paramount leader whose vision ought to inform and lead American politics – that was the "trust me" government for which he had condemned Carter and, decades earlier, Senator Fulbright. Reagan saluted "the American tradition of leadership at every level of government and in private life as well," calling it "a genius for leaders – many leaders – at many levels." But a multiplicity of leaders would make for chaos, or at least for division, unless their individual visions of the future were bounded and moderated by common values from the past, and unless those values were alive in the minds and hearts of the people, from which the leaders drew their visions. On the last count he appeared to have little doubt. A large majority of Americans already shared conservative or traditional American values; it was only the political expression of those values that remained latent, ready to be activated by the right kind of leadership.

Reagan played up the continuity of American values stretching from the Pilgrims to the present, but to do so he himself had to speak very abstractly. There was something real but insubstantial about "the community of shared values" he celebrated. Family, work, neighborhood, peace (replaced in the Second Inaugural by "faith," without explanation), and freedom – these were such elementary human goods that almost anyone, and any but the most oppressive political community, might embrace them. There was nothing peculiarly American about them. Lacking sharp edges, they did not encourage thoughts of tradeoffs or ranking, and gave little evidence of the role experience had played or could play in shaping them into a specific tradition. The "community" that embraced them had to operate at a high level of generality, and any consensus formed to advance or assert them would perforce be very watery. To say the least, it was hard to reconcile these values with the actual history of human, and especially American, political conflict, except to say, as Reagan did, that they were all under attack today from the Left. What's more, the "belief in change when necessary, but not just for the sake of change" did not provide any standards by which to judge purported necessity. Necessary for what, and says who? Besides, all "change" is not improvement and not all experience brings wisdom.

THE REVOLUTION MANQUÉ

Accordingly, what he sought from Americans in 1980 and 1984 was more a reaffirmation of values than a political revolution. In American history, the decisive partisan breakthroughs, as in the so-called "critical" elections of 1800, 1860, and 1932, involved sharp clashes over the meaning of justice, over the extent of freedom and equality, and over the purposes and limits of the Constitution. Such elections are comparable in their political effects to wars and revolutions. Reagan never quite asked for that kind of turning point, though he came close enough in 1980 to change "the trajectory of America," to recall Obama's celebrated pronouncement.

What did Reagan ask for? In 1977, speaking to CPAC, he declared that the nation needed a "New Republican Party" as the

vehicle by which Americans' community of shared values could settle down into "one politically effective whole." He specified he was
calling not for "simply a melding together" of social and economic
conservatives, but for "the creation of a new, lasting majority." He
was speaking to conservatives, of course, about the conservative
future. In general elections and to the general public he spoke more
guardedly, rarely mentioning "conservatism," though he would
occasionally employ "liberalism" as a pejorative. Then, as now, the
GOP was decidedly a minority party.

In the great election battles of the 1980s, he did not ask for that
partisan realignment. "I was a Democrat most of my adult life," he
said in his standard stump speech. "I didn't leave my party and we're
not suggesting you leave yours. I am telling you that what I felt was
that the leadership of the Democratic Party had left me and millions
of patriotic Democrats in this country who believed in freedom."
One might expect that the head of the Republican party would have
a *positive* argument for being a Republican, hence for disgruntled
Democrats and Independents to *become* Republicans, but one would
search in vain for such an argument in most of his speeches. It is
almost as if Americans were called upon to vote for Republicans
faute de mieux, there being no real Democrats left in control of their
party any more. But Reagan did not think he had to ask Americans to
make a sharp break with their habits or allegiances. They were
already on his side, after all. They already shared his values – or
rather, he shared theirs. He asked them only "to take a walk" with
him, echoing Al Smith's words as he broke ranks with Franklin Roosevelt in 1936. Far from repeating any of Smith's criticisms of FDR
as an un-American radical and collectivist, Reagan praised FDR for
his promises in 1932 to cut the federal budget and return authority
to the states, and promised to fulfill those promises in his own presidency. So wide was the consensus Reagan sought to build that he
emphasized it had plenty of room for supporters of FDR, Harry Tru-
man, and John F. Kennedy.

Reagan downplayed of course the predominant policies of the
New Deal, and what Roosevelt actually said about his opponents in
1932 and 1936. In his first presidential race, FDR had attributed the
GOPs' alleged trickle-down economic theory to "the party of Tory-

ism, and I had hoped that most of the Tories had left this country in 1776." Four years later Roosevelt associated Republicans with "economic royalists" and "the privileged princes of … new economic dynasties" who had "created a new despotism." In later years he would compare them to fascists. FDR's grand political strategy was to read the Republican party as previously constituted right out of American politics, to cast it as anti-American and beyond the pale of the Declaration and the Constitution, to pronounce it excommunicate and heretic and to anathematize its doctrines. At the same time he warned reactionary Democrats that "they are out of step with their party." Whereas Reagan appealed to Democrats as Democrats, asking them rather fancifully to vote for the genuine conservative principles of their party, which happened now to be in the GOP's custody, Roosevelt asked "nominal Republicans" to vote for *their* genuine principles, which belonged rightfully to the Democratic party. "Nominal Republicans" should really have been Democrats all along.

FDR recognized that, in 1932 as in 1776 and 1860, the great turning points in American politics involved the re-opening of the deepest issues concerning the meaning and bounds of republican government. What *ought* the values be that will define the American community? What new grounds of political consensus can and should be forged for the next generation or two? What sort of liberty and equality will the great American middle-of-the-road acknowledge and revere in the coming era? These questions, involving the ends of our common life, required a division of the house, a crisis, before they could be answered and a new consensus established. These kinds of elections involved, in effect, re-opening some of the fundamental issues of the American Revolution, including who among us count as patriots, as loyal and good citizens, and who are Tories, royalists, oligarchs, fascists, or Communists. Roosevelt set out quite deliberately to shatter and humiliate the Republican establishment – and to make his party the new majority party – and he succeeded.

Reagan did not appeal for such an indignant repudiation of the other party, though in his speeches he posed very clearly the question of us versus them – of self-government in keeping with the

American Revolution, versus rule by a self-appointed elite. At the crucial moments he seemed not to want to lead a revolution or a re-founding so much as to remind the majority of the compact to which it had already subscribed, whether it knew it or not – those "shared values," and the better future they almost guaranteed. It was as though the victory had already been won or was sure to come, and so the consolidation phase could begin.

Such an interpretation of Reagan's statesmanship risks underestimating his enormous political skill and the enormous labors he subjected himself to (e.g., he ran for president four times). If he had asked for more in the circumstances of 1980 and 1984, he might have gotten less. Nor should we forget how much he *did* accomplish – a revival of the economy that would spur growth for the next two decades, a foreign policy and military build-up that would help put the Soviet Union on the road to extinction. Two months after his second smashing victory at the polls, he took a sort of inventory in his 1985 State of the Union Address of what he and his administration had accomplished so far, noting the incipient signs of American renewal.

> Of all the changes that have swept America the past four years, none brings greater promise than our rediscovery of the values of faith, freedom, family, work, and neighborhood.
>
> We see signs of renewal in increased attendance in places of worship; renewed optimism and faith in our future; love of country rediscovered by our young, who are leading the way. We've rediscovered that work is good in and of itself, that it ennobles us to create and contribute no matter how seemingly humble our jobs. We've seen a powerful new current from an old and honorable tradition – American generosity.

Reagan got what he did ask for, in many respects, but this renewal of conservative values, without a broader and deeper victory for the Republican party and for the cause of constitutional governance, proved less enduring than he had hoped.

Reagan entered office calling for "a new beginning" in our politics. In 1984 he proclaimed, "We came together in a national crusade

to make America great again, and ... now it's all coming together....
Greatness lies ahead of us." At the meridian of his tenure, in the Second Inaugural, he elevated the goal to a "second American Revolution of hope and opportunity." In his Farewell Address, in 1989, he
rejoiced that the Reagan Revolution (a term he didn't coin but one
he accepted) had succeeded in creating millions of jobs and in reviv-
ing the national pride he called "the new patriotism." Nonetheless,
he regretted, in effect, that these worthy achievements had fallen
short of the second American Revolution he still thought necessary
to restore the country's health. We need a patriotism "grounded in
thoughtfulness and knowledge," he pleaded. And then this passage,
which, despite all of his administration's successes, came as close to
a poignant admission of defeat as anything he ever said or wrote:

> Those of us who are over thirty-five or so years of age grew up in
> a different America. We were taught, very directly, what it means
> to be an American. And we absorbed, almost in the air, a love of
> country and an appreciation of its institutions. If you didn't get
> these things from your family you got them from the neighbor-
> hood.... Or you could get a sense of patriotism from school.
> And if all else failed you could get a sense of patriotism from the
> popular culture.... But now we're about to enter the nineties,
> and some things have changed. Younger parents aren't sure that
> an unambivalent appreciation of America is the right thing to
> teach modern children. And as for those who create the popu-
> lar culture, well-grounded patriotism is no longer the style. Our
> spirit is back, but we haven't reinstitutionalized it.

Four years after he had hailed the recovery of American values,
five years after he had run for reelection on the theme "it's morning
again in America," he confronted some hard truths. Reagan had
grown up "in a different America," he admitted. He meant: America
had suffered a change of regime, and was a different country now.
Despite its many proud accomplishments, which in the speech he
modestly attributed to the American people, the Reagan Revolution
had not succeeded in restoring that earlier America or, more precisely, in sparking the "second American Revolution" that really was

needed. In this most comprehensive and important political task, he and his administration had not succeeded, and the disquieting proof was that even in Reagan's America an "unambivalent" patriotism could not prosper, much less dominate.

In his retirement, John Adams used to distinguish between the War for Independence and the American Revolution. The latter came first, he said. The American Revolution was in "the minds and hearts of the people" from 1760–1775, as the pamphlets and speeches of the era enlightened them to their rights and to their growing Union of political sentiment. The War, and the great events of what is usually called the Revolution, were a consequence of the real revolution that had prepared and forged American patriotism. Reagan's hoped-for political revolution depended on a deeper revolution, which he and the conservatives of his day were unable to inspire.

Being Reagan, he might put the point more optimistically: the great task of refounding American patriotism remained for his successors, for us, to accomplish. He had, after all, managed momentarily to thrust back to the center of American politics, for the first time since the New Deal, the question of the constitutionality and the justice of the modern state. Was the Constitution still the supreme law of the land – or was it being gradually, almost silently, displaced by a new form of autocracy operating behind the façade of the founders' Constitution? Had he pursued this question relentlessly – as, say, FDR did on behalf of the *living* constitution and against the Republicans of his day – Reagan might have discovered the key to the kind of "new beginning" he thought the country required. But he did not pursue the question, despite having warned throughout his political career that "freedom is never more than one generation from extinction." By 1984, he claimed it was "morning again," as though the new beginning had happened overnight while everyone was asleep. It had not.

A renewal of unambivalent patriotism would require renewed faith in the justice and goodness of America's principles and institutions. In 1980, he said that "renewing the American Compact" would require Americans "to trust your values – our values – and to hold me responsible for living up to them." Yet the prevailing *ambivalent* patriotism, he admonished as he left office nine years later, is the sign of a people that does *not* know or trust its values. What then becomes of the "special kind of compact" between the people and their leaders? By leaving leaders to be guided primarily by the people's values, Reagan, like Woodrow Wilson, left statesmen to that extent hostage to the *Zeitgeist*, unable to make a "new beginning," a revolution, by returning to first things and changing or restoring the form of government. His ends – "taking the country back to the Constitution," as he put it in 1962 – became increasingly discordant with his means – leading the people by advancing their enduring or strongest values.

Reagan liked to repeat Tom Paine's spirited boast, "We have it in our power to begin the world over again." He drew criticism from some conservatives for indulging Paine's radicalism. What Reagan was affirming, however, was that the American people had the power or the capacity to begin the world of American politics over again, to return to the spirit of American politics before modern liberalism. When ambivalent patriotism prevailed, it suggested to Barack Obama and other liberals that they had been right all along, in effect: the American people did not have the capacity to govern themselves, to choose to depart from the liberal path. Revolution was impossible; transformation was inevitable.

It is also possible, of course, that the people's leaders, including Ronald Reagan himself, were, so to speak, too progressive because they were too conservative: they could never make a clean break, even in thought, with the progressive canons of popular leadership, "values" and all, and with the progressive belief in a benevolent future. In other words, they didn't know how to be founders.

CHAPTER FOURTEEN

WHAT'S WRONG WITH CONSERVATISM?

For American conservatives, the late 1990s were a strange period of anticlimax and indecision. Crime rates were down, welfare rolls shrinking, the federal budget in surplus, fewer Democratic senators, congressmen, governors, and state legislators than in decades. Even more miraculously, the Soviet Union lay in history's dustbin. Yet despite these glad tidings, conservatives did not rejoice or even gloat. Nor did they aggressively follow up their successes, pressing liberalism on all fronts and striving for a decisive political breakthrough. Like General McClellan outside Richmond, conservatives felt proud to have come so far – but, uncertain of the kind of victory they sought and feeling an infinite need for reinforcements, were afraid to risk going much farther.

This frustrating paralysis did not stem from conservatives' having exhausted all their strategic or even tactical objectives, needless to say. The problem was – still is – their confusion about what their ultimate goals are, about the purposes that their strategy and tactics are supposed to serve. What is plaguing conservatism, in other words, is that its sense of mission – its devotion to a high, clear, and overarching cause – has deserted it, and recognition of this fact has begun to sink in among conservatives and liberals alike. Absent such a galvanizing purpose, even the most compelling conservative policies lose their urgency, and even the most faithful conservative politicians find themselves adrift. A glance at some salient events from the post-Reagan years will illustrate the point.

American conservatives have always been more confident of what they were against than what they were *for*. Sparked by their opposition to President Clinton's health care plan, for example, right-wing Republicans won an enormous electoral victory, capturing the House of Representatives and the Senate in 1994. Hopeful that American liberalism, like Soviet Communism, was historically doomed and needed only a final shove to topple it into the grave, Republicans led by Newt Gingrich (the first Republican Speaker of the House in forty years) tried to convert the public's rejection of ClintonCare into approval of the Contract With America, the initial installment of what they promised would be a positive agenda for conservative governance.

After most of the Contract's provisions had been acted on in the first hundred days of the new Congress, however, no new agenda came forward. The new Republican congressional majorities extemporized, lurching wildly from confrontation to conciliation with Clinton, apparently in the hope that if they just played for time the internal contradictions of liberalism would bring him down. Clinton was no Gorbachev, however, and his easy reelection, combined with the G.O.P.'s own sharpening divisions, left Gingrich and his allies dismayed. The future had failed them, and so had Gingrich's scientific futurism, based on his (oddly Marxist) confidence that a new mode of production (the microchip) would inevitably yield new relations of production, which would "demassify" the economy and society and undermine Big Government. Touted by Gingrich as the basis of a new conservative epoch, this technological tidal wave neither swept Clinton out to sea nor transformed the conservative coalition.

Still, the Contract With America was an admission that the Right needed new goals in order to move forward, some inspiriting goals beyond merely the defeat of liberal measures and liberal candidates. The deeper problem was that the Contract contained no such goals, inasmuch as its recommendations never rose above the level of specific policies. Its genesis in an off-year congressional election showed; it looked like (because it was) a document cobbled together by the House Republican Conference. The Contract lacked the unity and comprehensiveness that presidential politics at its best forces on political parties. At the deepest level, however, the Contract failed to spark a larger conservative resurgence because it was itself more an abdication than an assertion of any conservative principle. Vetted by political pollsters and honed by focus groups, it contained nothing that was unlikeable – e.g., it pledged that a Republican Congress would hold a vote on term limits, but it neither endorsed nor rejected any specific term limits plan.

To be sure, the Contract contained some sound provisions and had at least the merit of demonstrating that Republicans could keep their word – a useful corrective to the fiasco of President George H. W. Bush's 1990 budget deal. But it hardly amounted, in the Contract's own language, to "the end of government that is too big, too intrusive, and too easy with the public's money." At any rate, Bob Dole's feckless 1996 presidential campaign neutralized whatever good the Contract might have accomplished and re-emphasized its main vice. By then, "No Clear Principles" seemed to have replaced "No New Taxes" as the latest conservative Republican slogan.

So to put it mildly, conservatives had not yet achieved the top-to-bottom political realignment that they, and the Republican Party, have longed for ever since the New Deal. Despite the great electoral victories of 1980, 1984, and 1994, the American public had not trusted the G.O.P. with simultaneous control of the House, Senate, and the presidency in more than four decades – not since 1952–54. That goal was finally achieved in George W. Bush's first term, and again in the first two years of Donald J. Trump's administration. In neither instance did evanescent control of the three elective branches make a big difference. Facts are stubborn things, as Ronald Reagan used to say, and the failure to win an enduring realignment suggests that conservatism itself has failed, somehow, to engage the public's deepest passions and principles.

In what follows, accordingly, let us examine how the conservative movement came into being as both an intellectual and political force, what its character was and why it is now so perplexed, and what lessons we can draw for the revitalization of American conservatism.

BEFORE CONSERVATISM

The term "conservative" began to be used commonly in late nine-teenth-century America in order to distinguish the defenders of sound money and traditional constitutional and political arrange-ments from their sundry opponents – Populists, labor radicals, urban Progressives, and democratic tub-thumpers like William Jennings Bryan. Conservatives were then the Establishment, or at least were thought to be, and hence did not need to launch a "movement." Con-fusingly, however, these "conservatives" included everyone from the most corrupt apologists for big-city political machines to the most high-minded defenders of constitutional rectitude. In part, this lumping together was deliberate, an effort to taint the latter with the former's base motives. At its best, however, this conservatism had roots going back to Abraham Lincoln and to the Federalist-Whig interpretation of the Constitution, and its most serious exponents – e.g., Henry Cabot Lodge, Elihu Root, William Howard Taft – were renowned statesmen and judges. By and large, these men were legal or constitutional thinkers, a strength that was also their weakness. Although they fought courageously against a growing variety of novel assaults on the Constitution, they were usually on the strategic defensive. In an era whose main intellectual currents were increas-ingly hostile to individual rights and limited government, these emi-nent practitioners were unable to face down the philosophical challenges to the order they loved so well.

A sign of this debility was the increasing confusion, by the end of the nineteenth century, about the meaning of serious conserva-tism. Teddy Roosevelt spoke for many when he asserted that the true conservative was the reformer, the man in favor of gradual change or adaptation in order to keep American government in tune with the times. Reform beckoned as the sensible middle way between standpattism and revolution, and though he wasn't in the habit of quoting Edmund Burke, Roosevelt was in effect echoing Burke's admonition that "the state without the means of some change is without the means of its conservation." But Burke never meant that every change was a reform, or that all reforms were created equal.

Besides, in America, with a written Constitution that wisely was made very difficult to amend, conservative reform usually endeavors (in Walter Berns's useful phrase) to keep the times in tune with the Constitution rather than the Constitution in tune with the times. For the Constitution and its principles are grounded in human nature, which is the unchanging ground of our constantly changing experiences. And so the true conservative is not in the first instance the reformer who advocates gradual change but the man who knows the difference between what is changeable and what is not – the man who knows the *limits* of reform.

But in the twentieth century, this constitutionalist conservatism fell into a profound decline. Calvin Coolidge and Supreme Court Justice George Sutherland were perhaps its last major exponents. By the mid-1930s, the American Right was united in its opposition to Franklin D. Roosevelt but otherwise humbled, scattered, and confused, like the parts of a defeated army. There were conservatives aplenty, but no conservative movement.

CONSERVATISM AS AN INTELLECTUAL MOVEMENT

The first stirrings of renewal were intellectual. Around the end of the Second World War, a series of scholarly books began to appear that would gradually transform the terms of political debate. Friedrich Hayek's *The Road to Serfdom* (1944) led the way, followed soon by impressive works by Richard Weaver, Leo Strauss, Eric Voegelin, and Robert Nisbet. Russell Kirk's *The Conservative Mind* (1953) brought the notion of an embattled conservative legacy, not to mention the very term "conservative," to new prominence. A series of books by James Burnham emphasized the ominous new strategic threat of Communism; and Whittaker Chambers's autobiographical *Witness* (1952) elevated the anti-Communist cause into a transcendent battle for the soul of modern man. Harry V. Jaffa's *Crisis of the House Divided* (1959) and Milton Friedman's *Capitalism and Freedom* (1962) added important arguments on the nature of political and economic freedom.

But it was William F. Buckley, Jr., who set about to combine the factions of the American Right into a coherent movement informed by this new scholarship. *National Review*, the magazine that he founded in 1955 and edited for thirty-five years, was dedicated to shaking up the conformist status quo – to refuting the relativism and social utopianism that had seduced American professors and politicians. Fresh from college and his early fame as a critic of campus liberalism (*God and Man at Yale* had appeared in 1951), Buckley saw that the Left had conquered American politics by first besieging and occupying the high ground of the academy and journalism. Since "ideas rule the world," Buckley observed in the first issue, "the ideologues, having won over the intellectual class, simply walked in and started to run things." He concluded that an intellectual counterrevolution would be necessary before conservatism could organize as a political force. The diverse editors that Buckley assembled – ranging from traditionalists like Kirk to the most famous libertarian of the day, Frank Chodorov, and including powerful thinkers like Burnham and Willmoore Kendall – were testimony to the extent of *National Review*'s ambitions.

A movement must usually have a destination, of course, a shared goal by which its members define themselves and measure their progress. What were the principles that united these independent thinkers? Frank Meyer, a senior editor, claimed to have synthesized the precepts of libertarians and traditionalists into a new formula he called "fusionism," which became the magazine's unofficial credo. Meyer argued that both liberty and order (based on traditional morality) were important, that each depended to some degree on the other, and that the two could be squared by assigning to the state primarily the function of defending individual freedom, and to society (families, churches, schools, etc.) the task of teaching morality to its members. For philosophical support, Meyer leaned on Aristotle, who despite his reputation as a defender of order had actually maintained that virtuous acts had to be voluntary, and thus that virtue (Meyer claimed) could not be coerced by state action.

Yet Aristotle's contention depended on a factor that Meyer downplayed or ignored, namely, that moral virtue is a kind of habit and that a moral man's choices are shaped by his habits or character. So, for example, government cannot hesto-presto make someone into a just man, but by the influence of salutary laws it can encourage men to make themselves just. By rewarding just and punishing unjust actions, the law compels and teaches at the same time, holding citizens responsible for their actions (thus acknowledging human freedom) but also shaping their character, which is the product of their actions and choices over time. Even if it wanted to, then, government could not be indifferent to moral issues, since in punishing injustice in business dealings, cowardice in the armed forces, sexual abuse within families, and so forth, the law acts implicitly to direct our freedom towards certain moral norms or virtues.

Although impressive, Meyer's fusionism thus missed many of the hard questions about morality and politics. Like many traditionalists, Meyer loosely equated morality and religion, which, though overlapping and often mutually reinforcing, are not the same thing. And like most libertarians, he drew too bright a line between law and morality. In fact, his whole definition of the problem of freedom versus morality was fundamentally libertarian. Whatever its philosophical shortcomings, however, Meyer's fusionism provided a rough-and-ready basis on which to bring together the principal factions of conservative intellectuals in the 1950s and 1960s. In truth, these factions were not so much fused as glued together for the sake of fighting liberalism and, *a fortiori*, Communism. Communism threatened individualism, liberty, tradition, virtue – everything worth conserving; it was "the century's most blatant force of satanic utopianism," Buckley declared in *National Review*'s statement of principles. And so conservatism, consisting of "strange, discordant, and even, hostile elements ... gathered from the four winds" (to borrow Lincoln's description of the Republican party in the 1850s), coalesced, under Buckley's and his allies' influence, into the conservative movement. For the first time in this century, and after two waves of liberalism had washed over the country, conservatism became a self-conscious fighting force.

To be sure, libertarians did not cease to think of themselves as libertarians, and traditionalists remained loyal to their traditions; but acting in concert blurred some of the lines some of the time. The overwhelming practical imperative was to resist liberalism at home and defeat Communism abroad, and it would have been wrong to try to insist on other principles or conditions for such a necessary alliance. Against such enemies, then, each major conservative faction agreed to compromise: libertarians had to accept certain aspects of the "national security state," e.g., the draft, high defense spending, foreign alliances, an internal security apparatus; and traditionalists had to make their peace with the mass scale of modern life and warfare, the industrial economy, and the necessities of economic and scientific innovation.

The final piece of the conservative intellectual movement fell into place in the late 1960s when the neoconservatives began to discover their common outlook. Famously described by Irving Kristol as liberals who had been mugged by reality, most (though not all) of the neoconservatives had been liberal scholars whose indignation over the excesses of campus radicals and McGovernite Democrats had launched them on a pilgrimage to the Right. Intellectually, they represented a different and undogmatic kind of fusionism, blending a Burkean appreciation for the latent functions of social institutions and for the unintended (usually bad) consequences of liberal reform, with a Chicago School–like commitment to the methods of positivist social science. Although their respect for religious and philosophical traditions moderated this enthusiasm for social science, their principal contributions and discoveries were beholden to it nonetheless. In short, they launched a critique of liberal rationalism from the standpoint not so much of tradition but of a skeptical pragmatism. Armed with their own influential journals (especially *Commentary* and *The Public Interest*), the neoconservatives quickly established new standards in the scholarly analysis of everything from Great Society programs to Communist foreign policy.

The neoconservatives' defense of the "mediating structures" of civil society led them eventually to thoughtful reappraisals of the family, religion, and democratic capitalism. While extolling capitalism's freedom and creativity, however, most expressed reservations about its effects on human character (as did many traditionalists) and endorsed the welfare state's "ethic of common provision" as a useful corrective. This bold recommendation of a "conservative welfare state" dwindled over time to a defense of Social Security and little more, mostly because the inefficiency and inequity of government welfare and health care programs became increasingly evident. Thus the gap between neoconservatives and other conservatives narrowed. If Mark Gerson, a close student of neoconservatism, is correct, then as a separate intellectual force neoconservatism was a one-generation phenomenon. Its sons and daughters mostly call themselves conservatives.

Even so, it was a very important phenomenon that marked conservatism both intellectually and politically. It fueled a new kind of dissatisfaction with the reigning formulas of both libertarianism and traditionalism, and its hard-headed analysis of public policy combined with its scorn for the New Left made it, to a degree, a kind of intellectual defense of ethnic and working-class Democrats' worldview. Without exactly intending it, neoconservatism helped prepare the way, and even show the way, for Reagan Democrats (as they would later be called) to cross over into a grand conservative coalition.

CONSERVATISM AS A POLITICAL MOVEMENT

This coalition represented the consummation of a long political process, the roots of which stretched back a quarter century to modern conservatism's founding. Although *National Review* had concerned itself mainly with distilling the intellectual case for conservatism, it did not neglect practical politics. The magazine's firm rejection of the pre-War Right's isolationism helped set the boundaries of the national debate on the Cold War. Its refusal to tolerate anti-Jewish and nativist polemics and Birchite conspiracy theories was essential to the nascent movement's political health and sanity. More concretely, Buckley and his circle midwifed Young Americans for Freedom and the New York Conservative Party, on whose ticket Buckley would run for New York City mayor in 1965; Buckley's brother-in-law, Brent Bozell, became Barry Goldwater's legislative assistant and speechwriter (and ghosted his boss's *The Conscience of a Conservative*); and William A. Rusher, *NR*'s publisher, conspired with

Clif White and other conservatives in order to launch Goldwater's presidential campaign. Quite independently, Goldwater's backers in California, led by Holmes Tuttle and Henry Salvatori, hit upon Ronald Reagan as a pitchman only to realize that they had discovered a political talent far greater than the 1964 nominee. As a practical matter, of course, conservatism's electoral future lay in the South and West, and a small New York–based magazine could not hope to influence it in detail. Still, Salvatori had been one of *NR*'s initial investors, and Reagan one of its earliest subscribers, so the political effects of Buckley's project were far-reaching. He often said that he wanted to do for conservatism what *The New Republic* had done for liberalism – help to define it and guide it as a political creed – and Buckley accomplished this and much else.

It was Ronald Reagan, however, who led the way in adapting fusionist conservatism to the new political circumstances created by the third-wave, cultural liberalism of the Sixties and Seventies. He tempered Barry Goldwater's relentless attacks on the welfare state and his adherence to states' rights (Goldwater had opposed the *Brown* decision because he thought the federal government had no power over education). Whereas Goldwater had acerbically criticized the New Deal, Reagan claimed Franklin Roosevelt as his spiritual predecessor, albeit the somewhat illusory FDR of balanced budgets and lean government. Still, Reagan thought it important to reach out to a larger constituency, and invoking a Reaganite Roosevelt was one way to do it. Goldwater had called for dramatic cuts in federal spending, with tax cuts following apace, and Reagan did, too, in 1976; but by 1980 he had decided to lead with tax cuts, even promising that they would be revenue-neutral (i.e., that government spending would not have to shrink because of them). President Reagan did propose cuts – few of which he achieved – in domestic spending and in the number of federal agencies. But at the center of his economic agenda were cutting, and later flattening, tax rates, and moderating growth in the money supply – policies designed to promote long-term economic prosperity, to reaffirm the virtues of risk-taking and entrepreneurship, and to restore the economic and moral underpinnings of the American middle class, which had been dangerously eroded by the long stagflation of the 1970s.

In the 1964 campaign, Goldwater had indicted liberalism for the morally corrupting effects of farm price supports, aid to education, Social Security payments, and other federal benefits. While Goldwater's complaints had lost none of their libertarian cogency in 1980, more glaring abuses had in the meantime been thrust into view. The Supreme Court had elaborated a series of activist decisions narrowing religion's role in public life: mandating busing for racial balance in public schools, legalizing abortion in all fifty states, extending constitutional protections to pornography – and effectively propelling millions of evangelical Christians and ethnic Democrats into the conservative movement. These new social conservatives were worried about the country's moral tone and the perverse effects of the Counterculture – not the decline of agrarianism, the abandonment of aristocracy, or the other laments of many traditionalist intellectuals.

Reagan welcomed the social conservatives into the movement and they became an essential part of his electoral coalition. Building on Goldwater's success with Southern Democrats, Reagan had already proved in his two successful races for the California governorship that, by taking a tough stance towards campus protesters and urban rioters, he could attract significant Democratic and independent support. Unlike Richard Nixon, who rarely transcended the law-and-order aspects of these issues, Reagan knew how to parlay them into larger concerns over the moral law and order in America. In the 1980 presidential campaign, he broadened Goldwater's flinty individualism and Nixon's fealty to the Silent Majority into a warm, winning appeal to "all those across the land who share a community of values embodied in these words: family, work, neighborhood, peace, and freedom." President Reagan's policies were controversial but he was able to reassure public opinion while dividing it: his invocations of America's meaning and destiny – the "shining city on a hill" – lingered long after the controversies had been forgotten. Though he succeeded brilliantly at restoring America's self-confidence, he fared less well at rehabilitating the conservative movement, which admired more than it emulated him. At any rate, Reagan's Americanism was potent enough to delegitimize liberalism but not to reconstruct conservatism along more permanently attractive lines. For most conservatives, the "evil empire" always loomed larger than the "shining city on a hill."

IN SEARCH OF CONSERVATIVE PRINCIPLES

During the long decades of the Cold War, the conservative intellectual movement provided a rich political education for conservative candidates and officeholders. With the Cold War's end, however, it was increasingly clear that the conservative movement, as we have known it, is over. More and more, conservatism lacked a common message or focus, and the education it offered citizens and politicians was splintered into myriad discussions of specific policies. The range and intelligence of these discussions was unprecedented, but, absent a sustained attention to general principles, their overall effect was to trivialize conservatism's moral and political ambitions and, all too often, to emphasize conservatives' disagreements rather than the common goals they might be cultivating. Nor was there a political figure on the scene with anything like Reagan's stature who could, after absorbing the movement's teachings, modulate them with a view to America's national greatness.

Hence the conservative predicament. When faced by urgent threats from a common enemy, conservatives were strong and united; blessed with peace, prosperity, and the freedom in which to focus on their internal differences, they had grown restive and uncertain. All the good enemies are gone, complain conservatives, because after Soviet Communism's demise American liberalism seemed less threatening. No matter, for so long as conservatism remained basically anti-liberalism, the weakened condition of American liberals enfeebled conservatives, too, paradoxically.

But what more could American conservatism *be*, other than liberalism's nemesis? To begin with, it could be profoundly American. The most striking feature of traditionalist conservatism has always been how alienated it is from the roots of its own, that is, the American political tradition. Take Russell Kirk's *The Conservative Mind*, for instance, still the best expression of the traditionalist school.

Kirk enshrined a few Americans in his conservative pantheon – John Adams and John C. Calhoun, most prominently – but he had little room for George Washington, Thomas Jefferson (whose *"a priori* concepts" and "French egalitarian theories" Kirk distrusted), James Madison, Alexander Hamilton, or Abraham Lincoln, to name a few. Not that he renounced them, exactly, but he simply did not find in them the conservative disposition that he wished to celebrate, nor the conservative principles that he wished to canonize. In this respect, Kirk implicitly acknowledged distinctions that many of his readers may have missed. For none of these thoughtful American statesmen endorsed the quasi-Burkean love of prescription, inequality, and the Romantic-organic view of society that Kirk himself embraced.

Kirk's conservatism, therefore, was never peculiarly American. It was consciously Anglo-American; more specifically, it took Burke's useful half-truth that the British Constitution had been a product of slow evolutionary growth and adaptation, and applied the nostrum to America, whose Revolution then became a "conservative restoration of colonial prerogatives." So much for "the shot heard 'round the world"! Until about 1774, Americans had in fact argued in favor of various conservative adaptations of the British Constitution to colonial conditions; but from 1776 on, they insisted on new, emphatically republican constitutions of their own devising, based on the unalienable or natural rights of man. To quote Kirk's hero, John Adams, "there is no good government but what is republican," and the "only valuable part of the British Constitution" had been republican in effect if not in intent. The British political tradition contained valuable principles, then, which were sound not because they were British or traditional but because they were good, i.e., in accordance with human nature. In effect, the colonists exchanged their rights as Englishmen for their rights as Americans, precisely in order to secure their rights as men. They made a Revolution on behalf of human freedom, not "prescriptive freedom."

Kirk never admitted this, because he rejected freedom and equality as abstract principles and he loathed revolution. Like Burke, he spoke occasionally of the real or genuine rights of man – the moral order in which prescription or tradition was a chief part of the law of nature. Unlike his great model, however, Kirk allowed prescription to define virtually all of natural justice: as the "natural" part of natural law receded under his touch, the "law" part – the legal, customary, and conventional realm – grew apace. Hence Kirk's "traditionalism": the belief in the abstract principle that all abstract principles are nonsense; that justice is to be discovered at history's margins, not in nature's intentions; and that reason, at least moral and political reason, is always properly a child of its times. For traditionalists, revolution with a capital R, based on appeals to nature or to abstract truths like human freedom and equality, is the greatest of political evils. Indeed, Burke's opposition to the French Revolution was *the* inspiration for modern conservatism – and according to Kirk, the star by which conservatives should steer in all subsequent political upheavals.

But what of the American Revolution, which had boldly proclaimed its "new and more noble course" and its "new order of the ages," all in the name of certain unalienable and universal human rights to "life, liberty, and the pursuit of happiness"? Kirk denied or downplayed everything revolutionary about it, obscuring its real character. He was right, of course, that the Revolution was about more than abstract natural rights. Protestant Christianity, classical republicanism, and traditional British constitutional arguments all played important parts in the drama, but each of these received a new spin from the Americans' understanding of natural justice. Kirk was right, too, to insist that the American Revolution was quite different from the French Revolution, but it was not because the former was not revolutionary. The essential difference was that the French Revolution had been based on a Rousseauian theory of the rights of man, which robbed the rights of their foundation in an unchanging human nature and quickly abandoned them as a guide to political right in favor of the socialist authority of the general will. Then to make matters worse, this wrong-headed theory had been implemented by intellectuals leading a people with no experience in the habits and practices of self-government. It was a recipe for disaster.

After an initial burst of enthusiasm for the French Revolution – partly out of hope that it would be a sequel to or a continuation of the American experience – many American statesmen soon had second thoughts. For example, Adams shared with his then-opponent Jefferson the wish that the French people might eventually be free of civil and ecclesiastical tyranny; he disagreed sternly with Jefferson, however, about whether the French Revolution would ever emancipate the French nation. Adams went on to denounce the French experiment as foolish and irrational, and predicted, correctly, that it would be bloody. But whereas Adams blamed the French Revolution for being *irrational,* and therefore imprudent, Russell Kirk blamed it for being rational, or rationalistic. In their choice of epithets, one can see the great distance between the conservatism of the American founders and that of Kirk and today's traditionalists.

THE LIMITS OF TRADITIONALIST CONSERVATISM

For the truth is that traditionalism, and the type of conservatism based on it, have never been comfortable, really, with the American Revolution. They have tried to make peace with it by treating it as something neither very American nor very revolutionary, but the result has been to miss its major significance in American politics. Examples abound of contemporary conservatives' wariness of the "Revolution principles," as Adams called them, on which the founders took their stand. In fact, conservative politicians do not have to be self-conscious traditionalists to have absorbed this aversion to the concepts, indeed to the very language, of rights, equality, and justice. How many times, for example, has a Republican Congress ducked the chance to eliminate race and gender-based preferences in federal hiring, contracting, and grant-making? Republicans, including many staunch conservatives, flee the issue partly because they think it untimely, but mostly because they do not care to wage an uphill battle on an issue on which liberals presumptively command the moral high ground. In other words, they concede, without quite admitting it perhaps even to themselves, that equality and justice are liberal causes, to be defined by liberals, defended by liberals, and implemented by liberals.

There are honorable exceptions, to be sure, as in California, where conservative activists forced Proposition 209 onto the ballot and succeeded in laying low (at least temporarily) the state's regime of racial and ethnic favoritism. But such examples are rare. When conservatives in political office have to accost fundamental principles, they prefer to do so indirectly, from the shadows and behind many veils – by abstruse parliamentary procedures, say, or by deferring to the courts' future disposition of an issue, or by calling reflexively for a constitutional amendment. Conservatives avoid arguing about questions of justice whenever possible, which means they eschew politics (whose central issue is justice) whenever possible. They tend to shun any appeal that cannot be reduced to a matter of efficiency, economy, interest, or tradition. Tradition can be a great and a good thing, of course, but it is never so merely because it is traditional; slaveholders had their ancestral ways, too. To tell right from wrong within a tradition, or among traditions, requires a moral standard that has a validity or goodness independent of the tradition: it requires an abstract or reasonable principle.

Yet even in the familiar "social" disputes that agitate our politics, conservatives seem cut off from the principles of the American Revolution. They invoke "traditional family values," for instance, as though the phrase itself were traditional, which it is not. It is a very recent phrase, an untraditional term that tries, inadequately, to characterize and defend the American tradition of republican or democratic family life, rooted of course in the precepts of the Bible and of nature. Even worse, they invoke "traditional family values" as though being traditional were enough. (Even if the tradition they have in mind were the Judeo–Christian one, it is not valid *eo ipso* merely because it is traditional.) In practice, the new phrase often means little more than the "family values" that a majority in the past or at present would like to see prevail. Incidentally, this is where Kirkian traditionalism and the populist conservatism of the last few decades converge: at the core of traditionalism is a kind of historical majoritarianism (Chesterton called it "the democracy of the dead"). Traditions, after all, must be passed down by the major part of society (particularly in democratic ages) in order to be authoritative.

But wanting to keep "family values" traditional – i.e., majoritarian – does not establish that these "values" are good. Uncomfortable with moral argument, conservatives increasingly rest their case for morals legislation on majoritarianism, precisely because it appears to relieve them of the need to make moral arguments. They assume that they do not have to show why homosexual marriage, for example, is wrong if they can show that most Americans disapprove of it. When most Americans stop disapproving of it, however, these moralists are left speechless. The abortion issue is the massive exception to this tendency, precisely because conservatives cannot point with assurance to majority support for anti-abortion policies. Here moral arguments continue to be offered forthrightly in order to persuade the public. But the abortion issue is virtually the only part of the social or moral front where conservative troops are trying doggedly to advance; and the silent hunkering of the units on their flanks makes their efforts look fanatical rather than courageous.

On the premises of traditionalism, then, the conservative movement is ill-equipped to recognize, much less to rescue, a country largely defined by its traditional allegiance to universal principles of justice. This is not to gainsay the common conservative view that America's twentieth-century progressivist revolution is akin, somehow or other, to the various Communist revolutions of the twentieth century; nor that all of these contemporary upheavals are descended ultimately from the French Revolution. It is merely to deny that these later revolutions were organic extensions of the American Revolution. Returning conservatism to its American roots would in no way compromise the Right's principled opposition to these later revolts against human nature.

Yet many traditionalists, especially in the movement's once-flourishing neo-Confederate wing, claim exactly that. Willmoore Kendall and M. E. Bradford asserted long ago, for instance, that the Civil War was the precursor of the New Deal, the "Yankee Leviathan" the beginning of Big Government, and Lincoln's defense of human freedom and equality a fatal "derailment" of the American political tradition. In this humid version of Burke, the antebellum South became America's noble *ancien regime*, Lincoln became Robespierre, and slavery (or the agrarian way of life based on it) became an integral part of American freedom. But this was an interpretation that proved too much, insofar as it implied strongly that the American

Revolution was itself too egalitarian – all that loose talk of "all men are created equal" which now required explaining – and hence resembled the French Revolution more than American conservatives would care to admit. In the end, then, traditionalism seems to offer no alternative to making the United States. a colony of Great Britain, either by reinterpreting our principles in order to render them compatible with a tendentious version of Burke's account of the British Constitution, or by admitting in effect that it was a political mistake to break with hereditary monarchy and aristocracy in the first place.

THE LIMITS OF LIBERTARIAN CONSERVATISM

Today's libertarians display another sort of wariness towards the American founding. Although they are keen on individual rights and free markets, libertarians are divided on the question whether individual rights need a moral foundation besides utility. Most Chicago School economists (a powerful influence on modern libertarianism) believe that freedom *works*, in the sense of generating far greater social prosperity and individual utility than non-free or socialist societies can manage; and they do not see the need or, frankly, the possibility of justifying individual rights on any other basis. By contrast, most libertarian philosophers and publicists insist that liberty is and would be valuable for its own sake, even if it did not lead to greater individual and social prosperity.

Now, the utilitarian argument is true, so far as it goes; but it begs the question of why (and to what extent) economic prosperity is good, and it assumes, without proof, that every individual's utility should count equally. The "rights utilitarians," as they are sometimes called, try to explain why every person should count as one, but they disagree on the basis of this elementary equality and hence on its significance. Given these difficulties, the weight of the libertarian argument is on the side of bringing rights and utility as close together as possible, grounding the notion of individual rights in self-preservation and self-interest, and reducing the political morality of the American Revolution to the protection of mere life and a low sort of liberty. Conservative politicians of a libertarian stripe value freedom and individual rights much more highly than do their traditionalist allies, to be sure, but because the libertarian definition of liberty is almost synonymous with the pursuit of private desire, their public defense of it is much weaker than they think. Their "freedom" begins to sound suspiciously like a codeword for self-interest, an imputation that many of them would endorse! Libertarianism thus leaves citizens and politicians in much the same spot that traditionalism does: more at home with arguments about utility, efficiency, economy, and (spontaneous-evolutionary) order than about justice.

The ascending moral connections among life, liberty, and the pursuit of happiness cease to be a vital public concern for the libertarians, because for them happiness is mainly in the eye of the beholder. Even those who know better (Charles Murray, for instance), who recognize that there is some objective moral core to happiness, do not regard it as very relevant to the activities of government. Happiness is for the private sphere, whereas government is about the use of coercion to protect life, liberty, property, and the obligation of contracts. To be sure, there are several legitimate points in this analysis. In a country founded on the doctrine of natural rights, the general assumption is that citizens are free to pursue their happiness in any way not explicitly proscribed by law, because they have entrusted government only with limited power in order to secure their (pre-existing) natural or God-given rights. Moreover, the right of conscience – of worshipping God according to one's own lights, but in accordance with the same right and reciprocal social duties in others – makes one's relationship to God a lofty but primarily (though not exclusively) private matter, which means that majorities acting through government may not dictate true religion or force citizens to be pious. In this sense, supreme happiness and its various ingredients and prerequisites are certainly the highest concern of private life, and justify the purest freedom from government coercion in respect of our religious opinions.

All very well – but just because the law cannot know the conditions of supreme happiness in the next life does not mean that it cannot know anything about the elements of happiness here and now. The separation of church and state did not imply a parallel separation of morality and politics. Although human reason could not discern, by itself, the way to Heaven, reason could and did know much about the way to happiness. For instance, that courage was better than cowardice; wisdom better than ignorance or false knowledge; justice better than injustice; moderation better than intemperance – these moral propositions or truths were essential to a happy life, and to a free and self-governed life, as George Washington and virtually everyone else writing at the time emphasized. These virtues needed somehow to be inculcated in individuals, and in a people, who meant to use their life and liberty happily, as opposed to unhappily. And so to secure "the blessings of liberty" to themselves and their posterity, the American founders established a constitutional republic in which the people's capacity to govern themselves individually and collectively would be put to the test.

Laws inevitably shape morality (*pace* Frank Meyer), but the American founders did not believe that the laws alone could do so. In fact, they appreciated that the general laws of a distant federal government could play – and ought to play – only a very limited role in this task. Here their prudence agreed with today's libertarian preferences. At the same time, however, they expected state and local legislation to play a much larger role in encouraging the moral habits needed for self-government, through the exemplary sanctions of civil and criminal law – especially the wide scope for the states' police power, which dealt with the details of public health, safety, and morals – and through public-supported education. The statesmen of the early Republic realized, however, that even state and local legislation could accomplish only so much without the positive assistance of the primary character-shaping associations, families and churches.

In a republic, then, there is a public need for citizens with good character; but America's best statesmen have always understood that a public end does not solely or even necessarily have to be met by a public means. In the old days, for instance, the public need for a well-armed and regulated militia was met by acknowledging the private right to bear arms – supplemented, in some states, with the public duty to report for militia drills. Before the modern welfare state, the public need to assist widows, orphans, the sick, and the elderly was met not only in various ways by local governments, but also by state laws that encouraged the incorporation of charitable hospitals, self-insurance associations, and the like. Today, similarly, the public need for an educated citizenry may best be met by using educational vouchers and charter schools to encourage competition with, and even within, the public school system. In short, not every public need or end can be met directly by government. Nonetheless, the public may use government not only to protect life, liberty, property, and the obligation of contracts, but to elicit the character traits that help to keep limited government limited, and that help to make liberty a blessing rather than a curse.

THE AMERICANIZATION OF CONSERVATISM

One might combine these criticisms of latter-day traditionalism and libertarianism by saying that a reborn American conservatism, based on the principles of the American Revolution, would teach both morality and freedom, order and liberty, not as a fusion or agglomeration of opposites but as inferences from the same set of principles. Those principles are the rights of man under the laws of nature. Now, one of the great achievements of the scholars who helped, intentionally or not, to inspire the contemporary conservative movement, was their reopening of the question of natural right or justice. For the first time in perhaps a hundred years, it is now possible for us to return to the natural rights doctrines of the American founders in an intelligent way, to revive their moral and political enterprise and make it the heart and soul of a new American conservatism.

Practically speaking, this means a rediscovery of the moral basis and the moral argument for republican government. A restored Republic would entail a federal government that is much more limited than the present state, though energetic in pursuit of its limited objects. The inveterate conservative opposition to Big Government would shift in emphasis from hoarse calls to get the government out of our wallets and off our backs, to a new indictment of Big Government as an insult to our rights, an offense against our equality, and a violation of our Constitution. To be sure, Big Government has always been a reliable target of conservative denunciation. Yet often the grounds of the conservative attack on it have been sandy – a few perfunctory invocations of the Tenth Amendment, warmed-over anger at the unholy expense of it all, some boilerplate about the imperial judiciary. The modern state offends republicanism even more profoundly than it offends federalism, however, and conservatives should reformulate their attacks along more provocative constitutional lines – for example, stressing not only the cost of entitlement programs, but the manner in which they inveigle us into thinking that all our rights flow from government; or criticizing bureaucracy not only for its wastefulness and absurdity, but for its despotic tendency to concentrate legislative, executive, and even judicial powers into the same "expert" (and unelected) hands.

Even as economic conservatives ought to acknowledge that morality is essential to limited government, so religious and social conservatives should recognize that America is in many ways less free than it used to be. We suffer from too much license and not enough liberty. On the one hand, the modern state's social programs encourage personal irresponsibility by socializing its costs. On the other hand, Big Government narrows personal freedoms essential to republicanism: the right to use and be secure in one's property; to donate money to political campaigns; to count as an equal, regardless of race or ethnicity, in the eyes of the law.

So today's manifold threats to liberty and morality stem mainly from the same source: modern liberalism's rejection of the original American understanding of self-government. Reacting piecemeal to this affront, each faction of the existing conservative movement has seized an important part of the truth, but there is something missing that can be supplied only by a more American, and more political, conservatism. Though in some ways conservatism is now in a position to reconnect itself with the constitutionalist doctrines of the late nineteenth and early twentieth centuries, ultimately it is the conservatism of the founders that we are seeking. Their principles will not yield immediate solutions to every public policy issue: the Declaration of Independence will not tell us what to do about Google and Twitter. But their basic principles of justice and constitutional architecture will be relevant to our most important concerns, always

340 CONSERVATIVES AND THE TWO CONSTITUTIONS

assuming that we have the practical wisdom to apply them rightly.

The conservatives of a century ago had one advantage over us, however. They saw modern liberalism in its youth, at its most theoretically audacious and before its projects had become familiar. By rediscovering America's principles, conservatives have it in their power to encounter liberalism afresh, to see it anew and as a whole for the first time in many decades, and thus to learn how radical a departure from the founders' Constitution it actually was. Here, in truth, was where something like the principles of the French Revolution took hold of mainstream American politics and did not let go.

CHAPTER FIFTEEN

DEMOCRACY AND
THE BUSH DOCTRINE

GEORGE W. BUSH'S first presidency, devoted to compassionate conservatism and to establishing his own bona fides, lasted less than eight months. On September 11, 2001, he was reborn as a War President. In the upheaval that followed, compassionate conservatism took a back seat to a new, more urgent formulation of the Bush Administration's purpose.

The Bush Doctrine called for offensive operations, including preemptive war, against terrorists and their abettors – more specifically, against the regimes that had sponsored, encouraged, or merely tolerated any "terrorist group of global reach." Afghanistan, the headquarters of al-Qaeda and its patron the Taliban, was the new doctrine's first beneficiary, although the president soon declared Iraq, Iran, and North Korea (to be precise, "states like these, and their terrorist allies") an "axis of evil" meriting future attention. In his words, the United States would "not permit the world's most dangerous regimes to threaten us with the world's most dangerous weapons."

The administration's preference for offensive operations reflected a long-standing conservative interest in taking the ideological and military fight to our foes. After all, the Reagan Doctrine had not only indicted Soviet Communism as an evil empire but had endeavored to subvert its hold on the satellite countries and, eventually, on its own people. The Bush Administration's focus on the states backing the terrorists implied that "regime change" would be necessary, once again, in order to secure America against its enemies. The policy did not contemplate merely the offending regimes' destruction, however. As in the 1980s, regime *change* implied their replacement by something better, and the Bush Doctrine soon expanded to accommodate the goal of planting freedom and democracy in their stead.

CAPTIVE NATIONS

On this point, the Bush Doctrine parted company with the Reagan Doctrine. Although the Reagan Administration's CIA and other agencies had worked to build civil society and to support democratic opposition groups in Eastern Europe, Central America, and other strategic regions, these efforts were directed mostly to helping "captive nations" escape their captivity. That is, they presupposed a latent opposition against foreign, usually Soviet, oppression, or as in the satellite and would-be satellite countries, against domestic oppressors supported by the Soviets. The Russian people themselves counted as a kind of captive nation enslaved to Marxism's foreign ideology, and Reagan did not flinch from calling for their liberation, too. He always rejected a philosophical détente between democracy and totalitarianism in favor of conducting a vigorous moral and intellectual offensive against Communist principles.

But as a practical matter, the Reagan Doctrine aimed primarily at supporting labor unions, churches, and freedom fighters at the Soviet empire's periphery – e.g., Poland, Czechoslovakia, Afghanistan, Nicaragua, Grenada – rather than at its core. Even in these cases, the Administration regarded its chief duty to be helping to liberate the captive nations, that is, expelling the Soviets and defeating their proxies, rather than presiding over a subsequent democratization of the liberated peoples. Not unreasonably, the Reaganites thought that to those countries freed from totalitarian oppression, America's example would be shining enough, especially when joined to their visceral, continuing hatred for the Soviet alternative.

In countries where bad or tyrannical regimes were homegrown

or unconnected with America's great totalitarian enemy, the administration's efforts in support of democratization were quieter and more limited still. These involved diplomatic pressure, election-monitoring, and occasional gestures of overt support, such as the administration's endorsement of "people power" in the Philippines. Most importantly, Reagan wanted to avoid the Carter Administration's hubris in condemning the imperfect regimes of America's friends, while neglecting the incomparably worse sins of America's foes.

The distinction between authoritarian and totalitarian regimes, classically restated by Jeane Kirkpatrick in her article in *Commentary* that caught Reagan's eye, "Dictatorships and Double Standards," provided intellectual support for his administration's policies. Authoritarian regimes, like Iran's Shah or Nicaragua's Somoza, though unsavory, were less oppressive than totalitarian ones, Kirkpatrick argued. What's more, countries with homegrown monarchs, dictators, or generalissimos were far more likely to moderate and perhaps even democratize themselves than were societies crushed by totalitarian governments. And it was this potential of non-democratic but also non-totalitarian states to change their regimes for the better, in their own good time, that helped to justify America's benign neglect of or, at most, episodic concern with their domestic politics. Once freed from the totalitarian threat, countries like Nicaragua or Afghanistan could more or less be trusted to their own devices.

The wave of democratization that occurred in the 1980s, especially in Asia and South America, seemed to confirm the wisdom of the administration's approach. Even when America was called to play a role, as it was in the Philippines, our intervention was short and sweet, confined mainly to persuading Ferdinand Marcos to leave office.

By comparison, the Bush Doctrine put the democratization of once totalitarian, quondam authoritarian, and persistently tribal societies at the center of its objectives. The case of Afghanistan shows, to be sure, that the Reagan Doctrine had its drawbacks. Left to itself, Afghanistan after the Soviets' withdrawal did not resume its former ways, at least not for long, and certainly did not evolve into a democracy. Instead, it succumbed to the Taliban's peculiar Islamic totalitarianism. Nevertheless, the Bush Administration's policy was not merely to expunge the totalitarians there and in Iraq, but to ensure they never return by reconstructing the societies along democratic lines. Authoritarianism (at least in the Middle East) was no longer acceptable. The United States now proposed to liberate these nations from the captivity of their own unhappy traditions.

So far as it goes, that policy, or some version of it, might be justified by the circumstances and stakes of U.S. involvement, even as the American refoundings of Germany and Japan after the Second World War were justified on prudential grounds. Occasionally, the Bush Administration made this kind of argument. (The analogies were not exact, of course.) But usually this claim was mixed up with a very different one, more characteristic of the Bush Doctrine as such: America's supposed duty, as the result of our respect for human rights, to help the Iraqis and other peoples realize their democratic entitlement and destiny.

RIGHTS AND REPUBLICANISM

Political scientists James W. Ceaser and Daniel DiSalvo drew attention to this dimension of the Bush Doctrine when they observed, in *The Public Interest*, that "President Bush has identified the Republican party with a distinct foreign policy, which he has justified by recourse to certain fixed and universal principles – namely that, in his words, 'liberty is the design of nature' and that 'freedom is the right and the capacity of all mankind.'" Bush's appeal, in their words, to "the universality of democracy and human rights" is a watershed moment in the history of American politics, they argued, with enormous significance for the Republican Party and the conservative movement. "Not since Lincoln has the putative head of the Republican party so actively sought to ground the party in a politics of natural right."

Bush's revival of natural or human rights as the foundation of political morality was welcome, and should be taken seriously. Like Lincoln, Bush was, in his own way, looking to the American founding for guidance in charting his course through the dire circumstances that confronted him. But there was, in his use of these noble ideas, a certain ambiguity or confusion between the natural *right* to be free and the *capacity* to be free. The two are not quite the same.

The founders affirmed that every human being has, by nature, a right to be free. Unless men were endowed by nature with a certain minimum of faculties, inclinations, and powers, that right would be nugatory. Taken together, those endowments – which include reason, an access to morality (variously traced to reason, conscience, or the moral sense), a spirited love of freedom for its own sake, passions (especially the powerful desire for self-preservation), and physical strength – constitute the capacity or natural *potential* for human freedom. But this potential needs to be made *actual*, needs to be awakened by practice and habit.

James Madison, for example, writes in *The Federalist* of "that honorable determination which animates every votary of freedom to rest all our political experiments on the capacity of mankind for self-government." In the largest sense, those experiments aim to prove whether the latent capacity of mankind for self-government can, at last, after centuries of slumber, be activated, realized, and confirmed by the conduct of the American people – in particular, by their ratification of the newly proposed Constitution. Alexander Hamilton underlines the point in that work's famous opening paragraph: "It has been frequently remarked that it seems to have been reserved to the people of this country, by their conduct and example, to decide the important question, whether societies of men are really capable or not of establishing good government from reflection and choice, or whether they are forever destined to depend for their political constitutions on accident and force."

The human right to be free, in other words, does not guarantee the human capacity to be free. That capacity must be elicited and demonstrated, and its noblest and most persuasive proof is by the establishment of "good government," along with the habits necessary to perpetuate it – the habits of heart and mind that, among other things, allow a people's "choice" to be guided by "reflection."

Notice, too, that the founders are not content with (merely) democratic regimes, i.e., with governments that hold elections and empower majorities to rule. The test of mankind's political capacity is that its self-government should culminate in good government, in regimes that not only have elections but actually achieve the common good and secure the rights of individuals, whether or not they belong to the ruling majority. This blend of constitutionalism and republicanism is extremely difficult to attain. Well acquainted with the history of failed republican regimes, the founders by and large thought it the *most difficult* of all forms of government to establish and preserve. Hence good, republican government is an achievement, not an entitlement.

THE LIMITS OF REGIME CHANGE

Thus even with the improvements in political science celebrated by Madison, Hamilton, and the other founders, most of them never expected republican government to spread easily and universally across the globe. Though fervent believers in universal moral principles, they knew that these had to be approximated differently in different political situations. In this sense, they were students of Montesquieu and Aristotle, who taught that governments have to be suited to a people's character and conditions.

None of this implies, of course, that dramatic political change is not possible. America's founders could not have been *founders* if they did not think regime change possible and, in their own case, desirable. Founding is possible because culture is not destiny; politics can reshape a nation's culture. But they knew also that no founding is completely *de novo*. Every attempt at regime change begins from the existing habits and beliefs of the people for whom you are trying to found a new way of life. Accordingly, the founders would have been cautious, to say the least, about America's ability to transform Iraqis into good democrats.

In the last century, we saw in the cases of Germany and Japan that it is possible to remake even Nazi and imperial Japanese institutions into democratic regimes. But these are really exceptions that prove the rule: it is very difficult to pull off this kind of transformation. Germany and Japan were exceptional, first, because the U.S. and its allies had beaten them into complete submission. Then we occupied them for decades – not merely for months or years, but for the better part of a half-century. And both were civilizations that had the advantage of having enjoyed, before their descent into totalitarianism, a high standard of living, widespread literacy, and considerable political openness. Besides, America was reorganizing them at the beginning of the Cold War, when circumstances compelled them, as it were, to choose between the West, with its democratic institutions, and the East, with its bleak tyranny.

To his credit, President Bush recognized the difficulty of the task in Iraq. He acknowledged to the National Endowment for Democracy that "the progress of liberty is a powerful trend," but that "liberty, if not defended, can be lost. The success of freedom," he said, "is not determined by some dialectic of history." In his elegant speech at Whitehall Palace, he affirmed that "freedom, by definition, must be chosen and defended by those who choose it." And he warned that "democratic development" will not come swiftly, or smoothly, to the Middle East, any more than it did to America and Europe.

Nonetheless, he found strong support for the "global expansion of democracy" in human nature itself. "In our conflict with terror and tyranny," he said at Whitehall, "we have an unmatched advantage, a power that cannot be resisted, and that is the appeal of freedom to all mankind." In a speech in Cincinnati, he declared, "People everywhere prefer freedom to slavery; prosperity to squalor; self-government to the rule of terror and torture." Aboard the *U.S.S. Abraham Lincoln*, after announcing that "major combat operations in Iraq have ended," he said, "Men and women in every culture need liberty like they need food and water and air."

DEMOCRATIC FEELINGS

Here he stumbled, and stumbled badly. It is one thing to affirm, as the American founders did, that there is in the human soul a love of liberty. It is another thing entirely to assert that this love is the main or, more precisely, the naturally predominant inclination in human nature, that it is "a power that cannot be resisted." In fact, it is often resisted and quite frequently bested, commonly for the sake of the "food and water and air" that human nature craves, too. The president downplays the contests within human nature: conflicts between reason and passion, and within reason and passion, that the human soul's very freedom makes inescapable. True enough, "people everywhere prefer freedom to slavery," that is, to their *own* slavery, but many people everywhere and at all times have been quite happy to enjoy their freedom and all the benefits of someone else's slavery.

In his 2002 State of the Union Address, one of his best speeches, he amplified his point. "All fathers and mothers, in all societies, want their children to be educated and live free from poverty and violence. No people on earth yearn to be oppressed, or aspire to servitude, or eagerly await the midnight knock of the secret police." There was truth in the president's words, but not the whole truth. No one may want to be oppressed, but from this it does not follow that no one yearns to oppress. The love that parents feel for their children does not necessarily transfer to benevolence, much less equal solicitude, for the children of others. This is why "do unto others" is not a moral rule automatically or easily observed. This is why, when Abraham Lincoln distilled his moral teaching to its essence, he did not confine himself to the wrongness of slavery simply. "As I would not be a slave," he wrote, "so I would not be a master. This expresses my idea of democracy. Whatever differs from this, to the extent of the difference, is not democracy."

In other words, that "people everywhere" or "all fathers and mothers" have the same *feelings* for themselves and their own kind does not (at least not yet) make them believers in human equality, human rights, or democracy. President Bush, in effect, planted his account of democracy in common or shared human passions, particularly the tender passions of family love, not in reason's recognition – and imposition – of a rule for the passions. He did not insist, as Lincoln and the founders did, that democracy depends on the mutual recognition of rights and duties, grounded in an objective, natural order that is independent of human will. Bush made it easy to be a democrat, and thus made it easier for the whole world to become democratic.

HISTORY AND CULTURE

Yet democracy based on feelings or compassion has obvious limits. What takes the place of the rigorous moral teaching that once lifted compassion to the level of justice? What summons forth the embattled statesmanship and republican striving that sustain democracy, especially in crises? Despite his comments that democratic progress is not inevitable and that "the success of freedom is not determined by some dialectic of history," Bush found himself appealing again and again to a kind of providential or historical support for democracy. In the same speech in which he uttered the words just quoted, he concluded by saying: "We believe that liberty is the design of nature; we believe that liberty is the direction of history."

At Goree Island, Senegal, the slave ships' point of departure from Africa, Bush declared:

> We know that these challenges can be overcome, because history moves in the direction of justice. The evils of slavery were accepted and unchanged for centuries. Yet, eventually, the human heart would not abide them. There is a voice of conscience and hope in every man and woman that will not be silenced – what Martin Luther King called a certain kind of fire that no water could put out.... This untamed fire of justice continues to burn in the affairs of man, and it lights the way before us.

In this eloquent address, the president praised the role that John Quincy Adams and Lincoln, among others, played in the fight against slavery, but he saluted their "moral vision" as though that alone had been sufficient to doom the peculiar institution. In his words, "Their moral vision caused Americans to examine our hearts, to correct our Constitution, and to teach our children the dignity and equality of every person of every race." What happened to the Civil War, not to mention Jim Crow? Bush left the impression that "history moves in the direction of justice," and that once Americans were awakened to the Truth, they went with the flow. Yet the anti-slavery cause, at least in Lincoln's mind, did not depend in the slightest on history's support for the triumph of free labor and free men. Rather, it was a very close issue, requiring for its resolution all of Lincoln's genius and the Union's resources, not forgetting a considerable measure of good luck. And the triumph, so dearly won, soon gave way to tragedy and renewed tyranny in the South.

Bush's position recalled the important contemporaneous dispute between Francis Fukuyama and Samuel Huntington. Huntington insisted that, after the Cold War, international politics would be marked by the inevitable clash of civilizations, e.g., between Islamic and non-Islamic nations. Fukuyama argued that history is overcoming all such cultural clashes and culminating in liberal democracy, which is destined to spread all over the world. In this dispute, Bush seemed to be firmly on Fukuyama's side. At West Point, the president explained, "The twentieth century ended with a single surviving model of human progress, based on non-negotiable demands of human dignity, the rule of law, limits on the power of the state, respect for women and private property and free speech and equal justice and religious tolerance.... When it comes to the common rights and needs of men and women," he said, "there is no clash of civilizations."

If not dialectical, Bush's account of history certainly seemed Darwinian; history has winnowed itself down to a "single surviving model of human progress." He dismissed doubts that the Middle East will grow increasingly democratic as narrow-minded, if not downright prejudiced. From his 2004 State of the Union Address: "[I]t is mistaken, and condescending, to assume that whole cultures and great religions are incompatible with liberty and self-government. I believe that God has planted in every human heart the desire to live in freedom." Yes, but the question is whether some cultures and religions are less compatible with freedom and democracy than others, and if so, how he ought to adjust our foreign policy. He made it sound like a civil rights issue. Granted, too, that God has implanted in men a love of freedom, but cultures, rulers, and religions each diffract that love, accentuating, obscuring, or perverting it. Bush called those who raise such contentions "skeptics of democracy," when in fact they were skeptical mostly of his easy-going account of democracy.

The political scientist James Q. Wilson, with his usual insight and learning, took an empirical look in the December 2004 *Commentary* at the relation between Islam and freedom. He declined to inspect Islam and democracy, on the grounds that there are too few examples from which to generalize and that, in the long run, personal liberty is more important. From liberty, liberal democracy may spring; democracy without liberty is despotic (Fareed Zakaria reinforced this point in his book *Illiberal Democracy*). Wilson proffered Turkey, Indonesia, and Morocco as reasonably liberal Muslim states; of these only one, Morocco, is both Muslim and Arab. What these cases have in common, he suggested, is a "powerful and decisive leader" who can "detach religion from politics"; an army that "has stood decisively for secular rule and opposed efforts to create an Islamist state" (a condition that Morocco does not quite meet); the absence of "a significant ethnic minority" demanding independence; and the lack of major conflicts between Sunni and Shiite Muslims.

Iraq shared *none* of these advantages. Turkey soon abandoned several that it then enjoyed.

RETHINKING THE DOCTRINE

As far as it goes, it was heartening to see elections in Afghanistan, and eventually in Iraq. As the president said, "it is the practice of democracy that makes a nation ready for democracy, and every nation can start on this path." But not every nation will finish it, because democracy is not just a matter of elections. Democracy requires that majorities restrain themselves and sometimes undertake disagreeable tasks out of respect for law and for their fellow citizens. These tasks, in turn, require a willingness to trust one's fellow citizens that comes hard to tribal societies, whose members are not used to trusting anyone who is not at least a cousin.

Nevertheless, as against today's shallow culture of relativism, Bush's willingness to point out the plain difference between good and evil was bracing, and it recalled Ronald Reagan's denunciation of the Evil Empire. The problem is that in tracing the individual right to be free to ordinary human compassion or fellow-feeling, and then confounding that right with an entitlement to live in a fully democratic regime, Bush promised or demanded too much and risked a terrible deflation of the democratic idealism he encouraged.

In many respects, the Bush Doctrine was the export version of compassionate conservatism. Even as the latter presumed that behind the economic problem of poverty is a moral problem, which faith-based initiatives may help to cure one soul at a time, so the Bush Doctrine discovered behind the dysfunctional economies and societies of the Middle East a moral problem, which "the transformational power of liberty" may cure, one democrat and one democracy at a time. "The power of liberty to transform lives and nations," he admonished, should not be underestimated. But his administration underestimated the difficulty of converting whole societies in the Middle East into functioning democracies. By raising expectations – by making democracy appear as an easier conversion and way of life than it really is – Bush risked not only the erosion of liberal and pro-democratic support within Iraq, but also at home a loss of public confidence in the whole war effort.

For example, his version of compassionate democracy effectively neglected the problem of security. In most American wars, the reconstruction did not begin until the fighting had ended, until the enemy was subjugated and peaceful order imposed on the country. Vietnam was an exception, but not a successful one. Bush criticized previous administrations for making short-sighted bargains with Mideast kings and dictators, trading security for liberty in the region. Without liberty in the sense of free elections, he argued, there is no long-term security. Although he had a point, democracy presupposes a certain minimum security for life, liberty, and property that is woefully absent in much of Iraq. Earlier American statesmen, including the founders, would have been keenly aware of this requirement because their argument for republican government put great weight on the passion, and the right, of self-preservation. A government that could not protect the life and liberty of its citizens (better than they could left to themselves) was no government at all.

But the Bush Administration underestimated the problem of security because it overestimated the sentimental or compassionate grounds of democracy. Expecting the Iraqis quickly and happily to get in touch with their inner democrat, the administration was surprised that so many of them took a cautious, more self-interested view, preferring to reserve their allegiance for whichever side would more reliably protect them from getting killed. In general, the Bush team failed to recall that weak, contemptible, authoritarian regimes are not the only breeding grounds of trouble in the Middle East or elsewhere. Weak, contemptible democracies can be the source of great evils, too, as Weimar Germany attests. Unfortunately, the all-absorbing focus on bringing democracy to Iraq crowded out concern for the kind of constructive, wide-ranging statesmanship that was needed there and in other Islamic nations. Aboard the *U.S.S. Abraham Lincoln*, President Bush promised, "we will stand with the new leaders of Iraq as they establish a government of, by, and for the Iraqi people." But he should never have expected that they could reform themselves – much less that we could transform them – quickly or easily up to the standards of the Gettysburg Address.

CHAPTER SIXTEEN

CULTURE, CREED,
AND AMERICAN NATIONALISM

W HEN HE WAS VICE PRESIDENT, Al Gore once explained that our national motto, *e pluribus unum*, means "from one, many." That was a sad day for knowledge of Latin among our political elite – and for all those expensive private schools he'd been packed off to by his paterfamilias. It was the kind of flagrant mistranslation that, had it been committed by a Republican, say George W. Bush or Dan Quayle, would have been a gaffe heard round the world. But the media didn't play up the slip, perhaps because they admired its impudence. Though literally a mistake, politically the comment expressed and honored the multicultural imperative, then as now so prominent in the minds of American liberals: "from one," or to exaggerate slightly, "instead of one culture, many." As such it was a rather candid example of the literary method known as deconstruction: torture a text until it confesses the exact opposite of what it says in plain English or, in this case, Latin.

After 9/11, we didn't hear much from multiculturalism. In wartime, politics tends to assert its sway over culture. In its most elementary sense, politics implies friends and enemies, us and them. The attackers on 9/11 were not interested in our internal diversity. They didn't murder the innocents in the Twin Towers or the Pentagon or on board the airplanes because they were black, white, Asian-American, or Mexican-American, but because they were

American. (Although I bet for every Jew they expected to kill, the terrorists felt an extra thrill of murderous anticipation.)

In our horror and anguish at those enormities and then in our resolution to avenge them, the American people closed ranks. National pride swelled and national identity – perhaps the simplest marker is display of the flag – reasserted itself. After 9/11, everyone, presumably even Gore, understood that *e pluribus unum* means: out of many, one. Yet the patriotism of indignation and fear can only go so far. When the threat recedes, when the malefactor has been punished, the sentiment cools. Unless we know what about our national identity ought to command admiration and love, we are left at our enemies' mercy. We pay them the supreme and undeserved compliment of letting them define us, even if indirectly. Unsure of our national identity, we are left uncertain of our national interests, too; now even the war brought on by 9/11 seems strangely indefinite. And so Samuel P. Huntington (1927–2008) was correct in his 2004 book to ask *Who Are We?* and to investigate what he calls in the subtitle *The Challenges to America's National Identity.*

CREED VERSUS CULTURE

In Huntington's view, America is undergoing an identity crisis, in which the long-term trend points squarely towards national disintegration. A University Professor at Harvard (the school's highest academic honor), he wrote a dozen or so books, including several that are rightly regarded as classics of modern social science. (One of those, *The Clash of Civilizations and the Remaking of World Order,* [1996] was mentioned in the preceding chapter.) He was a scholar of political culture, especially of the interplay between ideas and institutions; but in this book he calls himself not only a scholar but a patriot (without any scare quotes). That alone marked him as an extraordinary figure in today's academy.

Though not inevitable, the disorder that he discerns is fueled by at least three developments in the culture. The first, as indicated, is multiculturalism, which saps and undermines serious efforts at civic education (see Chapters Five and Ten). The second is "transnationalism," which features self-proclaimed citizens of the world – leftist intellectuals like Martha Nussbaum and Amy Guttman, as well as the Davos set of multinational executives, NGOs, and global bureaucrats – who affect a point of view that is above this nation or any nation. The third is what Huntington terms the "Hispanization of America," due to the dominance among recent immigrants of a single non-English language which threatens to turn America, in his words, into "a bilingual, bicultural society," not unlike Canada. This threat is worsened by the nearness of the lands from which these Spanish-speaking immigrants come, which reinforces their original nationality.

Standing athwart these trends are the historic sources of American national identity, which Huntington describes as race, ethnicity, ideology, and culture. Race and ethnicity have, of course, largely been discarded in the past half century, a development he welcomes. By ideology he means the principles of the Declaration of Independence, namely, individual rights and government by consent, which he calls the American "creed" (a term popularized by Gunnar Myrdal). These principles are universal in the sense that they are meant to be, in Abraham Lincoln's words, "applicable to all men at all times." Culture is harder to define, but Huntington emphasizes language and religion, along with (a distant third) some inherited English notions of liberty. *Who Are We?* is at bottom a defense of this culture, which he calls Anglo-Protestantism, as the dominant strain of national identity. Although he never eschews the creed, he regards it fundamentally as the offshoot of a particular cultural moment: "The Creed ... was the product of the distinct Anglo-Protestant culture of the founding settlers of America in the seventeenth and eighteenth centuries."

Twenty-some years before, he took virtually the opposite position, as James Ceaser noted in a perceptive review in *The Weekly Standard*. In *American Politics: The Promise of Disharmony* (1981), Huntington declared, "The political ideas of the American creed have been the basis of national identity." But the result, even according to his earlier analysis, was a very unstable identity. The inevitable gap between ideals and institutions doomed the country to anguished cycles of moral overheating ("creedal passion periods") and cooling. He wrote the earlier book as a kind of reflection on the politics of the 1960s and 1970s, noting how the excessive moralism of those times had given way to hypocrisy, complacency, and finally cynicism. In a way, then, the two books really are united in their concern about creedal over-reliance or disharmony.

To bring coherence and stability to American national identity apparently requires a creed with two feet planted squarely on the ground of Anglo-Protestant culture. The creed alone is too weak to hold society together. As he argues in *Who Are We?*, "America with only the creed as a basis for unity would soon evolve into a loose confederation of ethnic, racial, cultural and political groups." It is not excessive individualism he worries about; he fears rather that individuals, steering by the creed alone, would soon be attracted to balkanizing group-identities. Therefore, the creed must be subsumed under the culture, if creed and country both are to survive; indeed, "if they are to be worthy of survival, because much of what is most admirable about America" is in its culture, at its best.

ANGLO-PROTESTANTISM

Huntington's argument provides a convenient starting point for thinking about the problem of American national identity, which touches immigration, bilingual education, religion in the public square, civic education, foreign policy, and many other issues. While agreeing with much of what he says about the culture's importance, I want to speak up for the creed and for a third point of view, distinct from and encompassing both.

Huntington outlines two sources of national identity, a set of universal principles that (he argues) cannot serve to define a particular society; and a culture that can, but that is under withering attack from within and without. His account of culture is peculiar, narrowly focused on the English language and Anglo-Protestant religious traits, among which he counts "Christianity; religious commitment;... and dissenting Protestant values of individualism, the work ethic, and the belief that humans have the ability and the duty to try to create heaven on earth, a 'city on a hill.'" Leave aside the fact that John Winthrop hardly thought that he and his fellow Puritans were creating "heaven on earth." Is Huntington calling for the revival of all those regulations that sustained Winthrop's earthly city, including the strictures memorably detailed in *The Scarlet Letter*? Obviously not, but when fishing in the murky waters of Anglo-Protestant values, it is hard to tell what antediluvian monsters might emerge. If his object is to revive, or to call for the revival of, this culture, how will he distinguish its worthy from its unworthy parts?

Huntington is on more solid ground when he impresses "English concepts of the rule of law, the responsibility of rulers, and the rights of individuals" into the service of our Anglo-Protestantism. Nonetheless, he is left awkwardly to face the fact that his beloved country began, almost with its first breath, by renouncing and abominating certain salient features of English politics and English Protestantism, including king, lords, commons, parliamentary supremacy, primogeniture and entail, and the established national church. There were, of course, significant cultural continuities: Americans continued to speak English, to drink tea (into which a little whiskey may have been poured), to hold jury trials before robed judges, to read (most of us) the King James Bible, and so forth. But there has to be something wrong with an analysis of our national culture that literally leaves out the word "American." Anglo-Protestantism – what's American about that, after all? The term would seem to embrace many things that our countrymen have tried and given up – or that have never been American at all, much less distinctively so.

Huntington tries to get around this difficulty by admitting that the American creed has modified Anglo-Protestantism. But if that is so, how can the creed be derived from Anglo-Protestantism? When, where, how, and why does that crucial term "American" creep onto the stage and into our souls? He allows that "the sources of the creed include the Enlightenment ideas that became popular among some American elites in the mid-eighteenth century." But he suggests that these ideas did not change the prevailing culture so much as the culture changed them. In general, Huntington tries to reduce reason to an epiphenomenon of culture, whether of the Anglo-Protestant or Enlightenment variety. He doesn't see – or at any rate, he doesn't admit the implications of seeing – that reason has, or can have, an integrity of its own, independent of culture. But Euclid, Shakespeare, or Bach, for example, though each had a cultural setting, was not simply produced by his culture, and the meaning of his works is certainly not dependent on it or limited to it. It is the same with the most thoughtful American founders and with human equality, liberty, and the other great ideas of the American creed.

THE CULTURAL APPROACH

Huntington's analysis is closer than he might like to admit to the form of traditionalist conservatism that emerged in Europe in opposition to the French Revolution. These conservatives, often inspired by Edmund Burke but going far beyond him, condemned reason or "rationalism" on the grounds that its universal principles destroyed the conditions of political health in particular societies. They held that political health consisted essentially in tending to a society's own traditions and idiosyncrasies, to its peculiar genius or culture. As opposed to the French Revolution's attempt to make or construct new governments as part of a worldwide civilization based on the rights of man, these conservatives argued that government must be a native growth, must emerge from the spontaneous evolution of the nation itself. Government was a part of the *Volksgeist*, "the spirit of the people." Politics, including morality, was in the decisive respect an outgrowth of culture.

But on these premises, how can one distinguish good from bad culture? What began as the rejection of rationalism quickly led to the embrace of irrationalism. Or to put it differently, the romance soon drained out of Romanticism once the nihilistic implications of its rejection of universals became clear. Huntington is right, of course, to criticize multiculturalism as destructive of civic unity. But he is wrong to think that Anglo-Protestant culture is the antidote, or even merely our antidote, to multiculturalism and transnationalism.

Multiculturalism likes to assert that all cultures are created equal, and that America and the West have sinned a great sin by establishing white, Anglo-Saxon, Christian, heterosexual, patriarchal, capitalist culture as predominant. The problem with this argument is that it is self-contradictory. For if all cultures are created equal, and if none is superior to any other, why not prefer one's own? Thus Huntington's preference for Anglo-Protestantism – he never establishes it as more than a patriot's preference, though as a scholar he tries to show what happens if we neglect it – is to that extent perfectly consistent with the claims of the multiculturalists, the only difference being that he likes the dominant culture, indeed, wants to strengthen it, and they don't.

Of course, despite their protestations, multiculturalists do not actually believe that all cultures are equally valid. With a clear conscience, they condemn and reject anti-multiculturalism, not to mention cultures that treat women, homosexuals, and the environment in ways that Western liberals cannot abide. Unless, perchance, such treatment is handed out by groups hostile to America; Robert's Rules of Multicultural Order allow peremptory objections against, say, the Catholic Church, that are denied against such as the Taliban. Scratch a multiculturalist, then, and you find a liberal willing to condemn all the usual cultural suspects.

Whether from the Right or the Left, the cultural approach to national identity runs into problems. To know whether a culture is good or bad, healthy or unhealthy, liberating or oppressive, one has to be able to look at it from outside or above the culture. Even to know when and where one culture ends and another begins, and especially to know what is worth conserving and what is not within a particular culture, one must have a viewpoint that is not determined by it. For example, is the culture of slavery, or that of anti-slavery, the truer expression of Americanism? Both are parts of our tradition. One needs some "creed," it turns out, to make sense of culture. I mean creed, not merely in the sense of things believed (sidestepping whether they are true or not), but in the sense of moral principles or genuine moral-political knowledge. If that were impossible, if every point of view were merely relative to a culture, then you'd be caught in an infinite regress. No genuine knowledge, independent of cultural conditioning, would be possible – except, of course, for the very claim that there is no knowledge apart from the cultural, which claim has to be true across all cultures and times. But then genuine knowledge would be possible, after all, and culturalism would have refuted itself.

HARD SELL

One of the oddities of Huntington's argument is that the recourse to Anglo-Protestantism makes it, from the academic point of view, less objectionable, and from the political viewpoint, less persuasive. As a scholar, he figures that he cannot endorse the American creed or its principles of enlightened patriotism as true and good, because that would be committing a value judgment. So he embeds them in a culture and attempts to prove (and does prove, so far as social science allows) the culture's usefulness for liberty, prosperity, and national unity, should you happen to value any of those. The Anglo-Protestantism that he celebrates, please note, is not exactly English Protestantism (he wants to avoid the national church), but dissenting Protestantism, and not all of dissenting Protestantism but those parts, and they were substantial, that embraced religious liberty. In short, those parts most receptive to and shaped by the creed.

As a political matter, Anglo-Protestantism is a hard sell, particularly to Catholics, Jews, Mexican-Americans, and many others who don't exactly see themselves in that picture. Huntington affirms, repeatedly, that his is "an argument for the importance of Anglo-Protestant culture, not for the importance of Anglo-Protestant people." That is a very creedal, one might even say a very American, way of putting his case for culture, turning it into a set of principles and habits that can be adopted by willing immigrants of whatever nation or race. This downplays much of what is usually meant by culture, however, and it is not clear what he gains by it. If that is all there is to it, why not emphasize the creed or, more precisely, approach the culture through the creed?

The answer, I think, is that Huntington regards the creed by itself as too indifferent to the English language and God. But there is no connection between adherence to the principles of the Declaration and a lukewarm embrace of English for all Americans. In fact, a country based on common principles (but not only on common principles) would logically want a common language in which to express them. The multiculturalists, tellingly, attack English and the Declaration at the same time. As for God, there is no reason to accept the ACLU's godless version of the creed as the correct one. The Declaration mentions Him four times, for example, and from the Declaration to the Gettysburg Address to the Pledge of Allegiance (a creedal document if there ever was one), the creed has affirmed God's support for the rational political principles of this nation.

REGIME CHANGE

Yet it is precisely these principles that Huntington downplays, along with their distinctive viewpoint. This viewpoint, which goes beyond culture, is the political viewpoint. It is nobly represented by our own founders and its most impressive theoretical articulation is in Aristotle's *Politics*. For Aristotle, the highest theme of politics and of political science is founding. Founding means to give a country the law, institutions, offices, and precepts that chiefly make the country what it is, and that distinguish it as a republic, aristocracy, monarchy, or so on. This authoritative arrangement of offices and institutions is what Aristotle calls "the regime," which establishes who rules the country and for what purposes. We hear much about "regime change" today but perhaps don't reflect enough about what the term implies. The regime is the fundamental fact of political life according to Aristotle. And because the character of the rulers shapes the character of the whole people, the regime largely imparts to the country its very way of life. In its most sweeping sense, regime change thus augurs a fundamental rewiring not only of governmental but of social, economic, and even religious authority in a country. In liberal democracies, to be sure, politics has renounced much of its authority over religion, society, and the economy. But even this renunciation is a political act, a regime decision.

Founding is regime change par excellence, the clearest manifestation of politics' ability to shape or rule culture. But even Aristotle admits that the regime only "chiefly" determines the character of a country, comparing it to a sculptor's ability to form a statue out of a block of marble. Much depends as well on the marble, its size, condition, provenance, and so forth. Although the sculptor wishes to impose a form (say, a bust of George Washington) on the marble, he is limited by the matter he has to work with and may have to adapt his plans accordingly. By the limitations or potentialities of the matter Aristotle implies much of what we mean by culture. That is, every founder must start from something – a site, a set of natural resources, a climate, and a population that already possesses certain customs, religious beliefs, family structure, economic skills, and laws. Aristotle chooses to regard this "matter" or what we would call culture as the legacy, at least mostly, of past politics, of previous regimes and laws and customs. By in effect subordinating culture to politics, he emphasizes the capacity of men to shape their own destiny or to govern themselves by choosing (again) in politics. He emphasizes, in other words, that men are free, that they are not enslaved to the past or to their own culture. But he does not confuse this with an unqualified or limitless liberty to make ourselves into anything we want to be. We are just free enough to be able to take responsibility for the things in life we cannot choose – the geographical, economic, cultural, and other factors that condition our freedom but don't abolish it.

Now it is from this viewpoint, the statesman's viewpoint, that we can see how creed and culture may be combined to shape a national identity and a common good. In fact, this can be illustrated from the American founding itself. In the 1760s and early 1770s American citizens and statesmen tried out different arguments in criticism of the mother country's policies on taxation and land rights. Essentially, they appealed to one part of their political tradition to criticize another, invoking a version of the "ancient constitution" (rendered consistent with Lockean natural rights) to criticize the new one of parliamentary supremacy, in effect appealing not only to Lord Coke against Locke, but to Locke against Locke. In the Declaration of Independence, the Americans appealed both to natural law and rights on the one hand, and to British constitutionalism on the other, but to the latter only insofar as it did not contradict the former. Thus the American creed emerged from within, but also against, the predominant culture. The Revolution justified itself ultimately by an appeal to human nature, not to culture, and in the name of human nature and the American people, the Revolutionaries set out to form an American Union with its own culture.

IMMIGRATION AND EDUCATION

They understood, that is, that the American republic needed a culture to help uphold its creed. The formal political theory of the creed was a version of social contract theory, amended to include a central role for Founding Fathers. In John Locke's *Second Treatise*, the classic statement of the contract theory, there is little role for Founding Fathers, really, inasmuch as they might represent a confusion of political power and paternal power, two things that Locke is at great pains to separate. He wants to make clear that political power, which arises from consent, has nothing to do with the power of fathers over their children. And so, against the arguments of absolutist patriarchal monarchy, he attempted clearly to distinguish paternal power from contractual, or political, power. But in the American case we have combined these, to an extent, almost from the beginning. The fathers of the republic are our demi-gods, as Thomas Jefferson, of all people, called them. They are our heroes, who establish the sacred space of American politics, and citizens (and those who would be) are expected to share a general reverence for them and their constitutional handiwork.

In fact, the American creed, together with its attendant culture, illuminates at least two issues highly relevant to national identity, namely, immigration and education. On immigration, the founders taught that civil society is based on a contract, a contract presupposing the unanimous consent of the individuals who come together to make a people. When newcomers appear, they may join that society if they and the society concur. In other words, from the nature of the people as arising from a voluntary contract, consent remains a two-way street: an immigrant must consent to come, and the society must consent to receive him. Otherwise, there is a violation of the voluntary basis of civil society. The universal rights of human nature translate via the social compact into a particular society, an "us" distinct from "them," distinct even from any other civil society constituted by a social contract.

Any individual has, in Jefferson's words, the right to emigrate from a society in which chance, not choice, has placed him. But no society has a standing natural duty to receive him or to take him in. Thus it is no violation of human rights to pick and choose immigrants based on what a particular civil society needs. In America's case, the founders disagreed among themselves about whether, say, farmers or manufacturers should be favored as immigrants, but they agreed that the country needed newcomers who knew English, had a strong work ethic, and possessed republican sentiments and habits.

As for education, from the creedal or contractual point of view, each generation of citizens' children might be considered a new society. But Jefferson's suggestion that therefore all contracts, laws, and constitutions should expire every generation (nineteen years, he calculated) was never acted on by him, much less by any other founder. Instead of continual interruptions (or perhaps a finale) to national identity, succeeding generations, so the founders concluded, were their "posterity," for whom the blessings of liberty had to be secured and transmitted. Perpetuating the republic thus entailed a duty to educate the rising generation in the proper creed and culture.

If certain qualities of mind and heart were required of American citizens, as everyone agreed, then politics had to help shape, directly and indirectly, a favoring culture. Most of the direct character formation, of course, took place at the level of families, churches, and state and local governments, including private and (in time) public schools. In the decades that followed the founding, the relation between the culture and creed fluctuated in accordance with shifting views about the requirements of American republicanism. Unable to forget the terrors of the French Revolution, Federalists and Whigs tried to stimulate root growth by emphasizing the creed's connection to Pilgrim self-discipline and British legal culture. This was, perhaps, the closest that America ever came to an actual politics of Burkeanism. Although the American Whigs never abandoned the creed's natural-rights morality, they adorned it with the imposing drapery of reverence for cultural tradition and the rule of law. In many respects, in fact, Huntington's project is a recrudescence of Whiggism.

By contrast, Jeffersonian Republicans, soon turned Jacksonian Democrats, preferred to dignify the creed by enmeshing it in a historical and progressive account of culture. They, too, were aware of the problem of Bonapartism, which had seized and destroyed French republicanism in its infancy; and in Andrew Jackson, of course, they had a kind of Bonaparte figure in American politics whom they were happy to exploit. But in their own populist manner they responded to the inherent dangers of Bonapartism by embracing a kind of theory of progress, influenced by Hegel though vastly more democratic than his, which recognized the People as the vehicle of the world-spirit and as the voice of God on earth. (You can find this in the essays and books of George Bancroft, the Jacksonian-era historian and advisor to Democratic presidents, as well as in popular editorials in the *North American Review* and elsewhere.) The people were always primary, in other words. Jackson and even the founders were their servants; every great man was the representative of a great people. Here, too, the creed tended to merge into culture, though in this case into forward-looking popular culture.

In his early life, Abraham Lincoln was a Whig, memorably and subtly warning against the spirit of Caesarism and encouraging reverence for the law as our political religion. But Lincoln's greatness depended upon transcending Whiggism for the sake of a new republicanism, a strategy already visible in his singular handling of the stock Whig themes as a young man. In fact, his new party called itself the Republican Party as a kind of boast that the new republicanism intended to revive the old. Their point was that the former Democratic Republicans, now mere Democrats, had abandoned the republic, which Lincoln and his party vowed to save. Rejecting Whiggish traditionalism as well as Democratic populism and progressivism, Lincoln rehabilitated the American creed, returning to the Declaration and its truths to set the face of American law against secession and slavery, to purge slavery from the national identity, and to reassert republican mores in American life and culture. This last goal entailed the American people's long struggle against Jim Crow and racial determinism, as well as our contemporary struggle against group rights and racial and sexual entitlements.

Lincoln and his party stood for a reshaping of American culture around the American creed – "a new birth of freedom." Because the creed itself dictated a limited government, this rebirth was not an illiberal, top-down politicization of culture of the sort that liberal courts in recent decades have attempted. Disciplined by the ideas of natural rights and the consent of the governed, this revitalization was a persuasive effort that took generations, and included legislative victories like the Civil War Amendments and the subsequent civil rights acts. Government sometimes had to take energetic action to secure rights, nonetheless, e.g., to suppress the culture of lynching. Nor should we forget that peaceful reforms presupposed wartime victory. As with the Revolution, it took war to decide what kind of national identity America would possess – if any. But war is meaningless without the statecraft that turns it so far as possible to noble ends, and that prepares the way for the return of truly civil government and civil society.

WE HOLD THESE TRUTHS

Modern liberalism, beginning in the Progressive Era, has done its best to strip natural rights and the founders' Constitution out of the American creed. By emptying it of its proper moral content, thinkers and politicians like Woodrow Wilson prepared the creed to be filled by subsequent generations, who could pour their contemporary values into it and thus keep it in tune with the times. The "living constitution" transformed the creed, once based on timeless or universal principles, into an evolving doctrine; turned it, in effect, into culture, which could be adjusted and reinterpreted in accordance with history's imperatives. Alternatively, one could say that twentieth-century liberals turned their open-ended form of culturalism into a new American creed, the multicultural creed, which they have few scruples now about imposing on republican America, diversity be damned.

To his credit, Huntington abhors this development. Unfortunately, his Anglo-Protestant culturalism, like any merely cultural conservatism, is no match for its liberal opponents. He persists in thinking of liberals as devotees of the old American creed who push its universal principles too far, who rely on reason to the exclusion of

a strong national culture. When they abjured individualism and natural rights decades ago, however, liberals broke with that creed, and
did so proudly. When they abandoned nature as the ground of right,
liberals broke as well with reason, understood as a natural capacity
for seeking truth, in favor of reason as a servant of culture, history,
fate, power, and finally nothingness. In short, Huntington fails to
grasp that latter-day liberals *attack American culture because they
reject the American creed,* around which that culture has formed and
developed from the very beginning.

In thinking through the crisis of American national identity, we
should keep in mind the opening words of the second paragraph of
the Declaration of Independence: "We hold these truths." Usually,
and correctly, we emphasize the truths that are held in common, but
we must not forget the "We" who holds them. The American creed
is the keystone of American national identity; but it requires a culture to sustain it. The republican task is to recognize the creed's pri-
macy, the culture's indispensability, and the challenge, which
political wisdom alone can answer, to shape a people that can endure
while also living up to its principles.

CHAPTER SEVENTEEN

TRUMP AND THE CONSERVATIVE CAUSE

A POLITICAL PARTY that allows seventeen candidates to compete for its presidential nomination is not a serious political party. A political party that allows its would-be presidents to debate one another silly – in every sense – is failing in its job, too. Happily, in 2016 the number of GOP debates was down from 2012 (when there were twenty-seven of one kind or another); but the number of candidates was up. You may recall that in the early exchanges they evaded and, occasionally, answered questions in flying squads of ten and seven, no existing television stage being able to hold them all.

Despite the Republican Party's fatuous and grueling process, however, the voters learned some valuable things. The vast field contained many accomplished politicians, though few truly distinguished ones. The senators (Ted Cruz, Lindsey Graham, Rand Paul, Marco Rubio, Rick Santorum) were young or implausible, the governors (Jeb Bush, Chris Christie, Bobby Jindal, Jim Gilmore, Mike Huckabee, John Kasich, George Pataki, Rick Perry, Scott Walker) successful but too numerous, stale, or busy for their own good. There was not the man of "continental character" that the framers had hoped would stand out. That left the "outsiders" or amateur politicians (Ben Carson, Carly Fiorina, Donald Trump).

The governors, with their records of domestic reform, dominated the early betting. As foreign policy issues (Russia, China, and the Middle East) flared up and the primaries began, the senators (except Rand Paul) enjoyed a surge. Only Kasich made it out of the governors' group; only Cruz and Rubio emerged from the senators; and the outsiders set the tone for the whole cycle. Dr. Ben Carson and businessman Donald J. Trump sat atop the polls for months. Carson's support finally melted away, leaving Cruz and Rubio (ignoring Kasich, as non-Ohio voters tended to do) to battle for the honor of saving the party from Trump.

Cruz outlasted Rubio, but in the end the man he had patronized for months as "my friend Donald" defeated him handily. Trump defeated them all handily.

CONSERVATIVE MINDS

What, if anything, can conservatives learn from Trump and from this episode? What, if anything, could *he* learn for the fights ahead … always assuming that he is willing to learn? To find out, conservatives would have to engage him. The Never Trump movement may be an understandable, even honorable reaction to the startling victory of a Johnny-come-lately Republican who never enjoyed a deep allegiance to the conservative movement. But it is hardly an adequate one. Conservatives cared too much about the party and the country to wash their hands of the 2016 or, for that matter, the 2020 election. A third-party bid would be quixotic. That leaves taking the measure of Trump, and offering advice and help, whether or not he has the sense to take it.

To abstain, in hopes of stimulating a recovery of full-throated conservatism in the next cycle, was sheer desperation, ignoring the weaknesses in the multiple forms of doctrinaire conservatism on offer in 2016: libertarianism (Paul); social conservatism (Huckabee, Santorum, Carson, Jindal); compassionate conservatism (Bush, Kasich); "reformicon" conservatism (Rubio); neoconservatism, at least in foreign policy (Graham); and self-styled "true" conservatism (Cruz). None succeeded in capturing the Republican imagination.

Trump helped to expose some of the problems latent in the current conservative movement and its agenda – without necessarily solving any of them. Aging baby-boomer conservatives were not that interested in sweeping reforms of Social Security, despite Chris Christie's admirable plan; and the candidates' evasiveness on how they would "replace" Obamacare, while hardly noble, was entirely understandable, given how difficult it will be just to keep the promises made by the pre-Obama welfare state, much less those added by a post-Obama one. (Trump finessed the problem by simply declaring Social Security and Medicare off limits to cuts, and pledging to unleash an American economy dynamic enough to grow us out of the problem.)

Ted Cruz's proposal to abolish the Internal Revenue Service fit the pattern: face large and intractable problems like the cost of government and the national debt by proposing a large and utopian solution to a different problem. No one expected Cruz's plan to be enacted, of course. It was a symbolic affirmation of "true" conservatism, just like the government shutdown. In general, many conservative "solutions" floated untethered from any political strategy that could have garnered sufficient popular and legislative support to enact them. It is always tempting for politicians to will the ends without willing the means. Only in our age do we call this idealism, however, or, in Cruz's favorite formulation, devotion to principle.

His case was perhaps the most interesting. It was Cruz, more than any other Republican, who throughout 2014 and 2015 led the populist revolt against the party leadership, exhorting the conservative rank-and-file to distrust, despise, and depose the party's grandees. It must be admitted that the leaders were of considerable help to him. Still, in 2014 the GOP had won historic victories in the Senate, in the House, and especially in state governorships and legislative seats. These wins could have been interpreted – with a little moderation and a few subsequent tactical victories – as a down payment, as preparation for the coup de grâce to be administered to the Democrats in 2016. Instead, expectations soared and crashed, embittering relations within the party and leading to a kind of crisis of legitimacy. This, in turn, prepared the way for an outsider, who turned out to be not Cruz but Trump.

CRUZ CONTROL

Cruz helped to breed his own nemesis. And what does he have to show for it? Is his style of "true" conservatism now the more popular, the more compelling, the better understood? For someone so intelligent and so renowned as a debater, it's hard to remember any of Cruz's arguments. Admittedly, he debated legions of opponents – a case where party leaders really did let the good candidates down, as mentioned above. Partly, however, his fluent arguments lacked a center, a focus.

He had two rhetorical modes – the preacher and the debater. One was earnest and revivalist, summoning ultimate appeals to right and wrong, salvation and damnation; the other was ceremonial, lawyerly, and dazzling, full of cut-and-thrust and aiming at applause and victory. Neither was presidential, strictly speaking, because the president doesn't preach and never has to debate anyone, at least officially. Cruz needed a third style, more deliberative and suited to fellow citizens. He needed to unite the principles of right and wrong with calm, deliberative judgments about what is advantageous for Americans to do here and now. In that way he – and the conservative movement – could have helped to cultivate what Abraham Lincoln called a "philosophical public opinion." Instead, Cruz let his forensic victories demarcate the boundaries of true conservatism – a string of positions each slightly to the right, coincidentally, of his main competitors.

Like Marco Rubio, Cruz entered national politics as a champion of the Tea Party, the populist-conservative reaction to the Great Recession and to the Bush- and Obama-led bailouts – and to Obama's cynical unwillingness to let a good crisis go to waste. He shared the Tea Party's longing to return American politics to some constitutional limits, an important and laudable principle. But neither he nor Rubio (nor, needless to say, any of the party elders) turned that vague longing into a compelling political case for an essential agenda. If the Constitution actually were imperiled, wouldn't you expect this to be the highest and probably most urgent message to voters? Yet restoring the Constitution remained a series of talking points (more elaborate in Cruz's speeches than in anyone else's, granted) rather than an organizing cause around which the conservative movement might reinterpret and realign itself. Doubtless, Rubio and Cruz would have picked federal judges with the Tea Party's concerns in mind. But decades of experience have proved that it takes more than one branch to halt, much less reverse, constitutional decay, and that the judiciary needs support, pressure, and direction from public opinion and the political branches in order to do its part under these circumstances.

This failure to take seriously the Tea Party's warning that corruption had eaten deeply into constitutional foundations, and that government was slipping beyond the control of the governed, left conservatives and Republicans searching, as usual, for a purpose. The sense of a dead end was reinforced by Chief Justice John Roberts's tortuous decisions saving Obamacare, twice, in 2012 and 2015.

If relimiting the government by constitutional means was not an option – as a lot of indignant Republican and independent voters concluded, in effect – then what was left but to use the system as it is, and try placing a strong leader, one of our own, someone who can get something done in *our* interest, at the head of it? After the Tea Party, the next stop on the populist train was Trump Tower.

THE TRUMP BUSINESS

There is no shortage of reasons to object to Donald Trump. They range from the aesthetic (that hair!) to the moral, political, and intellectual. But there's no reason to exaggerate. He is not a Caesar figure, though some conservatives sincerely fear that. Caesar's soul was ruled, said Cicero, by *libido dominandi*, the lust for mastery or domination. Trump wants to make great deals, build beautiful buildings, and shine in the public eye as a kind of benefactor. You might say he is interested in magnificence, not magnanimity. For good or ill, he lacks the deeply political soul. In a 1990 interview, *Playboy* asked him about his role models from history. "I could say Winston Churchill," he said, "but ... I've always thought that Louis B. Mayer led the ultimate life, that Flo Ziegfeld led the ultimate life, that men like Darryl Zanuck and Harry Cohn did some creative and beautiful things. The ultimate job for me would have been running MGM in the '30s and '40s – pre-television."

Trump is a very American character, a very New York character, the businessman who understands the world: the *sophos* who could bring efficiency, *toughness* (his favorite quality), and common sense to politics, if only he were listened to. In most of the world, populism is associated with distrust of business, with hatred of capitalism. In the United States it's more common to find populism linked to an admiration for the farmer and small businessman, for the entrepreneur who has pioneered new products and markets, or for the independent businessman who has fairly earned his own fortune. That's why Trump plays to a familiar Republican fantasy: the business leader who with cost control and double-entry bookkeeping could set government right.

It didn't work out so well for Herbert Hoover, Wendell Willkie, Ross Perot, Mitt Romney, Meg Whitman, or the many others who tried it at the national or state level because politics is actually quite different from business. For instance, there is hardly anyone to whom the president of the United States can say, "You're fired." He is pretty much stuck with the millions of federal employees already hired and protected by civil service, not to mention the judges and elected legislators. (Though to give him his due, it sometimes seems as if President Trump fired everyone he possibly could have.)

Plus, a businessman's instinct is to want to measure government's effectiveness by some single, or at any rate straightforward, standard, as a corporation can be measured by profitability, or a stock by earnings per share. But there is no comparable metric for politics that is so revealing and useful. The different branches have distinct powers and qualities (energy, deliberation, judiciousness, etc.) and the qualified independence that comes with them, for a reason. The temptation to be a political Louis B. Mayer, to produce the whole political show and insist on having *control* over all aspects of it, can lead only to a very frustrated presidency.

CULTURAL DECLINE

Of course, Trump's own business record was indistinguishable from his career as a celebrity. He stubbornly defends his crudity, anger, and egotism as integral to the Trump brand, which he promotes incessantly, and as in touch with the working class voters he covets. To conservatives enamored of the gentlemanly manners of Ronald Reagan and the Bushes, this indecency offends.

Yet it didn't disqualify Trump as a candidate, because it helps to certify him as a non-politician, a truth-speaker, and an entertainer. Trump seems to know the contemporary working class well, its hardships, moral dislocations, and resentments. Readers familiar with the new working class described by Charles Murray in *Coming Apart: The State of White America, 1960–2010* will have a roadmap to the America that Trump sees and that rallied to his side. As the Obama team got a jump on its rivals by exploiting new campaign software and technology in the 2008 race, so Trump got a cultural jump on his rivals in the 2016 primaries. He saw that the older, politer, less straitened America was fading among the working and lower middle classes. Downward mobility, broken families, disability and other forms of welfare support – these were increasingly the new reality for them.

This left them lots of time for TV (as Murray shows), especially for reality TV shows. Trump was more in touch with these developments, and also with the anxieties of the working part of the working class who feared falling into this slough of despond, than any of the other candidates. To put it in business speak, as *The New York Times* did, Trump "understood the Republican Party's customers better than its leaders did." It didn't help that much of the rank-and-file had lost confidence in those leaders. Trump ran rings around them, and employed new media to do it. Steve Case, the founder of AOL, described that part of the achievement in an email to the *Times* that had the odd rhythm of one of its subject's tweets. "Trump leveraged a perfect storm. A combo of social media (big following), brand (celebrity figure), creativity (pithy tweets), speed/timeliness (dominating news cycles)."

Every republic eventually faces what might be called the Weimar problem. Has the national culture, popular and elite, deteriorated so much that the virtues necessary to sustain republican government are no longer viable? America is not there yet, though when 40 percent of children are born out of wedlock (as they are now, alas) it is not too early to wonder. What about when Donald Trump became the Republican nominee for president, and then Chief Executive? George F. Will and many other conservatives thought the end is near.

I understand the question, but the surer sign of comprehensive decline was not Trump's success but the conservative candidates' failure, one by one, all sixteen of them. Trump himself has considerable, late-blooming political talents, and his vices have been exhaustively condemned but never examined in comparative perspective. Do obscenities fall from his lips more readily than they did from Lyndon Johnson's or Richard Nixon's? Are the circumstances of his three marriages more shameful than the circumstances of John F. Kennedy's pathologically unfaithful one – or for that matter, Bill Clinton's humiliatingly unfaithful one? The point is not to extenuate Trump's faults but to understand how millions of voters see him. They knew he was damaged goods, just as the Clintons are – and were, even back in 1992 – but they apparently regard him as more trustworthy, or at least more faithful to their interests, than any of his erstwhile GOP competitors.

One difference is that Nixon's, Johnson's, and Kennedy's sins were mostly kept behind closed doors. The culture in those days was intolerant of such vices (Nelson Rockefeller is the exception that proves the rule); *our* culture, not so much. Trump is not the first to benefit from our lower religious and moral standards – that would be the Clintons – and though his excesses shouldn't be condoned, most voters (so far) don't regard them, as Trump himself might say, as deal-breakers.

PRESIDENT TRUMP

Separation of powers, federalism, and the numerous other formal and informal folkways of American government constrained President Trump in ways that surprised him (while delighting others) and to which, all signs indicate, he had given very little thought. In his emphasis on *getting things done* by negotiating great deals between the branches, he sounded a little like Richard Neustadt, the political scientist who found the essence of presidential power not in the powers and duties vested in the office by the Constitution but in the president's personal ability to persuade. Although Neustadt, a Harvard professor, meant *persuade* in a more high-minded way than Trump does (*The Art of the Deal* says it all), Trump's raw understanding of the presidency appeared nevertheless to lie much closer to the liberal tradition stemming ultimately from Woodrow Wilson and Teddy Roosevelt than to the conservative or constitutionalist one. Wilson, not Trump, said this:

> The President is at liberty … to be as big a man as he can. His capacity will set the limit; and if Congress be overborne by him, it will be no fault of the makers of the Constitution – it will be from no lack of constitutional powers on its part, but only because the President has the nation behind him, and Congress has not.

Though Wilson reassured his readers that "the reprobation of all good men will always overwhelm [immoral or dishonest] influence," he stressed at the same time that "the personal force of the President is perfectly constitutional to any extent which he chooses to exercise it." "Personal force" – not far from Trump's praise of high energy, toughness, and strength in the ideal chief executive.

The big difference between Wilson's theory and Trump's reality, however, arises from the role of the political party. Wilson assumed that to be an effective leader of the nation, the president would first have to be a spirited leader of his own political party, organized around his own dominating vision. Trump thinks of himself as a man above party, or outside of party. His favorite metaphors come from boxing – not a team sport. At times he has been almost as estranged from other Republican officeholders, including his own cabinet members, as from Democratic leaders in Congress. A president caught between two parties, each suspicious of him and hostile to varying degrees, is a recipe for a weak presidency, like Andrew Johnson's after the Civil War. Trump has been saved from this fate not so much by his own cunning, though that's part of it, but by his popularity within his party. With ninety percent of Republicans consistently supporting him, according to the polls, there's little GOP officeholders can do except fall in line behind him, whether they like it or not.

POLITICAL CORRECTNESS

It's no coincidence that the two loudest, most consequential sociopolitical forces in America right now are Political Correctness and Donald Trump. One began life on college campuses, the other, as a political phenomenon, among working people. They have already begun to collide. At Emory University four years ago, someone scrawled "Trump 2016" in chalk on steps and sidewalks around the campus. About fifty students swiftly assembled to protest the incident, shouting, "You are not listening! Come speak to us, we are in pain!" Aghast at "the chalkings," the university president complied.

At Scripps College, at about the same time, a Mexican-American student awoke to find "#trump2016" written on the whiteboard on her door. The student body president, in a mass email, quickly condemned the "racist incident" and denounced Trump's hashtag as a symbol of violence and a "testament that racism continues to be an undeniable problem and alarming threat on our campuses." The student body's response, apparently, was underwhelming. Shortly the dean of students weighed in with an email of her own, upbraiding students who thought the student body president's email had been an overreaction. The dean noted that although Scripps of course respects its students' First Amendment rights, in this case the "circumstances here are unique." Note to dean: the circumstances are always unique.

The brave student journalist from whose account I take the Scripps story, Sophie Mann (who, incidentally, took two courses with me at neighboring Claremont McKenna College), closed her post about it in the *Weekly Standard* with this eye-opening statement: "In any event, I am hoping that this dies down before finals, because last semester, in the face of radical student agitation over minority victimization here, the student-run coffee shop was declared a 'safe space' for minority students. That was hard on those of us who need caffeine to study.'" In other words, the coffee shop was closed for several days *to white students*, who were officially forbidden its use, so that "students of color" could enjoy it safe from "white privilege" and oppression. It gives new meaning to the term "woke students"!

When P.C. world and Trump world collide, as these preliminary incidents show, there will be blood, or at least chalkings and coffee deprivation. In all seriousness, it's likely the campuses were primed to erupt in political disturbances of a sort not seen in decades, not out of affection for Joe Biden or any other Democrat but out of fear and loathing of Trump ... until the pandemic sent everyone home.

But the troubles can't be confined to the campuses. The Left has gotten used to the way it runs the universities – by a powerful, ideological majority so dominant that there isn't usually any effective opposition, or any opposition at all. What else can you expect when, as a recent study of eleven California colleges found, among sociology professors Democrats outnumber Republicans 44 to 1? In most other departments, Republicans are outnumbered by ratios ranging merely from 5–1 to 16–1. Republicans are much rarer than most of the groups usually singled out for affirmative action or other special admissions attention. Except for Jonathan Haidt and a handful of others, when did liberals ever complain about this imbalance?

The truth is they enjoy it; they regard it as natural, advantageous for students, and, increasingly, as a model for how the rest of the world should be run. What's worse is what they routinely do with their extraordinary power: they distribute rights and duties by race, sex, gender, politics, and ethnicity, as the coffee shop example illustrates. On campus, students are introduced to their roles and prepared to fulfill their functions as shock troops inside *and outside* the university: faculty members and administrators learn to assign equality and inequality, order atonement and punishment, and police the boundaries of speech, deciding who may be offended and by whom and for how long and why.

This is Political Correctness, and it is now the first of the Left's political institutions. It marks a new, ugly stage in liberalism, a new ensemble of required moral attitudes, as even a few sensitive liberals (e.g., Jonathan Chait) have begun to recognize and criticize.

P.C. is serious and totalist politics, aspiring to open the equivalent of a vast quarantine and reeducation camp for the millions of sick Americans infected with racism, sexism, classism, and so forth. This is most conveniently accomplished on college campuses, where few people expect toleration or civil equality these days; but it can also take place in the human resources divisions of major corporations, on social media, and in political campaigns.

It's the *basso profundo* under the Left's anti-Trump argument. The Democrats' criticism that he is "a loose cannon" arouses many fears – foreign policy blunders, the nuclear keys – but running underneath them, *sostenuto*, is the fear and outrage that he is always prepared to say things that offend a group that must not be offended. Debbie Wasserman-Schultz, the head of the Democratic National Committee, got to the heart of the matter when she tweeted four years ago, "Trump's racism knows no bounds," where "racism" is the Left's all-purpose condemnation for political incorrectness.

P.C. is the hard edge, the business end of what Emmett Rensin, in *Vox*, has called "the smug style" in American liberalism. Ever since the Democrats lost the working class, he argues, they signed their souls over to "the educated, the coastal, and the professional" classes. These overlords invented the smug style to answer the question, "What's the matter with Kansas?" as Thomas Frank titled his 2004 book, or more generally, How can the working class repeatedly vote against its own obvious (to a liberal) economic interests? Rensin's blunt epitome of the liberals' answer: "Stupid hicks don't know what's good for them." In their view, conservatism is not an attractive set of arguments or principles but a form of stupidity, of unknowing. Liberalism, by contrast, is a form of shared knowing, based not on knowledge, exactly, but on the presumption of knowledge. Hence the smug "knowingness" of the contemporary Left, most apparent and irritating in its smug contempt for working people who have rejected it.

Though his is a relatively mild case, Barack Obama cannot hide his smugness. As you may have noticed, the American people often disappointed him, clinging to their God and guns instead of cheering for his policies. Consider, for example, how quickly and shamelessly he switched from opposing, to supporting, gay marriage. He campaigned against it in 2008 *and* 2012. The only thing like it was how blithely the liberal justices on the Supreme Court pulled *their* switcheroo, assuring us that bigotry alone – not tradition, caution, or natural-law humanism – could ever have justified a prohibition on same-sex marriages. Obama almost winked at the American public: You knew all along I really wasn't against it, didn't you?

INCORRECT, AND PROUD OF IT

It's the spirited way Donald Trump has defied the P.C. mavens, I think, that's been the key to his success so far. He effectively made being anti–P.C. the centerpiece of his 2016 campaign. It proved a brilliant decision. The other Republican contenders might have done the same thing, but they were in thrall to their own versions of conservatism and the attendant policy agendas. They couldn't see that the ascendance of P.C. liberalism raised issues more fundamental and more urgent than the think-tank-approved litanies of tax, spending, and foreign policy reforms. Trump alone was willing, eager even, to *embody* political incorrectness, to own it, not merely to patronize it. And most politically incorrect of all, he got people to laugh with him as he did so.

Trump bet that 2016 was an election more like 1968 than 1980. Like Richard Nixon in '68, Trump felt that this election might test whether the center could hold, whether a silent majority could be mobilized on behalf of the country itself. The issue was not so much a showdown over liberal or conservative policies, but the simpler, more elementary question of whether a majority granted the premise – that the nation had once been great – and wanted America to be great again. Trump is more divisive even than Nixon, but perhaps he thinks the country is in worse shape, and that the majority needs to be angry, not merely silent.

Reaganism came with a full complement of urgent and intelligent policies. Nixon really had no "ism"; he thought the times demanded improvisation in the interest of conserving the nation, the only kind of conservatism he really respected. Trump is closer to Nixon. He is in no hurry to build out Trumpism into a political doctrine.

If there were a core to Trumpism, however, it would be his insistence on "America First," a phrase with unfortunate connotations, to say the least. To him, though, it seems to mean the legitimacy of preferring one's own people or country to others. Charity begins at home, in other words. The Declaration of Independence, notably, pays "a decent respect to the opinions of mankind" and appeals to "the Supreme Judge of the world for the rectitude of our intentions," but it speaks only "in the name, and by authority of *the good people of these Colonies.*" The Constitution is designed to "secure the blessings of liberty *to ourselves and our Posterity*" (emphasis added). It is not at all inconsistent with human rights to take care of your own first, and in fact it is a duty to ward off tyranny for one's own people before attending, to the extent prudently possible, to others.

Trump mentions America's founding principles often in the speeches he gives, but he has more urgent things on his mind in his pullulating tweets. Alas, he takes his tweets more seriously than his speeches. That is shortsighted and a mistake. Who knows if he can correct it? If he did, he could broaden the discussion from, say, the mores of Mexican immigrants to the mores of the Americans – "Americanization" being necessary not merely for naturalized citizens but also for the native born – which is the ultimate concern. But his savvy opposition to Political Correctness implies something like this defense of America, because there is nothing Political Correctness stands for so much as the denigration of America, its history and principles. P.C. liberalism doesn't stop there; its hostility extends to the theological, philosophical, literary, and scientific heritage of the West. But freedom, too, begins at home.

CHAPTER EIGHTEEN

THINKING ABOUT TRUMP:
MORALITY, POLITICS,
AND THE PRESIDENCY

Two months before the 2016 presidential election, the *Claremont Review of Books* published (in its digital pages) an essay that began: "2016 is the Flight 93 election: charge the cockpit or you die." The author, Publius Decius Mus, a pseudonym for Michael Anton, who later served as Deputy Assistant to the President for Strategic Communications on the National Security Council, noted that "you may die anyway" because there were no guarantees except one: "if you don't try, death is certain."

He allowed that his metaphor might strike many readers as "histrionic." It did. But it struck many more as galvanizing, especially when Rush Limbaugh devoted virtually an entire radio program to reading "The Flight 93 Election" excitedly to his listeners.

Not long after, a Never Trump friend took me aside to warn that the essay was "dangerous," by which he meant irresponsible, "the kind of argument that could be used to justify...." He didn't finish the thought, but I suppose he meant a calamity like a coup or the election of Donald J. Trump, assuming he could tell the difference. I pointed out the obvious, which is that the only non-metaphorical action the author urged Americans to consider was voting for the Republican presidential candidate. Nothing illegal about that, is there?

The broader point, of course, is that almost any spirited political appeal involves an element of exaggeration for effect. After all, in a democracy free speech often aims to awaken the public to a danger to which it is presently blind or complacent. A free people understands this and *enjoys*, in both senses of the term, the exuberance of political argument, which is its birthright.

During the Cold War, with the danger of nuclear annihilation hanging heavy in the air, fellow-traveling leftists often deployed a surrender slogan, "better red than dead," to which American conservatives liked to retort, jauntily, "better dead than red!" That qualified as an exaggeration, inasmuch as they were not looking forward to Mutual Assured Destruction, nor counseling, say, mass suicide in the event of a Soviet victory. More carefully stated, the slogan meant it was better to face the *possibility* of being dead than the *certainty* of being red: it was a rallying cry to resist the Communists. And by means of a vigorous, anti-Communist foreign policy, it might be possible, God willing, to end up being neither dead nor red, which was indeed how the Cold War played out not only for us but, more remarkably, for the Russians, too.

Is such freewheeling speech allowed anymore? That is a question for the Trump years, as we shall see. How amusing, in the meantime, that it is the president's opponents who now seem to be eyeing the cockpit, nervously. And not merely in anticipation of a heated 2020 get-out-the-vote campaign. Some of them fantasize, rather openly, about congressional "interventions," Twenty-fifth Amendment putsches, and other desperate steps that could be taken to remove the constitutionally elected president before he crashes Air Force One into the Majority Leader's office.

They are letting off steam, mostly. But what's remarkable is how little *light* they have shed on the object of their ire. After almost three years, American progressives and the conservative Never Trumpers are no closer to understanding the man and the political situation he's helped to create than they ever were. If we wish to make some progress in understanding him and the state of the country, we need to start from a different point of view.

BREAKING BAD

Teddy Roosevelt once congratulated his countrymen for never having elected a bad man as president. The critics' basic indictment of
Donald Trump, delivered with several variations, is that he is a bad
man, so bad as to be unfit for the presidential office. For most his
badness indicates moral vice, others cry up what might be called
temperamental or psychological failings, while a few insist the disorder is intellectual. Among the Never Trump oddsmakers, the theory that he aspires consciously to be a tyrant seems to have faded, to
be replaced by a more workaday worry over his "authoritarian personality," which might be said to comprise all three kinds of
badness.

The structure of the Never Trump argument is worth
examining.

▷ Bad men make bad presidents.

▷ Trump is a bad man.

▷ Therefore, Trump is, or will be, a bad president.

For the syllogism to hold, both the major and the minor premises
must be true. Let us stipulate, for the moment, that his critics are
right in their commitment to the minor premise: Trump is a bad
man. Does it follow that he must be a bad president?

There is certainly a lot of truth in the major premise. As the
ancient Greeks used to say, "ruling shows the man." That is, a man's
virtues and vices are clarified and magnified by his public actions
and words, especially in the case of a president. "Character is destiny," as Jonah Goldberg likes to say.

Yet two doubts or qualifications arise immediately. First, it is
possible for a bad person to do good accidentally, as it were, either
without intending to, or by intending quite deliberately to do so but
for the sake of another, further end that is immoral or amoral. As
Machiavelli argued (he wasn't the first), the prince may be persuaded to serve the people for the sake of his own personal glory.
That isn't virtue as Christian or classical ethics would define it. But it

can be productive of much public good, not as an intention but as a byproduct.

As it happens, the U.S. Constitution famously set up a series of institutional checks and balances to encourage ambitious men to vie with other ambitious men to serve the public good. The framers intended (a) to enable men of good character to have the powers and duties they needed in office to put their virtues and talents to work, consciously pursuing justice and the common good; and (b) to compel bad men to serve the public even if they would prefer not to. When working properly, the Constitution's incentives would, by repetition, help to make such service habitual, and thus improve the character of some, at least, of the imperfect human beings who would get elected in our democratic republic. John Adams put the point memorably at the end of his three-volume work of political science, *A Defence of the Constitutions of Government of the United States of America* (1787–88): "perhaps it would be impossible to prove, that a republic cannot exist, even among highwaymen, by setting one rogue to watch another; and the knaves themselves may, in time, be made honest men by the struggle."

Second, as these considerations suggest, a lot depends on what "bad men" actually means. Let's begin from the beginning, as it were. From the point of view of original sin, we are all bad, that is, fallen – deprived of the original justice and holiness God intended us to have. From this crooked wood of humanity – for there is no other – has come every so-called good, or even great, president. It shouldn't be surprising, then, that many old-fashioned readers of the Bible, and evangelical Christians in particular, have made their peace with President Trump more easily than outside observers might have expected. Christians are commanded to hate the sin but love the sinner. That doesn't mean they have to support Donald Trump. But his religious friends find it instructive that in the Bible, God repeatedly found ways to use even very flawed human beings for His purposes – from King David, who arranged for the death of Bathsheba's husband so as to continue his royal adultery with her, to Saint Peter, who fearfully lied about his association with Jesus.

Though commanded to strive for godliness, Jews and Christians do not expect to reach it in this world. But presumably that is not quite the point being raised by "bad men make bad presidents." All men, and all presidents, are not equally bad, nor bad in the same way. Many of Trump's most well-meaning critics are thinking "bad" not in the sense of falling short of God's glory but of falling short, through turpitude or vice (e.g., vanity, untruthfulness), of attainable human morality. Along these lines one of the less well-meaning critics, James Comey, the former FBI director, has said over and over, Trump is "morally unfit to be president." These critics are scandalized that Trump is not scandalized by his own misdeeds, especially involving women.

It's not uncommon, however, for bad men in this and similar senses to do good by the public. Gouverneur Morris, "the rake who wrote the Constitution," as Richard Brookhiser calls him in his excellent biography, felt a kind of calling to sleep with other men's wives. Martin Luther King, Jr., was a serial adulterer, as the tireless public servants in the FBI of his day knew well. These sins, which were habitual enough to be called vices, did not prevent – and detracted from, if at all, only slightly – the enormous public good they did.

Andrew Jackson killed a man in a duel, and would have killed more if he could. Ulysses S. Grant was a drunkard, at least for long stretches of his life. Grover Cleveland, an out-of-wedlock father through a dalliance that was Clintonian in its impetuousness, entered the presidency with chants of "Ma, Ma, where's my pa?" ringing in his ears, only to be defended by his fellow Democrats who chanted, "Gone to the White House, ha, ha, ha!"

Exhorting Americans to live up to the Declaration of Independence's principles as far as they could, that is, as far as circumstances would allow, Abraham Lincoln liked to appeal to the verse of Scripture, "Be ye therefore perfect even as your Father which is in heaven is perfect." But in accepting political allies among Know-Nothings (who hated Catholics, especially Catholic immigrants), Lincoln resisted counsels of perfection and appealed to another verse as the test of practical good: "By their fruits ye shall know them." That is, he asked: will bad or flawed men cooperate in delivering sound public policy (as measured by Lincoln's, not by their, standards), regardless of their moral and intellectual failings?

The leap from bad men to bad presidents is not certain or auto-matic. Bad character may be merely a distraction, or it may amount to a fatal flaw. Particulars matter. If we are talking tyranny, or trea-son, or bestial depths of viciousness, or psychological or mental incapacity – these and similar species of badness clearly make for bad rulers and bad presidents. But the inability of moral virtue to rule the world is an old discovery, understood by none more pro-foundly than by the truly magnanimous statesmen like Lincoln who were keenly aware of the rarity of greatness and goodness.

HARD AND SOFT

Good character remains more desirable and honorable than bad character – even if bad character does not necessarily make for a bad president, nor good character for a good president. Based on his crit-ics' account of him, the question about Trump would seem to be, at least from the conservative point of view: how comes such a bad man to do so much good? That is, is it really the case, as the Never Trumpers' minor premise asserts, that Trump is such a bad man? *So* bad that it was morally imperative to usher Hillary Clinton to the White House in his stead?

I'm reminded of Winston Churchill's line about the socialist Stafford Cripps: "He has all the virtues I dislike and none of the vices I admire." The Never Trumpers see no virtues in Trump, and admire none of his vices. The resulting portrait is a caricature, a rough, unrevealing one. No one would ever call him a moral paragon – not even the president himself. But the Trump universe theorized by the Never Trumpers is all dark matter; it doesn't acknowledge the traits we see with our own eyes, including some admirable vices, but also his distinctive virtues, whether we choose to dislike them or not. The critics seem to prefer an explanation of Trump that is, as the cosmologists say, non-luminous.

Michael Barone's *Hard America, Soft America: Competition vs. Coddling and the Battle for the Nation's Future* (2004) is a short book with a useful distinction that begins to illuminate the phenomenon of Trump. It describes two countries, as it were. "Hard America" is shaped by the marketplace forces of competition and accountability. "Soft America" is the realm of public schools, self-esteem, and government social programs. The latter, according to Barone, produces incompetent and unambitious eighteen-year-olds; the former hard-charging and adaptable thirty-year-olds. Somehow, uneasily, modern America includes both.

Donald Trump considers himself a kind of ambassador from hard America to soft America. Many (not all) of the asperities of his character are related to his career path. He calls himself "a builder," and America "a nation of builders." He knows his way around a construction site, and his virtues and vices skew to that hard, brazen, masculine world of getting things built quickly, durably, beautifully if possible, and in any case profitably. He wants to revive hard America's mines, factories, and building sites, in the face of what he knows is the growing power of its despisers in soft America.

Still, there are different districts in hard America. For example, Mitt Romney is a very successful businessman, too. But Trump comes from a different neighborhood. They divide along recognizable lines that until 2016 did not seem that interesting, because most commentators simply assumed that Romney's neighborhood had forever displaced Trump's. They pose sharp contrasts within the world of hard America: construction versus consulting, blue-collar versus white-collar, "deals" versus mergers and acquisitions.

For most of his life, Trump ran a prosperous and famous family business. Though he's had clients, partners, and customers, he's never had to report regularly to a board of directors, public shareholders, or regular capital markets, and it shows. He's used to being the boss, to following his intuition, to trying one thing and then another, to hiring and firing at will (and to hiring family members at will), to promoting himself and his companies shamelessly. Not every family entrepreneur is like this, but most could probably recognize a bit of themselves in Trump's exaggerated portrait. Whereas Trump is a wildcatter at heart, Rex Tillerson, his first secretary of state, the former CEO of Exxon, was Big Oil; it wasn't hard to predict they would clash.

As the quintessential Bain Capital private equity guy, Romney shunned big, old-line companies unless they were foundering. Like

Trump, he practiced a kind of creative destruction, but one that was planned, modeled, and financed as taught in the business schools (Romney is a joint Harvard JD–MBA). It was this spirit of cool expertise and willingness to sacrifice factories and jobs that helped to make so damaging Romney's leaked remark in 2012 about the "47 percent" who pay no income tax, whom he could never persuade "they should take personal responsibility and care for their lives." The only thing missing in his assessment was calling them "deplorables."

Trump also knows his way around a television studio. The hard reality of being a builder and landlord is combined, in his case, with being a longstanding reality-TV star. If the preceding president cast himself in the role of "no-drama" Obama, the current one plays all-drama-all-the-time Trump. From the beginning his kind of real estate verged on show business. Branding and selling his name, which have constituted the largest part of his business for a while, represented for him another step in the direction of show business. Show business is a business, however, and Trump likes to interpret what might be considered the softer side of his career in the hardest possible terms. He emphasizes numbers – the ratings, the advertising dollars, the size of his crowds. He has survived in several cut-throat industries, and intends to add politics to the list.

Whether in business or in politics, Trump disliked the airs and claims of "experts," detached from and above the subjects of their experiments. He distrusted their glibness, too. He identified with working men and women, and promised (at least) to *add* jobs, to boost economic growth, to "win" for pipe-fitters and waitresses, too. He defended their Social Security but blasted the fraud of Obamacare, whereas Romney had scorned the 47%'s "entitlements" but gave Obamacare (based, you may recall, on Romneycare) a pass. Romney lacked perhaps what Kanye West would call "dragon energy." When in a primary election he had done well among voters without a high school degree, Trump memorably declared, "I love the poorly educated." You'd never hear Romney, nor any other mainstream Republican, say that!

Romney is certainly not a bad man, but he was portrayed in the 2012 presidential campaign as cruel to animals, a bully, a liar, a religious fanatic, a sexist ("binders full of women"), a warmonger, and many other evil things by the campaigning Left. These days the Left is always campaigning; as is the Right. Under those conditions, moral criticisms shade quickly into aesthetic-political ones, and vice versa. It is not entirely clear whether his liberal and conservative critics disapprove of Trump because he violates moral law or because he is infra dig. The ease with which the one yields to the other might suggest that his conservative opponents in particular should take pains to specify their objections and check their own prejudices. Their favorite medium for getting these off their chest – Twitter – suggests that painstakingness is not the point.

At any rate, Trump was neither the first nor the last GOP presidential candidate to be caricatured as a very bad, very rich man. The ease with which businessmen of whatever precinct may be caricatured as immoralists shows that soft America is perhaps not as soft as Barone thought. Soft America, centered on our schools, is hard enough to have come up with Political Correctness, now the cutting edge of American progressivism. And hard America, at least its Fortune 500 slice, has proved soft enough to become the chief disseminator of Political Correctness to middle America.

IN SEARCH OF POPULISM

Trump is often called a populist, though it isn't a word he uses very often or to describe himself. Yet many of his alleged moral and political disqualifications are said to trace to his populism, whatever that means. In the age of big government or, more precisely, of administrative government, the word appears in country after country but always elusively. It responds to a need but never satisfies that need.

When the original American populists organized the People's Party in time for the 1892 election, their rallying cry was the people versus "the interests," meaning the railroads and large corporations that were squeezing farmers and small businessmen, and that allegedly dominated the two main political parties. So they started a new party calling for silver money and lots of it, nationalization of the railroads, a federal income tax, and other reforms including the initiative, referendum, and direct election of senators.

But in an age when the vast majority of federal laws are regulations passed by unelected bureaucrats, when state and federal courts
freely strike down state initiatives they dislike, when the money supply is controlled by the unelected members of the Federal Reserve,
when campaign finance laws make it difficult for new parties to form,
and when there is already a federal program for almost every imag-
inable social problem – what is "populism" supposed to do?

The post-1960s bargain that Americans made with their government, not quite knowingly to be sure, was to exchange more and
more aspects of popular control over government for a guarantee to
the people of new, constantly updated "rights," assigned by the government to economic, social, ethnic, racial, gender, and transgender
groups. The exchange of power for rights has left us addicted to the
rights but frustrated at the loss of power. The whole bargain seems
increasingly hollow. And it could get worse if the next Democratic
administration resumes President Obama's efforts to use treaties and
international organizations to upload more power to foreign courts
and bureaucrats, even further removed from the American people.

As a result, there are fewer and fewer levers by which the governed can make their consent count, by which an indignant people
can exert control over its own government. In the administrative
state there is little room for populism because there is no room for
an independent people. The "people" has been broken down into
claimant groups, and every group has been organized, the better to
mesh with the gears of the state. The only escape would be somehow
to revive the older political system, which limited government
enough so that the people could responsibly control the government,
directly via elections and indirectly through the Constitution. The
only populism that could make a difference, in other words, has at its
heart a return to constitutionalism.

That's a daunting goal, not particularly clear in its ultimate
demands. How to get there is just as daunting. In 2010 the Tea Party
cheered the ends but remained baffled by the means, and then
offered to let the Republican Party take over its thinking, which was
a fatal mistake. The GOP never got beyond opposing Obamacare,
declining to do the hard work of thinking seriously of a substitute.

Elections remain the people's primary means to control the

government, and it was through that door that Trump entered our political life, at the head of a popular movement that gradually gathered to oppose the existing Republican establishment, the torpor of the conservative movement, and the Politically Correct (and increasingly anti-American) Left. Several times Trump has pointed out that the movement he led lacked a name, and lacks one still. This reflects probably the sheer confusion of the political moment, as the popular resistance to the consolidation and expansion of progressivism – to eight more years of Obama-style transformation – measured its desperate goals against the field of seventeen contenders for the 2016 GOP presidential nomination. It reflects also, however, that Trump was not the origin of the discontent, however vital he was to its crystallization.

In the beginning it looked like a very impressive field, until Trump began to campaign against it. He announced his candidacy in June 2015, a day after Jeb Bush did. Bush already had raised $120 million, collected binders full of endorsements, muscled Romney out of the way, and stood near the top of every poll. Within a month Trump had overtaken him. Trump stayed at the top the rest of the way, with the exception of a few weeks of jockeying with Ben Carson.

The story of Trump's rise was also the story of Jeb's fall – of the whole Bush establishment's fall. Republican voters had come gradually to realize that George W. Bush's presidency, despite some glorious moments, looked more and more like a failure. The administration's occupation of Iraq and Afghanistan had curdled into endless war and self-deluded democratization. Its domestic agenda of compassionate conservatism had proved underwhelming, leading to a bigger federal role in education, a new Medicare entitlement, and failed efforts to implement "comprehensive immigration reform," meaning more immigration, multiculturalism, and Democrats. At the end of his tenure the economy collapsed into the Great Recession, prepared in part by his administration's compassionate distribution of mortgages to uncreditworthy borrowers.

Trump awakened the Republican Party to how alienated it was from its own titular leaders and their agenda, which agenda had been officially ratified by the Republican National Committee in its "postmortem" on Romney's loss in the 2012 election. The RNC recommended – demanded – more of the same, and especially a healthy dose of immigration "reform," for which Jeb, the former governor of Florida, was the perfect standard bearer. The only problem was that the party elites had completely misread the party base. They missed the huge popular (or was it populist?) wave that was building, the wave that Trump would ride to the White House.

CONSERVATIVE TORPOR

From George Herbert Walker on, Bush family politicians had fancied themselves not only as post-Reagan Republicans, though their eagerness in that respect was revealing enough, but as a better-than-Reagan, more generous, public-spirited class of leadership. The story, probably apocryphal, has Nancy Reagan listening to Bush the Elder's acceptance speech, in which he vowed to seek a kinder, gentler America. Afterwards she asked Ronnie, "Kinder, gentler than *who*?" Exactly. The history of the GOP post-Reagan – through its presidential avatars Bush 41, Bob Dole, Bush 43, John McCain, and Romney – is a history of barely contained jealousy and imaginary transcendence of Reagan conservatism.

In terms of its public policy successes, the conservative movement peaked in the Reagan years, launching a generation-long rejuvenation of the economy and preparing the defeat of Soviet Communism. The Berlin Wall, and soon after the Soviet Union itself, fell during H.W.'s watch, though mostly as the result of his predecessor's policies. After that, conservatives relaxed their vigilance, confident they were winning in a post-Soviet, post-socialist world. The GOP took the House of Representatives in 1994, for the first time in forty years. Didn't Bill Clinton declare that "the era of big government is over?"

Conservatives sank into a self-satisfied contentment, confident that what, in his brief heyday, Newt Gingrich called "the third wave" would conduct them safely and inevitably to shore. When the emerging Republican realignment did not emerge, many conservatives adjusted their timelines but did not despair. In the long run, they reflected, the alternation in power of conservatives and chastened liberals would produce an orderly progress toward moderate conservatism – or moderate liberalism, but in any event toward moderation. The price of this bargain did not seem too high: the Left only insisted on dictating the moral rules of the road, including the complete rulebook of racial and gender etiquette. As a result, affirmative action, in particular, was here to stay in college admissions and business hiring. Republicans hardly objected: what were human relations departments for, after all?

It was business as usual for the GOP and, to a lesser but still significant extent, for the conservative movement throughout the Bush era, from H.W. to Jeb. That era ended when Trump descended the escalator at Trump Tower to announce his candidacy. It's far from clear that the Trump Administration will end well, but it's perfectly clear that the Bush era – one might almost say the Bush–Clinton era – did not.

Perhaps only a genuine outsider could have smashed it. Although presidential candidates often present themselves as outsiders, Trump is the real thing: a complete novice in politics. Lacking experience or a deep acquaintance with history, he is forced to improvise. Sometimes that scrambling has the character of the best kind of entrepreneurial innovation, sometimes it seems like the worst kind of reality-TV blather, when the unscripted imperative is to say or do *something* – the more dramatic the better – and see what happens next.

His campaign was a case in point. It wasn't an accident that his children filled so many key positions in the early going. That wasn't nepotism, it was desperation. Trump didn't know the experienced strategists, fundraisers, pollsters, and politicos that a normal presidential campaign accumulates. Most of the outsiders who were attracted to him early were either complete unknowns or has-beens. (Everyone you'd ever heard of was working for one of the other sixteen GOP contenders.) Steve Bannon was virtually unknown then, and certainly had no political experience. It's possible to be a "populist" while being unknown by the people, but it isn't exactly a recommendation. Through Bannon's activities at Breitbart the term "alt-right," also hitherto virtually unknown, began to circulate. This was a boon to the liberal press, who needed a MacGuffin to pursue for the rest of the campaign.

It was a mess, but competent people eventually were found, and amid the confusion Trump's indictment of the party leaders continued to be heard, and welcomed. He had two conspicuous virtues that his Republican opponents, and Hillary Clinton too, lacked. One was a sense of humor. To address rallies for an hour at a time off the cuff and keep them laughing is very hard to do. His humor was not gentlemanly or self-deprecating like Reagan's; it was cutting, outrageous, and usually at the expense of his opponents and the press. But he connected with his audience even as Reagan did, because each spoke as a citizen to fellow citizens, without a trace of the policy expert's condescension, cosmopolitanism, or crocodile tears. The press never got Trump's humor.

His second virtue was a kind of courage in defense of one's own. This was a courage never tested in war or physical emergency, to be sure, but it was a large, and impressive, political fact. He was prepared to stand up for his family, his company, his campaign, his country, and for his country's jobs, workers, factories, and products. Courage never demands that one be a genius or morally pure, and he isn't, so this virtue fit his rhetorical needs and strength. America does not have to be perfect for him to defend her wholeheartedly against her enemies. He does not have to be perfect to seek or to assert the privilege of defending her. It's necessary only to love her.

Obama was constantly apologizing for America's past, present, and future sins. Hillary promised more of the same, only more gratingly. Trump regards this duty as, at most, a very small slice of the presidential portfolio; when vastly overdone, it becomes a moral nullity and a political con game.

One effect of his courage in defense of our own was to neutralize the effects in the campaign of what used to be called "liberal guilt." In truth, liberals long ago spread it to Republicans and conservatives. Part of the Bush dynasty's high self-regard had to do with its presumed sensitivity on this question. Why Republicans should feel so guilty over historic Democratic policies like slavery and segregation is itself a good question, but the tactic has worked for decades to paralyze conservatives' self-confidence and pride, and to induce them to take compensating positions on, say, immigration "reform" to prove their bona fides. Trump was the first GOP candidate and president in a long time to prove immune to this gambit. He appeared in public guilt-free.

In his confidence in America's principles and in the ultimate justice of the people, and his refusal to indulge in racial and sexual guilt-mongering, Trump resembles those brave conservatives like Clarence Thomas, Shelby Steele, and Thomas Sowell, who have turned their face against the contemporary politics of liberal guilt, including its insistence on never-ending affirmative action. Like them he believes in equal opportunity, which means a chance for anyone, male or female, black or white, to prove up to the job. But that requires the same standards for everyone. Like these prominent black thinkers, he doesn't mind that that makes him politically incorrect. In fact, he seems to enjoy it.

GREAT AGAIN

"Make America Great Again," Trump's slogan, presupposes of course that America once was great, and might be again. His courage in defense of her is thus not entirely blind to her faults and her glories. (You can love someone and still see the warts.) He assumes that her citizens ought to be proud of America, that she is something noble or capable of being noble.

These notions, which used to be the common sense of American politics, are now highly controversial. They are politically incorrect, rejected as "offensive" on many college campuses and increasingly in American politics. Today's freshmen, who are tomorrow's voters, soon learn (if they hadn't been taught already) to believe in the ubiquitous malevolence of "white supremacy" in American politics as earnestly as Puritans believe (or used to) in the depravity of human nature after Adam's fall. Needless to say, it's a very different thing to believe that *human* nature is inherently warped, and that white nature is. To disbelieve inherent white racism is itself, in contemporary parlance, proof of racism.

Trump has his eye on the contemporary Left's extremism, but this is not so much the statist Left that the libertarians oppose, nor the values-and-autonomy Left resisted by the religious Right, but the anti-American Left. This Left plunged its knife into our politics in the 1960s and has been twisting it ever since.

The Old Left had opposed American capitalism, the Progressives had condemned American plutocracy, but not until the '50s and '60s did a significant faction of the Left begin to blame the American masses, not the elite, for the country's sins. The people became the problem. They were racist, materialist, imperialist, sexist, and sexually inhibited, according to the original catalogue of sins; later the phobias were discovered – homophobia, Islamophobia, transphobia, and so forth. Together these comprise pretty much the irredeemable sins Hillary had in mind when she condemned Trump's voters as deplorable. His voters weren't the whole country, but they were close enough. (And to be fair, she said she meant to denounce only about half his voters.)

Far from being Trump's authoritarian fantasy, the Left's growing alienation from middle America, and hence from America, has been remarked and resisted in a series of major liberal books in recent decades: Arthur Schlesinger, Jr.'s *The Disuniting of America* (1991), Richard Rorty's *Achieving Our Country* (1998), and Mark Lilla's *The Once and Future Liberal* (2017). What these estimable volumes also have in common, alas, is ineffectiveness. They didn't stop or even slow the Left's self-alienation.

Increasingly, therefore, the effect of higher education is to turn our own children into aliens, and hostile ones at that. In truth, the difficulties of assimilating today's immigrants are due mainly to us, not to them; they are reluctant mostly because they are learning from us that America is not a country worth assimilating *to*. Trump alone among the 2016 candidates took an unflinching, *proud* stand against the multicultural dissolution and loathing of America. In that sense he was, as he occasionally indicated, a pro-immigration politician: great again, America would be a country worth immigrating to. "To make us love our country, our country ought to be lovely," as Edmund Burke observed. To be citizens again, Americans of all sorts must rediscover their country's loveliness.

That stand on behalf of America took not only courage but also a certain justice, another of his unsung virtues, which he expressed in very American terms. "When you open your heart to patriotism," he said in his inaugural address, "there is no room for prejudice." Donald Trump has gotten little credit for such virtues, but they are present amid the hurly-burly, the distractions, the mistakes, the tweets, the investigations, the exhaustion, and the shrewd public policy of the Trump Administration so far. His good qualities are the quietest part of his presidency.

ACKNOWLEDGMENTS

I began working on this book while on sabbatical leave from Claremont McKenna College, and I'm grateful for CMC's assistance in the endeavor. In the beginning, Petria Hoffpauir assembled a large stack of some of my writings in order to remind me just how foresightful I am. Passages, not to mention whole essays, which contradicted her thesis have been ruthlessly suppressed. I am indebted to her diligence, perseverance, and good humor. Ted Richards read the rudimentary manuscript with a critical eye, and Alex Sanchez gathered permissions to reprint or modify previously published works. Elliott Banfield, as he has for twenty years as Art Director of the *Claremont Review of Books*, provided the luminous illustrations. At Encounter Books, Andrew Shea copyedited with extraordinary care and grace, and Amanda DeMatto shepherded the whole project along without treating me as a herd animal. I'm grateful to each of them.

Nonetheless, anyone who read this book in its early stages – or who read the original pieces on which I drew for about two-thirds of it – would be surprised, I think, by how thoroughly it's been rewritten, and sharpened, in response to the worsening crisis of the two constitutions. Two friends who wouldn't be so surprised, with whom I've discussed matters along the way and who have generously provided research support at every turn, are Ryan Williams and Thomas Klingenstein, respectively the president and the chairman of the board of the Claremont Institute for the Study of Statesmanship and Political Philosophy. Without their encouragement, this book might never have appeared.

To the Claremont Institute itself, with which I've been associated for forty years, I owe a profound debt, which I indicate, in part, in this volume's dedications. Harry V. Jaffa was in many respects the Institute's intellectual inspiration, and laid the foundation for the "Claremont school" of conservatism, even though he never called it that. The Institute was founded by four of his graduate students at the time: Peter W. Schramm, Thomas B. Silver, Christopher Flannery, and Larry P. Arnn. We became fast friends.

Schramm was its founding president, and Silver the founding president of its (then) sister organization, Public Research, Syndicated. Schramm and Silver were joint editors of a volume, the Festschrift for Jaffa's 65th birthday, in which the earliest chunk of this book, on Woodrow Wilson's "statesmanship of progress," appeared. For that reason, and more, this book is dedicated to their memory and to Jaffa's.

My wife, Sally Pipes, was by my side every day – literally – as we dodged the coronavirus together and each wrote a book, she much more promptly than I. Thanks, Pinky.

* * *

For permission to incorporate parts or versions of the following works into these pages, I am grateful to the publishers:

"The Founders and the Classics," in *The Revival of Constitutionalism*, ed. James W. Muller, University of Nebraska Press, 1988, pp. 43–68.

"Education, Cultural Relativism, and the American Founding," in *The Intercollegiate Review*, Spring 1989, pp. 35–42.

"Federalist 10 and American Republicanism," in *Saving the Revolution: The Federalist Papers and the American Founding*, ed. Charles R. Kesler, The Free Press, 1987, pp. 13–39.

"Civility and Citizenship in the American Founding," in *Civility and Citizenship in Liberal Democratic Societies*, ed. Edward C. Banfield, Paragon House, 1991, pp. 57–74.

"Education and Politics: Lessons from the American Founding," in *The University of Chicago Legal Forum*, 1991, pp. 101–122.

"A New Birth of Freedom: Harry V. Jaffa and the Study of America," in *Leo Strauss, the Straussians, and the American Regime*, eds. Kenneth L. Deutsch and John A. Murley, Rowman and Littlefield, 1999, pp. 265–282.

"Woodrow Wilson and the Statesmanship of Progress," in *Natural Right and Political Right: Essays in Honor of Harry V. Jaffa*, eds. Peter W. Schramm and Thomas B. Silver, Carolina Academic Press, 1984, pp. 103–127.

"Separation of Powers and the Administrative State," in *The Imperial Congress: Crisis in the Separation of Powers*, eds. Gordon Jones and John Marini, Pharos Books, 1989, pp. 20–40.

"The Promise of American Citizenship," *in Immigration and Citizenship in the 21st Century*, ed. Noah M. J. Pickus, Rowman and Littlefield, 1998, pp. 3–39.

I Am the Change: Barack Obama and the Crisis of Liberalism, by Charles R. Kesler, Broadside Books, 2012, pp. xx–xxv, 223–226, 229–232, 234–237.

"The Reagan Revolution and the Legacy of the New Deal: Obstacles to Party Realignment," in *The 1984 Election and the Future of American Politics*, eds. Peter W. Schramm and Dennis J. Mahoney, Carolina Academic Press, 1987, pp. 245–264.

"Ronald Reagan and Modern Liberalism," in *American Culture in Peril*, ed. Charles W. Dunn, University Press of Kentucky, 2012, pp. 13–31.

"What's Wrong with Conservatism," Bradley Lecture at the American Enterprise Institute, June 8, 1998.

NOTES

1   Aristotle, *Nicomachean Ethics*, 1103b26–32, 1134b28–33, 1135a3–6, 1140a24–1140b8, 1141a15–1141b14, 1141b23–30, 1143b17–20, 1177b1–4; but cf. *Politics* 1325b14–24. For the general meaning of "theory" as observation, see for example *Nicomachean Ethics* 1098a31, 33; 1100b19; and 1104a11.

2   For the Hobbesian depreciation of prudence, see Thomas Hobbes, *Leviathan* (Harmondsworth, Eng.: Penguin Books, 1968), pp. 137–138, and *De Cive* II, 1, in *Man and Citizen*, ed. Bernard Gert (Garden City, N.Y.: Anchor Books, 1972), p. 123.

3   In this connection, one should consider the relation between Bernard Bailyn's famous *The Ideological Origins of the American Revolution* (Cambridge: Harvard University Press, 1967) and his views on historiography adumbrated in *The Ordeal of Thomas Hutchinson* (Cambridge: Harvard University Press, 1974). In the former, Bailyn disclaims that by "ideology" he means anything more than a system of ideas or a coherence of viewpoints and temperaments. But in the latter the disabling presuppositions with which the term is freighted are made clear. Bailyn explains that he is not writing heroic or Whig history, but a third kind which he calls tragic or contextual. What distinguishes tragic history from the partisanship and easy analogies of its predecessors is that it is "an ultimate mode of interpretation," displaying "a neutrality, a comprehensiveness, and a breadth of sympathy lacking in earlier interpretations." Concretely, this means that historians can now behold "the latent limitations within which everyone involved was obliged to act; the inescapable boundaries of action; the blindness of the actors – in a word, the tragedy of the event." What is this tragedy? Not the "sadness" or the "wrongness" of the Revolution, but our knowledge of the "circumstances of the time" – "material, cultural, political, even psychological" – that circumscribed all human thought and action in that time. Our knowledge corresponds, if not to the end of history, at least to the end of the historiography, which depends (to what extent he equivocates) on an Absolute Moment when everything becomes clear. (*Ordeal*, pp. viii-x.) It is only then that the

limitations set by the historical context reveal their decisive explanatory power.

4   See e.g., Richard M. Gummere, *The American Colonial Mind and the Classical Tradition* (Cambridge: Harvard University Press, 1963); Richard Beale Davis, *Intellectual Life in Jefferson's Virginia: 1790–1830* (Chapel Hill: University of North Carolina Press, 1964); Meyer Reinhold, *The Classick Pages: Classical Readings of Eighteenth-Century Americans* (University Park, Pa.: American Philological Association, 1975); Carl J. Richard, *The Founders and the Classics: Greece, Rome, and the American Enlightenment* (Cambridge: Harvard University Press, 1995); Carl J. Richard, *Greeks & Romans Bearing Gifts: How the Ancients Inspired the Founding Fathers* (Lanham: Rowman & Littlefield, 2009).

5   Bailyn, *Ideological Origins*, p. 26. Cf. the ingenious argument of Eva T. H. Brann, *Paradoxes of Education in a Republic* (Chicago: University of Chicago Press, 1979), esp. pp. 79–102.

6   Martin Diamond, "Democracy and *The Federalist*: A Reconsideration of the Framers' Intent," *American Political Science Review*, 53 (March 1959), pp. 52–68 reprinted in *The Constitution*, ed. James Morton Smith (New York: Harper and Row, 1971), pp. 171–91, at 183–84, 186. Cf. Diamond, "Ethics and Politics: The American Way," in *The Moral Foundations of the American Republic*, ed. Robert H. Horwitz (Charlottesville: University Press of Virginia, 1977). For evidence of Diamond's great influence on the contemporary understanding of the American regime, see, e.g., Walter Berns, *The First Amendment and the Future of American Democracy* (New York: Basic Books, 1976); Frank M. Coleman, *Hobbes and America: Exploring the Constitutional Foundations* (Toronto: University of Toronto Press, 1977); Irving Kristol, *On the Democratic Idea in America* (New York: Harper and Row, 1972); Herbert J. Storing, *What the Anti-Federalists Were For* (Chicago: University of Chicago Press, 1981); and such popular textbooks as James Q. Wilson, *American Government: Institutions and Policies* (Lexington, Mass.: D. C. Heath, 1980), and its many subsequent editions.

7   See Richard Hofstadter, *The American Political Tradition and the Men Who Made It* (1948; reprint, New York: Vintage Books, 1974); Louis Hartz, *The Liberal Tradition in America* (New York: Harcourt Brace Jovanovich, 1955); Carl Becker, *The Declaration of Independence: A Study in the History of Political Ideas* (1922; reprint, New York: Vintage Books, 1958). Though widely differing in details, these books share a moral and philosophical outlook arising from the historicism of the Progressive movement. For their common debt to the political thought of the greatest captain of Progressivism, see Chapter Eight of this volume. See also Bradley C. S. Watson, *Progressivism: The Strange History of a Radical Idea* (Notre Dame: University of Notre Dame Press, 2020).

8   Gordon Wood, *The Creation of the American Republic, 1776–1787* (New York: W. W. Norton, 1969), esp. chs. 1–3, 12–18, and 15; J. G. A. Pocock, *The Machia-*

vellian Moment: Florentine Political Thought and the Atlantic Republican Tra-dition (Princeton, N.J.: Princeton University Press, 1975), chaps. 14 and 15. Wood, who maintains that American republicanism as expressed in 1776 "embodied the ideal of the good society as it had been set forth from antiquity through the eighteenth century" (*Creation*, p. 59), vastly exaggerates the Founders' classicism, according to Gary J. Schmitt and Robert H. Webking, "Revolutionaries, Antifederalists, and Federalists: Comments on Gordon Wood's Understanding of the American Founding," *Political Science Reviewer* 9 (Fall 1979), pp. 195–229. Could it be that Schmitt and Webking exaggerate in the opposite direction? Consider how they pinch off the quotation from Jefferson's letter to Henry Lee (p. 199) on the sources of the Declaration of Independence. The full quotation will be discussed at length later. See also the thematic treatment in Paul Rahe, *Republics, Ancient and Modern* (Chapel Hill: University of North Carolina Press, 1994).

9   For a beginning, see Charles R. Kelser, "Is Conservatism Un-American?," *National Review* 37, no. 5 (March 22, 1985), pp. 28–37.

10 Joseph Cropsey, "The United States as Regime and the Sources of the Amer-ican Way of Life," in Cropsey, *Political Philosophy and the Issues of Politics* (Chicago: University of Chicago Press, 1977), pp. 1–15, at 7 and 13. See also Thomas L. Pangle, *The Spirit of Modern Republicanism.*

11 For the debate over the presence of the idea of the best regime in the Decla-ration of Independence, see, on the one hand, Irving Kristol, "The American Revolution as a Successful Revolution," and Martin Diamond, "The Revolu-tion of Sober Expectations," in *America's Continuing Revolution* (Garden City, N.Y.: Doubleday Anchor Press, 1976), pp. 1–21 and 23–40; and, on the other, Harry V. Jaffa, *How to Think about the American Revolution* (Durham, N.C.: Carolina Academic Press, 1978), pp. 49–140.

12 John Adams, *Novanglus* No. 1, in *The Works of John Adams*, ed. Charles Fran-cis Adams (Boston: Little and Brown, 1851). vol. IV. p. 15.

13 Jefferson in *The Writings of Thomas Jefferson*, ed. Andrew A, Lipscomb and A, E. Bergh (Washington, D.C.: The Thomas Jefferson Memorial Association, 1904), vol. XVI, pp. 118–19.

14 Thomas Hobbes, *Behemoth, or The Long Parliament*, ed. Ferdinand Ténnies, 2d ed. (New York: Barnes and Noble, 1969), p. 43. Cf. Hobbes, *Leviathan*, pp. 266–68, 369–70, 698–700.

15 See, for instance, the overview by Caroline Robbins, "Algernon Sidney's *Dis-courses Concerning Government*: Textbook of Revolution," *William and Mary Quarterly* 3d ser., vol. 4, no. 3 July 1947), pp. 266–96.

16 Consider, e.g., besides the letter to Henry Lee, Jefferson to John Norvell, June 11, 1807, in *The Writings of Thomas Jefferson*, XI, pp. 222–23; and the resolution of the Board of Visitors of the University of Virginia, approved during Jefferson's rectorship, March 4, 1825, *ibid.*, XIX, pp. 460–61. The lat-ter is especially revealing: "Resolved, that it is the opinion of this Board that

as to the general principles of liberty and the rights of man, in nature and in society, the doctrines of Locke, in his 'Essay concerning the true original extent and end of civil government,' and of Sidney in his 'Discourses on government,' may be considered as those generally approved by our fellow citizens of this, and the United States."

17 Algernon Sidney, *Discourses Concerning Government* (London: 3d edition, 1751), I.2, p. 5; I.6, p. 14; I.10, pp. 23–24; II.4, p. 75; II.6, pp. 85- 86; II.32, p. 247; III.4, p. 266; III.5, p. 270; III.16, p. 320; III.33, p. 406; II.36, p. 413.

18 Ibid., II.1, pp. 60–62; II.10, pp. 102–3; II.20, pp. 151–52; III.23, pp. 358–59.

19 Ibid., I.16, pp. 39–40; II.1, p. 60; II.11, pp. 104–6, 108; II.16, pp. 130–33.

20 Ibid., I.18, p. 45; II.20, p. 151.

21 See Jean-Jacques Rousseau, *Discourse on the Origin and Foundation of Inequality*, in *The First and Second Discourses*, trans. Roger D. and Judith R. Masters (New York: St. Martin's, 1964), pp. 102–4, 119,128–30, 149–51.

22 See Plutarch, *Publicola*, X.1–6, in *Plutarch's Lives*, trans. Bernadotte Perrin (London: William Heinemann, 1928), vol. 1, pp. 527–31.

23 All references to *The Federalist* will appear in the text and will be to the Signet Classics edition with introduction and notes by Charles R. Kesler. *The Federalist Papers* (New York: New American Library, 2003).

CHAPTER THREE

1 *Federalist* 14, p. 99. All references are to the Signet Classics edition, with introduction and notes by Charles R. Kesler, *The Federalist Papers* (New York: New American Library, 2003).

2 *Federalist* 14, pp. 99–100, No. 9, p. 67.

3 *Federalist* 9, p. 67.

4 Diamond was not the first, however, to discover the significance of the extended republic. The credit for that seems to belong to Douglass Adair. See his "The Tenth Federalist Revisited," originally published in 1931, and "'That Politics May be Reduced to a Science': David Hume, James Madison, and the Tenth Federalist," originally published in 1957. Both essays are republished in Trevor Colbourn, ed., *Fame and the Founding Fathers: Essays by Douglass Adair* (New York: W. W. Norton, 1974), pp. 75–106. For Adair's earliest reflections on the argument of *Federalist* 10, see his Ph.D. dissertation (Yale, 1943), later published as *The Intellectual Origins of Jeffersonian Democracy: Republicanism, the Class Struggle, and the Virtuous Farmer*, ed. Mark E. Yellin (Lanham: Lexington Books, 2000). For Adair, the extended republic offered a way to stabilize and moderate the republican form without having recourse to the mixed regime. Unlike Diamond, however, Adair regarded this as a fulfillment rather than a repudiation of the republican tradition that stretched back, in his view. to the sixth book of Aristotle's Politics. Adair was not of course the first to draw attention to the novelty of Publius's argument. See, for example, Charles Merriam, *A History of American*

Political Theories (New York: Macmillan, 1903). pp. 103–106; and much earlier, and with more attention to No. 14 than to No. 10, John Quincy Adams, "Life of James Madison," in *The Lives of James Madison and James Monroe* (Boston: Philips, Sampson, 1850), pp. 41–44. Cf. *Fame and the Founding Fathers*, pp. 71–79 and 84.

5   Martin Diamond, "The Federalist," in Leo Strauss and Joseph Cropsey, eds., *History of Political Philosophy* (Chicago: Rand McNally, 1972; 2nd edition) pp. 631–651, at 635, 646.

6   Martin Diamond, *"Democracy and The Federalist: A Reconsideration of the Farmers' Intent," The* American Political Science Review 53 (March 1959), pp. 52–68. See also Thomas L. Pangle, *The Spirit of Modern Republicanism: The Moral Vision of the American Founders and the Philosophy of Locke* (Chicago: University of Chicago Press, 1990). Diamond's essays are conveniently reprinted in *As Far As Republican Principles Will Admit: Essays by Martin Diamond*, ed. William A. Schambra (Washington, D.C.: AEI Press, 1992).

7   Diamond, "The Federalist," pp. 647, 649; *Federalist* 10, p. 73; cf. Diamond, "Democracy and *The Federalist*," pp. 188–189.

8   Diamond, "Ethics and Politics: The American Way," in Robert H. Horwitz, ed., *The Moral Foundations of the American Republic* (Charlottesville: University Press of Virginia, 1977), pp. 39–72, at 58–59.

9   Ibid., pp. 56, 59, 65; Diamond, "Democracy and The Federalist," p. 186.

10   Diamond, "Ethics and Politics," pp. 52, 63–67, 70; "The Federalist," p. 650. "Democracy and *The Federalist*," p. 190. It is not simply that in America virtue is subordinated to liberty, but that virtue is redefined in terms of liberty. Consider: "And Publius is aware that his scheme involves an enormous reliance on the ceaseless striving after immediate private gains; the commercial life must be made honorable and universally practiced." "The Federalist," p. 650.

11   See, for example, Walter Berns, *In Defense of Liberal Democracy* (Chicago: Gateway Editions, 1984). This interpretation of *The Federalist* takes center stage, too, in recent Catholic-communitarian or "rad trad" critiques of America. See especially Patrick Deneen, *Why Liberalism Failed* (New Haven: Yale University Press, 2018). Mention should also be made of Diamond's influence on the writing of American history, where his and Adair's interpretations have tended to reinforce one another. Cf. the treatment in Alan Gibson, *Interpreting the Founding: Guide to the Enduring Debates over the Origins and Foundations of the American Republic*, 2nd ed. (Lawrence: University Press of Kansas, 2009). For a grand overview and interpretation of ancients, moderns, and the American founding, see Paul A. Rahe, *Republics, Ancient and Modern* (Chapel Hill: University of North Carolina Press, 1994).

12   See Adair, "The Tenth Federalist Revisited," pp. 75–77, 82–88.

13   Charles Beard, *An Economic Interpretation of the Constitution of the United States* (New York: The Free Press, 1935; orig. ed., 1913), pp. 15, 156–158.

14 Ibid., pp. xi-xiii, xvi-xvii, 4–7, 13–18, 153–156.

15 Adair, "The Tenth Federalist Revisited," pp. 77, 86–88, 92; "'That Politics May be Reduced to a Science,'" pp. 97–106.

16 Diamond, "The Revolution of Sober Expectations," in *America's Continuing Revolution* (Garden City, N.Y.: Anchor, 1976), pp. 23–40; and cf. Diamond, "The Problems of the Socialist Party after World War One," in John H. M. Laslett and Seymour Martin Lipset, eds., *Failure of a Dream? Essays in the History of American Socialism* (Garden City, N.Y.: Anchor, 1974), pp. 362–379. This essay was originally a chapter in Diamond's unpublished Ph.D. dissertation, "Socialism and the Decline of the American Socialist Party," University of Chicago, 1956.

17 For a critique of Diamond along these lines, see Harry V. Jaffa, *How to Think About the American Revolution* (Durham, N.C.: Carolina Academic Press, 1978), pp. 75–140. In fairness to Diamond, he was not unaware of the problem. See especially his "Ethics and Politics," and the essays on the electoral college and on "Lincoln's Greatness" in Schambra, ed., *As Far As Republican Principles Will Admit.*

18 "In this and like communities, public sentiment is everything. With public sentiment, nothing can fail; without it nothing can succeed. Consequently he who molds public sentiment, goes deeper than he who enacts statutes or pronounces decisions. He makes statutes and decisions possible or impossible to be executed." Roy p. Basler, ed., *The Collected Works of Abraham Lincoln* (New Brunswick: Rutgers University Press, 1953), vol. 3, p. 27.

19 Alexis de Tocqueville, *Democracy in America*, trans. Harvey C. Mansfield and Delba Winthrop (Chicago: University of Chicago Press, 2000), p. 7.

20 Federalist 9, p. 67.

21 See chapter 1, *supra*, and Douglass Adair, "A Note on Certain of Hamilton's Pseudonyms, in *Fame and the Founding Fathers*, pp. 272–285.

22 *Federalist* 1, p. 27; Diamond. "The Federalist." pp. 633–634; David F. Epstein, *The Political Theory of The Federalist* (Chicago: University of Chicago Press, 1984), pp. 7–9.

23 *Federalist* 37, p. 220; No. 1, p. 27, cf No. 39, p. 236.

24 *Federalist* 2, p. 31; No. 3, p. 36.

25 *Federalist* 8, pp. 61, 63. See the fine discussion in Epstein, *Political Theory*, pp. 16–21, 26–28.

26 *Federalist* 36, p. 220, No. 37, pp. 220–222.

27 *Federalist* No. 1, p. 30; No. 37, p. 220, Epstein, *Political Theory*, pp. 61–63.

28 *Federalist* No. 8, p. 62; No. 9, pp. 66–68, No. 10, p. 71.

29 Federalist No. 9, p. 67. Cf. the ironical use of "enlightened" in Publius's later description of Thomas Jefferson's plan for securing the separation of powers in his draft constitution for Virginia. *Federalist* No. 49, p. 310.

30 *Federalist* 9, pp. 67–68, 71.

31 *Federalist* 9, pp. 67, 69, 71; No. 39, p. 237; Epstein, *Political Theory*, pp. 15–16,

59–62, 110, 118–125, 195–197; William Kristol, "Liberty, Equality, Honor," *Social Philosophy and Policy* 2, no. 1 (Autumn 1984), 125–140.

32 *Federalist* 9, p. 67.

33 *Federalist* 10, p. 71; No. 9, pp. 66, 70. The "firm" Union is in the end also the result of a firm opinion – an opinion confirmed by the Constitution. See No. 49, pp. 311–312.

34 *Federalist* No. 9, p. 68.

35 *Federalist* 10, pp. 71–72; No. 47, p. 304; No. 48, pp. 305–6; cf. No. 49, pp. 312–14. See also Epstein, *Political Theory*, pp. 61–63, and Diamond, "The Federalist," pp. 639–640. The best discussion of Publius's account of separation of powers remains William Kristol, "The Problem of the Separation of Powers: *Federalist* 47–51," in Charles R. Kesler, ed., *Saving the Revolution: The Federalist Papers and the American Founding* (New York: The Free Press, 1987), ch. 5. See also Harvey C. Mansfield, *America's Constitutional Soul* (Baltimore: Johns Hopkins University Press, 1991), ch. 9.

36 *Federalist* 10, pp. 72–73, and cf. p. 75. The "zeal for different opinions concerning religion, concerning government, and many other points, as well of speculation as of practice," mentioned on page 73, is the more remarkable for its making no impression either on Publius's statement of the problem or his statement of the solution to the problem of faction.

37 *Federalist* 10, pp. 72–73.

38 *Federalist* 10, pp. 72–73. I am indebted for this line of reasoning as well as many other elements of this interpretation to two splendid studies, William Kristol's *The American Judicial Power and the American Regime*, Ph.D. dissertation, Harvard University, 1979; and Mansfield's *America's Constitutional Soul*, especially chs. 1, 9, 11, 14, and 15.

39 *Federalist* 10, p. 73.

40 *Federalist* 10, p. 73; No. 43, p. 276; No. 57, p. 348; No. 62, p. 378.

41 *Federalist* 10, p. 73; No. 23, p. 149, cf. Diamond, "*Democracy and The Federalist*," pp. 183–184.

42 *Federalist* 10, pp. 73–74.

43 *Federalist* 9, p. 67, No. 10, pp. 73–74.

44 *Federalist* 10, pp. 73–74, 79; No. 51, p. 321; cf. Diamond, "Ethics and Politics," pp. 52–53.

45 *Federalist* 10, pp. 73–74.

46 *Federalist* 6, pp. 50–51. No. 7, p. 57; No. 11, p. 79; No. 12, p. 86; cf. No. 8, p. 63.

47 *Federalist* 10, p. 72; No. 11, p. 79, No. 12, p. 86.

48 *Federalist* 10, p. 74, No. 51, pp. 321–322.

49 *Federalist* 10, p. 78, No. 51, p. 321; Diamond, "The Federalist," p. 649. Cf. the insightful accounts in William B. Allen, "Justice and the General Good: *Federalist* 51," in Kesler, ed., *Saving the Revolution*, ch. 6; and Colleen A. Sheehan, *The Mind of James Madison: The Legacy of Classical Republicanism* (Cambridge: Cambridge University Press, 2017).

50 On the ambiguities of "interest," see James Madison's letter to James Monroe, October 5, 1786, in Robert A. Rutland, ed., *The Papers of James Madison* (Chicago: University of Chicago Press, 1975), vol. 9, p. 141: "There is no maxim in my opinion which is more liable to be misapplied and which therefore needs more elucidation than the current one that the interest of the majority is the political standard of right and wrong. Taking the word 'interest' as synonymous with 'Ultimate happiness,' in which sense it is qualified with every necessary moral ingredient, the proposition is no doubt true. But taking it in the popular sense, as referring to immediate augmentation of wealth and property, nothing can be more false. In the latter sense it would be the interest of the majority in every community to despoil & enslave the minority of individuals; and in a federal community to make a similar sacrifice of the minority of the component States. In fact it is only reestablishing under another name and a more specious form, force as the measure of right...." Cf. Harvey C. Mansfield, Jr., *The Spirit of Liberalism* (Cambridge: Harvard University Press, 1978), pp. 23–24. See also Gerald Stourzh, *Alexander Hamilton and the Idea of Republican Government* (Stanford: Stanford University Press, 1970), pp. 80–87, 90–94.

51 *Federalist* 10, p. 75; cf. especially No. 68, p. 412: "This process of election affords a moral certainty that the office of President will seldom fall to the lot of any man who is not in an eminent degree endowed with the requisite qualifications.... It will not be too strong to say that there will be a constant probability of seeing the station filled by characters preeminent for ability and virtue." On the Roman Publius, see Plutarch, *Publicola*, X.1–6, in *Plutarch's Lives*. trans. Bernadotte Perrin (London: William Heinemann, 1928), vol. 1, pp. 527–531.

52 *Federalist* 10, p. 75; No. 43, p. 279; cf. No. 10, pp. 78–79 with No. 49, pp. 312–314, No. 51, pp. 320–322, No. 78. pp. 463–469; No. 84, pp. 509–512, 514–515.

53 *Federalist* 10, pp. 75–76; No. 49, pp. 311–312, and consider No. 63, pp. 381–384. See also Diamond, "The Federalist." pp. 645–646; and the excellent discussion in Mansfield, *America's Constitutional Soul*, ch. 11.

54 See *Federalist* 2, pp. 32–35; No. 37, pp. 222–225; No. 38, pp. 228–229; No. 40, pp. 249–251.

55 *Federalist* 9, pp. 69–70; No. 10, p. 76; No. 14, pp. 95–96; No. 63, pp. 384–385.

56 *Federalist* 10, pp. 76–77; Epstein, *Political Theory*, pp. 124–125, 193–197. cf. Mansfield, *The Spirit of Liberalism*, pp. 1–20. On the importance of numbers, cf. No. 31, p. 194 with No. 55, p. 342.

57 *Federalist* 10, pp. 76–77, No. 68, p. 412, cf. Epstein, *Political Theory*, pp. 95–99.

58 *Federalist* 10, p. 78.

59 *Federalist* 10, p. 78; No. 11, p. 82.

60 *Federalist* 10, p. 78; No. 51, p. 325.

61   Consider *Federalist* 15, p. 101 and No. 49, pp. 311–314.

62   *Federalist* 1, p. 36; No. 9, p. 71; No. 10, p. 84, No. 63, p. 385.

CHAPTER FOUR

1   Aristotle, *Nicomachean Ethics* 1155a23–28.

2   In fairness to Parson Weems, his biography of Washington has not been read lately with the political sophistication it deserves. For the beginning of a correction, see Garry Wills, *Cincinnatus: George Washington and the Enlightenment* (Garden City, N.Y.: Doubleday, 1984), chs. 3–4.

3   Richard Brookhiser, *Founding Father: Rediscovering George Washington* (New York: Free Press, 1996).

4   Aristotle, *Nicomachean Ethics* 1123b17–1124a19.

5   Consider this passage from Gouverneur Morris's eulogy of Washington:

> Heaven, in giving him the higher qualities of the soul, had given also the tumultuous passions which accompany greatness, and frequently tarnish its lustre. With them was his first contest, and his first victory was over himself. So great was the empire he had acquired there that calmness of manner and conduct distinguished him through life. Yet those who have seen him strongly moved will bear witness that his wrath was terrible. They have seen, boiling in his bosom, passion almost too mighty for man; yet when just bursting into act, that strong passion was controlled by his stronger mind. Having thus a perfect command of himself, he could rely on the full exertion of his powers, in whatever direction he might order them to act... Hence it was that he beheld not only the affairs that were passing around him, but those also in which he was personally engaged, with the coolness of an unconcerned spectator.

> As Morris remarks, "None was great in his presence." J. Jackson Barlow, ed., *To Secure the Blessings of Liberty: Selected Writings of Gouverneur Morris* (Indianapolis: Liberty Fund, 2012), p. 294.

6   Cf. his letter of November 16, 1782, to the Reformed Protestant Dutch Church in Kingston: "Convinced that our Religious Liberties were as essential as our Civil, my endeavors have never been wanting to encourage and promote the one, while I have been contending for the other...." *The Writings of George Washington, 1745–1799*, ed. John C. Fitzpatrick (Washington: U.S. Government Printing Office, 1938), vol. 25, pp. 346–347.

7   Cf. *Cicero, De Re Publica*, I.25, Il.17–20.

8   Plato, *Laws* 624a.

9   Fustel de Coulanges, *The Ancient City* (Garden City, NY: Doubleday Anchor, n.d.; orig. pub., 1864).

10 See the discussions, from which I have learned much, by Harry V. Jaffa, "Equality, Liberty, Wisdom, Morality, and Consent in the Idea of Political Freedom," and "The American Founding as the Best Regime: The Bonding of Civil and Religious Liberty," in *The Rediscovery of America: Essays by Harry V. Jaffa on the New Birth of Politics*, eds. Edward J. Erler and Ken Masugi (Lanham, MD: Rowman & Littlefield, 2019), chs. 2 and 6.

11 The best discussion is Vincent Phillip Muñoz, *God and the Founders: Madison, Washington, and Jefferson* (Cambridge: Cambridge University Press, 2009), ch. 2. Debate over religion's proper role in politics did not end with formal disestablishment, of course. In some ways it only got going then. See John G. West, Jr., *The Politics of Revelation and Reason: Religion and Civic Life in the New Nation* (Lawrence: University Press of Kansas, 1996).

12 Despite the still memorable protest by John Courtney Murray in his *We Hold These Truths: Catholic Reflections on the American Proposition*, intro. Peter Lawler (Lanham, MD: Sheed & Ward, 2005; orig. ed., 1960).

13 Cf. Jefferson's description, in his First Inaugural, of America as "enlightened by a benign religion, professed, indeed, and practiced in various forms, yet all of them inculcating honesty, truth, temperance, gratitude, and the love of man ...." *Thomas Jefferson: Writings*, ed. Merrill D. Peterson (New York: Library of America, 1984), p. 494.

14 John Locke, "A Letter Concerning Toleration" in *The Works of John Locke*, 10 volumes (London, 1823), vol. 6, pp. 9–13. On the arguments of Washington's Farewell Address, see Matthew Spalding and Patrick J. Garrity, *A Sacred Union of Citizens: George Washington's Farewell Address and the American Character* (Lanham, MD: Rowman & Littlefield, 1996).

15 For an account of how this principle was translated into legal and constitutional practice, see Michael W. McConnell, "The Origins and Historical Understanding of Free Exercise of Religion," *Harvard Law Review*, vol. 103, no. 7 (May 1990), 1409–1517. For a dissent, see Muñoz, *God and the Founders*, pp. 17–20.

16 Thus Washington suggested that in America, on the basis of religious freedom, organized Christianity could achieve a purity and power it had never enjoyed before. "... [T]he consideration that human happiness and moral duty are inseparably connected, will always continue to prompt me to promote the progress of the former, by inculcating the practice of the latter," he wrote to the Protestant Episcopal Church in 1789. He continued:

On this occasion it would ill become me to conceal the joy I have felt in perceiving the fraternal affection which appears to increase every day among the friends of genuine religion – It affords edifying prospects indeed to see Christians of different denominations dwell together in more charity, and conduct themselves in respect to each other with a more Christian-like spirit than ever they have done in any former age, or in any other nation.

In W. W. Abbot, gen. ed., *The Papers of George Washington* (Charlottesville: University Press of Virginia, 1989), Presidential Series, vol. 3, 497.

CHAPTER FIVE

1   W. B. Allen, ed, *George Washington: A Collection* (Indianapolis: Liberty Classics, 1988), p. 256.

2   See, for example, *San Antonio Indep. School Dist. v. Rodriguez*, 411 US 1 (1973) (no constitutional right to equal per student expenditures across school districts).

3   See, for example, *Regents of the Univ. of California v. Bakke*, 438 US 265 (1978) (Constitution prohibits racial classifications in admissions, but race may be used as a "plus"); *Marshall v. Kirklan*, 602 F2d 1282 (8th Cir 1979) (Constitution limits use of race and sex in faculty hiring to situations in which such classification is substantially related to the achievement of an important governmental objective).

4   See, for example, *Guadalupe Organization v. Tempe Elementary School Dist.*, 587 F2d 1022 (9th Cir 1978) (no constitutional right to a bilingual education).

5   Reprinted in G. Brown Goode, "The Origin of the National Scientific and Educational Institutions of the United States," in *Papers of the American Historical Association*, vol. 4, part 2 (1890), pp. 82, 84 (emphasis in original).

6   For an overview of these criticisms, see Bradley Kent Carter and Joseph F. Kobylka, "The Dialogic Community: Education, Leadership, and Participation in James Madison's Thought," in *The Review of Politics*, vol. 52 (1990), pp. 32–63.

7   For this view, see, generally, Robert K. Fullinwider, "Multicultural Education," 1991 *University of Chicago Legal Forum* (1991), p. 75; Michael W. McConnell, "Multiculturalism, Majoritarianism, and Educational Choice: What Does Our Constitutional Tradition Have to Say?" *University of Chicago Legal Forum* (1991), p. 123.

8   Jean-Jacques Rousseau, *The Government of Poland*, trans. Willmoore Kendall (New York: Bobbs-Merrill, 1972), p. 5.

9   George F. Will, *Statecraft as Soulcraft: What Government Does* (New York: Simon & Schuster, 1983), p. 18. For his (silent) retraction or modification, see George F. Will, *The Conservative Sensibility* (Indianapolis: Hachette, 2019).

10   Id. at 40. See also Martin Diamond, "Democracy and The Federalist: A Reconsideration of the Framers' Intent," in *The American Political Science Review*, vol. 53 (1959), pp. 52, 64–68 (1959). For a more nuanced view, see Martin Diamond, "Ethics and Politics: The American Way," in Robert H. Horwitz, ed, *The Moral Foundations of the American Republic* (Charlottesville: University Press of Virginia, 1977), pp. 39, 56–68. See also Walter Berns, *Taking the Constitution Seriously* (New York: Simon & Schuster, 1987), pp. 130, 220–223; Robert A. Goldwin, "Rights Versus Duties: No Contest," in Arthur L. Caplan and

Daniel Callahan, eds, *Ethics in Hard Times* (New York: Plenum, 1981), p. 117.

11 Allan Bloom, *The Closing of the American Mind* (New York: Simon & Schuster, 1987), pp. 27–28, 329–30.

12 Sheldon Wolin, *Politics and Vision: Continuity and Innovation in Western Political Thought* (Boston: Little, Brown & Co., 1960), p. 389.

13 Benjamin R. Barber, "The Compromised Republic: Public Purposelessness in America," in Horwitz, ed, *Moral Foundations* at 19–20. For an intelligent critique of this view, see Carter and Kobylka, pp. 32–63 (cited in note 6).

14 See, for example, Gordon S. Wood, *The Creation of the American Republic, 1776-1787* (Norton, 1969); J. G. A. Pocock, *The Machiavellian Moment: Florentine Political Thought and the Atlantic Republican Tradition* (Princeton: Princeton University Press, 1975), chs. 14–15.

15 Rousseau, *Government of Poland*, p. 19 (cited in note 8).

16 See Jean-Jacques Rousseau, *On The Social Contract*, ed. Roger D. Masters (St. Martin's, 1978), pp. 67–70, 124–32. Rousseau is aware of the "exclusive and tyrannical" impulses in ancient religion that often made it "bloodthirsty and intolerant," but he still regards it as superior, from the political point of view, to Christianity. His own suggestion of a "purely civil profession of faith" based on toleration and love of civil duties is exposed to many of the same criticisms he directs at established Christianity, but is not for that reason otiose. See Hilail Gildin, *Rousseau's Social Contract: The Design of the Argument* (Chicago: University of Chicago Press, 1983), pp. 187–89.

17 Cf. Harry V. Jaffa, "The American Founding as the Best Regime: The Bonding of Civil and Religious Liberty," in *The Rediscovery of America: Essays by Harry V. Jaffa on the New Birth of Politics*, eds. Edward J. Erler and Ken Masugi (Lanham: Rowman & Littlefield, 2019), ch. 6.

18 See the discussion in Michael W. McConnell, "The Origins and Historical Understanding of Free Exercise of Religion," *Harvard Law Review* (1990), vol. 103, p. 1410.

19 Speaking of Massachusetts's first efforts to establish compulsory common schools (dating back to the seventeenth century), one historian remarks: "If perhaps Sweden be excepted, there was no precedent in the world's history for such universal education, through the agency of free schools as a civil institution. The attempt must have seemed, to the nations looking on, as the irrational presumption of a youthful colony." Richard G. Boone, *Education in the United States: Its History from the Earliest Settlements* 45–46 (New York: D. Appleton, 1889).

20 That education was undertaken solely by the state and local governments is not to say that the national government was indifferent to questions of inculcating morals. Hamilton acknowledges the propriety of certain kinds of morals legislation at the national level through, for example, his consideration of the possibility of a national excise tax that would discourage the excessive use of alcohol. *Federalist* 12 (Hamilton) in *The Federalist Papers* 90 (Signet,

2003). Indeed, it is those "practices on the part of the State governments which ... have occasioned an almost universal prostration of morals," to which *The Federalist* objects most vehemently; and to which it looks for correction from the salutary influence of the proposed Constitution. *Federalist* 85 (Hamilton) in *The Federalist Papers*, p. 521. For an excellent general account, see Thomas G. West, "The Rule of Law in The Federalist," in Charles R. Kesler, ed, *Saving the Revolution: The Federalist Papers and the American Founding* (New York: Free Press, 1987), pp. 150–67, 163–67. Nevertheless, the establishment and regulation of schools were tasks for state and local governments.

21   In both respects, the Founders' educational views are at odds with John Locke's. Locke insisted on private education with personal tutors living in the parents' home, and placed almost no emphasis on patriotism or civic education. See Thomas L. Pangle, *The Spirit of Modern Republicanism: The Moral Vision of the American Founders and the Philosophy of Locke* (Chicago: University of Chicago Press, 1988), pp. 220–21, 227.

22   Berns, *Taking the Constitution Seriously*, p. 130 (cited in note 10).

23   Id. at 222.

24   Id. at 219–20.

25   Robert Green McCloskey, ed., *The Works of James Wilson* (Cambridge: Harvard University Press, 1967) vol. 1, p. 81.

26   George Washington, Farewell Address, in Allen, ed, *George Washington* at 521–22 (cited in note 1).

27   John C. Fitzpatrick, ed., *The Writings of George Washington, 1745–1799* (Washington: U.S. Government Printing Office, 1938), vol. 28, pp. 13–14.

28   Josephine F. Pacheco, ed., *The Legacy of George Mason* (Plainsboro, NJ: Associated University Presses, 1983), p. 141.

29   George A. Peek, Jr., ed., *The Political Writings of John Adams* 103 (Indianapolis: Hackett, 2003), p. 103.

30   Robert M. Taylor, Jr., ed., *The Northwest Ordinance 1787: A Bicentennial Handbook* (Indianapolis: Indiana Historical Society, 1987), p. 61.

31   Ellwood p. Cubberley, *Public Education in the United States: A Study and Interpretation of American Educational History* (Boston: Houghton Mifflin, 2d ed., 1934), pp. 91–93.

32   Id. at 14–25.

33   Id. at 88–91.

34   Massachusetts Education Law of 1647, reprinted in Ellwood p. Cubberley, *Readings in Public Education in the United States* (Boston: Houghton Mifflin, 1934), p.18, citing *Records of the Governor and Company of the Massachusetts Bay in New England* (1853), vol. 2, p. 203. The original purpose of education in the colonies, particularly in New England, had been religious – to enable every believer to read and interpret the Scripture for himself. This purpose is manifest in the famous Massachusetts education law of 1647, which required that every township appoint a schoolmaster to teach children to

read and write, and that larger townships establish grammar schools to pre-pare better students for university study. The law's prelude reads as follows:

It being one chief project of the old deluder, Satan, to keep men from the knowledge of the Scriptures, as in former times by keeping them in an unknown tongue, so in these latter times by persuading from the use of tongues, that so at least the true sense and meaning of the original might be clouded by false glosses of saint seeming deceivers, that learning may not be buried in the grave of our fathers in the church and commonwealth, the Lord assisting our endeavors.... It is therefore ordered....

Id. at 18–19 (language updated).

35 Reprinted in Roy p. Basler, ed, *The Collected Works of Abraham Lincoln* (Rut-gers: Rutgers University Press, 1953), vol. 1, p. 108.

36 Edwin Grant Dexter, *A History of Education in the United States* (New York: Macmillan, 1984), p. 569.

37 Id., quoting American Lyceum general constitution.

38 Id. at 570.

39 See Basler, ed, *Collected Works of Abraham Lincoln*, vol. 1. p. 112. For a com-mentary, see Harry V. Jaffa, *Crisis of the House Divided: An Interpretation of the Issues in the Lincoln-Douglas Debates* (Garden City, N.Y.: Doubleday, 1959), pp. 182–232.

40 Gaillard Hunt, ed, *The Writings of James Madison, 1819-1836* (New York: G.P. Putnam's Sons, 1910), vol. 9, p. 103.

41 Noah Webster, "On the Education of Youth in America," in Frederick Rudolph, ed, *Essays on Education in the Early Republic* (Cambridge: Harvard University Press, 1965), pp. 43, 63–64.

42 Thomas Jefferson, "A Bill for the More General Diffusion of Knowledge," in Roy J. Honeywell, *The Educational Work of Thomas Jefferson* 199 (Cam-bridge: Harvard University Press, 1931), p. 199.

43 Id. at 201. History was emphasized to enable people to safeguard their rights against ambition and avarice in all of their protean forms. Id at 199. Benjamin Franklin emphasized the study of history for much the same reason. See Ralph L. Ketcham, ed, *The Political Thought of Benjamin Franklin* (India-napolis: Bobbs-Merrill, 1965), pp. 55–56.

44 See letter from Thomas Jefferson to Peter Carr, Sept 7, 1814, in Honeywell, *Educational Work of Thomas Jefferson* at 222–23.

45 Id. at 224.

46 Jefferson, "A Bill for the More General Diffusion of Knowledge," in Honey-well, *Educational Work of Thomas Jefferson* at 199. It should be noted that Jefferson did not imagine the "elite" to be a product of economic or social class. Instead, he envisioned his University serving the worthy "without regard to wealth." Id at 199. On Jefferson's intertwining of civic and liberal

education, see Thomas Jefferson, "Report of the Commissioners Appointed to Fix the Site of the University of Virginia," (Aug 1, 1818), also known as the Rockfish Gap Report, in Honeywell, *Educational Work of Thomas Jefferson* at 248; and see the broad discussion of the relation of civic and liberal education in Eugene F. Miller," On the American Founders' Defense of Liberal Education in a Republic," *The Review of Politics*, no. 65 (1984).

47 Adams concludes: "If you compare such a country with the regions of domination, whether monarchical or aristocratical, you will fancy yourself in Arcadia or Elysium." John Adams, "Thoughts on Government," in Charles S. Hyneman and Donald S. Lutz, eds, *American Political Writing During the Founding Era* (Indianapolis: Liberty Classics, 1983), vol. 1, pp. 402, 408.

48 See chapter 3, *supra*.

49 Gaillard Hunt, ed., *The Writings of James Madison, 1787-1790*, (New York: G.P. Putnam's Sons, 1904), vol. 5, p. 273.

50 But see the definition of multicultural education in Fullinwider, *University of Chicago Legal Forum* (1991), p. 77 (cited in note 7).

51 Thomas Jefferson, *Notes on the State of Virginia*, reprinted in Merrill D. Peterson, ed, *The Portable Thomas Jefferson* (New York: Viking, 1975), pp. 211–212.

52 *Federalist* 51 (Madison) in *The Federalist Papers*, p. 321.

53 The Founders' practice did not always live up to their theory, of course, but it was in light of their theory that subsequent generations were able to redress the evils of slavery, religious prejudice, and so forth. See Robert A. Goldwin, *Why Blacks, Women and Jews Are Not Mentioned in the Constitution, and Other Unorthodox Views* (Washington: American Enterprise Institute, 1990); and Chapter Ten, *infra*.

54 See Fullinwider, *University of Chicago Legal Forum* (1991), p. 75 (cited in note 7).

55 On the self-stultification of multiculturalism as it both silently presumes and insistently rejects a criterion of good and evil, see Stanley Fish, "Boutique Multiculturalism," in *Multiculturalism and American Democracy*, eds. Arthur M. Melzer, Jerry Weinberger, and M. Richard Zinman (Lawrence: University Press of Kansas, 1998), ch. 4.

56 *Federalist* 10 (Madison), in *The Federalist Papers*, p. 73.

57 *Federalist* 37 (Madison) in *The Federalist Papers*, pp. 223–224.

58 See *Federalist* 54 (Madison) in *The Federalist Papers*, p. 334 (emphasis added).

59 Basler, ed., *2 Collected Works of Abraham Lincoln*, vol. 2, pp. 405–06 (cited in note 42).

60 Id.

61 Thomas Jefferson, First Inaugural Address, reprinted in Peterson, ed., *Portable Thomas Jefferson*, pp. 291–292 (cited in note 58).

62 On the political implications of Jefferson's educational plans, see Honeywell, *Educational Work of Thomas Jefferson*, pp. 146–59 (cited in note 49).

63 Theodore Roosevelt, "American Ideals," *The Forum* (Feb 1895), reprinted in *The Works of Theodore Roosevelt* (New York: Charles Scribner's Sons, 1926), vol. 13, p. 3.

CHAPTER SIX

1   Harry V. Jaffa, *Thomism and Aristotelianism: A Study of the Commentary by Thomas Aquinas on the Nicomachean Ethics* (Westport, Conn.: Greenwood Press, 1979; orig. ed., 1952), p. 14.

2   Harry V. Jaffa, *Crisis of the House Divided: An Interpretation of the Issues in the Lincoln-Douglas Debates* (Chicago: University of Chicago Press, 1982; orig. ed., 1959), pp. 1–3, 10–14.

3   Leo Strauss, *Natural Right and History* (Chicago: University of Chicago Press, 1953), pp. 202–251; Strauss, *What is Political Philosophy? and Other Studies* (Westport, Conn.: Greenwood Press, 1973; orig. Ed., 1959), pp. 9–55, esp. pp. 49–51. Cf. *Ibid.*, pp. 302–305.

4   See, for example, Martin Diamond, "The Federalist," in Leo Strauss and Joseph Cropsey, eds., *History of Political Philosophy*, 2nd edition (Chicago: Rand McNally, 1972; orig. ed., 1963), pp. 631–651. "Other political theories had ranked highly, as objects of government, the nurturing of a particular religion, education, military courage, civic-spiritedness, moderation, individual excellence in the virtues, etc. On all of these *The Federalist* is either silent, or has in mind only pallid versions of the originals, or even seems to speak with contempt." Diamond, "Democracy and *The Federalist*: A Reconsideration of the Framers' Intent," in William A. Schambra, ed., *As Far as Republican Principles Will Admit: Essays by Martin Diamond* (Washington, D.C.: American Enterprise Institute, 1992), pp. 17–36, at 31.

5   See, for example, William Schambra, ed., *As Far as Republican Principles Will Admit*, chs. 7–8, 21; Walter Berns, *Freedom, Virtue, and the First Amendment* (Westport, Conn.: Greenwood Press, 1969; orig. ed., 1957); Herbert J. Storing, *What the Anti-Federalists Were FOR* (Chicago: University of Chicago Press, 1981); Paul Eidelberg, *The Philosophy of the American Constitution* (New York: The Free Press, 1968).

6   On Strauss's "authoritative exposition of Hobbesian and Lockean natural-right doctrine," see Jaffa, *Crisis of the House Divided*, p. 425n21.

7   *Crisis*, pp, 216–219, 325–327.

8   Cf. Leo Strauss, *Liberalism, Ancient and Modern* (New York: Basic Books, 1968), p. 207.

9   *Crisis*, pp. 211–214.

10 *Crisis*, pp. 212–217.

11 *Crisis*, p. 218.

12 See Mathew 25:21, "His lord said unto him, Well done, thou good and faithful servant: thou hast been faithful over a few things, I will make thee ruler over many things: enter thou into the joy of thy lord." Cf. Matthew 25:23, 26–30.

13 *Thomism and Aristotelianism*, pp. 116, 120–123, 138–140. In *Nichomachean Ethics*, Book X, Aristotle makes clear that the gods cannot have moral qualities because the divine good, as such, is contemplation, and the gods must be thought of as being perfectly self-sufficient. *Nicomachean Ethics* 1178b7–22. Cf. also *Metaphysics* 1074b15–35, and Jaffa, *Thomism and Aristotelianism*, p. 212n5.

14 *Thomism and Aristotelianism*, p. 140; Aristotle, *Nichomachean Ethics*, 1124b10–18, 1124b30–1125a4, 1125a15.

15 *Thomism and Aristotelianism*, p. 141. For a different view, see Rene Antoine Gauthier and Jean Yves Jolif, eds., *L'Éthique à Nicomaque: Introduction, Traduction, et. Commentaire*, 2nd ed. (Louvain: Publications Universitaires, 1970), vol. 2, part 1, pp. 272–273, 278–279, 283–284, 290–291, 293–296. And cf. *Crisis*, pp. 260–261.

16 In his 1972 Introduction, Jaffa remarked that *Crisis*, like the Lincoln-Douglas debates themselves, was a form of the Thomistic disputed question, which was itself a form of the Socratic dialogue. *Crisis*, pp. 8–9.

17 *Crisis*, pp. 218–219 and pp. 415–416n15. Consider also pp. 220 and 226.

18 *Crisis*, pp. 220–222.

19 Aristotle, *Nichomachean Ethics*, 1124a1–4, 14–21; 1146a10–17. Cf. *Crisis*, pp. 354–355.

20 On Lincoln's view of the inescapable limits to political salvation, see *Crisis*, ch. 10, "The Teaching Concerning Political Moderation," *passim*.

21 "For Brutus – at least Shakespeare's Brutus – although a man of purest intentions, was a guileless bungler. It was Cassius who possessed the wisdom of the serpent, who would have murdered Anthony instead of allowing him to speak at Caesar's funeral. The man who would be a match for Caesar must somehow combine the virtues *and* political capacity of which Aristotle speaks; he must somehow unite, in his single person, the goodness of Brutus and the wiliness of Cassius." *Crisis*, p. 215. Jaffa notes that "this interpretation of *Julius Caesar* was suggested to me by Prof. Leo Strauss." *Crisis*, p. 415n14.

22 *Crisis*, pp. 15, 215–216, 232, 261, 264. Cf. Jaffa, *American Conservatism and the American Founding* (Durham: Carolina Academic Press, 1984), p. 68.

23 *Crisis*, p. 211. Cf., e.g., Jaffa, *Equality and Liberty* (Oxford: Oxford University Press, 1965), pp. 137–138; *The Conditions of Freedom* (Baltimore: Johns Hopkins, 1975), pp. 150–153; *How to Think About the American Revolution* (Durham: Carolina Academic Press, 1978), pp. 40–42; *American Conservatism and the American Founding*, pp. 40–41.

24 *Crisis*, pp. 210–213, 217, 222.

25 Thus Jaffa quoted Lincoln's remarks on July 10, 1858: "It is said in one of the admonitions of the Lord, 'As your Father in Heaven is perfect, be ye also perfect.' The Savior, I suppose, did not expect that any human creature could be as perfect as the Father in Heaven; but he said, 'As your Father in Heaven is perfect, be ye also perfect.' He set that up as a standard, and he who did most towards reaching that standard, attained the highest degree of moral

perfection. So I say in relation to the principle that all men are created equal, let it be as nearly reached as we can." *Crisis*, pp. 316–317.

26 *Crisis*, p. 341.

27 *Crisis*, pp. 314–328.

28 *Crisis*, pp. 318–321.

29 *Crisis*, pp. 225, 318–327.

30 *Crisis*, pp. 328–329.

31 *Crisis*, pp. 342–346.

32 Jaffa deployed this interpretation of America as, in principle, a kind of regime in his later dispute with Martin Diamond, which concerned Diamond's contention that the Declaration provided "no guidance" as to the best form of government that Americans should adopt. See Jaffa, *How to Think About the American Revolution*, pp. 75–140. In this book, Jaffa contended that the views of Lincoln and the Founders on republicanism as the best kind of regime were virtually identical. But cf. his earlier remarks, in the context of the Supreme Court's "one man, one vote" decisions, in *The Conditions of Freedom*, pp. 158–159.

33 *Crisis*, pp. 322, 328.

34 *Crisis*, p. 306.

35 On this point, cf. *Crisis*, pp. 318 and 328. See Harry V. Jaffa, *A New Birth of Freedom: Abraham Lincoln and the Coming of the Civil War* (Lanham, MD: Rowman & Littlefield, 2000). For an early evaluation, see Charles R. Kesler, "A New Birth of Freedom," in *Claremont Review of Books*, Fall 2000, pp. 8–10. See also Lucas E. Morel, *Lincoln and the American Founding* (Carbondale: Southern Illinois University Press, 2020).

36 *Crisis*, pp. 237–245.

37 See, for example, *The Conditions of Freedom*, pp. 152–156.

38 Cf. *Crisis*, p. 211, and *How to Think About the American Revolution*, pp. 41–43, 104–111, 131–135.

39 See Jaffa, "Equality, Liberty, Wisdom, Morality, and Consent in the Idea of Political Freedom," *Interpretation* (January 1987), vol. 15, no. 1, pp. 24–28; and Jaffa, *The American Founding as the Best Regime: The Bonding of Civil and Religious Liberty* (Claremont: The Claremont Institute, 1990), 26pp. Both are now available in Edward J Erler and Ken Masugi, eds., *The Rediscovery of America: Essays by Harry V. Jaffa on the New Birth of Politics* (Lanham, MD: Rowman & Littlefield, 2019), chs. 2 and 6.

40 *Ibid.*

41 *The American Founding as the Best Regime, passim.*

42 Cf. *American Conservatism and the American Founding*, pp. 135–138. "I have, I think, sufficiently proved that the academic debate about the American political tradition is for the most part little more than a concealed (or unconscious) form of the political debate. Conducting my argument by political, rather than academic speech, is part of my attempt to restore to this debate

both its seriousness and its vitality." In so doing, Jaffa understood himself to be demonstrating "both the possibility and the necessity of natural right becoming political right." *Ibid.*, pp. 135, 138.

43 Jaffa, *Original Intent and the Framers of the Constitution: A Disputed Question* (Washington, D.C.: Regnery Gateway, 1994).

CHAPTER EIGHT

1 Aristotle, *Nicomachean Ethics* 1102a5–1103b25, 1140a24–1140b30, 1124a32–1142b34, and 1144b1–1145a7.

2 Woodrow Wilson, *The Papers of Woodrow Wilson*, ed. Arthur S. Link, 43 vols. (Princeton: Princeton University Press, 1966–83), 9: 130. Hereinafter cited as *Papers*. Wilson uses the term in the draft introduction to *The Philosophy of Politics*, his self-proclaimed *"novum organum* of political study," which he worked on episodically from 1885 to about 1892, never finished, but always hoped to take up again. For a description of the projected work, see the editorial note at 5:54–58.

3 See e.g., Arthur S. Link, *Wilson: The Road to the White House* (Princeton: Princeton University Press, 1947), pp. 31–35 and 122–132; but cf. Richard Hofstadter, *The American Political Tradition* (New York: Vintage, 1974), pp. 311–318 and 322–327.

4 *Papers* 10:22–23.

5 *Papers* 5:51–52; Wilson, *Constitutional Government in the United States* (New York: Columbia University Press, 1961; orig. ed. 1908), pp. 54–56.

6 *Constitutional Government*, pp. 41–44, 57; *Papers* 5:51.

7 *Constitutional Government*, pp. 54–56; Wilson, *The New Freedom* (New York: Doubleday, 1913), pp. 46–47; cf. Robert A. Goldwin, "Of Men and Angels: A Search for Morality in the Constitution," in Robert H. Horwitz, *The Moral Foundations of the American Republic* (Charlottesville: University Press of Va., 1977), pp. 10–12.

8 See Wilson, *Congressional Government: A Study in American Politics* (Baltimore: Johns Hopkins Press, 1981; orig. ed. 1885), esp. chs. 1–3, 6. For a description of the original constitutional balances, drawing not upon any official "literary theory" but upon John Adams, see *ibid.*, pp. 31–32. It is to be noted that Adams was the greatest American contributor to the doctrine of bicameralism, but not to the theory of separation of powers. Wilson conflates the two, in fact preferring the term "checks and balances," originally applied to the relations between the two legislative houses, to describe both bicameralism and the separation of powers. He thus gives to separation a peculiarly legislative reading, emphasizing what is common to the powers rather than what distinguishes them.

9 *Papers* 5:121; for Wilson's re-evaluation of his thesis of committee government in light of changing circumstances, see his Preface to the fifteenth printing of *Congressional Government*, pp. 19–23, and *Constitutional*

Government, ch. 4. The best discussion of Wilson's political science is Ronald J. Pestritto, *Woodrow Wilson and the Roots of Modern Liberalism* (Lanham, MD: Rowman & Littlefield, 2005).

10 *Papers* 5:345; cf. 9:102, 108–9.

11 George Fitzhugh, *Cannibals All! or Slaves Without Masters* (Cambridge: Harvard University Press, 1960), pp. 12–13, 71–72. Consider Leo Strauss, *The City and Man* (Chicago: University of Chicago Press, 1964), p. 11.

12 For a different interpretation, see Harry Clor, "Woodrow Wilson," in Morton J. Frisch and Richard G. Stevens, eds., *American Political Thought: The Philosophic Dimension of American Statesmanship* (Dubuque: Kendall/Hunt, 1976), esp. p. 217.

13 See the brilliantly oblique essay by Joseph Cropsey, "The United States as Regime and the Sources of the American Way of Life," in Horwitz, *op, cit.*, pp. 86–101. That this may not be his last word, however, may be inferred from "The Moral Basis of International Action," in Cropsey, *Political Philosophy and the Issues of Politics* (Chicago: Univ. of Chicago Press, 1977), pp. 172–188. For the interesting case of Allan Bloom, cf. my review of *The Closing of the American Mind*, "The Closing of Allan Bloom's Mind," in *The American Spectator* (August 1987), pp. 14–17. Herbert J. Storing sticks closer to the phenomena, but in locating the dynamics of American statesmanship in the tension between populism and scientific management, he views our politics through Wilson's lenses, despite the fact that he understands himself to be opposing Wilson. See "American Statesmanship: Old and New," in Robert A. Goldwin, ed., *Bureaucrats, Policy Analysts, Statesmen: Who Leads?* (Washington: American Enterprise Institute, 1980), esp. pp. 91–99.

14 Consider Leo Strauss, *What is Political Philosophy?* (New York: Free Press, 1959), pp. 50–51; and cf. Wilson, *Papers* 9:131 and Wilson, *The State* (Boston: D. C. Health, 1909), secs. 19–20, 1392.

15 *Constitutional Government*, pp. 56, 199; cf. *The New Freedom*, pp. 44–48; on the law of nature, see *The State*, sec. 1460.

16 "There is no country in the world where public statesmanship is so difficult as in this our own country," writes Wilson. *Papers* 16:12.

17 Wilson so recalls at *Papers* 7:129, but he regards it mainly as an indication of how prevalent was the "radical misunderstanding" of the subject at the time. That is, he uses the fact that Publius had to make an *argument* against extreme separation as an excuse not to study that argument.

18 Alexander Hamilton, James Madison, John Jay, *The Federalist Papers*, with introduction and notes by Charles R. Kesler (New York: Signet Classics, 2003), No. 47, pp. 297–299.

19 *The Federalist Papers*, No. 37, p. 224. On the character of Newtonian natural science, see Martin Heidegger, *What is a Thing?* (South Bend, IN: Gateway Editions, 1967), trans. W. B. Barton, Jr. and Vera Deutsch, pp. 76–88.

20 *The Federalist Papers*, No. 39, p. 236. See the excellent discussion in William Kristol, "The Problem of the Separation of Powers: *Federalist* 47–51," in Kesler, ed., *Saving the Revolution: The Federalist Papers and the American Founding* (New York: Basic Books, 1987), ch. 5.

21 Ibid., No. 51, p. 319; *Constitutional Government*, p. 56.

22 *The Federalist Papers*, No. 37, p. 224; No. 47, p. 298; No. 48, p. 305.

23 Ibid., No. 39, p. 237.

24 Ibid., No 49, pp. 311–312, 314.

25 Ibid., No. 49, p. 314; No. 51, p. 319.

26 *Papers* 7:367; *Constitutional Government*, p. 4.

27 Abraham Lincoln, *The Collected Works of Abraham Lincoln*, ed. Roy p. Basler (New Brunswick, N.J.: Rutgers University Press, 1953), Vol. III, p. 376.

28 *Constitutional Government*, p. 4.

29 Ibid., pp. 4–5, 22–23; *The State*, secs. 1074, 1394; *Papers* 5:304; and cf. *Papers* 7:363.

30 *Constitutional Government*, pp. 8–9, 27, 59; *Papers* 5:67–70.

31 *Constitutional Government*, pp. 25–28; *The State*, sec. 1414. For a revealingly different account of the stages of political development, see Wilson, "The Study of Administration," *Political Science Quarterly* 2 (June 1887), pp. 204–209.

32 *Papers* 6:228–231. Cf. *Papers* 5:62–67.

33 *Constitutional Government*, pp. 4–5, 57, 59.

34 *Papers* 5:304, 6:646–647. "Leaders of Men" is printed at 6:644–671.

35 Cf. the young Wilson's comment in an essay on Gladstone: "Great statesmen seem to direct and rule by a sort of power to put themselves in the place of the nation over whom they are set, and may thus be said to possess the souls of poets at the same time that they display the coarser sense and the more vulgar sagacity of practical men of business." *Papers* 1:628.

36 *Papers* 6:648–650, 662.

37 *Papers* 6:662.

38 Cf. William Graham Sumner, "The Absurd Effort to Make the World Over," in A. G. Keller and Maurice R. Davie, *Essays of William Graham Sumner* (New Haven: Yale University Press, 1934), Vol. I, pp. 105–106.

39 *Papers* 5:62, 65; 6:659, 663; 9:129; cf. 7:359–360.

40 *Papers* 6:659–660.

41 *Papers* 6:663. For Wilson's own politics of vision in the 1912 presidential election campaign, see his speeches in John Wells Davidson, ed., *A Crossroads of Freedom* (New Haven: Yale University Press, 1956), pp. 32, 34, 80–81, 92, 98, 147–148, 165, 242, 247, 270–271, 286–287, 324, 396, 401, 424, 426–428, 451, 459, 498–499, 518, and 520.

42 *Papers* 6:650; cf. 7:365.

43 *Papers* 6:661; *A Crossroads of Freedom*, p. 147; on the reformer's rhetorical

strategy, see "The Study of Administration," pp. 208–209, together with *Papers* 7:359–360, 365–367 and *The New Freedom*, esp. pp. 44–45. But cf. Clor, *op. cit.*, pp. 205–207.

44 The leader, Wilson writes, "rallies about himself, not mobs, but parties. He binds men to himself not by a vague community of sentiment but by a definite and decisive oneness of purpose. The people feel a keen charm in the knowledge of the fact that, though he is powerful, his power is derived from them and is dependent upon their favour. They are conscious of being represented by him in respect to their greater and soberer aims. They gain in dignity as he gains in beneficent powers. To follow him is to realize the greatest possible amount of real political life." *Papers* 5:87. On the connection between leadership and party government in Wilson's thought, see the excellent discussion in James W. Ceaser, *Presidential Selection: Theory and Development* (Princeton: Princeton University Press, 1979), pp. 188–207.

45 *Papers* 6:661, 663–4, 666; for the democratization resulting from the political discovery of compassion or sympathy, see Paul Eidelberg, *A Discourse on Statesmanship: The Design and Transformation of the American Polity* (Urbana, IL: University of Illinois Press, 1974), ch. 9.

46 *Papers* 5:61, 6:663–4. The first step toward the replacement of deliberation by interpretation – toward historicism, that is – can be seen in Hobbes's redefinition of deliberation as "putting an end to the Liberty we had of doing, or omitting, according to our own Appetite, or Aversion," and in his consequent redefinition of will as "the last Appetite in Deliberating." Consider Hobbes, *Leviathan*, Book 1, ch. 6.

47 *A Crossroads of Freedom*, p. 187; *The New Freedom*, p. 73; Clor, *op. cit.*, pp. 195–197; cf., *inter alia*, *A Crossroads of Freedom*, pp. 145–147, 326, 448.

48 *Papers* 6:661, 664; *A Crossroads of Freedom*, p. 147; *Papers* 5:90; Kent A. Kirwan, "Historicism and Statesmanship in the Reform Argument of Woodrow Wilson," *Interpretation* 11 (September 1981), pp. 350–351.

49 For example, consider Lincoln's peroration to his December 26, 1839, Speech on the Sub-Treasury, in *The Collected Works of Abraham Lincoln*, Vol. I, pp. 178–179; and Harry V. Jaffa, "On the Necessity of a Scholarship of the Politics of Freedom," *Statesmanship*, ed. Harry V. Jaffa (Durham: Carolina Academic Press, 1981), pp. 1–9.

CHAPTER NINE

1 For a dissenting review of Mounk's book, see my "Between Liberalism and Democracy," in *National Review*, June 11, 2018, pp. 36–37.

2 See, above all, John Marini, *Unmasking the Administrative State: The Crisis of American Politics in the Twenty-First Century*, ed. Ken Masugi (New York: Encounter Books, 2019), which is the best treatment of the subject. For the judicial side of the story, see Bradley C. S. Watson, *Living Constitution, Dying*

Faith: Progressivism and the New Science of Jurisprudence (Wilmington, Del: Intercollegiate Studies Institute, 2009).

3   See, in general, W. B. Gwyn, *The Meaning of the Separation of Powers* (New Orleans: Tulane University Press, 1965); M. J. C. Vile, *Constitutionalism and the Separation of Powers* (Oxford: Clarendon Press, 1967); and Harvey C. Mansfield, *America's Constitutional Soul* (Baltimore: Johns Hopkins University Press, 1991), ch. 9.

4   See the excellent discussion in Harvey C. Mansfield, Jr., *Taming the Prince* (New York: The Free Press, 1989).

5   Alexander Hamilton, James Madison, John Jay, *The Federalist Papers*, with introduction and notes by Charles R. Kesler (New York: Signet Classics, 2003), No. 47, p. 298.

6   See Harry V. Jaffa, *How to Think About the American Revolution* (Durham: Carolina Academic Press, 178), pp. 131–32; George Anastaplo, "The Declaration of Independence," *St. Louis University Law Journal*, vol. 9 (1965), p. 390.

7   *Federalist* 48, p. 305; 51, p. 319.

8   *Federalist* 48, pp. 306–10.

9   *Federalist* 48, p. 305; cf. 37, p. 223; 39, p. 237; and see Aristotle, *Politics* IV.14–16.

10   *Federalist* 9, p. 67. For examples of the "deadlock" thesis, see Woodrow Wilson, *Constitutional Government in the United States* (New York: Columbia University Press, 1908); James MacGregor Burns, *The Deadlock of Democracy: Four-Party Politics in America* (Englewood Cliffs, N.J.: Prentice-Hall, 1963); and Robert Dahl, *A Preface to Democratic Theory* (Chicago: University of Chicago Press, 1956).

11   *Federalist* 68, p. 412; Mansfield, *America's Constitutional Soul*, pp. 124–25.

12   *Federalist* 10, p. 77; 51, p. 319; 73, pp. 441–44.

13   For a pathbreaking account, see James Ceaser, *Presidential Selection: Theory and Development* (Princeton: Princeton University Press, 1979).

14   *Federalist* 49, pp. 311–312.

15   Woodrow Wilson, *Congressional Government: A Study in American Politics* (Baltimore: John Hopkins University Press, 1981; orig. ed., 1885), pp. 27, 215.

16   *Constitutional Government*, pp. 56–57.

17   *Federalist* 10, p. 76. See Woodrow Wilson, "Leaders of Men," in *The Papers of Woodrow Wilson*, ed. Arthur S. Link, 43 vols. (Princeton: Princeton University Press, 1966–83), 6:644–71. Reprinted in R. J. Pestritto, ed., *Woodrow Wilson: The Essential Political Writings* (Lanham, MD: Lexington Books, 2005), pp. 211–229. For a commentary, see chapter Eight, *supra*.

18   *Constitutional Government*, pp. 66–67.

19   *Constitutional Government*, pp. 68–69.

20   Consider in this connection *Constitutional Government*, pp. 80–81. For a thoughtful account of the Constitution's view of the executive power, which

Wilson was rejecting, see Joseph M. Bessette and Gary J. Schmitt, "The Powers and Duties of the President: Recovering the Logic and Meaning of Article II," in Bessette and Jeffrey K. Tulis, eds., *The Constitutional Presidency* (Baltimore: Johns Hopkins University Press, 2009), chapter 2.

21 *Congressional Government*, pp. 197–98.

22 Jeremy Rabkin, "Bureaucratic Idealism and Executive Power: A Perspective on *The Federalist*'s View of Public Administration," in Charles R. Kesler, ed., *Saving the Revolution: The Federalist Papers and the American Founding* (New York: The Free Press, 1987), chapter 9, at p. 200.

23 *Federalist* 68, p. 413.

24 *Federalist* 63, p. 38; 71, pp. 430–31; 78, p. 465. See Paul Eidelberg, *A Discourse on Statesmanship* (Urbana, Ill.: University of Illinois Press, 1974), pp. 296–304.

25 *Congressional Government*, p. 203.

CHAPTER TEN

1 W. B. Allen, ed., *George Washington: A Collection* (Indianapolis: Liberty Classics, 1988), 548.

2 George Washington, "General Orders," April 18, 1783, in Allen, *George Washington: A Collection*, 237; "Letter to the Volunteer Association of Ireland," December 2, 1783, in *Writings of George Washington*, ed. John C. Fitzpatrick, vol. 27 (Washington, D.C.: *Government Printing Office*, 1931–44), 254. Cf. Matthew Spalding, "From Pluribus to Unum: Immigration and the Founding Fathers," *Policy Review*, Winter 1994, 35–41.

3 On the peculiar, and continuing, effects of black slavery on the character of U.S. citizenship, see Judith N. Shklar, *American Citizenship: The Quest for Inclusion* (Cambridge: Harvard University Press, 1991). For a historical summary, see James H. Kettner, *The Development of American Citizenship*, 1608–1870 (Chapel Hill: University of North Carolina Press, 1978).

4 For further details, see Reed Ueda, "Naturalization and Citizenship," in *Harvard Encyclopedia of American Ethnic Groups*, ed. Stephen Thernstrom (Cambridge: Harvard University Press, 1980), 734–48.

5 Rogers M. Smith, *Civic Ideals: Conflicting Visions of Citizenship in U.S. History* (New Haven: Yale University Press, 1997), 36–37. See also Shklar, *American Citizenship*, 7–8, 13–14.

6 For an intelligent overview, see Will Kymlicka and Wayne Norman, "Return of the Citizen: A Survey of Recent Work on Citizenship Theory," *Ethics 104* (January 1994): 352–81.

7 Robert W. Johannsen, ed., *The Lincoln-Douglas Debates* (New York: Oxford University Press, 1965), 196. For the grounds and limitations of Douglas's argument, see Harry V. Jaffa, *Crisis of the House Divided: An Interpretation of the Lincoln-Douglas Debates* (Chicago: University of Chicago Press, 1982).

8 Willmoore Kendall, "Equality and the American Political Tradition," in

Willmoore Kendall Contra Mundum, ed. Nellie D. Kendall (New Rochelle, N.Y. Arlington House, 1971); reprinted in William F. Buckley, Jr., and Charles R. Kesler, eds., *Keeping the Tablets: Modern American Conservative Thought* (New York: Harper & Row, 1988), 71–83, at 71.

9   See Edmund Burke, *Reflections on the Revolution in France*, in *The Writings and Speeches of Edmund Burke* (Boston: Little Brown, 1901), vol. 3, 259: "A state without the means of some change is without the means of its conservation." Cf. 974–75 and 455–57. Cf. Friedrich A. Hayek, *The Constitution of Liberty* (Chicago: University of Chicago Press, 1960), 54–70.

10   Madison, in *The Federalist Papers*, intro. Charles R. Kesler (New York: Signet Classics, 2003), no. 42, 262–63.

11   Madison, *The Federalist Papers*, No. 54, 334.

12   This is not Kant's own position exactly, because he distinguished between moral and legal duty. Pure or categorical morality made it one's duty never to break the established law, even if it is very imperfect, according to Kant. Nonetheless, he distinguished sharply between the mere "political moralist" and the admirable "moral politician," whose goal is to make politics bend its knee before right. See Immanuel Kant, "To Perpetual Peace: A Philosophical Sketch," Appendix I, in *Kant's Political Writings*, ed. Hans Reiss (Cambridge: Cambridge University Press, 1970), 116–25; and Kant, "The Metaphysics of Morals," in *Kant's Political Writings*, 143–47.

13   Johannsen, *The Lincoln-Douglas Debates*, 304. Lincoln is quoting from his speech on the Dred Scott decision, originally delivered in 1857.

14   Frederick Douglass argued that it was in the slaves' own interest for the Constitution to be ratified, even with its compromises over slavery, because the alternative was a sundering of the Union and thus a much greater chance for slavery to expand and perpetuate itself across the South and the rest of the continent. "My argument against the dissolution of the American Union is this," he wrote. "It would place the slave system more exclusively under the control of the slaveholding states, and withdraw it from the power in the Northern states which is opposed to slavery." Frederick Douglass, "The Constitution of the United States: Is It Pro-Slavery or Anti-Slavery?" in *The Life and Writings of Frederick Douglass*, ed. Philip S. Foner, vol. 2 (New York: International Publishers, 1950), 478.

15   Cf. Aristotle, *The Politics*, trans. Carnes Lord (Chicago: University of Chicago Press, 1984), 1327b23–33.

16   Fustel de Coulanges, *The Ancient City*, trans. W. Small (Garden City, N.Y.: Doubleday, 1956); originally published in 1864.

17   Aristotle, *The Politics*, 1253a30–31.

18   Aristotle, *The Politics*, 1228b12–13, 1229a27–33. Cf. Aristotle, *Topics* 105a5–8, 115b32–35.

19   Aristotle, *The Politics*, 1275a2–23. For good commentaries, see Harry V. Jaffa, "Aristotle," in *History of Political Philosophy*, ed. Leo Strauss and Joseph

Cropsey, 2nd ed., (Chicago: Rand McNally, 1972), 94–116; Harvey C. Mansfield Jr., *Responsible Citizenship, Ancient and Modern* (Eugene, OR: University of Oregon Books, 1994), 4–12; and Mary p. Nichols, *Citizens and Statesmen: A Study of Aristotle's Politics* (Lanham, MD: Rowman & Littlefield, 1992), 55–61.

20   Aristotle, *The Politics*, 1275a2–1275b20, 1284a3–17, 1284b25–34, 1288a17–29.

21   Aristotle, *The Politics*, 1276b16–1277b32, 1287a1–1287b35.

22   See Mansfield, *Responsible Citizenship*, 6.

23   Aristotle, *The Politics*, 1275b21–33.

24   Allen, *George Washington: A Collection*, 271.

25   For further discussion, see Chapter 4, above.

26   Thomas Jefferson, letter to Roger Weightman, June 24, 1826, in *Thomas Jefferson: Writings*, ed. Merrill D. Peterson (New York: Library of America, 1984), 1517.

27   For exhaustive proof of the universalism of the Founders' basic principles, see Thomas G. West, *Vindicating the Founders: Race, Sex, Class, and Justice in the Origins of America* (Lanham, MD: Rowman & Littlefield, 1997). See also his *Political Theory of the American Founding* (Cambridge: Cambridge University Press, 2017).

28   Religious disestablishment was primarily the work of state governments, not the federal government, which under the First Amendment was clearly forbidden to establish a national church, but not empowered to abolish the established churches then existing in some states. Virginia's disestablishment of Anglicanism in 1786 led the way; and by 1833 the last of the state churches had been swept away.

29   William B. Allen argues that the American Founders' account of sovereignty "replaces the nation-state with the state-nation .... Nationality no longer operates to secure the relevant distinctions, which consist primarily in determinations of the extent to which rights are guaranteed .... The existence of the state serves to create de facto that class of human beings whose nominal rights are actually enforceable in contrast to those whose rights are subject to abuse .... Modern sovereignty requires the death of nationality or community membership, not as vital memory, but as a primary and active basis of civic association." Allen, "The Truth About Citizenship: An Outline," *Cardozo Journal of International and Comparative Law 4* (Summer 1996), 355–72, at 368–69.

30   West, *Vindicating the Founders*, 157. Emphasis added by West.

31   Philip B. Kurland and Raiph Lerner, eds., *The Founders' Constitution, vol.* 1 (Chicago: University of Chicago Press, 1987), 11.

32   West, *Vindicating the Founders*, 156.

33   Max Farrand, ed., *Records of the Federal Convention, vol.* 2 (New Haven: Yale University Press, 1966), 258. Quoted in West, *Vindicating the Founders*, 157. In a sense, immigration and naturalization became the model for citizenship.

As Reed Ueda comments, "Since naturalization had been central to the process of forming colonial societies, the colonists began to see political allegiance as reflecting the essential character of naturalization itself and to hold that allegiance was volitional and contractual." Ueda, "Naturalization and Citizenship," 756.

34 On the subject of tacit consent, see John Locke, *Two Treatises of Government*, ed. Peter Laslett (New York: Mentor, 1965), II, secs. 104–12, 116–22.

35 Samuel Eliot Morison, ed., *Sources and Documents Illustrating the American Revolution* (New York: Oxford University Press, 1923), 164. Cf, Emer de Vattel, *The Law of Nations, Or The Principles of Natural Law*, trans. Charles G. Fenwick (Washington, D.C.: Carnegie Endowment, 1916), 37–38, 88–91, 140–41, 151, 154–55.

36 Vattel. *The Law of Nations*, 91–93; and Smith, *Civic Ideals*, 525–42.

37 Letter to John Augustine Washington, June 15, 1783, in Allen, *George Washington: A Collection*, 256.

38 Allen, *George Washington: A Collection*, 515.

39 See Noah M. J. Pickus, "'Hearken Not to the Unnatural Voice': Publius and the Artifice of Attachment," in *Diversity and Citizenship: Rediscovering American Nationhood*, ed. Gary Jeffrey Jacobsohn and Susan Dunn (Lanham, MD: Rowman & Littlefield, 1996), 63–84; and chapter 3, *supra*.

40 See *The Federalist Papers*, No. 49, 311–14; and No. 37, 226–27.

41 *The Federalist Papers*, No. 37, 226–27 and No. 49, 314; cf. No. 78, 466–68.

42 *The Federalist Papers*, No. 78, 465–69; cf. No. 51, 319–20.

43 Benjamin Franklin, "Information to Those Who Would Remove to America," in *Benjamin Franklin: Writings*, ed. J. A. Leo Lemay (New York: Library of America, 1987), 975–83, at 978–82.

44 Franklin, in *Benjamin Franklin: Writings*, 982.

45 Smith, *Civic Ideals*, 159–60.

46 In his famous discussion of slavery's injustice in *Notes on the State of Virginia*, Query 18, Jefferson hopes eventually for "a total emancipation … with the consent of the masters, rather than by their extirpation." He admits that in the event of a violent "revolution," however, "The Almighty has no attribute which can take side with us in such a contest." Remarkably, Jefferson refers to slavery as a condition in which "one half the citizens … trample on the rights of the other," thus acknowledging, at least rhetorically, that black slaves were or ought to be equal citizens. Peterson, *Thomas Jefferson: Writings*, 288–89.

47 Peterson, *Thomas Jefferson: Writings*, 210–12.

48 The first U.S. naturalization law (1790) set the residency requirement at two years, which was raised to five years (1795) and then fourteen years (1798). Jefferson's proposal for immediate naturalization was not passed, but the Democratic Republicans did reset the requirement to five years (1801), where it has remained since. See Ueda, "Naturalization and Citizenship," 737.

49 Smith, *Civic Ideals*, 153–70, 190–92; West, *Vindicating the Founders*, 154.

50 Alexander Hamilton, "The Examination," nos. 7–9 (1802), in *Papers of Alexander Hamilton*, ed. Harold C. Syrett et al., vol. 25 (New York: Columbia University Press, 1961–79), 491–501. Quoted in West, *Vindicating the Founders*, 154–55.

51 The British naturalization laws of 1740 and 1761, which permitted foreigners in the colonies to become British subjects without special appeals to King or Parliament, had contained religious tests in addition to residency requirements. The 1740 law, in fact, prohibited the naturalization of Catholics. The effect of the U.S. naturalization act of 1790 and its successors was to replace religious tests with a test of "good character" as a prerequisite for U.S. citizenship; and, of course, to replace allegiance to the Crown with allegiance to the Constitution. See Ueda, "Naturalization and Citizenship," 735, 737–38.

52 Much scholarly work has been done on the republican virtues, as it were, immanent in liberalism. See, e.g., Stephen Macedo, *Liberal Virtues: Citizenship, Virtue, and Community* (Oxford: Oxford University Press, 1990); and William Galston, *Liberal Purposes: Goods, Virtues, and Duties in the Liberal State* (Cambridge: Cambridge University Press, 1991).

53 See chapter 5, *supra*.

54 Iris Marion Young, "Polity and Group Difference: A Critique of the Ideal of Universal Citizenship," *Ethics 99* (January 1989): 250–74, at 267. The argument is elaborated with reference to contemporary theorists of distributive justice (e.g., John Rawls and Ronald Dworkin) in her *Justice and the Politics of Difference* (Princeton: Princeton University Press, 1990). Cf. Herbert Marcuse, "Repressive Tolerance," in Robert Paul Wolff, Barrington Moore Jr., and Herbert Marcuse, *A Critique of Pure Tolerance* (Boston: Beacon Press, 1965), 81–117.

55 Young, "Polity and Group Difference," 250–51.

56 Young, "Polity and Group Difference," 269.

57 Young, "Polity and Group Difference," 269.

58 Young, "Polity and Group Difference," 272. Will Kymlicka distinguishes, in his more moderate version of differentiated citizenship, between "multicultural" or "polyethnic rights," intended to help citizens express their particularity and cultural pride but without hindering their integration into society, and "self-government rights," belonging to distinct cultures or peoples occupying a given homeland or territory, who wish to maintain, like the Quebecois, their separate cultural and even political identity. Kymlicka, *Multicultural Citizenship: A Liberal Theory of Minority Rights* (Oxford: Oxford University Press, 1995). For a perceptive postmodernist critique, see Stanley Fish, "Boutique Multiculturalism, in *Multiculturalism and American Democracy*, eds. Arthur M. Melzer, Jerry Weinberger, and M. Richard Zinman (Lawrence: University Press of Kansas, 1998), ch. 4, esp. p. 86.

59 Young, "Polity and Group Difference," 259–60.

60 See Alexis de Tocqueville, *Democracy in America*, trans. Harvey C. Mansfield and Delba Winthrop (Chicago: University of Chicago Press, 2000), 180–86, 485–503.

61 Young, "Polity and Group Difference, 259–60. On "thrownness" (*Geworfenheit*), see Martin Heidegger, *Being and Time*, trans. John Macquarrie and Edward Robinson (New York: Harper & Row, 1962), secs. 29 and 38.

62 Young, "Polity and Group Difference," 260, 268–69.

63 Young, 'Polity and Group Difference," 260.

64 Young, "Polity and Group Difference," 261–62.

65 Young, "Polity and Group Difference," 262.

66 Young, "Polity and Group Difference," 258, 262, 270–71.

67 Young, "Polity and Group Difference," 262–63.

68 Young, "Polity and Group Difference," 261. "In short, everyone but healthy, relatively well-off, relatively young, heterosexual white males," comment Kymlicka and Norman in "Return of the Citizen," 374 n26.

69 Young, "Polity and Group Difference," 262.

70 Young, "Polity and Group Difference," 263. Young does criticize Habermas for retaining "an appeal to a universal or impartial point of view from which claims in a public should be addressed," as opposed to her emphasis on "the expression of the concrete needs of all individuals in their particularity." Cf. Seyla Benhabib, *Critique, Norm, and Utopia* (New York: Columbia University Press, 1986), for a similar critique.

71 Young, "Polity and Group Difference," 264, 267.

72 Young, "Polity and Group Difference", 264–65.

73 The "test of whether a claim on the public is just," Young writes, "… is best made when persons making it must confront the opinion of others who have explicitly different, though not necessarily conflicting, experiences, priorities, and needs." "Polity and Group Difference," 263.

74 Young, "Polity and Group Difference," 265.

75 See Ross M. Lence, ed., *Union and Liberty: The Political Philosophy of John C. Calhoun* (Indianapolis: Liberty Fund, 1992), 3–78, 369–400, 565–70.

76 James Madison, "Majority Governments," in *The Mind of the Founder: Sources of the Political Thought of James Madison*, ed. Marvin Meyers (Indianapolis: Bobbs-Merrill, 1973), 520–30, at 528, 530.

77 Young, "Polity and Group Difference," 265–66.

78 T. Alexander Aleinikoff, "A Multicultural Nationalism?" *The American Prospect*, January-February 1998, 80–86, at 84.

79 Young, 'Polity and Group Difference," 261.

80 Abraham Lincoln, speech at Chicago, July 10, 1858, in *Collected Works of Abraham Lincoln*, ed. Roy T. Basler, vol. 2 (New Brunswick, NJ: Rutgers University Press, 1953), 499.

INDEX

obsolescence of, 269; natural rights (critique of), 19; qualitative, 160; quantitative, 160; rejection of self-government, 339; Sixties, 144; "smug style" in, 380; today's elderly appearance of, 268; turned anti-American (1960s), 298; as value judgment, 265. *See also* Obama, Barack (future of liberalism and) liberalism, waves of, 143–168; "affleuent society," 160; American founders, view of man of, 148; anti-Americanism, 158–168; anti-trust policies, 153; assertive doctrine, liberalism as, 143; "bourgeois" values, 167; consciousness-raising, 164; Constitution, Progressive critics of, 148; cover-up, 146; Darwinism, 150; economic truths, 154; economic tyranny, 157; entitlements, 144, 156, 157; FDR's politics, continuation of, 145; Four Freedoms, 159; Great Society, 162; "liberal century," 143; natural-rights individualism, rejection of, 150; New Deal, 144, 155; New Freedom and Progressivism, 144; New Left narrative, 167; new rights, moral hazard of, 156; "Progressive historians," 147; progressive statesmen, 146; progressivism and living Constitution, 147–152; "purge" campaign (FDR), 158; qualitative liberalism, 160; quantitative liberalism, 160; redistribution and second Bill of Rights, 152–158; reform movements, previous, 144; second Bill of Rights, 253; silent majority, 160; Sixties existentialism, 166; Sixties liberalism, 144; social democracy, awakening of, 147; State, as social organism, 150; Students for a Democratic Society, 163; tyranny, 152; underconsumption, 154;

Vietnam War, 163; view of man, 163; "war socialism," 153; Watts riots, 162
Life of Washington, 100
Lilla, Mark, 398
Limbaugh, Rush, 383
Lincoln, Abraham, 119, 268; "derailment" of American political tradition by, 222; idea of democracy, 348; Lyceum address, 110, 127, 264; moral vision of (Bush), 349; nonconservative disposition of (Kirk), 330; personal interpretation of Constitution, 300; philosophical public opinion, 372; promise of American citizenship, 255–256; task set before, 100; test of practical good (Scripture), 387
living constitution: creed transformed by, 367; implication of, 293–294; Obama and, 294; progressivism and, 147–152; Reagan Revolution and, 294, 296; ruling class of, 296
Locke, John, 84, 97; influence on founders, 9–10, 34; natural rights, 363; "natural universal liberty" of mankind, 18; private property and state of nature, 121; republican liberalism of, 20; *Second Treatise of Government*, 34, 203, 364
Lodge, Henry Cabot, 321

Machiavelli, Niccolò, 5, 54, 385
Madison, James, 234, 235; capacity of mankind for self-government, statement on, 345; nonconservative disposition of (Kirk), 330; pseudonym of, 21; statement refuting Calhoun, 254
Mann, Sophie, 379
Mao Tse Tung, 160
Marcos, Ferdinand, 343
Marcuse, Herbert, 165, 244, 283
Marx, Karl, 51, 244, 277

A NOTE ON THE TYPE

CRISIS OF THE TWO CONSTITUTIONS *has been set in Jonathan Hoefler's Mercury types. Originally created for the* New Times *newspaper chain and later adapted for general informational typography, the Mercury types were drawn in four grades intended to be used under variable printing conditions – that is, to compensate for less-than-optimal presswork or for regional differences in paper stock and plant conditions. The result was a family of types that were optimized to print well in a vast number of sizes and formats. In books, Mercury makes a no-nonsense impression, crisp and open, direct and highly readable, yet possessed of real style and personality.*

DESIGN & COMPOSITION BY CARL W. SCARBROUGH